WOMEN WRITERS
of the
CONTEMPORARY
SOUTH

WOMEN WRITERS
of the
CONTEMPORARY
SOUTH

Edited by
Peggy Whitman Prenshaw

UNIVERSITY PRESS OF MISSISSIPPI
Jackson

This book has been sponsored by the
University of Southern Mississippi

Southern Quarterly Series

The University Press of Mississippi thanks *The Southern Review* for permission to reprint "Why There Are No Southern Writers," Autumn 1982, pp. 755–66. Copyright by Daphne Athas.

Library of Congress Cataloging in Publication Data
Main entry under title:

Women writers of the contemporary South.

  (Southern quarterly series)
  Bibliography: p.
  1. American fiction—Southern States—History and criticism—Addresses, essays, lectures. 2. American fiction—Women authors—History and criticism—Addresses, essays, lectures. 3. American fiction—20th century—History and criticism—Addresses, essays, lectures. 4. Southern States in literature—Addresses, essays, lectures. I. Prenshaw, Peggy Whitman. II. Series.
  PS261.W65   1984   813'.54'093287   84-5165
  ISBN 0-87805-222-4

Contents

Introduction

The subject of this collection of essays is the fiction of a group of Southern writers whose first novels or collections of short stories were published after 1945. Taken together, these writers share a view of the South that differs in many respects from the South reflected in the fiction of the Southern Literary Renaissance of the 1920s and 1930s. They differ perhaps most noticeably from earlier twentieth-century writers in their depiction of a Southern region more typically urban than rural and in their portrayal of characters more mobile and transient than rooted in the Southern past.

The South portrayed by this younger generation of writers generally has little to do with the agrarian life, except by way of memory through parents and grandparents and through recollections of cherished country places of childhood. Here is a South where people live largely in towns and cities, visiting the countryside for an occasional outing or a family reunion at an old homeplace. Still, their connections to an earlier twentieth-century South are vivid and change slowly. While the fiction of the post-1945 South shows many alterations in landscape and demography, a strong sense of place continues to shape the Southern characters' view of themselves, especially their consciousness of being "Southerners."

In earlier fiction, the portrait of the Southerner was indistinct, almost unimaginable until the character's racial identity was set. "Is your man white or black?" The question put to Huck Finn and explored in various ways in Faulkner's *Light in August,* Robert Penn Warren's *Band of Angels,* and many other Southern novels has not lost its potency in recent Southern fiction. This fiction has been profoundly influenced, however, by the nearly revolutionary change in laws, customs, and attitudes governing racial relations of the past thirty years. Particularly in the fiction of the late

1960s and 1970s, there is little of the old rigid sense of social place defining the roles of black and white Southerners. Rather, there is an atmosphere of ambiguousness and tension, from which original, highly individualized characters emerge. Every portrayal of blackness or whiteness is heightened by the writer's knowledge of change, that which has already come and that which is on the way.

Just as these recent writers reflect a consciousness of evolving racial mores, so do they portray the sometime subtle, sometime startling changes in relations between Southern men and women. The writers who are the subject of these essays are all women, grouped together here not so much by sex, however, as by gender—that is, by a shared social sense of the world they have grown up in as women, a world they have come to know as daughters, sisters, wives, mothers. If the South has sought to conserve its traditions regarding the races, no less has it sought to maintain its time-honored roles for women: the Southern lady, the belle, the sheltered white woman on a pedestal, the pious matriarch, the naive black girl, the enduring black mother. Unable to ignore the legacy of expectations for women, these writers have nonetheless interpreted the roles variously, depicting them frequently as constraining, artificial, simplistic, often something of a sham, but occasionally even as ennobling. Rarely does the Southern woman of fact or fiction ignore the region's old binding stereotypes; rather, she acknowledges and reacts to the roles with rebellion or accommodation, or both, in what becomes finely turned irony. For the contemporary Southern writer, especially if she is a woman, and for the Southern heroine of recent fiction, the changing patterns of womanhood (or ladyhood) are as problematic and as intensely interesting as the comparable shifts in racial roles.

Obviously, the writers discussed here do not write exclusively about women. Their broad range of interest and vision, in fact, greatly circumscribes the generalizations one can make about the characters and themes of their fiction. I trust that the essays included here will reveal the diversity, as well as the artistry, of their fiction. Finally, I should like to note that, because these are all writers whose careers are still very much underway, these essays represent something of a criticism in progress. That the analyses offered here almost certainly will be subject to revision in light of later fiction to come is nothing but business as usual for literary critics undertaking to discuss contemporary writing. Compensating for the inevitable tentativeness one feels in writing about a canon in progress, however, is the pleasure of anticipating new fiction to be read and enjoyed, new pleasures and insights ahead from writers still at work.

In the opening essay, Laurie L. Brown interviews seven of the writers about their careers as artists and their experience as Southerners and as women. Next, Doris Betts discusses the evolution of the narrative methods and themes of Anne Tyler's eight novels, concluding with the 1982 *Dinner at the Homesick Restaurant.* Thadious Davis likewise examines the distinguished literary career of Alice Walker, showing Walker's use of "patterns of generations" to portray her concern with "familial identity, continuity and rupture, and with social roles, order and change."

Discussing the themes of Southern womanhood in five novels by Gail Godwin, Carolyn Rhodes concludes that only in the 1982 work, *A Mother and Two Daughters,* does Godwin portray women who achieve an admirable balance in their lives, who "without fleeing the South" manage "to achieve autonomy and to define grace and duty in their own ways." If not "balance," then an exuberant acceptance of life is what Merrill Skaggs finds in the protagonists of Beverly Lowry's three novels. Lowry's heroines, who are never "passive female victims of anything or anybody," elude Southern stereotyping. What Lowry gives us instead, especially in the most recent novel, *Daddy's Girl,* is a heroine of complex and wonderful appetites, and strong and loving heart.

Concentrating on the short stories of Shirley Ann Grau, Mary Rohrberger traces the development of Grau's fictional technique and the evolution of her themes in stories beginning with a 1948 publication written when she was an undergraduate at Tulane. In her essay on Lisa Alther's *Kinflicks* and *Original Sins,* Mary Anne Ferguson discusses Alther's handling of a familiar theme in recent Southern fiction: "home as viewed from the perspective of a native who has left and returns." Ferguson shows that Alther employs a cyclic narrative structure to portray her characters' experience of homecoming, a return that finally leads less to transcendent insight than to ironic, ambivalent attachment to the Southern homeland. In a survey of Ellen Douglas's six books of fiction, Carol Manning focuses upon the recurrent themes of the individual's responsibility for others and one's obligation to search out and tell the truth about the past.

Writing of Doris Betts's 1981 novel, *Heading West,* Dorothy Scura

observes that the book is the first of Betts's four novels to be set outside
the South and the first to portray a strong, single woman at the center of
the action. Scura finds in the protagonist Nancy Finch a "heroine for the
1980s—smart, strong, intuitive, loving, funny, possessed of integrity,"
and she concludes that with *Heading West* Betts "comes into her own as a
novelist with a distinctive voice and a comic view of the world." Similarly,
I discuss the heroines of the later fiction of Elizabeth Spencer, beginning
with her fourth novel, *Light in the Piazza*, which like Betts's *Heading
West* was Spencer's first novel set outside the South and the first to
feature a female protagonist. Discussing three subsequent novels and
several short stories, all of which include central female characters, I trace
Spencer's portrayal of heroines who move from various states of depen-
dency to autonomy and self-possession.

Mary Lee Settle's series of novels known as the Beulah Quintet is the
subject of Nancy Carol Joyner's essay. Noting the elaborate detail and
construction of the novels, as well as the complex connections between
the works, Joyner analyzes one of the major themes of the quintet, "class
consciousness and the resultant conflict such awareness engenders." Joyner examines Settle's technique for embodying this theme in various
images of dress and decoration of houses, as well as in more overt statements about family status and wealth.

Focusing upon Berry Morgan's *Pursuit* and *The Mystical Adventures of
Roxie Stoner*, Margaret Jones Bolsterli explores Morgan's "androgynous,
bi-racial vision." Bolsterli notes that, as the cultures of men and women
and of blacks and whites grow less distinctive in the future, the broad,
inclusive vision of a writer like Morgan may become more common. "For
now it is still a rare circumstance, worth celebrating when it occurs in
Southern or any other culture."

Surveying both the fictional and nonfictional writing of Rita Mae
Brown, Martha Chew points out the different audiences to which Brown
has directed her early political writing and her fiction. Chew sees in the
rebelliousness of Brown's fictional heroes, however, evidence that "her
concerns as a lesbian feminist underlie and inform her portrayal of Southern women and link her early political vision with her imaginative vision
as a Southern novelist."

Nancy D. Hargrove reads Toni Cade Bambara's *Gorilla, My Love* for
the stories' remarkable portraits of black life. Hargrove compares Bam-

bara's fiction with classic literary studies of youth, but she notes that in giving us protagonists who are "female, black and generally preadolescent," Bambara contributes a new perspective to the genre. In their essay on Ellen Gilchrist's *In the Land of Dreamy Dreams* and *The Annunciation,* Jeanie Thompson and Anita Miller Garner discuss Gilchrist's portrayals of "the workings of a complex female psyche through a variety of women of all ages." They observe that Gilchrist, pursuing "a very straight and narrow path of realism," has created women who are "anguished but tenacious" and who demonstrate in the recent novel the "courage to face the truth about themselves."

In a richly detailed reading of Lee Smith's stories and novels, Anne Goodwyn Jones finds that Smith's "eye for, ear for, love for . . . the 'gross world' is entirely compelling." She discusses Smith's technical virtuosity, as well as her themes, concluding that what Smith offers her readers is "the sometimes heroic, sometimes comic, sometimes sneaky and petty ways in which Southern women and men try to salvage a sense of self within a system that tries to define that self for them."

In discussing the fiction of Joan Williams, Judith Bryant Wittenberg considers the problems inherent in any assessment of a writer's career at midpoint, particularly a writer like Williams, whose career she finds "still very much in progress." Wittenberg examines the relation of Williams's life to her work, noting the effect of a "powerful male mentor," a "somewhat turbulent personal life," and a need "to come to terms with her Southernness in the North where she lives and with her femaleness in what has been for her largely a male-dominated world." Maureen Ryan discusses Bobbie Ann Mason's 1982 work, *Shiloh and Other Stories,* her first published collection of stories. Mason's present-day South, set in western Kentucky, is one very much marked by change, and her characters, observes Ryan, "stumble through their lives in this protean world, puzzled by intimidating new mores." Ryan finds Mason's South paradigmatic of the region, and in many ways typical of the rest of the country, with the pressures wrought by rapid change often producing in her characters contradictory impulses, "the temptation to withdraw into the security of home and the past, and the alternative prospect of taking to the road in search of something better."

In the final essay, provocatively entitled "Why There Are No Southern Writers," Daphne Athas surveys the current literary scene in the South and finds that Southernness no longer is to be found in distinctively regional characters and conflicts. Athas, who is herself the author of four novels and numerous stories and poems, sees the 1940s as a turning point when Southern women no longer had to foreswear or hide their ambition and freedom to be regarded as successful, admirable women. What happened, Athas shows, was that many of the old prototypes yielded to new transformations, or as she says, many of the old aristocratic idols and urges of Southern writers turned plebian. For the new generation of readers and writers, a beauty like Scarlett O'Hara may yet live, but her vitality lies not in her looks but in the "scrapping, spunk, schemes, determination, marrying, working, and even in the slapping of other women who fail to have her guts." And the type of "sensitive girl-adolescent of winsome pain" made famous by McCullers and others has been transmuted by the later generation of writers into a character whose charm lies not in her pain but in her intelligence. "The brilliance analyzes the pain, and the characters do not have physical defects and do not consider themselves ugly, deformed, or crazy." Although Athas finds the old Southern prototypes transformed in recent fiction by Southern writers, particularly by the women who "are analytical now and in content devoid of disguise," she yet finds a residue of Southernness in their style. Their vision may be "defiantly plebian," but in the subtle prose and sophisticated voice of these contemporary writers, one may detect hints of the aristocratic—evidence, albeit slight, of a persistent Southernness.

All but three of these essays appeared originally in the summer and fall 1983 numbers of the *Southern Quarterly,* published by the University of Southern Mississippi. Daphne Athas's essay, "Why There Are No Southern Writers," first appeared in *Southern Review,* 18 (Fall 1982), 755–66. The essays by Maureen Ryan and Judith Bryant Wittenberg were written for this collection. This volume, with the checklist of primary and selected secondary sources, is part of the University Press of Mississippi's *Southern Quarterly* series. All parenthetical references in the text are to the sources listed in the checklist at the conclusion.

Peggy Whitman Prenshaw
February 1984

WOMEN WRITERS
of the
CONTEMPORARY
SOUTH

Interviews with Seven Contemporary Writers

LAURIE L. BROWN

Following is a mosaic of interviews in which seven writers—Lisa Alther, Ellen Douglas, Gail Godwin, Shirley Ann Grau, Mary Lee Settle, Elizabeth Spencer and Anne Tyler—share their views on writing as a vocation. When, I wanted to know, did they start writing? What ideas or beliefs have shaped their fiction? How do they reconcile the necessarily private nature of writing with social and family responsibilities? What other kinds of relationships enter a writer's life, and how influential are readers, critics, other writers?

The answers to these questions do not fall so easily into categories. Nor are these slender threads intended as archetypes. "It is kind of you to think of me," wrote Mary Lee Settle in response to my request for an interview, "I wonder if I'd suit you—I'm more of a writer's writer than a woman writer—as a composer friend of mine says—I am a woman and I am a composer, but not at the same time!" Anne Tyler, too, would write: "I see no essential difference between the sexes when it comes to writing and I'd have to be a great pretender to present myself as a Southern writer. (I wasn't born in the South, and was only raised on the outskirts looking in.)" I have tried, then, to avoid interpretation, and to present these women, who are as incorrigibly individual and specific as their statements, as persons and as writers, rather than as representatives of a particular sex or region.

The variety in style, tone and length among the responses is attributable to more than just incorrigible individuality, though. Distance, time, and personal preference dictated the approach I took with each writer. Lisa Alther, Gail Godwin, and Elizabeth Spencer (Southerners now removed), responded to my questions through the mail. Anne Tyler also asked for an interview by mail: "I find that letter-answering can be sched-

3

*uled at two a.m., if that's where my free time falls, while interviews at two
a.m. are often difficult to arrange." Mary Lee Settle talked with me on the
telephone for nearly two hours. The remaining interviews, with Ellen
Douglas and Shirley Ann Grau, were done in person. I would like to thank
all these writers, who gave generously of their time and their ideas.*

> Peering inside, she saw the copy of Baudelaire's poems . . . and the
> two or three other books she kept by her bed: a Bronte book, *Villette,*
> which she had not re-read since freshman days, but which had given
> her a firm idea of how life could center around a woman's impressions
> of it.
>   —Elizabeth Spencer, *The Snare*

*All of these women—all of these writers—have centered life around their
impressions. But in learning to reconcile imagination and observation, in
constructing a fictive world from the actuality of day to day existence,
they have not necessarily had such a clearly defined role model, or even a
strong sense of vocation. Variously motivated, some encountered obstacles, some did not; they bumped up against society, or fled confrontation.
How did it begin? When did "the writer" emerge? Were they encouraged
by those close to them at the time? Did they ever consider alternatives to
writing?*

Anne Tyler, who began writing "as soon as [she] knew how to put words
on paper," planned to be an artist. She remembers, "Both of my parents
supported and encouraged anything their children did that was creative
in any way whatsoever." After college were graduate school, marriage,
and a succession of "non-intellectual, non-draining jobs to supplement
our income," but no real sense of urgency or commitment. "If you don't
count writing for pure fun, I started writing after leaving the Duke job [as
a Russian bibliographer at the university library]. I'd begun a novel
haphazardly during the job, lost one manuscript on a plane when we
moved to Montreal, decided it wasn't worth going back to the airport for,
recovered the manuscript by accident weeks later, then couldn't find a
job for six months and finished the novel in order to keep busy. I received
notice of its acceptance the day I finally started a new job."

Lisa Alther did not plan to be a writer either, though she wrote for her
high school and college newspapers. "I planned to work in publishing

after college, took a course in that at Radcliffe, and worked at Atheneum Publishers for about 6 months before moving to Vermont, where I did freelance writing for several years. I first wrote fiction in a creative writing course when I was 18, and continued writing stories on the side when I was working at Atheneum." Her family always encouraged her to do what she wanted to do, "but since I didn't know while I was living at home I wanted to write, there wasn't a lot of overt encouragement. But there was covert encouragement because both parents read a lot and there were many books throughout the house."

Gail Godwin wrote her first story at the age of nine. Her mother, who was divorced, wrote fiction to supplement her earnings as a journalist, and provided encouragement as well as example: "She always took it for granted I would be a novelist . . . if I worked as hard as she thought I ought to work." Godwin never seriously considered becoming anything other than a writer, though she claimed "I planned for my failure by preparing for a career that could support me, but that was simply to assure myself I could earn a living."

A decade earlier, sexual barriers in the legal and academic worlds made it simpler for Shirley Ann Grau to reverse the process. "I probably— ordinarily—would have gone into law. But in those days—you've got to remember—in the very early fifties, late forties, there was a good deal of dislike of women in the general legal world . . . I've never exactly been entranced by the thought of going into a field where you are ever so handicapped. The same thing, in those days, was true of teaching. Women taught *below* the college level." As a student at Sophie Newcomb College in New Orleans, she had been "fairly determined" to go into Classics and teach: "But . . . soon it became terribly obvious that the demand for Classics scholars is about as great as the demand for French horn players. . . . Classics was closed not only because there were so few openings, but because of the enormous prejudice against women at the time. So I shifted to English because I *like* the academic life. It simply feels comfortable to me. I wanted to go into English teaching. Again, I ran into the absolute point blank dead end. You couldn't even get a teaching assistantship at Tulane. The head of the department, who has since gotten into a great deal of trouble over his misogynist tendencies, simply would not have it. So, rather than fight it—some of my friends insisted and fought it—I just shrugged my shoulders and said 'you don't have to do that.' So I shifted into writing, which is probably a less routinized life, heaven knows."

Ellen Douglas, on the other hand, grew up with the knowledge that she wanted to be a writer—which is to say, "A sense of vocation, yes. A conviction that I could succeed, no." She talked about the effect that being a woman had on her decision: "I think that at the time I was growing up, a life, a career in art was more possible for a woman writer than for any other kind of female artist, that you would feel more comfortable in your role as a writer because there were so many good and successful female writers to think about and to *read* and to know about. Where, for example, if you were a musician, symphony orchestras were composed almost entirely of men, and it would be almost impossible to make a successful career. Certainly you would run into *enormous* barriers to being a composer or conductor. Even now, still dreadful barriers. And I don't understand exactly why. The world of painting, sculpture, art is much more radically confined to males, so there are fewer successful women at that. But not so for writers. I didn't have any trouble thinking about writing, as I would have, certainly, if I had been thinking of going into music, or even if I'd been thinking of going into law or some other male-dominated profession. It doesn't seem to me that was true for a writer, or has been, since the eighteenth century. After all, we've got people like Jane Austen, George Eliot, and George Sand—all those people to look back at and see that they did it. Just being able to take it for granted that there weren't going to be those difficulties, *probably* not going to be those difficulties in getting published—just in beginning to make one's way. The main difficulty was being good enough, being lucky enough—a combination of those two."

Elizabeth Spencer has written movingly about women who are restricted by social or familial obligation, but she is reticent about drawing a parallel to her own experience as a young woman drawn to a life as a writer: "It would be a strange family who would want a young girl to turn into a serious novelist—strange, I mean, in the sense of being quite outside the ordinary. Families often run counter to their children's talents for the idea they have of what is good for the children. My parents were somewhat divided, I think, about my writing: my mother wished me to continue, my father wanted the whole nonsense stopped." Being a woman was not the issue, however: "If I had been born a boy I might have found more freedom in living as I chose, but as a young man wanting to write I would certainly have faced much stronger opposition, as a man's 'career' was thought to be much more important than a woman's and had to be on firm economic and social ground."

> There is a time when all that we have done, or thought, or dreamed, meets in a moment that no matter how deeply buried in us is always in the present tense.
> —Mary Lee Settle, *The Killing Ground*

The circumstances of one's birth and the society one grows up in may impose restrictions or provide opportunities that determine choice of vocation. An awareness of how a writer's work has been influenced by religious, political, or social structures can provide insight into the subtle and often ambiguous relationships between life and art, experience and imagination. Do religious or political convictions influence their writing in any way? How autobiographical is their fiction? Do they locate those first, fictional impulses in their imagination or the 'real world' of experience?

Ellen Douglas: "I was raised in a very devout Presbyterian family, and certainly, although I'm no longer a Presbyterian, or even, perhaps, a Christian, that religious background influenced me very strongly. There's a collection, a series of books, that are in all old-fashioned Presbyterian-Southern households, really devout ones. There are about twelve of them called *Line Upon Line, Precept Upon Precept:* and so I guess I was raised "line upon line," "precept upon precept." So that, certainly, was a strong influence. The predicament of the South and the deep racial problems from the time I was old enough to think seemed overwhelmingly important to me, and *that* was a strong influence. The business of trying to come to terms, trying to decide what to think about the world one grew up in, lived in, was really heavy because of all that." Writing was not a process of discovering her values or beliefs, however: "I think the impulse to make fiction was more the impulse to tell stories and that those are some of the things that formed the kind of stories I was interested in telling. Then, as far as the outside world is concerned—or maybe it's the inside world—I grew up in a large and complex extended family in which everybody was compulsively interested in everybody else's character and personality, and there were lots of tale-tellers and people who enjoyed listening to tales. And that, too, was a strong influence. All those things."

The sources of her fiction can be found in both the outside and inside worlds: "*Where the Dreams Cross* started with an idea about a character, particularly about the notion of a woman who's intelligent, and strong, and attractive, but who has been taught by the world she has grown up in that she must present herself as a kind of artifact. *The Rock Cried Out* started with two things. One, I wanted to write a book about young people in the sixties and early seventies—a time we'd just lived through, a time of terrible and complex crises. And then I chose the place, and the place was exceedingly influential on the course of the novel. Only certain things could happen in that place, and to those people. . . . That whole business, for the writer, is so fascinating to think about: the business of the interplay between what one knows of one's experience and what one invents out of one's imagination. The place in *The Rock Cried Out,* except for changes in geography that were necessary for the plot, such as moving the lake around, and things like that, is very close to the place that my family owns in south Mississippi. The *voice* of the narrator Alan is certainly based to some extent upon my youngest son, Brooks's, voice. Brooks and his eldest brother Richard at that time were fixing up a cabin on that place. . . . But the events of the novel, and the characters—the Levitts, and the Boykins and Leila and so forth—are all inventions and the story is an invention." Is there ever a point at which truth and the fiction merge? "I can see that it might happen. If you transformed a situation you knew, wrote about it, and as you wrote changed it so that it became something else, then the fictional world might influence your memory of the real world and you might come to think the fictional thing was the real thing. That interplay between reality and fiction is strange. Sometimes I don't know if I'm remembering my books or my life."

Mary Lee Settle's most recent novel seems to erase the distinction between reality and fiction through exposition of a character whose books have—literally—become her life. Hannah McKarkle, the narrator of *The Killing Ground* and author of five novels collectively known as "The Beulah Quintet," shares just those affinities with Settle. McKarkle's imaginative reconstruction of a past both personal and historical provides structure for *The Killing Ground* and rationale for "The Beulah Quintet." Reconstructing the circumstances of her brother's death, "setting out on a long trail of cleansing whys," back to seventeenth century England, she is the clear embodiment of Settle's belief in writing as a means of understanding experience. But the resemblance ends with the obvious: "I wrote the books and so did she," points out Settle; "I had to make her a writer: How else would she know to see her own past with objective historical training?"

According to Shirley Ann Grau, the things one can say about the influences of a writer's life on her works "are just truisms and they're hardly worth saying—you know, that one's life inevitably conditions views of the world. Many writers are autobiographical by choice. It seems to me a perfectly valid approach to the problem of subject matter. Others try not to be. I suppose the most ridiculous example is Mailer, who, whatever he's writing about, manages to write about Mailer. I'm almost the other extreme. I don't think writing's self-expression in that sense. Writing is story-telling and if it's to be successful—or to be anything beyond story-telling—it has to have some sort of—I hesitate to use the word 'philosophical'—point to it: it has to have some meaning beyond the simple action story. But I don't think any person can continue an autobiographical thing for too long. I think that's probably why American writing has so many one-and-two-book people. It just runs out. Now in *theory* it needn't, but unfortunately, theory doesn't very often come through. I think the failure to look outward means a writer's got a short career, if he's going to keep developing in any sense. . . . The 'cult of personality' has always bothered me, because it runs into—what? Bit of a circus, bit of a showman, probably even more of an actor. Ideally, the writer is an observer, an interpreter, but not in himself a part of what he's interpreting. A filter, I guess. The writer as interpreter—not of himself, but of everything else."

For that "everything else," what Mary Lee Settle calls the "raw material" of fiction, Grau often relies upon newspapers. She is quick to point out, however, that "It has nothing to do with current events at all. I never read the first page. I read the obituaries. Obits are great—they're little, encapsulated *things*. There was a period in my life when people gave me newspapers for presents. I had the Miami paper, the Atlanta *Constitution*, Louisville *Courier-Journal*, New York *Times*, *Wall Street Journal*, San Francisco *Chronicle*. And occasionally the Chicago newspapers—the *Sun-Times* I think I still get. But it's certainly not for the first page. The first page is so monotonous. It's as if city editors made the same page all over the country: same position, same story. But I find the back pages a constant source of interest, amusement—and stir it all up and you'll get characters out of it. It's such a nice way to do it, for me."

In "A Writing Woman," Gail Godwin quotes Gide ("The best means of learning to know oneself is seeking to understand others") to mark a turning point in her writing efforts. Six books later, she regards the transition from memory to imagination as a matter "of instinct, of learning to shift gears," as she writes of a world plausibly close to the one she must enter and leave each day. But Gail Godwin denies the autobiographical element, and the wholesale value of Gide's advice when applied to writers: "Am I Roger Jernigan? Am I Ambrose Clay? Francesca Bolt? 'M'? I am not Nell, or Cate, or Lydia. Or even Violet Clay. Some of my experiences are similar to Jane Clifford's, but I am not Jane, either. Our temperaments are worlds apart. Everyone's 'objective' in writing is different. Some write to win love, admiration, fame, money. Some to explore. Some to save their souls. Some to convert others. Some to share important information." Her social, religious and political influences are unsurprising: "I am closer to middle class people with cultural and intellectual concerns. I don't write about blue-collar workers or manicurists, but if I needed one, I wouldn't hesitate to imagine him/her into a story. Religious beliefs: 'There are more things in this world, Horatio, than are dreamt of in your philosophy.' I am open to miracles, the unexpected. The possibility of a FATE. Political: I vote, I hate wars. I hate stupid, conniving, opportunistic politicians." What Gail Godwin likes—and names as influential in her own development as a writer—are "Austen, Eliot, Dickens, James, Charlotte Bronte, Lawrence, Cather, Wharton. Doris Lessing before she left the world." Her fictional impulses differ from book to book: "*A Mother and Two Daughters* started with an anecdote a friend told me about a disastrous vacation she took with her mother and her sister. *Violet Clay* with a theme: Is there a *time* when an aspiring artist either becomes one or fails to do so? My present novel began with a vision of a country landscape and an idea that 'something' is going to befall a young person. The theme: how the young learn from and take from people who may be very helpless or dangerous in themselves."

Writing, for Anne Tyler, is "simply a way of living other lives," and her books are generally provoked by daydreams: "Just about everything I've written has been based upon 'what if.' What if I led such-and-such a life instead of the one I do lead? What if that person I see standing at the bus stop were to go home and find out such-and-such had happened?" Her childhood efforts attest to this same source: "So far as I can remember, mostly I wrote first pages of stories about lucky, lucky girls who got to go West in covered wagons." She would grant neither religion nor politics a place in her writing, but conceded that growing up in an experimental Quaker community had an influence: "It set me far enough outside the regular world so that I have been able to view things from a certain distance—which is sometimes good for my writing, sometimes bad. So far as I know, nothing else has influenced me." Literature? "I hope you won't think I'm being facetious when I say that my earliest and perhaps strongest literary influence was a children's picture book called *The Little House* by Virginia Lee Burton. I still read it; my copy is in rags. It has everything that matters: insidious change, the passage of time, giving in to change, struggling against change. . . ."

"I think everything I've ever read has influenced me, for better or for worse!" responded Lisa Alther. "The Southern women writers made a big impact—O'Connor, Welty, Porter, McCullers. Doris Lessing. The Southern men writers to a lesser extent. The standard classics."

Presumably, the social and political activism in her novels mirrors Alther's concerns, but she has not been involved to the extent that some of her characters are: "The movement I've been most directly involved in is the women's movement. My involvement in other political movements has been more peripheral, limited to sympathizing, attending occasional functions, trying to understand what's going on. I do, however, feel I've benefited enormously from the atmosphere created by the woman's movement—the significance that is now being granted to female experience, the freedom to explore formerly taboo topics."

> All she saw of him was the seamless exterior—sculptor at work. She never guessed at the cracks inside, the stray thoughts, tangents of memory, hours of idleness, days spent leafing through old magazines or practicing square knots on a length of red twine or humming under his breath. . . .
>
> —Anne Tyler, *Celestial Navigation*

Picture the writer, too, poised between the solitude of his or her imagination—tangents of memory and thought—and the world which labors it. What lies behind the seamless exterior? How does writing fit into a life?

Where and when do writers obtain the solitude and the distance that seem requisite?

Gail Godwin manages through "Country existence. But with a telephone and a car and bus tickets to N.Y. City. And a few interesting friends. I work best alternating between an *input* of experience, social life, other chores, even other writing (essays, reviews) and then a deep plunge into the clear, still, waters of repose, reverie and meditation." She does not agree that being a writer makes living a "normal" life difficult: "No, a good writer needs as much life as possible. However, your discrimination becomes more acute. You choose your 'normal' activities for sharpness and quality. There is not time for the second-rate. Unless, of course, you are writing a story about the second-rate. Then you may have to subject yourself to a boring afternoon."

Mary Lee Settle emphasized the discipline—"a hell of a lot of discipline"—required; the importance of routine—sitting down to write *every* day—and something she called "the will not to will." She defined this as the will *not* to put out the garbage, check on the coffee pot, start the laundry ("No writer up until the twentieth century had to cook their own food or do their own laundry"); but to "wait in your own silence until it happens." She will spend all morning on a first draft and then spend the rest of the day getting ready for the next morning. Revising? "No! Loosening up! Gardening, cooking, talking, seeing friends . . . belly scratching . . . watching *M.A.S.H.* I can't spend my time wrapped up in the novel or in some intensely intellectual conversation. Not until I get to the very end of the novel: then I could write for twenty-four hours straight if I had the energy." The need for energy to sustain the book or the idea, she added, can control your day to the extent that "when I'm writing I'm like an athlete in training. I can't drink too much, I can't stay out too late."

"It's hard to write without clear quiet space around me," responded Elizabeth Spencer. "I rent a small studio—only one large room really—over in East Montreal where I know scarcely anyone." A solution modified somewhat by Lisa Alther: "When I was first writing it was much more difficult to get going. Sometimes I'd go away for several days at a time, rent a room somewhere, and do nothing but write, sleep, and eat." Now she works while her child is at school and her husband at work. She added: "At the moment I don't have an outside job, though I've taught, worked in publishing, and done freelance writing. I enjoyed my jobs and learned a lot from them, though I did find it difficult to have as much uninterrupted time as I require for fiction writing. But when I do nothing but write, I can feel quite insular and cut off. I think it's crucial to find a balance."

Anne Tyler follows a similar routine—one of the peculiar advantages she ascribes to being a writer that almost makes things easier: "For one thing, I have never had to choose between tending children at home and working away from home; I can have my cake and eat it too." One radical solution to the problem of time and energy is dismissed: "Living alone is the start of one of my favorite fantasies. But the end of it is when I realize that, having got everything arranged exactly to my liking and all distraction dispensed with, I would probably look around me and ask, 'Why was it I imagined I wanted this?'"

Ellen Douglas published her first novel at the age of forty, after working on it intermittently over the course of six years, while raising three sons. She talked about the discipline of writing as it affects women in general, and her own response to the demands of being both mother and writer: "The business of being at home, in a house, constantly surrounded by the people whose lives you're involved in, is a problem for a woman, as it isn't for a man. Particularly if you're raising children. Just having children underfoot is a problem for a female writer—to make a space, a time, to work in. When my children were very small I never wrote in the summertime, because they were home, and it was impossible to get away. I wrote in the wintertime; when everybody left for school, I sat down to work. I was a Southern woman in a particular period in history when it was possible to have servants; and that's probably why it was possible for me to do the work I did. If I had had the care of a house, and the raising of children entirely on me, I probably wouldn't have had the time to do it. Again, that's bad, too: it's not good for you to be dependent upon someone else to do the scut-work, but that's the way it was." Thinking back to those half-days of relative freedom when her children were at school, she added: "The fact that I only worked half a day didn't have anything to do with my children being around: I still don't work but half a day. At noon, my brain gives out. I can do proofreading, or that sort of thing in the afternoon, but most of the time I only write in the morning."

Shirley Ann Grau succeeded at raising a family and writing her books by having "very healthy kids." "I suppose," she continued, "if you were unlucky enough to have a very sick child it would be devastating. Mine weren't—they just went their own ways. So that's no problem at all. Well, you were sleepy at times—and there were years when I was sleepy most of the time. But I wrote—whenever. I don't have to have a time. You fit it in, that's all. It's a neat arrangement—having children *is* for the young; because after a certain age I don't think you could do that anymore. Get on with such *little* sleep. Nor could you compartmentalize your thought quite that much." Solitude? "Again, it's relative. I can sit here and work and keep half an ear on the workings of the house. You know, I can answer the door, answer the phone. I've long ago trained myself. Writing is only part of a life, you see. It's not a precious kernel to be sheltered and nurtured. It's part of the ordinary, human, complicated set of jobs, relationships. It's got to be fitted in and balanced with everything else. Now, I know writers—darn good ones—who've kept little offices and go there to work. But I've always preferred not to move, because I'm lazy. It is easier to climb a few steps and be there. Also, when I get home there isn't a pile-up of details that have to be dealt with—you know, everything from 'the car battery's dead' to 'the gardeners couldn't start the mower,' or something like that. There is every *possible* way of dealing with the problem of fitting writing into everyday life. I know one guy who vanishes, literally, for weeks on end. That's probably the most endearing thing about writing—that it has room for so many eccentric patterns of behavior. Can you imagine advertising, say, allowing that kind of thing? There's only one test in writing: does it work? If you wanted to write standing on your head, I'm sure the test would be exactly the same. Do you produce anything? So in that way it's a very simple life. It's almost not fair to speak of writing as a field, as if it were unified. The end may be a book, but it's produced by *enormously* different people, working in *enormously* different fashions. And not really wanting to adopt each other's work patterns."

> Sometimes, too, she felt singular to the point of being waiflike, as though she'd moved to a distant city and had no society in the world of other women.
>
> —Elizabeth Spencer, *The Snare*

Solitude, when it is required, is by necessity, rather than choice; reinforced by habit or circumstance. ("When I do nothing but write, I can feel quite insular and cut off. I think it's crucial to find a balance.") *To be sure, cooking, gardening, and bus tickets to N.Y. City provide compensation of sorts; but how many writers seek to redress their isolation through friendship with other writers? How valid is the notion of a literary community, particularly among women writers, in this country?*

Gail Godwin has "a few friends who happen to be writers. We write letters, see one another, exchange chapters."

"I have a good many friends who know my work and follow it," responded Elizabeth Spencer. "And a handful who seem to understand it so well that showing my work to them is a great help. I love to share what is share-able."

Anne Tyler: "Very few of my friends are writers. A good many aren't even readers. I am superstitious about showing, or even discussing, work in progress with anyone at all. Probably the same superstition keeps me from advising—I get anxious for other people when they discuss their work at any length." (Her husband published his first novel when he was a medical student in Iran, and he still writes—in a language which precludes much literary camaraderie with his wife, who commented: "I do speak some Persian, but barely struggle through the alphabet when it comes to reading.") The notion of a literary community had obviously not crossed Tyler's mind before, but she was reluctant to damn the possibility: "Maybe," she responded, "I live in the wrong area for that."

Lisa Alther was equally perplexed, particularly at the notion of a community of women writers: "If such a thing exists, I'm not aware of it. There are certainly lots of fine women writers in America, many of whom have strong feminist convictions and are in touch with and supportive of each other. But 'community' seems to put it a bit strongly, since the country is so vast, and connections, sporadic. Maybe a community exists in N.Y.C. and other large cities, where women can get together more easily, but there's not much sense of 'community' (at least as we use the term in the South) for those of us in rural areas."

Instead, she admits to the kind of casual network of friends that Godwin maintains: "Usually four or five friends read a second or third draft, and I incorporate some of their suggestions into the next draft. I do the same for several friends."   .

"Even if writers know one another—I suppose I've known *most* of the important writers," said Shirley Ann Grau—"I don't necessarily think they talk about writing. Now in New Orleans—New Orleans is having a sort of 'rebirth', to use a ridiculous phrase, of writing self-consciousness—there is a terribly active, brand-new group called Louisiana Writers Guild or something like that. It's state-wide, it's very active, it's growing. They just published—because as beginning writers they had difficulty getting published (it's terribly hard to get started now)—a collection of short pieces. Some are good, some are bad, some are really very professional, some are terribly amateurish. But the important thing is that it's out. That they did it at all is rather amazing. And they're already planning another one, so this is the sort of thing that's rolling. I think beginners probably need more support—just the comfort of knowing there are other people in the same situation. That's the value of writing classes. It certainly doesn't teach you to write. But it gives you an ego boost—enough confidence to let you go on by yourself."

Indeed, for many writers, and many more would-be writers, the union of art and fellowship takes place in the classroom. The teaching of creative writing, and all the literary paraphernalia associated with the process, has become, in Gail Godwin's words, "an industry—and a thriving one!" Although she was "stimulated" at Iowa and by her teacher in London, and generous in her estimation of colonies like Yaddo and MacDowell (". . . a quiet place to work, free meals, a respite from the world's demands. I am all for them"), Godwin feels that workshops and conferences are not really an asset to apprentice writers: "They encourage a dismal sameness of material depending on the literary fashion of the moment."

Lisa Alther, like Godwin, has never taught creative writing, but took a couple of courses in college, and thinks classes are helpful to the extent that they force the writer to show his or her work to other people: ". . . in hearing their criticisms and suggestions, you realize that there are many ways to state the same point, that words aren't sacrament."

"I'm all for the teaching of creative writing," responded Anne Tyler. "At the very least, it imposes some structure and applies a little pressure to people at a stage when they might otherwise be aimlessly waiting for 'inspiration'; and if you have a good teacher it speeds up your progress by shortcutting through reams of trial-and-error. Reynolds Price was really the rarest kind of teacher, and I feel blessed to have had him. I have never been to a workshop or writer's colony, and suspect I would be completely unproductive in one, but I would love to have one of those little lunchbaskets at my workroom door every noon."

Ellen Douglas has taught creative writing for the past six years, the first three at Northeast Louisiana University, and now one semester a year at Ole Miss. She doesn't think it's possible to teach people how to write, but rather, "you can lead them up to a way of teaching themselves. You can help people find the kinds of books they ought to read and find ways of criticizing themselves. . . . So many young people in colleges think they want to write, but they haven't even *begun* to acquire—to read—English and American literature. If you start like I did, you start at the front and go back. I mean, you start with contemporary writers and move back into the past. I think you can help teach young people, who have been raised on television, mostly, and movies, that reading is marvelous, and that if they're going to write, they have to read, read, read. And then I think you can begin to teach them how to teach themselves to think, how to give themselves some critical standards. But past that, the writer has to do it for himself."

> Sitting alone in a room reading a book,
> with no one to interrupt me. That is all
> I ever consciously wanted out of life.
> —Anne Tyler, *Celestial Navigation*

Miss Vinton, the bookstore clerk in Anne Tyler's novel, is repeatedly confounded by the knowledge that "things rarely work out the way the magazines would lead you to expect," and is perhaps less absorbed in reading than she is in her search for privacy. But as an observer, as a fictional character who interprets reality in terms of what she has read, we can use her as a kind of link between the two worlds of reading and writing. For it is in the realm of the imagination that reader and writer come closest. Who are the readers? Are writers conscious of a reader as they write?

Not Anne Tyler. "If I were, I think I would dry up. My only thought of readers comes at the end of a book, when I read it the last time with an outsider's eye (as nearly as possible) to see if something literally doesn't make sense."

For Gail Godwin, too, writer becomes reader "as I re-read what I have written." She noted that she receives letters from "93 year old women and sixteen year old boys and all the in-between versions," and took issue with the assumption "that women write for women and are read by women. I write for people who care about the things I care about—how to live life bravely and well and fully and curiously."

"I write with an ideal reader in mind," said Ellen Douglas. "The ideal reader is intelligent, sensitive, and puts his attention on the book. But other than that, I don't write with a reader in mind. I think that's a fatal error, you can't do that. John Cheever said he had no idea who read his books. He was always astonished to think there were, say, 15,000 or 50,000 people out there who bought his books. It *is* mysterious who your readers are."

Mary Lee Settle, amused by her own, somewhat existential pursuit of the question, admitted that she'd never seen anyone on a train reading *O Beulah Land.* Working on her third book of juvenile non-fiction, she makes an exception and does project a reader out there: "Myself at ten or eleven—very smart-alecky and very questioning."

Elizabeth Spencer, long an advocate of writing which communicates, likes to think she is understood "without a sacrifice of subtlety or making things easy and cheap. I think the convoluted style Faulkner was prone to in later work, and Joyce's densities in *Finnegan's Wake* are both self-defeating if one wants to be understood by a considerable audience. Both have found an audience, so perhaps I am mistaken. I seek to communicate as widely as possible—I love clarity—without sacrificing meaning. About my readers, I can't say beyond my acquaintance and people who write me. Judging by the letters I get they are varied indeed."

"I've absolutely no idea who buys books—anybody's books—least of all who reads them," was Shirley Ann Grau's response. "Or, indeed, when people read them, I'm not sure they're reading, that we're reading, the same things. You get some very literate, informative letters sometimes, and I can't *believe* that they're talking about the story they're talking about. Because that isn't what I've put in there. Now as far as I know, no aesthetician has ever worked on that: the independent life of a piece of fiction. Because it can say exactly *opposite* things to people. It's as if a story had a life all its own and that it went its own way."

Still, Grau believes that writing "is less self-expression than communication. And that to communicate you have to, in some basic way, always remember the reader. I don't mean 'remember the reader' in the sense that popular books are tailored to a certain audience. Not the way Silhouette romances, say, are tailored to a certain female audience of a certain reputation or a certain age. I don't mean 'think of the reader' that way at all. I think that's the death of good fiction. I think a writer of quality fiction has got to always remember the other side of the page— because he's got to communicate with it, he's got to get his message across. You lose so much—one loses so much, anyway, in the transmission of ideas. What starts out as an idea in a writer's head loses—what?—a third maybe; the writer loses a third putting it down on paper. The reader, taking it off the page, loses I don't know what percentage—so what's actually communicated is a very tiny percentage of the original idea. So in that sense, sure, you have to think of the reader. But you think of him as a way of forcing yourself to take great care in getting your message across, because words have a funny way of simply not carrying the meanings you think they carry. This accounts for all the 'stunting'—all the points of view, all the images. It's just an attempt to get through. Another school says you just express yourself and devil take the reader if he doesn't get it. But that's a little more self-centered than I care to be. I suppose my emphasis is not very much on the individual, personal side of writing at all—it's on the message, if you will, the meaning side."

If the act of publication affords the writer an audience of readers, who are to varying degrees sympathetic and perceptive, or hostile and misdirected, it also exposes the book to the equally various, and more pervasive, judgments of critics and reviewers. Reviewers are uniquely, almost unforgiveably, dependent upon writers. What can be said about the other side of the relationship? How do writers feel about criticism? Do they read reviews of their own work? Do they write reviews? Does this enable them to be more objective about their own work?

Mary Lee Settle, who wrote for years without publication, claimed she has been "discovered" three times; but despite critical neglect, she was never neglected by other writers: "The recognition of people you respect sustains you." In tones which conveyed acceptance rather than approval, she spoke of the "curious way" in which neglect—"of a woman as a brain and so forth"—enabled her to work in "conscripted secrecy," freed of the demands that fame ushers in. Those early years left her with a dismissive, shrug-of-the-shoulders attitude toward the vicissitudes of critical favor: "A bad review stops me writing for about three days; a good review stops me for two days."

"I remember being quite disappointed," wrote Elizabeth Spencer, "when some of my best efforts went unnoticed by critics, while some not so good were praised, but more recently I've come to accept this as part of the general gamble taken by anyone in the arts. The effort is always maximum and totally sincere—the results are uncertain."

Anne Tyler responded: "I have nothing against reading reviews, but gradually, almost unconsciously, I seem to have stopped. I think it might be because, while I believe that reviews are valuable for the reader, I don't see much but negative results for the writer. Whether they approve or disapprove, they still make the writer self-conscious. I think criticism is necessary as a kind of Consumers Report Service. But it troubles me that a single review, in a major paper, can make or break a book. After all, we're only talking about one person's opinion. I play around a lot with thoughts of alternatives—capsule reviews of every book, compiled on one page, a kind of Gallup Poll of the critics? Or nothing but positive reviews, however long it takes for a book to filter down to someone who likes it? (If a reviewer wrote, 'I love this book because the hero is handsome and the heroine is beautiful,' the reader would still guess what was what.)" A frequent reviewer, Tyler continued, ". . . I do believe reviewing has sharpened my thought processes. I used to read books like eating chocolates—I like it, I don't like it, toss it aside and reach for the next—but reviewing has forced me to stop and analyze what makes a book work or not work."

When asked whether she wrote book reviews, and whether they enabled her to view her own work more objectively, Gail Godwin responded: "Only for books I am interested in. Only in that I know I am hurting or pleasing another ego, as mine has been hurt or pleased."

Shirley Ann Grau had an equally pessimistic view of the state of book reviewing: "I read review after review and I find it impossible to discover the basic thing—'what's the book about?' Book reviewers tend to make themselves out to be terribly clever fellows, and forget that they're supposed to be communicating something about the book. So when I get annoyed at that I write one, and I flatter myself that mine always describe the book pretty precisely. I also don't like the fairly common reviewer habit of ego gratification by destroying a book. So I don't do negative reviews, period. There's never a reason to do a negative review—if the book is no good, pass over it. Somebody else has got a good book. I gave up reading reviews of my own work a long time ago. I was reading one and it said, in effect: 'There's one marvelous short story in this: let me tell you the plot. This is the finest story in the book.' End of review. Well, it may have been a good story—it wasn't mine. Gosh knows where the story came from, but the poor dear soul was so muddled he had given me credit for someone else's short story. If they can't keep the contents page straight, I can't really pay too much attention to anything else."

> I spend my life working at what seems to some people no better than playing—unless, of course, you're lucky enough to earn a lot of money at it.
> —Ellen Douglas, *The Rock Cried Out*

The economic and social difficulties of making a living as a novelist have been at least partially eclipsed by the rise of public and private foundations supporting the arts (and the artist), and by our celebration of the writer as a marketable commodity. And while these writers tended to minimize the financial disadvantages of a writing career, it should also be noted that many of them hold other jobs (Ellen Douglas, Elizabeth Spencer, and Mary Lee Settle teach creative writing part of each year), and all of them—save Gail Godwin—are married. The transformation of writer to celebrity (remuneration not withstanding) is more vexing, however, probably because it is accomplished at the expense of literature. Are writers concerned with fame? Do they think in terms of immediate reward or ultimate recognition?

"I don't like what I have seen of fame in the most popular sense," wrote Anne Tyler. "It baffles me that people keep mixing up the book with the person who wrote it. But I am concerned with ultimate critical reputation, yes. I would like for people to read my books and take them seriously. I'd like them to get lost in my characters' lives for a while." Being well known, however, hasn't affected her life much: "Luckily, it's been gradual enough so that I learned to say 'no' along the way—a most valuable word—and I figure that by the time I'm ninety, I'll have reached a hundred percent of 'nos' and be leading a completely happy life."

"More money / more mail / more invitations / more visibility" is the way

Gail Godwin summarized life after success. "Fame concerns me, now that I have had a share of it, in that I feel that the world rewards a writer for good work by making so many demands it is hard for that writer to get on with more good work." She concluded: "I very much hope my work outlives me."

"I used to be ambitious," answered Lisa Alther, "wanted a book published and reviewed in the *New York Times*. But I wrote for 12 years—2 unpublished novels, 13 short stories, many articles, 250 rejection slips—without that happening. During those 12 years I had to find other rewards, which I did in the pleasure of feeling myself improve at my craft, and the pleasure of understanding through writing fiction issues I hadn't understood before. So that by the time I got published, I'd almost ceased to care about publication and recognition. Though they've certainly been pleasant. Now I approach fiction writing as a learning experience. It's how I make sense out of the world around me, and that seems to me to be reward enough. Though if what I write rings a bell for someone else, I'm always delighted, partly because it seems to confirm my own perceptions and leaves me feeling more linked up with other people."

Shirley Ann Grau dismissed the question of "fame" in a slightly different way: "I don't think anybody thinks that way. It breaks down to a series of problems that have to be solved. When you finish one book, there's the problem of the next. Whatever you do, there's far more that you haven't; so you don't—by and large—think of anything except the next problem and what to do about it. You always have many more novels than you're ever going to do—they're more or less standing in line, and how you select, I don't know. But you pick from the possibilities."

The Fiction of Anne Tyler

DORIS BETTS

I often speculate about how the college courses we teach in writing—which usually means in writing the short story—may be changing the form of the contemporary American novel.

We teach the short story not because it is an easier form to learn—I agree with Faulkner that after poetry, it is the most difficult—but for such practical reasons as classroom time constraints mingled with the impatience of sophomores, and the teacher's need to evaluate finished fictional units.

The result is that a rare student whose creative mind and vision might promise the scope of Tolstoy will instead practice exclusively the skills of an Edgar Allan Poe: brevity, focus, compression, and intensity—much as Anne Tyler did when she was a student of Reynolds Price at Duke University. (At Broughton High School both Price and Tyler had been the writing students of a locally famous teacher in Raleigh, Phyllis Peacock.) At Duke Tyler's favorite author, and Price's, was Eudora Welty, more a short story writer than a novelist, whose effects are most often wrought less from event than from plumbing the depth of her characters and their memories.

What difference, we might ask, can it possibly make if a painter trains his young eye and brush on the miniature or cameo, only later to be commissioned chiefly for murals or chapel ceilings? Which of her early habits would such a painter decide to abandon or modify or—conversely—to practice stubbornly and transmute? By insisting on detail and concentration, by preferring focus and unity over breadth of development and scope, can such an artist modify OUR expectations of what a mural *does* or what a novel *is?*

Anne Tyler's nine novels over seventeen years trace her own accommo-

23

Photo: Diana H. Walker

Anne Tyler

*Born in Minnesota (1941), Tyler spent her childhood in North
Carolina. She received her education at Duke (B.A.) and Co-
lumbia University. Since the publication of her first novel in
1964,* If Morning Ever Comes, *she has published eight novels
and numerous short stories, essays, and reviews. Her reviews
appear frequently in the* New York Times Book Review.

dation of the methods of the short story, methods geared to change and revelation, until they become adapted to her more novelistic conclusions about a Reality which changes very little, but waits for its runaways to come home and learn at the dinner table how to tolerate even their next-of-kin.[1]

Of course novels and stories are subgroups, not separate species, but the focused structural method and the revelatory intent of the short story mark Tyler's first three novels, which zero in to choose the spot from which the past may be understood and the future implied. Just as Poe's "Tell Tale Heart" has all three verb tenses in its opening sentence and thus makes time radiate, most short stories seek to enter time where they can suggest all three time levels and almost stop their clocks so that yesterday and tomorrow, lying on either side of the moment, can be better understood. Eudora Welty's *Losing Battles,* an example of this structure raised to the size of the novel, may be seen as an older, wiser, cousin to Anne Tyler's first novel, *If Morning Ever Comes* (1964). Both use the same gathering-home; both look through the keyhole of present time at a long past and its meaning.

Short story trainees in our classes prefer summoning characters to those settings where time will cluster most naturally, to home ground, for holidays, reunions, ceremonies, crises, deathbeds—wherever the situation will allow shared memory to solidify. A story writer's second favorite place to arrest time and motion is the circumscribed encounter, sometimes in train stations or airports (Hemingway, Raymond Carver, etc.) where lives intersect for travelers carrying their pasts like undeclared baggage. A story writer attempting a first novel may retain focused time, focused setting, or both. Katherine Anne Porter floated her microcosm out to sea to make her characters hold still for examination in *Ship of Fools.* Styron's first novel, *Lie Down in Darkness,* enters time at a crucial funeral, and recounts the past by flashback.

Early in her career Tyler retains brief times, flashback and restricted setting. Instead of recounting the gradual passage of time before the reader's eye, Tyler enters it at a still spot near some point of change, insight, or decision for her protagonist. Robert Browning's poetry contains even tinier examples often cited in story classes, since Browning, too, can enter a lifetime with a pinprick: showing, for instance, how the only poised chimney sweep we notice is the one about to fall or, in "My

Last Duchess," hanging an immobile woman's portrait on the wall, to cause the Duke unwittingly to reveal himself and their entire marriage. Such a revelatory stillspot, or poised moment, is the jugular for which natural story writers have an instinct.

Two of the short stories Anne Tyler wrote for her Duke college class, "Nobody Answers the Door" (*Antioch Review*, Fall 1964) and "I Never Saw Morning" (*Archive*, April 1961), are testing points for her first novel, (1964). Both early stories occur sooner in time than the novel, as if Tyler were walking around the lives of her characters, feeling for a jugular. Like so many short stories, Tyler's first novel has a circular rather than linear structure and concentrates on the *implications* of small events more than the pressure of accumulating cause-effect acts onstage. Its surface ongoing time-level covers just over five present days in the life of Ben Joe Hawkes coming home to Sandhill, N.C., but by memory and association—favorite devices by which stories use moments to suggest entire lives—Tyler draws forward into this five-day period not only Ben Joe's twenty-five years but those of his relatives, including the sister who has also come home and who may now leave.

This novel, like the stories where she tested it first, pierces time instead of tracing Ben Joe chronologically from birth to the present. Even in her first novel, however, Anne Tyler's outlook differs from that of most short story writers who choose the off-balance chimney sweep, a character near the point of change. Tyler has always said she doubts that people *do* change very much,[2] thus her novels more often snap open a shutter on characters who want to change and try, but in the end become what they were fleeing. Because from the beginning her epiphanies have been so calm and slow, if not downright ambiguous, Tyler's development is her reconciliation of a theme of slow-developing realism with modified prose techniques meant for rapid, flashing disclosure. At twenty-three in this first book, Tyler relies on short story method, but has since been steadily tinkering to adjust it to the more ponderous inevitability which magnetizes her rebellious characters home.

Her second novel, *The Tin Can Tree* (1965), still has a dense center to which events cling for resonance and insight. Her plot direction still moves down through layers of meaning, not across time from left to right. This novel is as chronologically compact as the first, six successive days, and again enters time at a selected crisis point—Janie Rose's funeral and the disappearance of her brother. But Tyler has now begun tinkering with the unity of story, and her first attempt to increase the size of one of fiction's elements is the most obvious: she increases her cast of characters. She crowds members of *three* separate but interdependent families into a single house, still keeping unity of surface time and place, but entangling more, and more complex, relationships. Again the novel's structure drills down into grief and guilt to the bedrock of past causes, but diversity of character saves the action from seeming static. Though this second novel seems neither longer nor larger in size than the first, it *does* feel heavier. This compressed weight, which will become a Tyler trademark, predicts one way her novels develop, from a round marble to a round ball bearing, from china to steel.

Like Eudora Welty, Tyler chose early to make character bear her heaviest load of meaning. Outlining any Tyler plot will illustrate Welty's definition of plot as the "why" of story, the steady asking of "why?" and having the question replied to "at different depths."[3] Tyler's strategy keeps but deepens and weights the basic strategy of Katherine Anne Porter's story, "The Grave," where a forgotten incident thrusts itself across twenty years' time to become clarified while the narrator is walking a street in another country. And Tyler has also learned to walk Welty's "Worn Path," not pursuing any buildup of suspenseful events, but because the real journey is the deep descent into the life of Phoenix Jackson. Or perhaps Tyler absorbed her time structure from Faulkner's story, "A Rose for Emily," where the entire present action occurs on one day of Emily Grierson's funeral but below that day, like a mine shaft, drop sixty years of past events, all forced upward to claim their true meaning in the grisly discovery waiting up the stairs in a dusty bed. These good story writers (as well as talented novelists tinkering with their methods) suspend time long enough to drive readers down the layers asking "why?" with such aroused curiosity that they forget the more primitive question of "what happened next?"

By her third novel, *A Slipping Down Life* (1970), not only Tyler's structure but recurring themes seem clear. Her microcosm is the family, containing its two extremes, the stay-at-home and the runaway. Dare I call them types of the Classic and Romantic? In Tyler's family cacophonies one lonely individual voice sounds stronger among other lonely voices, recalling Frank O'Connor's famous study of the short story, *The Lonely*

Voice, which identifies the mood of the form. Other persistent Tyler motifs are: leaving and returning; the desire for dream-parents and dream-lives but the confrontation with real ones; conflict between individual freedom and duty to others; the pull between private and social life. Often Tyler's novels end with reconciliation (some call it resignation) to a reality which may include drudgery, in homes where possessions threaten to own their occupants. (Some resolutions are made with a passivity which my liberated women students find very close to masochism. Last month we read Tyler's *Earthly Possessions* just after Fowles's *French Lieutenant's Woman;* the coeds want and fully expect to become Sarah Woodruff, and never Charlotte Emery.)

By Tyler's third novel, *A Slipping Down Life,* she decides to tinker with her surface time span. Suddenly it flowers from a few days into a full year in the life of Evie Decker, a fat teenager who carves with nail scissors the name of a rock singer on her forehead. Evie is one of many Tyler characters with a longing to be set apart from the rest, at least by a mark, at best by full bodily escape. But Evie is also more *vivid* than earlier characters. According to Stella Nesanovich, Tyler has described the characters in her first two novels as "bland" ("Individual" 7), so in this gloomier novel she not only spreads time but outlines its occupants with darker lines, like Roualt. This time she shrinks again the size of her family unit as if abandoning the experiment with mere numbers in favor of experimenting with intense individual portraits, almost to the point of caricature. Critics have called this her most Gothic novel. Here again are the Tyler themes: escape, kidnapping, non-communication, the final return home— although here Evie will enter an empty house to examine the stopped-time smiling photograph of her mother whom no one now living remembers. (Tyler's use of photographs, especially in *Earthly Possessions,* will be more fully treated later, since a short story is to a photograph what a novel is to a motion picture.) But Tyler's biggest adaptation of story form to novel intent in *A Slipping Down Life* is the more novelistic time span in which she uses more sharply etched character.

With her fourth book, *The Clock Winder* (1972), Tyler covers an entire decade, 1960–70, and for the first time begins tinkering with point of view. Most modern short stories achieve unity and impact through tight viewpoints, and Tyler's early novels have been persistently focused through one character, *The Tin Can Tree* through two. In *The Clock*

Winder, Tyler enters many more characters, though still treating each like a protagonist in a separate short story, with assigned chapters in each one's point of view. These divisions make the novel's structure match its controlling metaphor since each character, even when synchronized with the others, will tick separately in the novel, just as many clocks tick in separate rooms in the Emerson household. Again Tyler's favorite themes recur: families, individuals escaping families, with focus on the title character Elizabeth Abbot, who can wind all the clocks properly to keep the same time, who in future novels will be the almost inadvertent, half unwilling, nurturer of others. Elizabeth, incidentally, believes in reincarnation, surely Tyler's ultimate expression of the motif of departure and return!

In this fourth novel, Tyler not only tinkers with viewpoint and extends her scale, but also expands her unified story writer's setting. Elizabeth, a native of North Carolina, comes to live with the Emersons in Baltimore, so for the first time Tyler has *not* located past and present in the same place. Although shifting points of view can easily become separate stories, her increasingly novelistic overview is also larger, more interlaced. She even tries here a section of letters, and provides more action and triggering action before the reader's eye instead of retrospectively.

She keeps but modifies further her viewpoint expansion in *Celestial Navigation* (1974), perhaps her most revealing novel about her own literary progress. This time-coverage extends to thirteen years, most of them spent in a dark, three-story boarding house (still vertical space, not horizontal) on a narrow street in Baltimore, where the boarders who come and go resemble an extended family. The return of two sisters for their mother's funeral again opens the novel but, significantly, despite reliance on memory, this novel moves forward along events which occur after this entry point of crisis. Unlike Tyler's now familiar survivor-women, Jeremy Pauling seems a new kind of character, Tyler's first portrait of the artist, whose development from collage to sculpture seems to parallel Tyler's literary progress from story to more and more complex novel. Jeremy begins his career with pasteups inside fixed borders, using items which, selected and clustered, suggest a whole which reveals even more than its parts. He progresses to more intricate collages, then thickens their layers to bas relief, and at last molds sculptures, a steady progress in dimension, a steady move toward using human character. The process takes Jeremy a decade; Anne Tyler in ten years and five novels has also enlarged her story skills through a process of added dimension.

When asked, Tyler called Jeremy Pauling "wholly imaginary " ("Individual" 123), a character barely suggested by an ex-mental patient she knew for only one day—more than sufficient time for a story writer's trained laser vision. Besides, when most writers call a character "wholly imaginary," we often mean secretly that we went down deeper for him than we knew or cared to tell, that we formed him by feel alone of our unconscious dust in the dark. As a girl, Tyler has said, she wanted to be an artist, not a writer ("Still Just Writing" 13).

Artist Jeremy Pauling also provides one answer (perhaps the answer creative women have historically given) to the artist's eternal question about choosing between the life and the work. Despite complaints, even allowing for his eventual withdrawal from the interruptions of family living, Pauling's art is first brought alive and nourished by the intrusion of children, clutter, love. In his life first, then his art, he makes a parallel shift from the use of objects in his collages to inclusion of human beings.

Six years before *Celestial Navigation* appeared, Tyler's writing teacher Reynolds Price also published a novel animated by Yeats's question, called *Love and Work* (1968). I hope a critic will someday compare the two, for *Celestial Navigation* seems almost a response to Price's, a yes-but response; and both novels contain similar content. Price's protagonist does choose work over life; though in the end Jeremy rejects life for art as well, the final images of his moored boat moving only in circles, of his old age spent in a locked and darkened house, seem to say that a high cost has been exacted for the "great, towering, beautiful sculptures" he makes late in his isolated life.

Anne Tyler's essay "Still Just Writing" details her own conflict between life and work. Like so many writers who are also wives and mothers, she chose both; she stayed home with art practiced the hard way against the contrary pull of domesticity; but she has said her children have deepened her and her work. "Who else in the world do you *have* to love, no matter what?"(9).

A stronger resemblance between Tyler and Jeremy, then, may be the way he sees life in a series of brief flashes which arrest motion in midair, faster even than photographs, the other metaphor Tyler uses in almost every novel. Story critics have compared the photograph with Hemingway's "Hills Like White Elephants," Irwin Shaw's "Girls in Their Summer Dresses," even William Carlos Williams's "The Use of Force," calling these stories the polaroid shots of literature. Click. The black and white essence, caught. Click. Stopped movement. Sufficient. Yet mysterious.

Jeremy's clicking eyesight is specified early in *Celestial Navigation.* "That was the way his vision functioned: only in detail. Piece by piece. He [Jeremy] had tried looking at the whole of things but it never worked out"(45). Even as an artistic child, Jeremy could not draw an entire room, but would produce a closeup of wallpaper pattern showing one electric wall socket with "its screws neatly bisected by microscopic slits." Although Mary Tell (one of Tyler's simultaneous rebels and nurturers) will bear Jeremy's four children, they will always *see* different things. She has left one husband and will eventually leave Jeremy, but although Jeremy (who early reminds us of Bartleby) rarely leaves his house, he deduces the entire world from evidential detail observed through his third floor window.

This vantage point of seeing, this use of detailed parts arranged inside a frame, sounds like Tyler's developing literary method. She remains a writer who selects her time entry points but heads toward magnitude, whose life is both private and domestic but who prefers not to teach writing courses much as Jeremy finds art students an ordeal. Nor will you hear Anne Tyler speaking at the South Atlantic Modern Language Association; she has said, "I will write my books and raise the children. Anything else just fritters me away. . . . I hate leaving home" ("Still Just Writing" 15).

And as Jeremy's art work thickens with glued-in layers of ordinary objects like Dixie cups and shoestrings, so have Tyler's novels. Family and its clutter remain her metaphor for life. She does not examine political, social, class, or economic movements, but like Jeremy keeps increasing texture, depth, dimension, of the small, earthly possessions which come to hand. Olivia calls one of Jeremy's structures "a cross section of a busy household." Anne Tyler's later novels, Jeremy's later art and the symbolic photographs can all be described by another character in *Celestial Navigation*, Mrs. Vinton. "Moments that you just witnessed are suspended forever while you yourself recede from them with every breath you take. The moments grow smaller and yet clearer. You see some sorrow in them you have never before suspected"(145).

Following her portrait of the developing artist and his developing art, Tyler's last four novels consolidate her gains, the short story form now so imbedded inside the larger novel that its overlapped, glued-down edges blend and hardly show. Novel number six, *Searching for Caleb* (1976), like Jeremy's final towering sculptures, is Tyler's largest family and longest time coverage—five generations of Pecks who look alike but aren't. Their 1912 runaway, Caleb, was always drawn away from the others by any stray music he might hear. Once more Tyler unravels time backwards, since Caleb disappeared sixty-one years before the novel opens; but this great volume of time has become historical, affecting generations, with older causes, longer meanings, below the surface action. In *Searching for Caleb*, Tyler has also grown more comfortable with enlarged scope, relaxed enough to be more humorous. Though the actual finding of Caleb and his second disappearance will occur over the span of one summer, this time Tyler also tinkers with the breadth of her persistent themes. Her runaway/stay-at-home conflict has sometimes warred within one character, then between two, or between one family member struggling with the rest; but among the Pecks of fashionable Roland Park, whole groups of kin of all ages have these contrasting natures. Having multiplied the conflict, she also synthesizes it by joining one representative of each type, Justine and Daniel, in partnership to find Caleb. More than usual, in this novel Tyler seems to choose sides with the vagabond family group, allotting this time to the runaways those qualities she typically affirms—steadfast endurance and the will to keep on loving. In the end Justine is moving on, but stripping her house not of love—only the family furniture.

The distance is not great from that scene to Tyler's seventh novel, *Earthly Possessions*, in which Charlotte Emery also wants to strip herself of all encumbrances, objects, possessions, perhaps even people, in order to take alone the long refugee march of her life away from the romantic homeland of childhood, toward the revised, improved, romantic true country of dreams.

Tyler's frequent use of photography becomes in this novel a central metaphor which functions much like Jeremy's art. I was reminded of Jeremy's quick flashes by a recent exhibition at UNC-Chapel Hill of thirty-five of the black-and-white photographs Eudora Welty made during her 1930s work with the Mississippi WPA. Reynolds Price has called

Welty's the "keenest eyesight in American letters." Tyler's eyesight is also keen and her shutter snaps open and shut in many novels, even the first, when Ben Jo finds his captured younger self photographed riding a long-ago wrecked tricycle. In *The Tin Can Tree* a main character is a professional photographer, Joan Pike photographs the family and thus makes visual her absence from it, and a dead child is outlived by her printed image, the mortal features beginning to fade among surrounding splotches of Queen Anne's lace which have since withered. The photographs, like Jeremy's art, "suspend moments forever, while we recede from them with every breath" (*CN* 145), and see their hitherto unsuspected sorrow.

In *Earthly Possessions* photographs are most consistently used to freeze time and to pin people inside its case like collected butterflies. Photographer Charlotte Emery, who drifts into using the studio she inherits from her father, discovers that using props (a sword, a flaring lace shawl) can coalesce personalities on film and develop the ghostly true image up through the routine identity. Photographs can also be used to do what Faulkner said the writer does, to "say no to death," though sometimes Tyler's seem to say yes to it. Early in *Celestial Navigation* a photo holds somehow at home the father who "went out for a breath of air 34 years ago and never came back." And just as Jeremy's collages turn ordinary objects into symbols, just as mortality and transience are challenged and admitted by the photograph, Anne Tyler's literary entries into time bring back and save those arrested moments which imply the whole. In *Caleb* one photo of Caleb playing the cello in a stable loft is said by the pose alone to reveal not Caleb, but the personality of the photographer.

In her later novels, having married story's methods to novel's goals, Tyler can flash into place a single face before it shows the grim genetic trait, can glimpse through her camera lens, though inverted, the start of loving desire just as it metamorphosizes into the propagation of the tribe. The mood of the short story, like that of the lyric poem, is youthful, trusting illumination or luck; but Tyler has now learned to tell us at length that the more things change, the more they stay the same: caught forever, lost forever, all at once, like photographs.

Photographs may be too neat a metaphor as *Earthly Possessions* seems too neat a book. It is her most criticized, perhaps because her tinkering here has become too conscious, not gently relaxed as *Caleb* was. Her tinkering with viewpoint has become first person, too thin a wire on which to hang so much. Her tinkering with structure this time seems arbitrary and mechanical, an alternating sequence of past and present chapters, dividing past from present far more neatly than seems Tyler's habit. Perhaps she wanted the reader to feel he was turning in rhythm from this year's photograph album to focus on an older one. An undergraduate called this novel "overworked," too patterned, with too many then-and-now kidnappings to be plausible, too many pre-and-post insights, too many neat black-and-white parallels developed.

Many readers prefer her eighth novel, *Morgan's Passing* (1980), which began, Tyler writes in "Still Just Writing," with a bearded character who wandered into her mind and who, if "organized," might cause a novel to "grow up around him"(3). By accident Morgan also enters in 1967 the lives of two puppeteers and becomes their impromptu obstetrician. This novel moves progressively twelve years to 1979, though it circles to end at another puppet show. Popular because of the vitality and appeal of the scene-stealer Morgan Gower, for that very reason it recalls Kay Boyle's famous discussion of short story technique and her description of what she called the "wallpaper story." In such a story one character, often eccentric and memorable, enters lives, makes a certain pattern, and exits; by his very nature he will probably move on and repeat the same pattern in the next life in the next town. A story example she cites is Carson McCullers's "A Tree, A Rock, a Cloud." The tramp, the wise old man, the good witch, the childlike spokesman for innocence, the philosophic clown, are typical wallpaper characters. Though Morgan seems to come home to love Emily and will not continue to produce long patterns of twined leaves and rosy ovals in other lives, he *could;* he could easily *keep* passing, could easily go, like Caleb, off to Wyoming without notice just a few more pages beyond the novel's end.

Far more satisfying is Anne Tyler's most recent novel, *Dinner at the Homesick Restaurant* (1982)—still set in Baltimore, still centered on one family, the Tulls, still opening at the crisis point when the mother, Pearl, is dying at eighty-five. As usual, the narration moves back thirty-five years to reveal Pearl deserted by her traveling-salesman husband and dandy, a figure Tyler sometimes makes a paradigm of male mobility. Here Mary Tell, Charlotte Emery, and Elizabeth Abbot, among others, live in their kinsman Ezra Tull—for sometimes Tyler's separate families from all nine novels seem like one large family, like a clan even larger than the Pecks. They even sound alike: Tell and Tull, Peck and Decker, Peck and Pike, Emery and Emerson. Unlike Jeremy, Ezra Tull does not expect art from life; he only wants to create a restaurant with a family atmosphere, a homesick restaurant—the name expresses Tyler's usual paradox: sick FOR home, sick OF home. In spite of all Ezra can do, the Tull family meals end in squabbles and quarrels. Yet the family is curiously bound together in spite of desertion, child abuse, and the betrayal of one brother by another. Tyler's homes are not merely broken but often crazed like a glass vessel but the vessels still hold; blood is still thicker than water. That the family should all be nourished at the same dinner table, despite estrangement, despite those members who fling down their napkins midway and go, seems Tyler's perfect symbol.

If Ezra is Pearl Tull's stay-at-home boy as Jeremy was Mrs. Pauling's, and if he is outwardly also the novel's loser, Cody and Jenny are this family's runaways. Cody even takes with him in a kind of latent kidnapping for jealous revenge the woman, Ruth, whom Ezra meant to marry. Again there is homecoming for Pearl's death, the revealed contrast of their different memories of what she, the mother, and they, the children, were really like. Even their father Beck Tull, who like Jeremy's father ran away years before, will come home now to eat the funeral meats at Ezra's homesick restaurant.

This runaway father seems to summarize for Tyler what she considers semi-heroic. Beck Tull admires but cannot be like those who can endure "the grayness of things, the half-right and half-wrongness of things," the stay-at-homes who cope. But since Beck Tull will leave again as soon as possible, and because Tyler must evidently keep working through her long stay-and-go conflict over and over, book after book, we might measure her stay-at-home allegiance and her vision as only 60–40, that is, 60 percent a classic vision.

In Murray Krieger's study, *The Classic Vision*, he concentrates on those authors who know what extremity is and means, but reject it and "turn away toward the wholly compromised human condition,"[4] without illusion, sentimentality, or false expectations. He says they are the Leech Gatherers, the Michaels. They are Dostoevsky's remarkable peasant women of faith who have no idea that they are remarkable. And they are Anne Tyler's self-sacrificers, although some 40 percent of her heart is always running away from this compromise and fleeing for dear life with the non-conformists.

If Tyler were depicting them in short stories, her dutiful characters intensely rendered closeup might appear simple-minded, perhaps saccharine, whereas a novel like *Stoner* by John Williams, or one like *Dinner at the Homesick Restaurant* can give dimension to the sad but "good" person.

Anne Tyler has been learning dimension at a rate of one novel every two years, from age twenty-three to age forty. By tinkering she has learned also how to outwit the weaknesses most writers risk when they first switch from short story to longer novel form. One risk is that their themes will be too small to stand up under coverage of 80,000 words or more without being watered down; early in Tyler's career she already had a classic vision, at least 60 percent, which demanded size. Another risk is that a cast of eccentric, overblown characters will be transposed in full hyperbole to the longer work, and seem narcissistic there, and too theatrical. Some of Tyler's characters are, but she imbeds these deep in the collage of the others and she gives her longest attention to ordinariness. A talent for story writing and for short bursts of intensity can produce nervous though vivid novels peopled by static navel-gazers. Like Jeremy Pauling, Tyler has avoided that risk by her steady thickening of realistic representational work, and by her willingness to avoid sensationalism, the way Jeremy carved his friend's head in "wood, because that is slow and takes patience." Some story writers who take up novels cannot break the habit of producing each chapter like a mini-story, one bead on a string of beads. Last month, by accident, I met Anne Tyler's mother, Phyllis, who told me every titled chapter in *Homesick Restaurant* had been designed so it could be published as a separate story. I had not noticed.

Though Tyler's range does not aspire to *War and Peace*, though her work with time and family does not become Faulkner's historical South, though there are subjects she passes over with minimal treatment—sex and philosophy; and though some complain that she never experiments much with her very competent style, her persistent tinkering with story methods has produced a distinctive, dense, Tyler-type novel, dependent on character, made resonant by memory. About 60 percent of the time, she continues to do variations on the unfashionable and rather Southern theme that those who can live generously in close quarters at home are facing the world as it is, not as it should be. The other 40 percent of the time, Anne Tyler runs off with her vagabonds and rebels in their capes and costumes.

Her ratio is just about right. Any writer who has been more than 60 percent tamed, even when entering her forties, is probably not vivid enough nor honest enough to make us pause in our own preference for running away, to hear her home truths.

NOTES

[1] Even more than these endnotes might show, my observations on Anne Tyler's novels are indebted to earlier work by two women scholars, and have been affected by and enriched by both. The first was a paper read in 1981 (before *Homesick Restaurant*) by Susan Hull Gilbert (Meredith College) entitled "Returning Home in Anne Tyler's Novels: or Ending at the Beginning." The second source is the only dissertation on Tyler's work, "The Individual in the Family: a Critical Introduction to the Novels of Anne Tyler" (1979) which was written by Stella Nesanovich at Louisiana State University; she is now teaching at McNeese State University. In addition to the novels, Nesanovich makes use of other sources, correspondence, and stories, in tracing her theme through Tyler's seventh novel, *Earthly Possessions* (1977). Her recommendation in her conclusion that the influence of Welty might be a fruitful subject first suggested this brief essay on short story structure itself. Both she and Gilbert comment in even more detail on Tyler's use of photography.

[2] See Nesanovich dissertation, 74, citing Tyler's 1972 interview with *National Observer.*

[3] See Eudora Welty, "Looking at Short Stories," in *The Eye of the Story* (Random House , 1970), 90.

[4] See Murray Krieger, *The Classic Vision* (Baltimore: Johns Hopkins Univ. Press, 1971), 44.

Photo: Coleman Library, Tougaloo College

Alice Walker

A native of Georgia (b. 1944), Walker attended Atlanta's Spelman College before transferring to Sarah Lawrence (B.A.). Her first collection of poetry appeared in 1968, and she has since published two collections of poetry, two collections of short stories, a biography, and three novels. Her most recent novel, The Color Purple, *won both the American Book Award and the Pulitzer Prize. She is currently an editor for* Ms. *magazine.*

Alice Walker's Celebration of Self in Southern Generations

THADIOUS M. DAVIS

Perhaps Alice Walker alone of her generation of black women Southern writers persistently identifies herself and her concerns with her native region—the deep South of Georgia and Mississippi. "No one," she has concluded, "could wish for a more advantageous heritage than that bequeathed to the black writer in the South: a compassion for the earth, a trust in humanity beyond our knowledge of evil, an abiding love of justice. We inherit a great responsibility . . . for we must give voice to centuries not only of silent bitterness and hate but also of neighborly kindness and sustaining love" ("Black Writer" 26). Her heritage is complex; nevertheless, like Louisiana native Ernest Gaines, Walker grounds her fiction and poetry primarily in the experiences of the South and Southern blacks. Her three volumes of poetry, three novels, and two collections of stories, all depend upon what black life is, has been, and can be in a specified landscape that becomes emblematic of American life.

While Walker's paradigm communities are nearly always black, rural, and Southern, they become viable emblems by means of her creation of familial and social generations that underscore her concerns with familial identity, continuity and rupture, and with social roles, order and change. In shaping her fiction and much of her poetry according to patterns of generations, she has established a concrete means of portraying who her people are and what their lives mean.

Though her dominant themes (spiritual survival and individual identity, as well as freedom, power, and community) link her to the literary heritages of both Southern and black writers, her structures and forms address most clearly the uniqueness of her particular vision within these traditions. Walker weds her intellectual themes to the life experiences of "just plain folk" who are also black and mainly poor; she has said of them, "their experience as ordinary human beings" is "valuable," and should not be "misrepresented, distorted, or lost" ("Saving the Life" 158). In her literary works, she stresses her own history and by extension the cultural history of Southern blacks and American blacks. "It is," Walker asserts in the novel *Meridian*, "the song of the people, transformed by the experiences of each generation, that holds them together, and if any part of it is lost the people suffer and are without soul"(205–06). Her own works are, in a sense, "the song of the people" celebrating and preserving each generation.

Walker's heritage and history provide a vehicle for understanding the modern world in which her characters live. "Because I'm black and I'm a woman and because I was brought up poor and because I'm a Southerner, . . . the way I see the world is quite different from the way many people see it," she has observed to Krista Brewer: "I could not help but have a radical vision of society . . . the way I see things can help people see what needs to be changed" ("Writing to Survive" 13). Her vision, however, is a disturbing one to share. Walker relies upon sexual violence and physical abuse to portray breaches in black generations. Typically, she brings to her work a terrible observance of black self-hatred and destruction. While Walker does not negate the impact of a deleterious past, she rarely incorporates white characters as perpetrators of crimes against blacks. Her works simply presume, as she states, that "all history is current; all injustice continues on some level" ("One Child" 129). Her images of people destroyed or destroying others originate in a vision of cultural reality expressed matter-of-factly, such as in the poem from *Revolutionary Petunias*, "You Had to Go to Funerals": "At six and seven/ The face in the gray box/ Is nearly always your daddy's/ Old schoolmate/ Mowed down before his/ Time"(7). Walker's racial memory of a tangible, harsh reality succeeds in focusing experience, holding it fixed, and illuminating some aspects of brutality that might well be overlooked or obscured.

Walker's fiction expresses the outrage that she feels about the injustices of society; "I think," she has stated, "that growing up in the South, I have a very keen sense of injustice—a very prompt response to it" ("Writing to Survive" 14). It may well be that some of the brutal depictions of life in her writings are ways of responding to both particular and general injustices suffered by blacks throughout their history in the United States. Gloria Steinem, for instance, has concluded after interviewing Walker that "the rage and the imaginings of righteous murders that are in her writing are also in her. You just have to know her long enough to see the anger flash" ("Do You Know" 93). There are hidden layers in Walker's handling of injustice, so that it is not so easy to follow the logic behind it in her fiction. She herself has confessed, "It's true that I fantasize revenge for injustices, big and small. . . . I imagine how wonderful it must feel to kill the white man who oppresses you. . . . Lately . . . I've come to believe that you have some help when you fight. If a country or a person oppresses folks, it or he will pay for it. That happens more often than not. Years after the Indians died in the Trail of Tears, Andrew Jackson, who had been President at the time, had to be wrapped like a mummy to keep the flesh on his bones" ("Do You Know" 93). Her fictional use of rage, however, is more often than not contained within a family environment and directed toward self or kin, rather than towards outsiders.

One scene in *Meridian* delineates the everyday quality of familial rage in Walker's fiction. A woman who believes that her family and community, as well as the racial barriers and social order of the South, have all combined to rob her of a full life irons into her children's and husband's clothes her frustrations and her creativity. Instead of loving her family openly or accusing anyone explicitly, she uses her ordinary domestic chore to enclose her children in "the starch of her anger," as Walker labels it. This character, Mrs. Hill, includes her children in her victimization, and in the process she excludes them from any meaningful, close relationship with her. The result is a tension- and guilt-ridden existence, both for Mrs. Hill and for her family. The scene suggests how personal outrage and anger stemming from social and historical forces (particularly ignorance, discrimination, racism, exploitation, and sexism) become warped and distorted in Walker's world.

In fact, Walker has discussed her writing, and need to write, in terms that articulate her deflection of rage and her reconciliation with it. After the birth of her daughter, she put her frustrations and her energy into her work: "Write I did, night and day, *something*, and it was not even a choice, . . . but a necessity. When I didn't write I thought of making bombs and throwing them. . . . Writing saved me from the sin and *inconvenience* of violence—as it saves most writers who live in 'interesting' oppressive times and are not afflicted by personal immunity" ("One Child" 127). She does not have to add that her writing absorbed the violence, especially emotional violence, in the lives of her characters. Walker's recollection and the scene from *Meridian* add a situational context to the prevalent violence and excessive pain found in all of her fiction, but they do not fully address the motivational context for the choice of family as the expressive vehicle.

Walker creates a multiplicity of permanently maimed and damaged souls within the family structure who feel no pressure for responsible living or assume exemption from the demands of responsibility. There may be occasions of optimism or hope; for example, when Sarah, a Southern black art student in "A Sudden Trip Home in the Spring," returns from New York for her father's funeral, she comes, with the help of her brother, to understand her father's life after years of resenting his flaws, and she resolves to learn how to make her grandfather's face in stone. But more pervasive in Walker's fiction is despair: women who commit suicide, such as the wife in "Her Sweet Jerome," who sets fire to herself and her marriage bed; men who maim or kill, such as the father in "The Child Who Favored Daughter," who cuts off his daughter's breasts; people who allow themselves to become animals, such as Brownfield in *The Third Life of Grange Copeland,* who, accepting a "nothingness" in himself, shoots his wife in the face while his children watch; and people who simply give up on life, such as Myrna in "Really Doesn't Crime Pay?" who spends her days softening her hands and thwarting her husband's desire for a child.

Walker assumes that by revealing negative actions and violent encounters, she may be able to repair the damage done by unreflective people who are unable to recognize that their actions have more than personal consequences, that they may rend bonds between generations and thus affect all members of a family, community, race, or society. In her depictions of abuse and violence, Walker takes the risk of misrepresenting the very people whom she seeks to change. Yet her unrelenting portraits of human weaknesses convey her message that art should "make us better"; "if [it] doesn't . . . then what on earth is it for?" ("Do You Know" 94). Her message, postulated in her novels, is that the breaches and violations must be mended for health and continuity, for "survival *whole,*" as her character Grange Copeland declares.

Reparation or redemption may be undertaken by a single individual in whom Walker vests the responsibility for survival, because it is the action of a single individual that has caused the breakdown of experience or identity in private lives, and ultimately in the public or social life of the group. Individual characters acting alone become repositories of decent behavior, as well as harbingers that the messages embedded in the lives of generations of blacks will not be lost. One example is Elethia, a young woman who masterminds the retrieval of "Uncle Albert," a mummified black man who is all teeth, smiles, and servitude as a decoration in the window of a "whites only" restaurant, despite the reality of his having been a rebellious slave whose teeth were knocked out for his efforts to remain human. Elethia knows that Uncle Albert's denigration to a subservient happy waiter cannot be allowed. She and her cohorts break the plate glass, reclaim the mummy, burn it, and save the ashes. She aims to rid the world of all false, stereotypical images of blacks, especially men, and to recover the past, rectify its misrepresentations, and preserve the truth for future generations. Elethia realizes that the work will not end with rescuing Uncle Albert, but that it will extend over her lifetime. Walker's individual Elethias understand that breaches may have occurred between succeeding generations, but that progress in the present and towards the future depends upon reconstruction of the bridges that, as Carolyn Rodgers says in her poem "It Is Deep," one generation has "crossed over on." Although "Elethia" is not one of Walker's most successful stories, it adheres to her belief that the world, her reality, is filled with connections, oftentimes unsuspected connections, which she as an artist can illuminate.

Walker believes that as a writer she must work towards a larger perspective, which she describes as "connections made, or at least attempted, where none existed before, the straining to encompass in one's glance at the varied world the common thread, the unifying theme through immense diversity, a fearlessness of growth, of search, of look, that enlarges the private and the public world" ("Saving the Life" 152). For her, one way of structuring "the common thread" is by means of generations; she values the strength and purpose black generations have given to her writing, but she refuses to reduce their meanings to platitudes or to ignore the complexities of their lives.

"It is not," Walker stresses, "my child who has purged my face from history and herstory and left mystory . . . a mystery; my child loves my face . . . as I have loved my own parents' faces . . . and have refused to let them be denied, or myself to let them go" ("One Child" 139). Repeatedly, she uses the image of her mother's face "radiant," "ordering the universe in her personal conception of beauty. Her face . . . is a legacy . . . she leaves to me" ("In Search" 64). Walker treasures and preserves in her works not merely her parents' faces and her own, but those of her grand-parents and great-grandparents and all her blood and social relatives as well. For instance, in the poem from *Goodnight Willie Lee* entitled "talk-ing to my grandmother who died poor (while hearing Richard Nixon declare 'I am not a crook')," she concludes: "i must train myself to want/ not one bit more/ than i need to keep me alive/ working/ and recognizing beauty/ in your so nearly undefeated face"(47). It is in her grandmother's "so nearly undefeated face" that Walker reads at what cost her people have survived.

Her conception of the black writer and herself is inextricably linked to survival. She has said, "Only recently did I fully realize . . . that through the years of listening to my mother's stories of her life, I have absorbed not only the stories themselves, but something of the manner in which she spoke, something of the urgency that involves the knowledge that her stories like her life must be recorded" ("In Search" 64). Derived partly from the urge to retain her parents' faces and their stories, her sense of black writers is that they are involved in a moral and physical struggle "the result of which," as she points out, "is expected to be some kind of larger freedom" ("Saving the Life" 152). Walker attributes this search for freedom to a black literary tradition based upon slave narratives which foster the belief in escape from the body along with freedom for the soul. Indeed, while the oral tradition, essential to even the most literary of slave narratives, such as Frederick Douglass's, is a prominent part of Walker's writing, its strength as a mode of telling in her work may be more immediately linked to her mother's voice. "Do you actually speak with your mother's voice?" Mary Helen Washington has asked Walker. The response is forthright: "Just as you have certain physical characteris-tics of your mother's—her laughter or her toes or her grade of hair—you also internalize certain emotional characteristics that are like hers. That is part of the legacy. They are internalized, merged with your own, trans-formed through the stories. When you're compelled to write her stories, it's because you recognize and prize those qualities of her in yourself" ("Her Mother's Gifts" 38).

Because of her conception of art and the artist, as well as her recognition of the value of her mother's stories and her family's faces, Walker displays an enormous sympathy for the older generation of Southern women ("Headragged Generals") and men ("billy club scar[ed]"), whose lives were sacrifice. As she has revealed in "The Women" from *Revolutionary Petunias:* "They were women then/ My mama's generation/ . . . How they battered down/ Doors/ . . . To discover books/ Desks/ A place for us/ How they knew what we/ Must know/ Without knowing a page/ Of it/ Themselves (5, 7). The poem celebrates the generation that preceded Walker's own, those men and women who opened doors through which they themselves would never pass and who were unafraid to attempt personal and social change in order to restructure subsequent generations. Walker acknowledges their achievement, but also their adversities.

Her older men, in particular, have experienced troubled, difficult lives, such as those of Grange Copeland and Albert in *The Color Purple.* These men have been abusive in their youths, but they come to an essential understanding of their own lives and their families' as they learn to be reflective, responsible, and expressive individuals. Although they may seem to reflect her anti-male bias, they are more significant as portrayals of Walker's truth-telling from a particular perspective that is conscious of their weaknesses—weaknesses that they distort into violence against other blacks, especially women and children—and conscious, too, of their potential for regeneration. Walker's men to whom sexuality is no longer an issue are redeemed by learning to love and assume responsibility for their actions. In presenting these men, Walker first depicts what has come to be the stereotypes of blacks, essentially those set destructive patterns of emotional and psychological responses of black men to black life, their women, children, friends, whites, and themselves. Then she loosens the confines of the stereotype and attempts to penetrate the nexus of feelings that make these lives valuable in themselves and for others.

Much of the redemption, nevertheless, is only potential as Walker portrays it. The nameless husband in *The Color Purple* becomes "Albert" in his later years, because, like Grange Copeland in Walker's first novel, he discovers reflection which makes him a defined person who can accept the responsibility for his mistakes and the suffering he has caused, especially his abusive treatment of his wife whom he had denigrated ("You a woman . . . you nothing at all,"176). Despite his contemplative demeanor at the end of the novel, Albert remains in the realm of potential. His apparent psychological return to roots, though inadequately motivated, is primarily a portent of a healing process.

Walker names this healing a "wholeness" in her essay, "Beyond the Peacock: The Reconstruction of Flannery O'Connor," in which she, like her characters, returns to her roots in order to regenerate herself and to comprehend the pervasive impact of social environment. Her attitude is clear in the poem from *Once,* "South: The Name of Home," which opens: "when I am here again/ the years of ease between/ fall away/ The smell of one/ magnolia/ sends my heart running/ through the swamps. / the earth is red/ here—/ the trees bent, weeping/ what secrets will not/ the ravished land/ reveal/ of its abuse"(39–40). It is an environment that is not without a history of pain, but it nonetheless connects generations of blacks to one another, to a "wholeness" of self, and to "the old unalterable roots," as in "Burial": "Today I bring my own child here;/ to this place where my father's/ grandmother rests undisturbed beneath the Georgia sun/ . . . Forgetful of geographical resolutions as birds/ the farflung young fly South to bury/ the old dead" (*RP* 12–13). One key to "wholeness," even if it is rarely achieved, is the development of self-perception by means of generational ties to the land.

The achievements and dreams that emerge from the connected experience of generations are expressions of freedom and beauty, of power and community. The primary dream, usually voiced in terms of the creation of art, is that of freedom to be one's own self, specifically to be one's own black self and to claim, as do Walker's blues singers Shug Avery in *The Color Purple* and Gracie Mae Still in "Nineteen Fifty-Five," one's own life for one's self and for future generations.

Walker transforms the individual, so much a part of the special characteristics used to define the white South, into a person who is black and most often female. In the one-page story "Petunias" from *You Can't Keep a Good Woman Down,* she individualizes an unnamed woman with a history and a sense of herself. The woman writes in her diary just before her death in an explosion of a bomb her son intends for the revolution: "my daddy's grandmama was a slave on the Tearslee Plantation. They dug up her grave when I started agitating in the Movement. One morning I found her dust dumped over my verbena bed, a splinery leg bone had fell

among my petunias"(40). This woman and others in Walker's canon are
the stereotyped, the maimed, the distorted blacks who still rise, as Maya
Angelou entitles one of her works, "Still I Rise." These characters become
redeemed as individuals with an indelible sense of self. But that act of
rising out of the depths of degradation or depression is accomplished by
means of the person's coming to terms with the truth of his or her community, with his or her social and historical place among others who have
suffered, grieved, laughed, and lusted, but who miraculously have held
on to dignity and selfhood. Characters, such as Sammy Lou, a woman on
her way to the electric chair for killing her husband's murderer, pass on a
powerful legacy of individual identity; Sammy Lou leaves her children
the instructions: "Always respect the word of God," and "Don't yall forget
to *water* my purple petunias" (*RP* 29).

Walker operates within this legacy. She keeps before her the vision of
her own mother, who cultivated magnificent flower gardens, despite her
work from sun up to dark either in the fields or as a domestic for less than
twenty dollars a week. Walker refers to her mother's gardens as her "art,"
"her ability to hold on, even in simple ways" ("In Search" 64). That garden
is her recurrent metaphor for both art and beauty, endurance and survival; it is essentially, too, Walker's articulation of the process by which
individuals find selfhood through examining the experiences of others
who have preceded them. As she has stated, "Guided by my heritage of a
love of beauty and a respect for strength, in search of my mother's garden,
I found my own" ("In Search" 64). In fact, her very first novel, *The Third
Life of Grange Copeland,* directly involves the gardens of the character
Mem as emblems of her tenacious will to survive in beauty and in love.

In celebrating her people (characters, mediums, models, and family),
Walker demonstrates a deeply-rooted consciousness of her role as an
artist in a socially and politically complex world. "To acknowledge ancestors means," she states, "we are aware that we did not make ourselves. . . . The grace with which we embrace life, in spite of the pain, the
sorrows, is always a measure of what has gone before"(*RP* Preface 1). By
acknowledging ancestors, she acknowledges that she is part of a black
tradition of artists, particularly that strain stemming from Southern slave
narrators, folk tellers of tales, and literary artists. These include Zora
Neale Hurston, one of her major influences, and Margaret Walker, her
fellow poet and novelist who in the 1940s paid tribute to blacks in "For

My People" and in the process celebrated her roots "deep in Southern life" and her "grandmothers . . . strong . . . full of memories."[1] Similarly, Alice Walker derives meaning from the historical experiences of her foremothers, because she insists, "nothing is ever a product of the immediate present" (O'Brien, *Interviews* 197).

She takes into account the dynamics of collective identity along with the demands that social codes place upon the group, and she considers the structure of personal identity with its unreflected social relations, especially family. She shapes her fiction so that both collective and personal identities become keys to character, theme, and plot. At the same time, she structures the experience of identity in terms of social and familial generations that have the potential to transform black life.

In her first novel, *The Third Life of Grange Copeland,* three generations of Copelands converge to create Ruth's identity, and three generations form the stages or lives of the patriarch and title character, Grange Copeland. When any one member of the Copeland family or of a particular social generation of blacks (from 1920 to 1960) ignores the dynamics of family structures or forgets the historical perspective that the structures are maintained through necessity and love, he or she loses the capacity for primary identifications with race, family, and community, and loses as well the major basis for defining one's self and one's humanity. The most detailed illustration presented in the novel is Brownfield, the son of Grange and a member of the middle generation in the work.

Brownfield Copeland becomes one of "the living dead, one of the many who had lost their souls in the American wilderness" (*TL* 138). He reduces his murder of his wife to a simple theorem: "*He liked plump women. . . . Ergo,* he had murdered his wife because she had become skinny"(161). Because of his twisted logic, Brownfield "could forget [his wife's] basic reality, convert it into comparisons. She had been like good pie, or good whiskey, but there had never been a self to her"(162). Not only by means of the murder itself, but also by the process of his reasoning about it, he strips himself of his humanity when he negates his culpability with the negation of his wife's existence as a human being.

Brownfield's physical death sadly, though appropriately in Walker's construction, comes at the hands of his father Grange and over the future of his daughter Ruth. But his spiritual death occurs much earlier "as he lay thrashing about, knowing the rigidity of his belief in misery, knowing he could never renew or change himself, for this changelessness was now all he had, he could not clarify what was the duty of love"(227). He compounds one of the greatest sins in Walker's works, the refusal or inability to change, with his dismissal of meaning in family bonds. Ironically, his death makes possible the completion of change in his daughter's life that had been fostered by his father, who late in his life understood the necessity of moving beyond the perverted emotions constricting the lives of the Copelands.

In *Meridian*, Walker's second novel, the heroine divests herself of immediate blood relations—her child and her parents—in order to align herself completely with the larger racial and social generations of blacks. Meridian Hill insists that although seemingly alone in the world, she has created a fusion with her generation of activist blacks and older generations of oppressed blacks. The form of the work, developed in flashbacks, follows a pattern of Meridian's casting off the demands made by authority and responsibility within the conventional family and traditional institutions. Unlike Brownfield's rejection of responsibility, the rupture in this novel is ultimately positive, despite its being the most radical and mysterious instance of change and acceptance in Walker's fiction. It is positive because the novel creates a new basis for defining Meridian's self and for accepting responsibility for one's actions. In fact, the controlling metaphor is resurrection and rebirth, an acting out of the renewal impossible for Brownfield. By the end of the novel, Meridian's personal identity has become a collective identity. "There is water in the world for us/ brought by our friends," she writes in one of her two poems, "though the rock of mother and god/ vanishes into sand/ and we, cast out alone/ to heal/ and re-create/ ourselves" (*M* 219). In spite of her painful private experiences, Meridian is born anew into a pluralistic cultural self, a "we" that is and must be self-less and without ordinary prerequisites for personal identity. And significantly, because she exemplifies Walker's recurrent statement of women as leaders and models, Meridian leaves her male disciple Truman Held to follow her and to await the arrival of others from their social group.

Truman's search, structurally a duplication of Meridian's, is part of personal change that is more necessary for men than for women in Walker's fiction and that becomes social change through the consequences of actions taken by individuals who must face constraints, as well as opportunities, in their lives, but must also know why they act and what the consequences will be. Truman resolves to live the life of an ascetic so that he might one day be worthy to join Meridian and others "at the river," where they "will watch the evening sun go down. And in the darkness maybe [they] will know the truth"(227). The search for truth leads Truman, like Meridian, to a commitment to the social generation of blacks to which he belongs. He follows Meridian's rationale for his action: "i want to put an end to guilt/ i want to put an end to shame/ whatever you have done my sister/ (my brother)/ know i wish to forgive you/ love you"(219). By so doing, Truman accepts his personal duty towards all blacks, discovers his own meaning, and commits his life in love to both present and future generations.

Perhaps Walker's third novel most effectively conveys her messages and evidences her heritage as a black Southern writer. In *The Color Purple*, which won the Pulitzer Prize for fiction in 1983, she takes a perspectivistic or "emic" approach to character delineation and cultural reality. She sees and portrays a world from the inside outward; she uses the eyes of Celie, a surnameless, male-dominated and abused woman, who records her experiences in letters. Celie is not a "new" character in Walker's fiction; she is similar to one of the sisters in "Everyday Use," the bride in "Roselily," and the daughter in "The Child Who Favored Daughter," but unlike these other silent, suffering women characters, Celie writes her story in her own voice. She tells her life as only she has known it: a girl, merely a child, raped by her stepfather whom she believes is her natural father; that same girl bearing his two children only to have them stolen by him and to be told that they are dead; the denial and suppression of that girl's actual background and history, as well as her letters from her sister.

In Celie's epistles, Walker makes her strongest effort so far to confront the patterns in a specified world and to order and articulate the codes creating those patterns. In effect, she uses the uncovered patterns to connect, assimilate, and structure the content of one human being's world and relationship to that world. Celie writes letters—her story, history—to God and to her sister Nettie. She writes out of desperation and in order to preserve some core of her existence. In love and hope, she writes to save herself, just as Walker has said of her own writing: "I have written to stay alive . . . I've written to survive"; "writing poetry is my way of celebrating

with the world that I have not committed suicide the evening before"
("Writing to Survive" 12, *Interviews* 197). Celie writes from the heart,
and grows stronger, more defined, more fluent, while simultaneously her
intensely private, almost cryptic style develops into a still personal, subjective style, but one which encompasses much more of the lives surrounding her.

While social interactions and institutions typically define human reality, these do not ultimately define Celie's. She is isolated and alone,
despite the numbers of family members and others impinging upon her
world. Slowly and cautiously, she builds a reality that is different, one
based upon her singular position and the abstractions she herself con-
ceives in the course of her everyday life. Her inner life is unperverted by
the abuse and violence she suffers. Only when she has formulated the
outlines of her private identity in writing does her interaction with others
become a significant factor in making sense of social codes in the public
world. When she reaches her conclusions, she has rejected most of the
available social models for personal identity; she is neither Shug Avery,
the hardliving blues singer who gives and takes what she wants in being
herself, nor is she Nettie, her sister who can experience the wider world
outside the social environment of her childhood. Yet, Celie passionately
loves both of these women, and has tried at different stages to emulate
them. Celie's own subjective probings lead her to confirm her individual
interpretation of herself and of her situational contexts. Nonetheless, she
does arrive, as invariably a Walker bearer of responsibility must, at her
place in the spectrum of life, her relationship to others, and her own
continuity.

Celie affirms herself: "I'm pore, I'm black, I may be ugly and can't
cook, a voice say to everything listening. But I'm here" (*CP* 176). Her
words echo those of Langston Hughes's folk philosopher, Jesse B. Semple
(Simple): "I'm still here. . . . I've been underfed, underpaid. . . . I've
been abused, confused, misused. . . . I done had everything from flat feet
to a flat head. . . . but I am still here. . . . I'm still here."[2] Celie's verbal
connection to Hughes's black everyman and the black oral tradition extends her affirmation of self, so that it becomes racial, as well as personal,
and is an actualization, rather than the potentiality that most often appears in Walker's work. Celie *is*, or in her own black folk English, she *be's*
her own black, nappy-haired, ordinary self in all the power and pain that

combine in her writing to reveal the girl, the female becoming totally a woman-person who survives and belies the weak, passive exterior her family and community presume to be her whole self. Her act of writing and affirming is magnificent. It is an achievement deserving of celebration, and perhaps not coincidentally, it is Walker's first "happy ending," not only for her character Celie, but for most of her fictional family as well.

Celie's progeny will make the present and future generations. Her two children—Adam, who takes the African name "Omatangu" and marries an African woman, and Olivia, who promises to be a sister to her brother's bride Tashi—exist without the blight affecting their mother and their aunt, even though their lives as children of missionaries in Africa have not been without the problems of colonialization and oppression. Adam's and Olivia's return to America, to the South, and to Celie at the end of the novel may be contrived, but it signals the continuity of generations, the return (ironically perhaps) to the "old, unalterable roots." Their return is cause for a larger hope for the race, and for celebration within the family and community, because they have survived "whole," literally since they miraculously survive a shipwreck and symbolically since they have acquired definite life-affirming attitudes.

Near the end of the novel, Celie's stepson comments on a Fourth of July barbecue, and in the process provides a commentary on the letters Celie has written and the novel Walker has produced; he says, "White folks busy celebrating they independence from England. . . . Us can spend the day celebrating each other" (*CP* 243). *The Color Purple*, with its reiteration of "purple" as the motif symbolizing the miracle of color and life apparent in all of Walker's works, is a celebration of "each other," individual selves inextricably linked in social and familial generations. In the celebration is an inexplicable strength, which Walker attributes to her own optimism, "based," she states, "on what I saw of the courage and magnificence of people in Mississippi and in Georgia. . . . I saw that the human spirit can be so much more incredible and beautiful than most people ever dream . . . that people who have very little, . . . who have been treated abominably by society, can still do incredible things . . . not only *do* things, but can be great human beings" ("Writing to Survive" 14–15).

Despite her concentration on the brutal treatment of black women and the unmitigated abuse of children, Walker believes in the beauty and the power of the individual, and ultimately of the group. And because she does, she is willing to gamble on ways of articulating her unique vision. She is not always successful; the experimental stories of *You Can't Keep a Good Woman Down* are an example, as are the unconvincing letters from Celie's sister Nettie in Africa. However, even in the less effective works, Walker validates the necessity of struggling out of external constrictions to find meaning in one's own life. It seems quite appropriate that both her dedication and statement at the end of *The Color Purple* reaffirm and invoke the spirits of people who fill her head and her work with their voices and their presence, with the selves that come to *be* within the pages of her writing.

Certainly, in the composition of much of her work so far, Alice Walker must have felt as she did while writing "The Revenge of Hannah Kemhuff," a work inspired by one of her mother's own stories: "I gathered up the historical and psychological threads of the life my ancestors lived, and in the writing . . . I felt joy and strength and my own continuity. I had that wonderful feeling that writers get sometimes . . . of being with a great many people, ancient spirits, all very happy to see me consulting and acknowledging them, and eager to let me know through the joy of their presence, that indeed, I am not alone" ("Saving the Life" 157). Perhaps this consoling vision of interconnections is one reason why Alice Walker can capture the deep layers of affirmative and destructive feelings in human beings who must live and make their lives known, and why she can compel readers to heed their messages.

NOTES

[1] See Margaret Walker, "Sorrow's Home," "Lineage," in *For My People* (New Haven: Yale Univ. Press, 1942), 12, 25.

[2] See Langston Hughes, "Final Fear," in *Simple Speaks His Mind* (New York: Simon and Schuster, 1950), 112–13.

Gail Godwin

Born in Alabama (1937), Godwin spent her childhood in the South. She received her education at the University of North Carolina (B.A.) and the University of Iowa (M.A. and Ph.D), where she taught English and creative writing. The first of her five novels, The Perfectionists, was published in 1970. She has also published a collection of short stories.

Gail Godwin and the Ideal of Southern Womanhood

CAROLYN RHODES

Gail Godwin's fiction has reflected many of the myths and manners of the South.[1] Some of her most sympathetic characters have been Southern women whose struggles toward self-discovery required them to reject traits demanded by the traditional ideal of Southern womanhood. In her novels published during the 1970s, Godwin often depicted that ideal as alive and deadly: it entailed a set of values bent toward restraining Southern belles to narrow notions of grace and duty. In her social criticism, Godwin spoke even more explicitly of the dangers of the old ideal of "Southern Womanhood," with its constricting effects on the docile daughters of the misguided mother who tried to model and impose the tradition of shallow ladyhood.[2] Only in her latest novel have the three featured Southern women attained the balance that Godwin admires: without fleeing the South, they manage to achieve autonomy and to define grace and duty in their own ways.

All five of Godwin's novels feature the quests for identity of women who fear failure, and who are distracted by differing notions of what their best selves might be and become.[3] In her three longer novels, those published in 1974, 1978, and 1982, the protagonists are Southern-born, Southern-bred, and aware of the ambiguities of their heritage. Similar characters appear in some of her short stories. Godwin has also discussed the stereotypes of Southern Womanhood in journalistic commentary. This author's writing, then, conveys her explicit and implicit views on the Southern heritage as a shaping factor in the lives of certain women of the twentieth century, groups identified carefully by class and age and attitude toward an ideal of womanhood. In both article and fiction, she distinguishes the stereotype from the individual, and she often depicts Southern women in the context of the traits she attributes to heritage-

bound Southern mothers and their fleeing daughters.[4] Godwin also focuses upon the confrontations which set women free, which she describes
directly as social critic and dramatically in fiction when her protagonists
confront their Southern constrictions and attempt to break out of them.

In her article, "The Southern Belle," on the ideal of Southern
womanhood in *Ms.* in 1975, Godwin analyzed two contemporary generations of women and their responses to each other and to the typical
expectations set up for them as Southern Belle and Southern Lady. She
begins by insisting that only the Southern region of the United States
places such an explicit list of ladylike goals before its young women. And
although they may be directed primarily toward white women of the
would-be-leisured classes, the distinctive traits are known not only to
other Southerners but to others throughout the nation. Only in the South
does a growing girl find "an image of womanhood already cut out for her,
stitched securely by the practiced hands of tradition, available for her to
slip into, ready-made, and hence-forward 'pass' as a 'lovely person'"(49).

Demands imposed on females by the idealized image have changed
little in two hundred years, whether glorified as archetypal or satirized as
banal.[5] Many Southern women still seek to merge into the myth and to
lure their daughters toward embodying its traditions. Godwin finds their
ardor for the past admirable when it encourages grace and courtesy, yet
dangerous in its refusal to recognize reality. As she lists the "trademarks
of the tradition," she prepares readers for her conclusion that loveliness
may not fully compensate for the shallowness and evasion inherent in
them:

> . . . soft hands and soft voices; first concern for others, not self; refusal to dwell
> on subjects of ugliness, unpleasantness, violence, tension, strife: sauve short-
> circuiting of all "embarrassing questions"; cultivation and veneration of tradition
> and beautiful things; impeccable manners; spotless "reputation."(52)

Throughout the essay, Godwin dramatizes with piercing anecdotes the
small daily traumas that beset a wife and mother who strives to live in the
Southern ideal, who must appear always hospitable, congenial, and
charming while resorting to deceptions and avoidances so as to keep the
surface of her life looking smooth. She will "minister, forestall, deflect,
prevaricate, suffer martyrdoms"(51) rather than allow any scene to occur.
Godwin points out that the Southern Lady has to take hypocritical and
ultimately self-deceptive stances to preserve the semblance of fulfillment

in her limited life: she avoids all, honest recognitions of sexuality, politics (especially racial relations), and violence (so that she shudders away from much of current history). To her tractable daughters, she can overtly teach the skills of a hostess and home manager, while covertly conveying subtle methods for the management of men, particularly how to win "maximum benefits . . . without threatening masculinity"(52). While never seeming rude, she can show those docile daughters the use of indirect remarks so that they too can snub, demean, or evade unwelcome topics or unacceptable people.

Godwin perceives, and illustrates with sometimes tender humor, that the mother who devotes her life to indoctrinating the Ideal of Southern Womanhood, dutiful to *her* mother's model, sadly misses a most significant aspect of selfhood. Godwin explains the vagueness, the elusiveness, of such a woman, lacking opinions or goals beyond her domestic sphere, becoming blank because she is dedicated to others in that small world. Accepting the boundaries of the Southern heritage, she has dutifully found ways to count her blessings but has never turned inward to assess her uniqueness:

> Many a Southern woman has died, and more will die, without ever having once strained toward what Jung called "the task of personality," without ever having once confronted her true reflection beyond the quicksilver image of what her heritage has prepared her to be. (51)

Godwin's explicit, journalistic, portrait of Southern motherhood in service to the old ideal is certainly a sorry picture.

No such dismal stereotype is developed at length among Godwin's characters who are Southern mothers. And yet, ticking off the stereotypical traits one by one, readers will find most of them in the two mothering women who represent the ancestry of Godwin's best known heroine, Jane Clifford, the protagonist of *The Odd Woman*.[6] Transmuted by love and eased with wit, the Southern foibles of her mother and grandmother have charm for Jane and for the reader. Moreover, they are richly self-aware as personalities and thus they escape the last damning accusation that Godwin directs at the stereotypical Southern mother. Yet their taboos and withdrawals constrict them and narrow their worlds.

Edith Dewar Barnstorff, Jane Clifford's grandmother, epitomizes the "original Southern lady" (*OW* 170). Born in the 1890s, living until the 1970s, she ardently tries to shape both her daughter Kitty and her granddaughter Jane by her standards of purity and gentility. Purity for Edith means enduring, not enjoying, sex within marriage, and knowing that other sexuality is wicked and will probably bring doom to women who indulge in it. Gentility's ramifications involve pride and propriety, the pride of knowing who we were, long after the old landholdings are gone, and the propriety of fine manners, carriage, and dress. Jane recalls that Edith's favorite disciplinary sentence was "Nice people don't act that way" (377). In her youth, Edith succeeded as a belle, fainting into the arms of the doting man who would be, for her, the perfect husband—awed, protective, considerate of her delicate sensibilities, and away from home often. She has carried intact through the murky twentieth century the clear standards of her nineteenth-century Southern heritage. While Jane can envy the certainty of Edith's choices, she perceives that the decisions are easy because they are dictated by formulas, "based simply on what tradition expected of her . . . written out in some etiquette book copyrighted about 1890"(48).

Kitty, Edith's daughter and Jane's mother, was a flamboyant belle, unwilling to forego the sensual when young, but converted by her matronhood to a philosophy of renunciation. She enjoyed her heyday as enchantress, beset by suitors, though none of them were quite the flawless gentleman her mother wished. Kitty has in her middle years become a searching person, deeply religious and considerably more complex than the hollow stereotype of the Southern Lady as Indoctrinating Mother. However, Kitty can be as crafty as the shallowest woman. She tosses coy catch phrases to her daughters in efforts to mend their manners, and she manipulates her adoring husband, resorting even to tears—shamelessly, Jane thinks. Worse, she tends to reject her own self as "silly"(195). The subjects that Kitty shared with Jane, then later dismissed as silly to recall, were her young dreams and her uneasiness about her later place in the moving world. She tries to tell her daughter how encompassing her yearnings had been: "I wanted it all. I wanted love. I wanted a career . . . everything eternally beautiful, with no compromise"(177). And she wanted a marriage, not just of esteem, like her parents, but of passion, too. She confesses to Jane that she is "sick to remember" the power of her desires, and advises her daughter to dream more sanely, not to ache for the impossible. Such cautions may be universal, since older generations, male as well as female, repeatedly warn the young to try not to care too much. But Kitty's comments on the way dreams must be limited place her views on delusive hope in a very Southern context. "I was brought up," she says, "to believe woman's best virtue was that of renouncing herself"(178). So she was torn between the love of others (husband, babies) and wishes for herself that she had to call selfish and try to dismiss as "silly." Kitty believes herself born too late to find the old Southern certainties that had guided her mother; yet she feels that she and her daughter Jane have been born too soon to take part in the coming time of the new settled patterns.

As Kitty compares herself with her mother, so does Jane measure herself by contrast with both her mother and grandmother. Jane sometimes wishes she could learn the social deftness of her woman forbears, and she admires the serenity of their acceptance of roles. Yet she can feel only disdain for many mannerisms of typical Southern women. For instance, she is glad that she and her best friend Gerda have never exchanged "those insincere little kisses and hugs" which Southern women "lavish on each other in public," even women "who detest each other"(412). The ideal of Southern Womanhood, the full panoply of traits, horrifies Jane. The perfect Southern lady of her mother's generation appears in *The Odd Woman* as the dull and proper Cousin Frances, Edith's niece. She embodies traits that Jane has fled from, even though they are the exact trademarks that pass for gentility. Frances is correct, solicitous, well-kept in every sense.[7] Smooth routines structure her life: entertaining, shopping, her country club and women's clubs—she takes pride in belonging to both the United Daughters of the Confederacy and the Daughters of the American Revolution(140). Her clothes are in the best taste and her hair and hands show that she is frequently groomed by "some respectful slave at the beauty parlor"(141). Jane asks herself if she would have enjoyed being Frances, "safe and secure on my husband's thousand acres"(140). Her answer is "Perhaps. If I had . . . a lobotomy first"(141).

In her *Ms.* article, "The Southern Belle," Godwin writes of Southern daughters—those who stay and those who flee. She emphasizes the difficulty for any woman who questions her Southern heritage but would like to stay in the South without taking some traditional role; her peers will gently, firmly ostracize her, pulling her "back onto the beaten path"(51). Thus, the rebellious woman, if she "begins to succeed" in her search for new images of selfhood, is likely to be made so uncomfortable that she must flee the South—"depriving future generations of girls of her example"(51). Moreover, the fleeing rebel leaves the land to the spiritual clones of their Southern mothers, clones shaped with a "repertoire" of superficial graces known to be attractive to the "right" sort of man for the production of still other generations of spiritual clones.

The author's comments parallel her handling of Southern protagonists in her novels up until *A Mother and Two Daughters*. Venturesome, questioning daughters flee the South, yet they cannot fully escape it. In Kitty and in Jane, Godwin conveys the truth that every mother had a mother. Many of Edith's graces live on in Kitty. And Jane is spiritually the daughter of both. She partly inherits, along with their Southern accents, not a few of their Southern values and qualms, transmuted because she does question them, yet still haunting her.

The title character in *Violet Clay* is another Southerner, born and bred in Charleston, who reacts to Southernness by fleeing from it. Fatherless before birth, and motherless since infancy, she is still the daughter of an insistent heritage of the South. She compulsively measures herself with reference to those who reared her, the grandmother and uncle who instilled dear old lies, or perhaps half-truths, of the family's heritage. These lady and gentleman kindred, rather than her motherline, provide her models. She has little contact with her mother's people, simply mill-country folks. Ironically, these proud Charlestonians who molded Violet's sense of the South have wasted their lives, perhaps not without a certain pride in being as doomed as their homeland. Pride is even more evident in the energy both find to support keeping up appearances of decorum while glossing over their failures. Grandmother, as everyone knows, is a secret alcoholic, skillful in using gracious manners to enchant the world into sharing her pretenses of dignity. She confides in her granddaughter that she succumbed to her beau because of secret fears of failure in her potential career as a pianist (29) and because of her pride as a belle who could capture the 32-year-old who had rejected so many other belles (28). She was totally won at last by the myth, the "subversive, tempting picture" which could lead even an ambitious woman of 1919 from dreams of self-fulfillment to dreams of traditional glory:

> The picture was of that lady so feted in our day—her praises were sung in every women's magazine—the accomplished wife and mother who turns her gifts to

the enhancement of Home. I saw myself, safe and rich and beautiful, seated at a nine-foot grand in Charles's ancestral home. (29)

Violet leaves the South and succeeds in New York as a commercial artist, yet plays variations on the ancestral tensions. She cannot respect her own work, a craft that usually is crass. She sells romantic covers for Gothic novels, depicting women running away from houses. And her deepest fears are fears of failing if she should dare to aspire to higher art.

Violet also compares her life to her Uncle Ambrose's, whose role as Failed Southern Gentleman is relevant because he served as surrogate parent, modeling self-deceit and ultimate hollowness. After publishing a promising, though excessively romantic first novel, he then lived on for decades as a writer of fading promise. His Southern charms serve mainly to seduce a series of women into supporting him emotionally, even to an extent economically. Finally, he commits suicide. Even that gesture fails in one way; he does not carry it off as gracefully as intended. Violet lingers over her recurring sense of descent from a line of failed artists, sometimes finding wry consolation in her intent to fail with grace. She thinks she could go down as "a dignified loser . . . if it came to that" reminding herself that her part of the country "had made its biggest loss into a sort of debonair victory"(266).

Women in most societies may find it more difficult than men to rebel from the demands of tradition, since they are expected to transmit received truisms as unquestioned truths. They have fewer chances to test socially-accepted rules, fewer chances to gain varied experiences which help a searcher to tell truth from tradition. During the 1970s what Godwin wrote about the American South shows her concern with the customs and taboos which make the traditional roles of women even more inflexible. Southerners who believe in the heritage of the old South try harder to turn women into exemplars and transmitters of its old virtues. When those are shallowly defined, and Godwin sees how often they are mere forms, the most admired mothers perpetuate falseness. Dutiful daughters replicate their mothers, and questing daughters "flee for their lives." Even after their flights, they are hampered in their searching for honesty and autonomy because of lingering fear of all that is disruptive. Raised voices, the threat of a scene, whatever her mother would call ugly or strident, will tend to disgust even the expatriate daughters, will often send them into trembling retreat. Away from home, they do have the courage of some quite liberated convictions about sexuality. Nonetheless, they often think of "what people will say," and sometimes trim their behavior accordingly. Their shudders over "scenes" make particularly interesting the processes depicted by Godwin as essential to growth. They often achieve breakthrough insights by means of intense, even angry and loud, confrontations with their friends.[8]

Until her latest book, *A Mother and Two Daughters,* Godwin held out little hope for daughters who stayed at home. They simply relived the Southern fallacies. She presented dramas of psychological progress featuring the growth of the venturesome ones who abandoned the South. As social critic, she wrote of the typical ex-Southerner Carter Stephens having a chance to grow, to break out of the "vicious circle" (*Ms.* 51) of heritage-bound continuity. Breaking the old spell depends, for Carter, upon getting in touch with the reality of a black woman, that home-bred alien who abhors the heritage. Marianne, her black acquaintance, and Carter have met as women with careers in the North. Both are eager to "work hard at being friends"(84) and know how much they have in common, such as their love of books and their strains with men and the larger problem of designing their lives. Both take pride in broadmindedness: they intend not to be "petty nor isolationist nor heritage-handicapped"; both "like being women" but find "being human more important"(84). Their friendship meets its test when Carter defends the Southern habit of false-sweet pretendings; she likes making things nicer. Marianne challenges not just her social values but her maturity by asking, "Don't you think it's time you outgrew all these meaningless trappings of the privileged elite?"

Before Godwin lets Carter reply, the writer comments pointedly that a "portion of social history hangs in the balance" while Carter weighs her choices (85). She can take the old-Southern condescending option of avoiding a scene, feeling smug because Marianne hadn't had the advantages which would have taught her not to be rude and critical. Then Carter considers being honest, recognizes her anger and her need "to challenge . . . and be challenged in return," to have the furious encounter that "only friends and equals can have."

Do they win an open, lasting, taboo-free friendship by letting all hell break loose, airing out their particular hell-bent heritages? Godwin asks the cogent question: Can either of them get beyond her particular identity, blackness for one and Southern breeding for the other? Do they really want to outgrow their pasts, either of them?

> If they do, they may stay up shouting at each other all night, asking and answering the kinds of embarrassing questions that would rock the traditional Southern home] on its foundations. Marianne will explode into flames of rage at the injustice of centuries and Carter will dissolve backward into tears of nostalgia for that life of her mother's, where no dangerous questions are broached and the troublesome self is negated.(85)

Godwin chooses to let her readers decide whether the two women work through their furies, and survive the long night of rage and nostalgia. But she praises the benefits of such confrontation: when women keep trusting each other, articulating and sharing their versions of their pasts, individual and cultural, painful yet necessary, maturity will evolve. This 1975 article reaches the conclusion that only after such sharings can we "be one day nearer" to the happy time "when all constricting, debilitating stereotypes," including those of traditional Southern Womanhood, will be "relegated to the archives of human evolution"(85).

In *A Mother and Two Daughters*, Godwin's three protagonists do not succumb to the debilitating stereotype of Southern Womanhood in the least. Most of the traits of the Southern Lady seem to them amusing anachronisms. The novel suggests that Godwin can foresee prospects for the best hopes of her 1975 analysis coming true. Yet faint variations of the types she noted do appear in the form of a rebel daughter and a docile daughter. Cate, the rebellious troublemaker, questions all injustices, worries her family with her protestings, and seems to be bound to flee forever from the South. But she returns at the end to her roots in the hills of North Carolina, as a base from which she travels to earn her venturesome living. Lydia, the docile daughter, and Nell, the mother, preserve the graces of Southern ladies while avoiding the pitfalls of hypocrisy and shallowness. All three women relish "the task of personality" and each in her own way is both sensual and self-determining.

The novel is a comedy. Witty talk and wry perceptions pervade it, and it is also comic in that larger sense of happy endings—prizes are distributed and journeys lead to lovers meeting. Some of the humorous moments feature old concepts of Southern Womanhood. Throughout her life Nell has taken pride in keeping a critical distance from traditional Southernness, remaining an observer who "masqueraded adequately . . . as a

'Southern Lady.'" Yet Godwin juxtaposes this conscious pride in her freedom from the stereotype with a lasting distress at Cate's greater freedom from it, Cate's disordered life: Nell cannot forgive her rebel daughter "for not making more of an effort to blend gracefully into the landscape"(6). Lydia, the second daughter, indoctrinated in docility by her traditional father, only gradually breaks away from the formulaic successes of the Southern belle. As stages in her awakening to the task of personality, she leaves her husband and home, studies sociology and feminism, develops a true sisterly friendship with a black woman, and takes a lover. Lydia tries to envision her life in neatly labeled compartments, and even after her unconventional independence has been attained, one of these compartments reads "STILL A LADY"(253). Lydia's discovery of a career depends upon her ladylike air and her absorption with Southern life. She becomes a TV celebrity, charming her audiences with visits to the sites of gracious living.

Light touches, then, play upon the manners and graces of the South, while debilitating flaws are mostly "relegated to the archives of human evolution," as Godwin wished in her *Ms.* article. Racial bigotry, for example, has been transcended by all of the featured characters, even though the off-stage activities of realistically vicious bigots have cruelly changed the course of the lives of the two major black characters before the close of the novel. On stage, more hopeful trends are dramatized. Crucial to Lydia's development was her friendship with Renee Peverell-Watson and her guidance from Calvin Edwards. In the novel's epilog, set five years after its major events, Renee's daughter has married Lydia's son. The only members of either family who feel strain about this interracial marriage are blacks: on the bride's side, Renee's brother, the patriarch of the Peverells, and on the groom's side, Azalea, Aunt Theodora's maid-companion, who opposes "mixing" on principle (547). Amusingly, the concept of the lady in the South of 1984 (the date of the epilog) has been quite detached from concern with color, although not from beauty and grace and demeanor. Camilla, the bride, impresses her white mother-in-law as "a perfect lady"(535) and the matriarchal Aunt Theodora agrees.

In summary, Godwin's writings dissect the conservative feminine myth of the South not just to expose its debilitating central demand for a selflessness that precludes self-discovery, but also to present remedies. This author recognizes the beauty of ordered lives, and clings to hopes that Southern grace in its best sense can be cherished, can still enhance the old South's new daughters. But more emphatically she cautions that traditional roles when merely traditionally fulfilled endanger the spiritual lives of two generations: both the Southern mothers who model such roles and the daughters whom they dutifully try to mold toward the confining Ideal of Southern Womanhood. Women reared to reenact the traditional values must learn, Gail Godwin insists, to see their fallacies, explore them openly among critical friends and find new ways to be themselves, continually self-creating. And the three Southern women delineated in Godwin's latest work, A Mother and Two Daughters, all manage to sustain their self-creativity without permanent flights from the South and without romantic denials of contemporary realities; as a result they can be shown moving into a wholesome future, not problem-free by any means but free of the problems imposed by the rigid model of constraining Southern Ladyhood.

NOTES

[1] Contemporary interest in Gail Godwin's work is shown by her inclusion in the "Books" section of Time (10 Jan. 1983, 46–47) in an article by J. D. Reed "Postfeminism: Playing for Keeps." There with Joyce Carol Oates, Anne Tyler, Joan Didion, Ursula LeGuin, Alice Walker, Ann Beattie and several others, Godwin appears among women writers of novels who are "moving beyond doctrine." The article notes that "Godwin, 45, has taken up the theme of self-sufficient women with passion and precision," and observes that her "women face their trials with refreshing distance, like the author." Her work has attracted critical attention since the publication of The Perfectionists in 1970. She is included in Lina Mainiero's American Women Writers: A Critical Reference Guide from Colonial Times to the Present (New York: Unger, 1979), as well as in a number of similar reference works. Among the best of these is the entry by Carl Solana Weeks in the Dictionary of Literary Biography: American Novelists Since World War II, Vol. 6, Second Series (Detroit: Gale Research Co., 1980), 105–09.

[2] Of interest here is Anne Firor Scott's The Southern Lady: From Pedestal to Politics 1830–1930 (Chicago: Univ. of Chicago Press, 1970). Speaking of a time two generations earlier than the period in which Gail Godwin dramatizes the lives of Southern women in The Odd Woman (1974) and Violet Clay (1978), Anne Firor Scott reaches a strikingly optimistic conclusion about women's hopes for autonomy in the South: "the options were there and would continue to multiply. Southern women had begun to shake loose from the tyranny of a single monolithic image of women and were now free, for better or worse, to struggle to be themselves"(231). While Godwin's novels of the 1970s are less optimistic than Scott's views, Godwin's 1982 work, A Mother and Two Daughters, shows a trio representing two generations of self-determining Southern women moving confidently into 1984.

[3] Gail Godwin's first two novels are not relevant for the topics examined in this paper: The Perfectionists originally published in 1970, and Glass People in 1972.

[4] Gail Godwin's collection of short stories, Dream Children (1975), includes four stories which feature Southern characters or settings: "An Intermediate Stop," "False Lights,"

"Interstices," and "Some Side Effects of Time Travel." None deals with the clusters of traits which define the ideal of Southern Womanhood, but in "Some Side Effects of Time Travel," the leading character, Gretchen Brown, has a mother and grandmother who resemble some aspects of the characters in the maternal line of Jane Clifford. These generations of women are interesting to compare with Godwin's actual mother and grandmother as recalled by the author in her autobiographical memoir tracing the history of her creative efforts, "Becoming a Writer," in *The Writer on Her Work*. This is an expanded version of an earlier essay, "A Writing Woman," *Atlantic*, Oct. 1979, 84–92.

[5] Pressures which prevent the development of autonomy in women have been widely depicted in contemporary fiction. Mary Allen's *The Necessary Blankness: Women in Major American Fiction of the Sixties* (Urbana: Univ. of Illinois Press, 1976) includes perceptive analyses of the passivity and victimization of female characters. The study shows that the leading writers of the period (women as well as men, e.g. Oates, Plath, Bellow, Updike) all tended to depict female characters as cowed or shallow or despairing.

[6] All page citations are to the paperback edition (New York: Warner Books, 1979).

[7] Irony heightens the impact of Frances's prim decorum. The family keeps secret her birth as the illegitimate child of Edith's sister, Cleva, who died after being seduced and abandoned by an itinerant actor. Their aunt's story has become a classic cautionary tale as Edith alerts her daughter and granddaughter to the risks of sexuality and the wages of sin. Jane's later search for "the villain" who ruined Cleva is also featured in the novel.

[8] In both *The Odd Woman* and *Violet Clay*, the protagonists attain significant new perspectives through confrontations with close female friends. Gerda exposes Jane's evasions of reality; she describes Jane's illusions and qualms as the mannerisms of a "fence-sitting Southern bitch" who retreats to "lovely old nineteenth-century lies"(407). Samantha, Violet Clay's friend, has neither the savvy nor the articulate force of Gerda, yet she serves better to cure Violet's Southern defeatism than Gerda did to counteract Jane's romanticism. Sam's courage and independence enable Violet to learn that she is not doomed to re-enact her family tradition of futility, using Southern charm to cover self-indulgent failure. Samantha's autonomy gives Violet faith in her own potential strength. With help from their very different friends both Jane and Violet grow to realize that they can choose not to be heritage-bound. The novel *A Mother and Two Daughters* also builds toward a vivid confrontation. But in this case the conflicts of Cate and Lydia are not couched in terms of Southernness. Nor does the confrontation between the sisters result immediately in curative recognition of faults. Rather it appears to lead towards grudging tolerance and slow growth.

Eating the Moment Absolutely Up:
The Fiction of Beverly Lowry

MERRILL MAGUIRE SKAGGS

One comes to look forward to several specific pleasures when reading the great Southern women writers of fiction—Ellen Glasgow, Katherine Anne Porter, Willa Cather, Eudora Welty, Flannery O'Connor, Anne Tyler. First, perhaps, is that sense of a distinctive place, created through specific details which are rendered interesting by clever metaphor and analogy. In tandem with that initial expectation is a sense of lives lived out in a community context. The reader expects to meet a wide spectrum of the social types making up that Southern microcosm, from founding fathers to alcoholic mothers and on to obstreperous children. One learns to anticipate a gallery of grotesque human types contained within any Southern city limits. And for protection from the horror, one relies on so lively an irony that it can turn dismay into laughter. One goes to reportedly excellent Southern fiction anticipating most of these characteristics. One finds them all in Beverly Lowry, as well as a great deal more.

Lowry's first two novels, *Come Back, Lolly Ray* (1977) and *Emma Blue* (1978), in fact seem written self-consciously to help Lowry find her place, and claim her territory, within this distinguished tradition. The novels are both set in the same fictionally made-to-order small Southern town—Eunola, Mississippi—which can convincingly supply all the verbal artifacts we wish, by long training, to discover there. So we recognize, in one book or the other, Walker Percy's levee, Robert Penn Warren's destructive modern highway, Katherine Anne Porter's grannies, Flannery O'Connor's users of reverberating clichés. We can spot William Faulkner's abstracted, narcissistic mother, who acquires Mr. Compson's drinking problem before committing Quentin's suicide. No matter. The literary references seem self-conscious enough to be interesting and intentional. The novels advance Lowry's assertion to other Southern writers that she is "one of us."

Photo: Susie James

Beverly Lowry

Born in Tennessee (1938), Lowry spent her childhood in Mississippi. She attended the University of Mississippi but transferred to Memphis State University where she received her B.A. She has contributed stories, articles and reviews to a number of magazines and newspapers and has published three novels. Her first novel, Come Back, Lolly Ray, *appeared in 1977.*

Some ambitious young Southerners are, of course, put off by so many handy yardsticks for measuring their new literary talent. But those who can stand the comparison are also profoundly lucky in having so profuse a variety of geniuses to learn from. The truly determined newcomer can thus be energized by the competition. And whatever else she may be, Lowry is unmistakably one of the most determined and ambitious of the recently recognized Southern talents.

With her first novel, Lowry clearly signaled the world that she did not intend to be ignored. The "electric" fictional character who conveys this announcement is Lolly Ray Lasswell, a virtuoso baton twirler who dominates the important pageants and public events of Eunola. Though Lolly Ray turns out to be anything but impregnable, in fact must finally leave Mississippi and end the novel in order to bear her bastard out of public sight, she nevertheless provides, in her public-school years, the town's most compelling image of glory. Eunola does not live happily ever after, without her.

Quickly following that starburst beginning, *Emma Blue* keeps the Lasswell story moving. Emma, Lolly's high-school-aged illegitimate daughter, has grown up in the care of her dippy grandmother and gleefully malicious great-grandmother. Three generations (skipping Lolly) live together in Lolly's old childhood home, a trailer anchored permanently on the edge of town. In this second novel, Emma learns both how to protect her isolation, her outsider status, and also how to dig her way into community—an enterprise she compares to archaeology. Emotionally richer than her mother, Emma learns to see herself not merely as an unrivalled focus of community attention—Lolly's goal—but rather as part of a social and historical context. If Lolly learns to excel, Emma learns to relate to others. Neither lesson is easy. Yet at the end, Emma not only gets her diploma but also graduates smiling. She enters a world which has already offered her several attractive options, including a prestigious marriage; it has always permitted her to walk, symbolically and literally, on her own feet.

The most arresting of Lowry's novels, the latest and the best, is her third which appeared in 1981, *Daddy's Girl.* Set in the Houston, Texas, suburbs, though including a side trip to Pine Bluff, Arkansas, it is much less self-consciously "Southern" than her preceding two. Here Lowry no longer bothers to prove she can do all the Southern tricks just as well as her mentors. Here she finds her own style, and a distinctive one it certainly is. Both style and book are more sophisticated, more subtle, more maddening, more demanding, and certainly more challenging than Lowry's others. This novel requires us to work, and work hard, to read it. It also repays our closest attention.

One concedes at once, however, that a number of the details and incidents of this third novel also appear in the preceding two. For example, Sue Muffaletta's ties to her father, "Big Daddy" Jim Stovall, are not unlike those Lolly shares with *her* doting and attentive father, Frank Lasswell. Though a daddy's girl, Sue tries to recover some sense of her mother Linda's earlier days through her mother's old journal, just as Emma tries to comprehend her mother Lolly's personality by reading Lolly's old diary and scrapbook. "Big" regards Sue's performances as June Day, the country singer, just as ambivalently as Frank Lasswell viewed Lolly's twirling. Frank will wait to take Lolly home, as Big will babysit for Sue's children, but neither father will watch his daughter strut in public. Sue's performances as singer June Day—or M. S. Sue, a songwriter—are directed as straightforwardly toward helping her enter "the limelight; my noblest self" (*DG* 63), as Lolly's twirling once was. Lolly speaks for all Lowry's young women when she concludes, "To be out front that way. Was everything" (*EB* 55). Emma complains of her mother Lolly that "all her stories were the same. About herself" (*EB* 54). Yet all these women are egotistical. In *Daddy's Girl*, Sue's mother Linda writes pornographic fairy tales that she claims are always about herself; and Sue's narrative songs grow unmistakably, as the novel demonstrates, from Sue's personal experience. All their stories germinate in the same personal plots of ground.

Such similarities as these bring up an important point about Lowry's heroines which should be understood from the beginning. Whatever else she does, Lowry never bothers to sketch passive female victims of anything or anybody. Her most passive woman, Lolly's mother Lucille, finally learns by the end of *Emma Blue* that there's no hope of rescue from her life which will ever come from outside herself: "Rescue: there had never been the least hope of it, not from him [her estranged husband] or anybody else" (*EB* 162). If anything is to change, Lucille must change it herself, rescue herself.

All the other young women Lowry creates appear to discover this truth as naturally as breathing. From the first page of Lowry's fiction, when we watch with a curbside crowd for Lolly to appear, the typical Lowry heroine propels herself down the street way in front of the trailing band, on her own steam, asserting her own right to recognition. All Lowry's women act self-consciously, in their own self-interest, to gratify themselves. They don't watch out for others, they move. They don't intuit nuances, they choose. They make their own (often pathetic and often hilarious) mistakes. Even the alcoholic Lady Cunningham, wife of the town's wealthiest citizen, drinks because she chooses to do so—out of boredom. It is an intense reader's pleasure to meet female characters who are selecting their own routes, just like regular human beings with wills of their own. Fully human potential adults who are female! It is a consummation we have devoutly wished.

There are other details in Lowry's work to feast a feminist eye. For one thing, Lowry is masterful with the telling detail especially associated with a typical female life. For example, in *Daddy's Girl* a nursing mother drops off to sleep with an exposed breast still caked with milk; or a woman, through mirrors, wonderingly experiences her own act of childbirth and admires the beauty of a placenta; or a mother of a middle-aged boy experiences a familiar anger she never expresses, upon seeing him eat the bacon she has fried to treat herself, when he doesn't like bacon.

Lowry is also good at depicting family networks, especially the intricate networks of women. She insists we recognize that all characters are compounds of many familial ingredients, and that all the generations affect each other. In *Daddy's Girl*, for example, Linda's mother Dolly has labeled her a *"little toy. . . . Made for sex"* (73). Linda has wanted literary style as well as sex, and has in turn produced a daughter, Sue, who, somewhat more openly than Linda, acknowledges her own ambitions about writing. But in her domestic hours, Sue thinks of herself as Mama Two to Linda's Mama One. Sue in turn rears a daughter Caroline, who is fifteen in the novel's present time and obviously having some trouble becoming a woman. Her menarche is delayed; she also faces the problem of resolving the conflicting signals she picks up from Sue and Linda. She seems emotionally to volley between them and to recapitulate all the problems of forging an acceptable female identity which each of them faced in turn.

Needless to say, the path to adulthood ne'er runs smooth. In Lowry's first novel, Lolly Ray never really makes it there—to a semblance of emotional maturity. That, in fact, is one of this first novel's major problems. In *Come Back, Lolly Ray* Lowry devises this splendid symbol: the female highschool hero as much the target of all eyes, as thoroughly the dominator of sports events, as consummate a narcissistic egoist, as ever a Young Studs Lonigan or Rabbit Angstrom dared to be. Like those male figures, Lolly will never again regain so absolute a glory as she knows in her youth. As a convincing female agent of such power, Lolly is an extraordinarily believable literary symbol. Unhappily, she never seems nearly so real as a human being who encourages our attachment. Perhaps Lolly's whirling acrobatics kept Lowry at a distance, too. Lolly is supposed to be a twentieth-century hollow woman, but she remains so hollow she echoes.

Emma, on the other hand, is her mother's ultimate nightmare: "Ordinary, just as she had thought" (*EB* 206). In the one occasion Lolly returns to the trailer, her eyes suggest to her daughter, "No life, no hope, no vision" (*EB* 208). After finally seeing Lolly, Emma concludes, "The Mama was a pumped-up dead woman" (208). Thereafter, Emma can jettison her obsession with her mother. Yet Emma herself fails to secure more than lukewarm continuing interest. At the end, she grins broadly, knowing her life will be all right. We have no reason to contradict her hope but little more reason to care, one way or the other. Only when Lowry gets to *Daddy's Girl* does she devise a protagonist who is ordinary enough to be fully human, but extraordinary enough to promise almost any jaw-dropping surprise.

As *Daddy's Girl* begins, we are plunged immediately into a distinct rhythm, immediately puzzling, unexpected, and apparently unrelated to our presumed everyday lives: "And-two-and-hit-it." We quickly discover that the rhythm is that of a country blues song, and is the particular beat of a singer whose voice speaks to us over the song and introduces herself as June Day, the narrator. We learn that this narrator has many names, as well as many rhythms or beats. She's a young suburban widow and mother of three, named Sue Muffaletta. She's a song writer named M. S. Sue. She's her father's darling: "Sweet Sue"—Sue Shannon Stovall; and she's a housewife volunteer presently serving as her son's Little League team father. Which identity, which name, is most real is anybody's guess: but the most preposterous—*June Day*, whose rhythm introduces us to the tale—is actually connected to traceable fact. It is derived from her mother's real maiden name of Day. In fact, her mother's pseudonym— Shannon Day—is also true to fact, for she was born Linda Shannon Day. So fantasy and reality blend here at every turn.

Obviously, the narrator Sue not only has many names but also many secret selves. Significantly, the first person we meet is the secret self who sings in the limelight and gives Sue her intensest pleasure. Our first order of business, that is, becomes meeting Sue's most important and most secret of all selves—the one who can control and manipulate audiences, who can sing at dusk in a parking lot with a live band and then go straightaway into a former meat locker and make love with a restaurant owner. The first thing this novel is about, we infer, is how to put all these secret selves together into a whole and integrated personality.

To complete that task Sue must face the fact that secret selves are not mysterious and bizarre. They are rather part of being human and alive. Everybody has them. In fact, her mother tells her towards the novel's end that she has had a secret self since her babyhood: it began to walk, then ate dirt, then learned to run away in order to mess in its pants. From infancy, a part of Sue has been breaking rules and fleeing the humdrum. At the end, Sue has taken some apparently constructive steps, not to eliminate her secret selves but simply to consolidate them: June Day is going to engulf M. S. Sue, the writer, and become June Day, the writer-performer, who is daughter of Linda Shannon Day, the successful shaper of salacious adult fictions.

Before that constructive simplification, however, Sue has required her audience to confront with her the fact that all the people she knows best are fragmented into many selves about which each person is secretive. Daughter Caroline's secret self is Princess Grace, a snob. Neighbor Jane's secret self is a promiscuous woman of voracious sexual appetite who will park her kids anywhere to make a quick pickup. Grandmother Stovall's secret self plans a revenge on her family so effective that it will operate to the third or fourth generation. Sue inherits her capacity to invent frag-mented identities directly from *both* father and mother. Her adored father is called variously Chunk, Big, Baby, The Kid, Daddy, Big Daddy, and Jim Stovall. Towards the end, he reveals still another innermost secret self he has apparently always lived with: "one-nut, short-dick Stovall"(225). Sue's mother Linda once identified herself as the Queen of

Shades, Sue discovers. And only at the end does Linda in fact manage to discard one cast-off identity and divorce her estranged husband, Jim Stovall. All the important characters in this novel move slowly toward an open acknowledgement of their capacity for secrets and their "normal" need for secrecy.

A major part of the family charm, and a game Big initiates all his children and grandchildren to, is the inclination to spell names backwards and then invent stories about the new-old fabrications. Alucard, the family demon, is known to the uninitiated as Dracula. But Frankenstein and Wolfman submit to the family's seachange as well. As a group this family is both Stovall and Llavots, the latter being their *more* real, because privately shared, identity. From the beginning we learn that Big's family behaves the way it does because it is "so whacko, so haywire"(22). Big Jim Stovall's bizarre behavior at the end, requiring his incarceration in the psychiatric ward, is therefore in some way normal for him and for them all.

To maintain their air of happily shared secrecy, the essential family unit—Sue, her three children, and her father—share a more elaborate secret signal system than merely reversed names and words would indicate. These exchanges themselves acquire symbolic overtones before the novel ends. "Shall we leave?" / "I'm ready"—a standard question-and-answer sequence—becomes instead, "Shall we dance?" / "Jive and mambo." And of course, secret languages always sound like jibberish to those who cannot understand them. So towards the novel's close, when Big has grown "atilt" and cannot talk normally or communicate with anyone for long, his association of dance with significant movement still conveys sense to his worried daughter. Having learned to accept her father's recurrent lack of focus, his abnormality, Sue still learns that the more things change, the more they stay the same. Throughout the novel, the idiom for getting along is, "we do our dance"(9). Anticipating a delightful trip to Memphis, she ends the novel saying characteristically, "Never mind weather, I'm going. Turn up the music. I plan to dance."

One implication of Lowry's fiction is that no amount of modern sophistication can erase the simple, primitive intensity of some relationships (father-daughter, for example); no amount of "enlightenment" can shield a father's heart from some kinds of pain: "That their baby girls carry diaphrams in their purses next to lipstick flatly breaks daddies' hearts, however updated 1980s they profess to be, wearing beards and chains, buying *Good Sex For All* (40). With all the flimflam modernity and breezy sophistication of the present year, Lowry asks, how does one face, much less deal intelligently with, those unsophisticated basic problems springing from basic human relationships? These problems are not rendered intelligibly easy or orderly here; if anything, they are depicted as more intense than one would have easily admitted.

Sue has identified herself, in her youth, as "the girl all daddies adore" and the girl of everybody's standardized dreams, the "all-American honor girl"(10). Having admitted that "Daddy and I have terrible dreams," and that "Sometimes we wake up and have had the same one"(51), Sue divulges that they have been caught in the same bad dream, the same nightmare, from time to time. She even asks rhetorically who steals whose dreams. By the end of the book, their shared dreams—obscene, impertinent, impolite, amusing, unspeakable, and true—are realized. Big's haywire perceptions become everybody else's central nightmare. By this time Sue, having sat on his lap (on the way to his sister's funeral), slept in his room (because space is at a premium at the family home), and grasped his penis (to prevent his exposing himself by his sister's grave), indeed shares intimately in Big's bad dream. She becomes the Big Mama who alone can remain stable enough to see Big through and get him safely over the nighmare stretch of road he must travel in order to get back home. Thus they literally steal each other's dreams and nightmares, in living so intensely each other's lives.

But they do not do so in isolation from a surrounding world. No writer more than Lowry, it seems to me, has with more effective compression presented more convincingly the theory that no human being lives a life, or enters a relationship, alone. One brings parents, grandparents, siblings and children with one into any moment, and must then relate to those same forces operating in mysterious ways on others. Every significant encounter is like a family funeral—populated by distant relations one wouldn't even have recognized on the street. But the existence of that throng who crowd into and around a single encounter does not make it impossible to express exactly one's personal opinions of a central character—the corpse, for example—in one profoundly simple gesture. At the end of this novel's funeral, Big simply urinates an avalanche into his sister's grave. He thus digs the hole a little deeper where her face will go.

A joy of *Daddy's Girl* is the way in which style or technique becomes theme, or perhaps vice versa. In any case, Linda says at one point, "The truth is in bits and pieces. You connect them up in your mind"(182). Lowry has moved more securely into this style made of bits of pieces with every novel. In each novel she in fact gives us sharper shards which we are obliged to connect in our minds if we are to find coherence. The sections sometimes seem a Chinese box of pieces, a tour de force puzzle, all commenting on all others. In the section of *Daddy's Girl* entitled "Little Big and SSS" (25 ff), for example, stories constantly intercut other stories and each other, expanding the major topics of the section: how well Big tells stories and how he finds the stories he tells. Yet the section is also part of Sue's story about Big and about story-telling. In it, Big's set piece story is compared to his primary family-history (which is Sue's story), and both are compared to television reruns of the kind Sue's sons habitually watch for the joys of experiencing the repetitions. But the present family which Sue heads also provides a context for Big's childhood story. And Big's story is in turn repeated in Sue's family—like a repeated story or a rerun.

Lowry also juxtaposes her fragmented bits and pieces deliberately, to allow each to make a comment on the others. For example, Sue resolves to try to persuade her sons to switch the television from *Bonanza* to "a decent late movie if there is one" and then remarks, in passing, "later on, dreams"(107). Immediately thereafter we have a short passage entitled "The Girl of My Dreams #3," in which the third version of self as dream girl which coheres in Sue's head is erotic, upsetting, and obscene. We must splice together for ourselves this scene with throwaway lines about hating to sleep because sleep always brings upsetting dreams. To "read" a Lowry novel appropriately, then, one must not only grasp the facts as they unfold but also grasp the insignificant phrasing, the sequences and the context and order in which the unfolding occurs. Like an elaborate recipe, the ingredients are added in particular sequences for particular chemical effects.

Of particular interest in this novel is the narrative voice. For example, it is a great jolt, after the novel begins so clearly in the voice of Sue Muffaletta, who also uses pseudonyms, to find ourselves receiving information Sue could not know, though in sentences typical of Sue. We are suddenly out of Sue's head and into her father Big's consciousness. Next we find ourselves in Big's dreams. It is reasonable to be thoroughly confused, until we recall that Sue says she *shares* Big's dreams and may even dream them first. We then conclude that Sue and Big share thoughts as well as dreams, and can therefore know what the other experiences. Having accepted this assimilable unconventionality and breathed a sigh of relief, however, we are jolted and disoriented again (not unlike Big will be in his upcoming bout with perceptual vertigo) to discover that narrator Sue eventually enters *every* head of *every* character in her immediate family, including her mother, her children, and her brother Steve. All are parts of her thoughts and she is part of theirs. Eventually she tours the dreams of her sleeping kin, as gently intrusive as Walt Whitman's persona in "The Sleepers." She shares all their dreams, not just her daddy's. When, at the end of the book, "Big is atilt and so the world is"(214) atilt also, she thinks, "It's like he's inside a dream"(223). But by then we have been with Sue inside a number of dreams, and so we understand Big's condition. It seems, under these circumstances, a kind of outer-fringe normality, especially for a "Llavots head."

Initially, the narrative voice has seemed slangy, brave, humorously self-deprecating, self-satirizing, mildly ironic, folksy, and very familiar *with* the reader ("I ask you."). In that voice, Sue makes distinctions between "my June Day style" and the "at home" look. By the end of the novel, we're very familiar with all these styles and with the fact—the thematic statement—that they're all her own forms of speech. Each gives us a new way of seeing her character and predicament.

The way Lowry uses this narrative voice to advantage suggests the large degree to which her fiction has been influenced by film techniques. Years ago, Kuleshov demonstrated that the expressions or emotions a viewer perceives in one shot of a motion picture will depend on the juxtaposition of the next shot or the preceding shot. Thus a neutral face placed beside a bowl of soup will look hungry; the same face beside a coffin will look sad; against a playing child will look happy, and so forth. Cinematic artists manipulate their audience by the care with which they arrange their shots, the sequences in which images occur. Kuleshov's theory explains why our thoughts about the character of Sue depend on whatever the narrative voice describes next to Sue. Lowry certainly knows these tricks of arrangement. But in other ways as well, she appears to have been heavily influenced by the movies.

As *Lolly Ray* opens, for example, a whole crowd looks one way, alerting us to something important and preparing us to identify immediately that important person, object, or act the instant it appears. As in a hundred movie openers, the credits seem to roll over unimportant figures until the crucial moment when the right speck appears in the upper right-hand corner to which all heads are turned. Then the distracting print disappears, and the action gets under way: Lolly rounds the corner and prances into sight, a golden image sparkling in the sun.

In *Emma Blue* we repeatedly get a general statement of a scene, what cinematographers call the master shot, which precedes any detailed action, introduces an episode, and clarifies a location or furnishes a context. After the inclusive master shot, the camera moves in, first to one close-up and then to another. Always, however, we can return to the "master shot" when the need arises, when we need to remember that context. For example, having identified a particular morning, we see Lucille listening to the radio, Emma plodding toward Mattie Sue's house, Granny Peavey waking up disruptively, and Mattie Sue dressing herself and structuring her day. We realize that we are receiving quick impressions of a representative cross-section of Eunola's population. Opposites exist here. Mattie Sue thinks of her life, "it had never been fair but she knew better than to use herself up hating and blaming and fighting what never paid off, even—*even*—if you won" (63). What Granny Peavey thinks is "*Shit!*" (60). Among the younger generations, Carroll Cunningham wonders what meaning he will ever find, while Emma plunges forward, impatiently forging ahead to find the trail of her destiny. The cross-cutting makes a social collage of the kind invented by D. W. Griffith.

Most interestingly, in *Daddy's Girl* the novel begins with a scene of a country singer, costumed in a precisely described way to convey precisely libidinous signals. But the sound of the song fades quickly, once it has been identified, and what we hear is the voice of a narrator, speaking with much the same effect as a cinematic voice-over. As she grows more experienced, in fact, Lowry seems to rely ever more heavily on these techniques of film: fancy cross-cutting, flashbacks, background music to build mood, zooms in for closeups alternating with long shots. It is surely a major characteristic of her "modernity."

Lowry's strongest claim to recognition, however, as well as her most distinctive stylistic characteristic, is her humor. Not only is her prose stocked with wit aplenty, and from the first novel; the comedy also grows through each subsequent novel in both subtlety and variety. With *Daddy's Girl* Lowry achieves a comic tour de force of major power. One can find in Lowry's three books, in fact, an author moving steadily from predictably standard Southern comic devices to a humor distinctively her own.

Consider the titles Lowry chooses. *Come Back, Lolly Ray* is in itself mildly comic. It issues a plea to a female whose name, by Southern fictional conventions, signals that she is lower-middle-class and probably tacky. That such a figure could be important enough to plead for her return tips us off to expect a comic novel. The title's *cri de coeur* is too personal, too intense, too vulnerable to tempt our sympathy. By embarrassing us, it creates the distance necessary for derisive laughter. Spotting this title, we expect to find here that humorous exploitation of absurd smalltown manners which Eudora Welty mines in *The Ponder Heart* and other works. This kind of humor assumes that creator and reader understand what good taste is, and also understand that certain smalltown Southern types don't have it.

The title *Emma Blue* creates a different effect. This is a spirit-deflating name, and the title doesn't indicate beyond its suggestion of lumpish dumpiness what the proper attitude will be to the major character it identifies. We know instantly that this major character, whom we are to take seriously, with or without affectionate sympathy, is not the object of laughter. In fact, the humor in this novel is more quiet and ironic.

In *Emma Blue* we find many touches of the Southern humorists' exploitation of the tawdry or tacky; but in hindsight we can see Lowry moving toward the interesting demands she places on us in her third novel. In *Daddy's Girl* the narrator is *both* exuberantly tasteless and unrestrained—a veritable female ringtailed roarer—and *also* the captor of our sympathies. Lowry finally learns to create humor which allows her to have her cake and eat it too. She learns to create a character who seems both pathetic and strong, serious and silly, vulnerable and assertive, comic and profoundly wise, all at once. The *Daddy's Girl* title conveys a number of these stylistic complexities. First, it is an exact statement of the novel's primary subject matter; second, it is a succinct summary of the protagonist's psychological quandary. Thus the title precisely describes the novel's contents. But it also indicates a certain judgmental recognition of emotional immaturity, of a fixation and developmental stoppage at too young a level. Such neurosis is too threatening to provoke much besides nervous, discrediting sniggers or derisive, disgusted headshakes.

The distance such a suggestion of a violated taboo establishes between characters and their taboo-observing readers also creates the necessary leeway for the raunchy-raw, unbuttoned humor Lowry provides those with the appetite for it. And some of Lowry's sexual one-liners are unsurpassed for slack-jawed splendor: "I do love men's tits. Like erasers to gnaw"(56). Or describing a male whom women respond to: "You'd suck his toes"(93). What Lowry's humor seems to do, in fact, is move from smartaleck quickies and surefire smirk-starters, towards puns and aphorisms, to extended set-pieces of satire and then beyond.

Among the dependable pleasures of *Daddy's Girl* are the labels which reduce people, emotions and things to their essence. One loves these boxes for containing things neatly. For example, a theatrical director with whom Sue has a casual affair is called only Al Theater. A Presbyterian preacher's wife who adores her husband too ostentatiously remains My Wife Evelyn. A black Chief Resident in Neurosurgery who behaves as a professional robot is Fast-and-Tense. Even more plentiful are the Stovall family's reductions-to-a-word which convey what it feels like to be in a particular place at a particular time. A scoured house is labeled Mr. Clean City. Sleeping late is Sweet City. Breakfast is Banana City. Houston, where quick money is made, is Snake Oil City. A long-absent but now returned capacity for orgasm is Angel Wing City.

Such flashes of delight lead to somewhat longer phrases, which Lowry supplies through puns both verbal—"After Big came, M. S. Sue was born"(67)—and visual—Daddy's girl Sue lives in a suburb abbreviated on street signs as POP. An apartment complex is described as "a place of government sameness and one-foot-and-then-the-other occupants"(45). These puns and allusions suggest a self-conscious attention to the shape, rhythm, and compact intensity of a line. That attention produces, in a few gifted writers, the aphorisms toward which Lowry's prose is clearly moving. Some sentences in *Daddy's Girl* appear to originate in so deeply-felt a knowledge that they will almost scan: "But when babies are little, time for mothers turns gray"(62), or "I have done the married man waltz and left the floor"(81). In her best passages, Lowry can capture Sue's nervous and sporadic flashes of insight as well as the residue of wisdom they leave behind: "Fact: some things you get past but not over. Time's a famous healer but there are limits. Never's a fact as well as someday"(72).

Within this whole work are also satiric set-pieces which provide interludes of particular intensity. In them Lowry takes time out to eviscerate her personal *bêtes noires.* Her description of Writers' Conferences is just what one has always suspected they deserve: she defines them as events about selling, not writing, which are designed to permit the predatory incursions of "experts," who mostly make love to the students ineptly. But Lowry also satirizes the kind of writing such students offer: housewives' poems about "how sad I was, what terrible things had been done to me, how awful it was to sit in the back room of your house writing poems, how lonely"(63).

Perhaps the best of all Lowry's satiric set-pieces is contained by the family funeral Sue and Big attend back in Arkansas. Among the outer rings in Lowry's targets are the vocal mannerisms Arkansas develops in its women: on the telephone, an Arkansas matron turns each declarative sentence into a question, the intent of which is, "Are you remembering / following / listening?" One keeps the statement / questions flowing by murmuring "uhmm" in each decent interval. In the flesh, an Arkansas female addresses every other female as *girl,* regardless of name, age or condition.

Once in Pine Bluff, Sue and Big must enter the Pine Bluff dream: a house so stripped of personality, so modern and improved, that it is only a set of noises: "The low rumbling underscores the bink of digital clocks moving time ahead, the switching gears of the refrigerator-freezer, the filling of the ice-making machine, the tinkle of chandeliers, the sounds of a nighttime new house"(*DG* 148). Finally, however, the malicious highpoint comes with a description of Cousin Louanne's new behavior patterns, derived from her "nut-sect us-and-not-you church"(140). They produce Louanne's finest scene: "Louanne, mourning the death of her mother nut-church fashion, is sitting at Lou's head making a noise that sounds like a nail going across a blackboard as she turns her hands back and forth over her dyed Church-of-God hairdo"(186). The tense becomes present here while all those present tense-up into future-time-denying knots.

The malice here is familiar enough to admirers of Welty or O'Connor. What's distinctive is the fact that we must face this delicious malice in a narrator who is also our emotional home base within the story. Lowry's narrator Sue shares with us, the readers, *both* our amused recognition of aberrant behavior and also the malice she's willing to express about her own family. In other words, the sympathetic narrator is also self-consciously part of and related to the targets she is presently attacking: she is both attacker and target, whom we both dismiss and care for. And thus the satire turns serious, its sharp edge blunted. For part of the point is that these crazies are as representative of the crazy Stovall family as Sue, the storyteller we must trust. And ultimately the craziest of the Stovalls becomes Big Daddy Stovall himself. That most treasured one, who enters a room or narrative bringing life, stability, and laughter, turns out to be the craziest of all. And Big has no hope in sight for a total recovery. He's going to *stay* a little crazy, just like them all.

What is beyond Lowry's satire? Not so much more humor as good-humored acceptance of the inevitable: Big will make perfect sense some of the rest of his time; and some of the rest of his time, he'll be atilt, out-of-focus, underwater, with cows swimming by. Sue will discover more thoroughly that she can operate independently and become Mama Number One, in charge. But she'll never outgrow her need to have her Daddy close at hand, in whatever focus he must be. Whatever her attached and continuing dependence will mean, Sue conveys her acceptance of her life and her secrets and selves. Not only does she know what she is and accept all of it. She also clearly commits herself, at the end, to accept and enjoy her life, "mean as it is." She's strong-heartedly planning to eat her moments "absolutely up." A typical Lowry heroine, she is ready to dance.

Shirley Ann Grau and the Short Story

MARY ROHRBERGER

The problem with Shirley Ann Grau is that she has consistently refused to stand still and conform to the stereotypes critics and reviewers have created for her. The problem of course, is not hers but ours, for we have consistently failed to understand the complexity of her statements and the excellence of her forms. Rather than try here to treat the corpus of her fiction, I have decided to examine the short stories, starting with the earliest and coming to ones she is currently working on for collection in a new anthology. My hope is to demonstrate not only her extraordinary skill in the short story genre, but also the development of that skill, and by so doing to stimulate a continuation of the recent flurry of scholarly activity devoted to examination of her work.

Had critics and reviewers been familiar with Grau's first published stories, their initial judgments concerning her proper métier might have been different, for the stories published during her college years exhibit a range more in line with catholic than regionalist tendencies.

"For a Place in the Sun" appeared in April 1948 in *Surf,* an intercollegiate magazine published at Tulane University. Grau was then a nineteen-year-old sophomore at Newcomb College. The protagonist of the story, a young man named Dan, has been injured by a falling crate and is unable to take a job driving a large van. The job signifies for him escape from his cramped and penurious circumstances, but it also signifies the advent of manhood and the assumption of a power role.

Dan is his mother's favorite son and subconsciously he seeks comfort in and from her. At the same time, he wants her approval and her admiration. Though injured, he is trapped not by his body but by his state of mind. The fuzzy whiteness in the form of tiny puffs of clouds that he hallucinates, the blades of grass he tears from the ground and scatters, his

Shirley Ann Grau

*A native of Louisiana (b. 1929), Grau received her B.A. from
Newcomb College, Tulane University, where she also did graduate work. The first of her two collections of short stories,* The
Black Prince and Other Stories, *appeared in 1955. She has
published five novels, one of which,* The Keepers of the House,
won the Pulitzer Prize.

throbbing pain replicated in the landscape, the fog and marshes and odor of decay are all correlatives of his inner being.

His mother is also of two minds. Torn between her desire to care for her first born and her knowledge that she must at least try to motivate Dan to activity despite his injury, she speaks to him cautiously and fearfully. Struck by what she says but unable to deal with it, he escapes to the barn, to a milking stool where he sits breathing heavily and gazing vacantly at a row of milk cans. His vacant gaze is similar to the painful void and the dank hollows he wants to escape. Enshrouded by fog and blinded by his own egoism, seeing only shadowy forms, Dan opens the gate to the pasture lot, knowing the animals' escape will prevent his brother Will from taking the job Dan believes is his.

Although the plan to thwart his brother succeeds, Dan does not prevail. Will realizes what has happened; moreover, the knowledge does not bother him. Secure in himself, he is neither annoyed nor angry, and he has no need to tell his mother or to lash out at Dan. In the end, Dan stretches his leg in the sun to ease his pain, but "not even the clear yellow rays that seeped through the cloth could ease it or warm the cold loneliness within him."

This remarkable story is told in fewer than two thousand words. Nothing is stated overtly; everything is related indirectly through image patterns. The notable skill of the storyteller is evident from the first image of expected pain to the cyclic return to pain at the end of the story. The details of setting and action function to reveal the psychologic makeup of the characters as well as their inner conflicts. Modern in form with an *in medias res* beginning and lack of complicated plot, the story ends with an epiphany that embodies the entire experience.

The first issue of a new literary magazine, *Carnival*, published at Tulane in May 1949, contains a second story, "So Many Worlds," a short-short story, less than one thousand words. This time Grau handles a different kind of people, a different social class, and uses a somewhat different form. In "So Many Worlds," two people enter a restaurant and are seated by a waiter. The young wife, clothed in fur and diamonds, clearly dominates and manages her confused and gesticulating husband. A short paragraph moves the couple to the outside. It is after a rain, and he points to a puddle: "Look, a world at your feet." "That," she says, is the "other side of the looking glass," the "upside-down world." As she hurries him away, his glance falls back to the puddle of blackness where "their two reflections lay bent and grotesque, and made a single pattern." In "So Many Worlds," rising action moves to what in a traditional story would be climax. But instead of climax a transitional paragraph begins the pattern of images that builds to the epiphany.

The December 1949 issue of *Carnival* provides another story, "The Shadowy Land," not long by any means, but better than twice as long as anything Grau had done before. The story's more complex plot is arranged in a traditional order—exposition, conflict, complication rising to climax and falling then to denouement. With more characters and a mingling of social classes, this story is Grau's first "Southern" story. Set in New Orleans during the Mardi Gras, the story contains white "masters" of French extraction and black "servants." Her skill at handling dialect at this early stage in her career is evident here, as well as in the speech of the poor whites in "For a Place in The Sun" and the speech of the moneyed class in "So Many Worlds." The protagonist is a white girl child named Barbie, who is dressed for the Mardi Gras as a "little southern lady" (in the words of a passing drunken Yankee) and is carried about for most of the day on the shoulder of her "faithful servant" John. John, whose own little boy is left behind, is called into service because Dilsey, Barbie's black nurse, refuses to take her. Dilsey, with wide white apron and knife strapped to an inner thigh, is going out to look for her husband who has left her, and she means to kill him. Barbie, in her role of naive protagonist, is carted about all day, while the drama of the chase takes place just outside of her immediate consciousness. But Barbie is not entirely innocent. Indeed, it is in this ambiguity that the power of the story resides, for no costume or role can hide the thrill the child experiences when she feels the knife on Dilsey's thigh and understands its purpose or the fear she experiences over that which she is too young to analyze. Barbie wakes into a shadow land in which the shadows are never dispelled, and her day is peopled by antic figures acting out grotesque patterns replicating nightmares. Nor is there hope of spring awakening consequent to the penitential fasting. At the end of the story, still being carried on John's shoulder, Barbie drowses while the cold wind blows the tears on her cheeks.

As a college senior, Grau published two more stories in 1950 in *Carnival*, in the October and December issues. Another four-thousand word story, "The Lonely One," focuses on a black family, particularly on Cissy, who believes her lover Brett is not coming back to her. Brett, the very model of a machismo figure of legend who drinks more, fights better and loves stronger, does however come back, and of course kills Cissy's new friend Sam. Based more in simple irony of circumstance than in the power of image, "The Lonely One" is the least successful of Grau's early stories, though her evocative skill is still evident in such descriptive passages as the first paragraph, where she speaks of the "hemlock shoulder of the ridge," or in the descriptions of the dancing couples or the trumpet player "wailing great mistakes."

"The Things You Keep" is also based in irony of circumstance. May's lover comes home to their small apartment to tell her he is leaving her. At the end of this very short piece, May stands before a mirror watching herself cry. Not as simple as this summary indicates, the story is carried forward on two levels—the overt level of linear plot resulting in the man's leaving and a covert level composed of patterns indicating that trouble spots should have notified her long before he did. Both levels come together in the final paragraph.

The last story published by Grau in *Carnival* appeared in the October 1951 issue at a time when she had entered graduate school and was working on a master's thesis. She never finished the master's thesis but during this period she began to write the stories that would appear in *The Black Prince*.

"The Fragile Age" is like nothing she had done before. It is a comic piece, a carefully controlled satire on literary study and the vagaries of the university. Mrs. Perse has disappeared into the library for four days before her husband realizes her absence and takes his problem to the dean. The ineffectiveness of the dean, the creeping and laborious working of Perse's aged mind, and the tottering Mrs. Perse, whose excitement at locating a source which can result in the birthing of a lifetime dream, generate sufficient energy to delineate and define the objects of satire and lead to the story's humorous climax. In the vaults of the library, at the far end of one of the corridors, Stravos and Michaels, two graduate assistants, find Dr. Perse illuminated by a lamp and glowing with inner light. His wife is absent, but her manuscript is there on a desk. She has, Perse exclaims, located the source of *Beowulf!* Her pursuit has not been in vain. Concurrent with Perse's announcement, Stravos and Michaels find in the center of the polished seat of the library chair a "little pile of grey dust." Evidently, like the one-horse shay, Mrs. Perse goes off all of a piece—"all at once and nothing first," her excitement acting like an orgasm sufficient to shatter her into particles of dust but not great enough to scatter the particles and disperse them into the air. In locating the source of *Beowulf* she finds her own source, too, in the little pile of grey dust. The title, "The Fragile Age," seems perhaps too restricted in its application if it is taken to apply only to the actually aged, but if as metaphor it is attached to the whole academic community whose pursuits are dry as dust, the story takes on considerably more meaning. The metaphor, of course, can be carried further, but Grau makes little attempt to do so, seeming content in this story lightly to skim surfaces.

The Black Prince, published by Knopf in 1955, contains nine stories, three of which were published earlier: "Joshua" in *The New Yorker;* "White Girl, Fine Girl," in *New World Writing* and "The Black Prince," in *The New Mexico Quarterly.* Several differences are apparent among the stories published in *Carnival* and the stories published in *The Black Prince:* the later stories are considerably longer; more fully developed plots follow either the traditional or the epiphanic line; more characters are involved and they are developed in more complex ways. Despite the additional complexities made possible by the additional length, however, basic devices remain the same. The writing style remains poetic and evocative; images still cluster into patterns, subsurfaces function in analogical modes.

In the move to longer stories, Grau's effort was toward a more careful and precise rendering of the experiential, while at the same time holding to that rich suggestiveness made possible by symbolic structures. The distinction to be made is not exactly between the romantic and the real-istic or the intuitive and the empirical. That would be too easy. Rather, it is more between the direct and the subtle. What Grau was aiming for was a realistic rendering of a total experience, but only if "total experience" is taken to mean a meshing of the affective and the cognitive. Grau makes the point herself in her comment on "The Black Prince" prepared for an anthology of literature:

> Fiction, as I see it, is basically and always realistic. What else can it be? I know nothing beyond my experience and the experiences of people like me. If my expression becomes too personal, my symbols too intimate, my readers no

longer understand. The demands of communication force me—partially at least—into the common mold of thought. I find myself dancing around the edges of meaning, trying to cut off a bit of the truth here, a bit there, trying to express, to shake the limitations of experience, above all to communicate my vision of the world. And, like most writers, I sometimes lose patience and abandon the reasonable realistic paths for the simple direct truths of myth-making.[1]

In this comment made thirteen years after the publication of *The Black Prince,* Grau was not suggesting that "The Black Prince" is easier to understand than stories which do not partake of the quality of legend. She uses both the words "direct" and "oblique" to describe her method and she is talking about means of communicating.

I should like to extend her points by suggesting that the "college" stories in their brevity and concentration on essence, are marked by a common analogical mode. Indeed, most of the stories in *The Black Prince* collection are closer to the dream mode than to the realistic. Five of the stories portray black characters in situations common to folk ballads. The other pieces of the collection, with the exception of "Fever Flower," are initiation stories, told in the first person by a white adolescent (two female and one male). But even these in one way or another partake of the stuff of legend. There is a pattern whereby Grau moves increasingly toward the more realistic, but we need to remember that the stories in *The Black Prince* are also early stories. And though movement can be seen away from the college stories, similarities persist.

In "White Girl, Fine Girl," the opening story in *The Black Prince,* the voice of a storyteller is clearly evident; the tone is conversational, the overt purpose descriptive, the style imagistic, subtly rendering areas of thematic concern. Just released from prison, Jayson Paul Evans tests his manhood and his will. When he leaves the road to enter a field, he moves at a jogging trot, taking long steps and swinging his arms, testing his "flight." It is difficult to avoid identifying Jayson with jay birds. The first clue appears when Jayson talks to a "dusty black crow" that is scratching on the "bare red earth." Aggressive and boastful, Jayson wants to drive away other "birds," throws stones and has stones thrown at him, sings a song without either rhyme or meter, steals food, "borrows" a skiff from two boys by the force of his size and determination.

Jayson is determined to seek out Aggie, the woman for whom he went to prison, and to assume the authoritative role not only in her and her daughters' lives but also in the reestablishment of his former business. But Jayson has reckoned without Aggie, who will have nothing to do with him, and he has not counted on his daughter acting out a stereotypical female role. His acceptance of the "Jax Poster" girl who is "white or nearly white" as a substitute for Aggie satisfies for the moment his need to prove himself and to assert the dominance of his position. Trusty lieutenants await his wishes; the girl of his dreams is his. His triumphant entry into town is completed, his masculinity restored. How long it will last is a question providing ironic overtones for the end of the story. Similarly, the title of the story sets the irony at the beginning, and image patterns throughout the story reinforce the irony, identifying town and prison, Jayson freed and Jayson trapped, Jayson as potent force and Jayson as impotent, the rebellion of the women and their submissiveness, white girl, fine girl and the Jax beer poster.

Many similarities exist between Jayson Paul Evans and Stanley Albert Thompson, the black prince of the title story who "comes walking out of the morning fog." Both men are associated with jays (as is Jay Mastern, who impregnated Maggie Mary Evans); both exude virility; both use songs in their association with women, though Jayson's songs are harsh and sometimes scolding and Stanley Albert Thompson's song is soft and melodious; both have superior muscle prowess and "win" their fights. There are, however, essential differences. Stanley Albert Thompson is a real figure of myth, a supernatural power, a force so seductive he can attract all women and enrage all men, a dispenser of death and of everlasting life, a successful wooer of the woman he chooses—Alberta. The seduction scene where Stanley Albert Thompson woos Alberta is one of the most memorable in all of Grau's writing—chiaroscuro joins with rhythms of sound and meter arranged in circular patterns to lead to the night flight of the betrothed couple. Alberta is a fitting mate for Stanley Albert Thompson, a woman made to his specifications to fit the role of princess of the night. Filled with devil lore (the flight through the air, the silver bullet, the alchemy, the play on the name—S.A.T.A.N.), the story has the dimensions of legend, being at once powerful and lyrical in its effect.

"Miss Yellow Eyes" presents a variation on the theme of the perfect couple. Where Stanley Albert Thompson and Alberta are purely black, Chris and Lena have had their color so mixed with white that their skin is light enough for them to pass over the color line, and this is their ambition. They will go to Oregon where it is easy to pass, and they will be white. They are a handsome couple—Lena, all gold colored with light brown hair and ivory skin and eyes flecked with yellow, and Chris, with pale blue eyes and a suntanned face and brown gently waving hair. The narrator of the story is Lena's younger sister Celia, who calls Chris the handsomest man she has ever seen and says she is more than half in love with him herself. For Celia, Chris becomes a model of conduct and stature whose actions are honest and straightforward and noble. Called into the Army during war time, Chris believes he has an obligation to go. Pete, brother to Celia and Lena, has a different opinion. He is angry and frustrated over the segregated life he is forced to lead, over the fact that the country drafts black men as well as white men but allows black men few other equalities.

Three other characters, two actually present in the story and one not, complete the cast of persons: the old grisgris woman whom Lena goes to in time of despair (after she goes to a priest); Lena's mother, a cook in "one of the big houses on St. Charles Avenue"; and the absent father, whose presence is marked by a photograph. The missing husband and father becomes a symbol for all the men unable to function in a society that takes away their manhood. The war kills Chris. Pete, whose effort to cut off his finger to save himself from the draft results in his cutting off his hand instead, is left maimed and too angry and bitter to function. Only the women are left—the mother, still working as a "fancy" cook; Lena, broken and empty in spite of her prayers to supernatural forces; and Celia, her good sense and moderate responses replaced by the hysterical outbursts of the closing scene.

With Chris dead, Pete believes himself justified, and he taunts mother and sister:

> "But me, I'm breathing. And he ain't. . . . Chris was fine and he ain't breathing. . . ."
>
> "Chris boy . . . you want to cross over . . . and you sure enough cross over . . . why, man, you sure cross over . . . but good, you cross over."

Unable to take anymore of Pete's taunting, Lena attacks him, and accidentally hits him on the stub of his arm. Missing his footing, he falls, screaming softly to himself: "Jesus, Jesus, Jesus, Jesus."

Pete's call on Jesus, together with a motif of "crossing over," strongly suggests the image of Moses leading his people across the waters and, as in the spiritual, a cry to the Pharaoh: "Let my people go." Moses, a prototype of Christ, is successful; but Chris (a modern Christ?) is unsuccessful in leading his people to freedom.

"The Way of a Man" and "Joshua" complete the roster of stories about black people. The former, a heavily ironic story of the initiation of a young man into a world of crime and debt, contrasts with the latter, another initiation story, but one whose protagonist finds through his initiation some positive values.

In "The Girl with the Flaxen Hair," Grau uses a first person narrator, the young girl Lily, who tells the story from an adult perspective. The point of view is particularly useful both in the presentation of the voice of the protagonist and in the perspective provided, for time, memory, and voice are major themes. Lily, a "tomboy" type, has a mother enamored of a misty Southern past and a down-to-earth dentist father who tries to keep "reality" in the forefront of his life and that of his wife and daughter. The Ramond family that moves nearby is a reverse image of the first family. There is a father who apparently cannot cope with reality, a mother attempting to live a lie, and a daughter Rose, a "sheltered" type, who accepts the lie. It is in the interaction of the two families and the conflict that arises that the tension of the story lies. Images also participate in the counterpoint—the wounded limbs, for example, Lily's cut hand ripped open by a splinter that she virtually ignores and her mother does not even notice, and Rose's wasp stings that create chaos and confusion and that are still wrapped long after the ache is gone; Lily's father's slow moving hand wounded by the bite of a child who was having his teeth examined and Mr. Ramond's hands moving so fast over a piano keyboard that they become a blur; Lily's black hair and sun-tanned skin and active life and Rose's yellow hair and fair skin and languid movements; the mother's real possessions which she values less than Mrs. Ramond's imagined ones; Rose's dream vision of a fairy tale marriage to a phantom groom and the coffin in the baggage car she lies in for her ride back to Jefferson City; and most important of all, the real father whom Lily forgets and so makes disappear and Mr. Ramond who actually disappears.

"The Bright Day," also told in the first person, is the slightest story in the collection. Charlotte, a young woman recently married, finds herself caught in a moral dilemma that threatens to break up her marriage. Unable to stand firm against the family, she gives in, and although she halfway realizes that timber and brick and cement do not create a home, she will not let herself come to complete realization. When she feels faint because of her subconscious recognition of the truth, she blocks that recognition and attributes her condition to the heat of the day.

If "The Bright Day" is the slightest story in the collection, "Fever Flower" is the best. On first perusal the opening paragraph seems innocent of symbolic overtones, but, as the story continues, patterns emerge, and one can be shocked to discover (so easy is the reading) that the images presented in this paragraph will later coalesce to form the major metaphor of the story, extending it beyond local significance to microcosmic proportions. A single word "Cadillacs" in the first paragraph carries over to the second, where locale magically becomes particularized as the modern South and limited even further to the affluent members of that land together with their servants. Before long, however, locale is identified with artificial growth, forced feeding, tropical gardens and attitudes that create tropical gardens, hot houses where children can only writhe and burn. The fever flower of the title refers both to the hot house orchids, blooms forced to grow outsized and defying normal time patterns, beautiful, exotic, and soon used up, and to Maureen, small daughter of Katherine and Hugh Fleming, who will be formed beyond her years and so distorted, her normal growth perverted by the environment in which she lives.

Identification of Katherine and Maureen is skillfully made by means of the orange juice both mother and daughter drink and spill and by Katherine's vision of the proper kind of room appropriate for a child of three—not a nursery, but a young girl's room with vanity table and mirror and perfume atomizers and ruffled organdy. Another device Grau uses to establish identification is the montage, a kind of voice-over projection into the future, typically presented as inset or parenthetical passages. In these we learn what will happen when mother and daughter, both used up, both not quite human, settle into lives of narcissistic display.

The sexual base of the forced growth is suggested throughout the story but comes to climax at the story's end, which identifies Annie's vision of torment and destruction prior to the apocalypse with the child's burning up with fever. Annie is the child's Irish nurse who desires the child for her own and hates both mother and father for their interference and for their lusts. A Bible reading woman, she prefers the New Testament to the Old. But her preference for the Epistles marks her fixation on lusts of the flesh, and though she thinks she cannot understand the Apocalypse, she creates her own vision of torment: "Joy. The lusts of the flesh. The chaff which shall be cast in the fire. Hell Fire. Which was like summer sun, but stronger seven times."

Annie's vision for Maureen resides in a Gaelic song: "A love to have . . . And strong arms to carry you away." Perhaps Annie does not realize that the man she summons for Maureen is called too soon, though the little lady appears in her feverish sleep already to have received him. Her hair is damp and sticks to her skin; her cheeks are flushed; her color is high. Shadows give her face the illusion of age. At the end her crying has stopped and she lies there "beautiful and burning."

"One Summer" is an initiation story told in the first person by an adolescent boy who finds that the death of his grandfather miraculously propels him into the role of a man. With his new status come realizations frightening in their implications as the boy experiences his first presentiment of death. Like the other stories, the surface of this one is gloss, so smooth and effortless to read that the rendering of the texture of the experience seems its only purpose. But beneath the surface, underpinnings of image patterns made clear by means of repetition and juxtaposition point to meaning worth reaching for.

At its publication *The Black Prince* received rave reviews from all of the right critics and places. But though the critics wrote in superlatives, the superlatives were based in initial impressions, and no one went further in an effort to analyze the stories to see just where their merits lay. Indeed, the major impression that the critics seem to have taken away with them was that the stories were written by a young Southern woman and that she would carry on the tradition of Southern writers, especially women, and take her place among other Southern regionalist writers of the time. Novels followed the publication of *The Black Prince,* all published by Knopf: *The Hard Blue Sky* (1958), *The House on Coliseum Street* (1961), the Pulitzer Prize winning *The Keepers of the House* (1964), *The Condor Passes* (1971)—each succeeding one better than the last, though it was becoming more and more difficult for reviewers to make their assumptions about Grau's work jibe with the work she was producing. And all the while she continued to write short stories, publishing them regularly both in the popular magazines and in the literary journals. A number of these were collected in the volume, *The Wind Shifting West* (1973).

Stories in *The Wind Shifting West* demonstrate many of Grau's mature interests, as well as her continuing and remarkable narrative skill in the genre of the short story and her ability to handle forms and points of view extraordinary in their range and gradation. A fiction that can loosely be classified as a "ghost story" ("Three") or one in the "science fiction" mode ("The Last Gas Station") takes its place in the same collection with pieces of topical interest ("The Other Way," "Eight O'Clock One Morning"), with stories that circle back to Grau's earlier interests typified in *The Black Prince* ("Pillow of Stone"), to those that adumbrate novels to come ("The Patriarch," anticipating *Evidence of Love*, 1977, and "Stanley," *The Condor Passes*), and with stories, including several of the above, that demonstrate a continuing effort to hide the technical and formal underpinnings in a dazzling and seemingly effortless surface display. The volume also exhibits virtuosity in perspectives employed. Whereas point of view in *The Black Prince* was basically limited to children or primitives, viewpoint in *The Wind Shifting West* extends to include people of all ages, both sexes, and different social classes in a variety of settings.

"The Wind Shifting West," the title story, is set not on a Southern coast but on one in the Northeast; point of view is third person focused through the protagonist, Caroline, a woman approaching middle-age; and nothing more spectacular happens than a first infidelity. Caroline and Robert Edwards, with their nine-year-old son Guppy, have for ten years been joining the rest of the Edwards family in their summer houses on the coast. Routines are so well established that people and actions fit into their places as easily and neatly as Mrs. Edwards, the matriarch of the family, fits words into her Double Crostics. Though it is very early in the season, Robert is enthusiastically preparing to sail across the sound in a visit he makes annually. Caroline stays home to tend the geraniums and then visits the home of her mother-in-law where other members of the family have gathered, including Giles van Fliet. Half English and half Dutch, with his continental ways and speech patterns, Giles seems even more out of place in the Edwards family than does Caroline. Both are physically different; both ostensibly accept the Edwards pattern of living but, consciously in Giles' case and subconsciously in Caroline's, secretly despise it; both are inlaws, unrelated to each other.

Caroline's dissatisfactions seem trivial—displayed as they are in an array of small incidents which begin as soon as the story does. In ten years of marriage she has not learned the right terms for the accouterments of a boat; in ten years she has not succeeded in diminishing the use of her son's nickname or in influencing her son to her own point of view; in ten years she has never really fitted into the family or its interests; and in a year and a half she has not kissed her husband goodbye because Robert does not want to embarrass their son. Caroline's preoccupation with her age is another indication of her frame of mind. The "little twinge" in her back is also a "twinge in her soul"; she responds with annoyance to her nephew's pleasure in her physical appearance, to her mother-in-law's blunt comments, to Giles' cool presence.

A ship to shore call begins the intensification of the conflict. A mast has been ripped from Robert's new boat, and he and Guppy are stranded at their friend's place. The ship to shore conversation between Caroline and Robert acts as an objective correlative for their growing estrangement. Robert is annoyed because she does not know the procedures necessary for communication. He and Caroline talk at the same time and at cross purposes with neither hearing the other. When Giles takes the phone, he begins a pattern of action to which Caroline acquiesces as the story continues. Giles' obvious admiration for his mother, whose fidelity to her husband he comments on, is in stark contrast to his own behavior. When Caroline realizes that he keeps bathing suits in a variety of sizes on his boat for the women they will accommodate, she questions him about his marriage. His response makes it clear that his own infidelities are kept separate from his marriage and in his own mind have no bearing on it.

Giles, who handles his power launch with the same skill he apparently handles women, is set in counterpoint to Robert, the "sailor who has just lost his mast." Ironically, Caroline uses Robert's symbolic "unmanning" as part of her rationalization for her behavior and eventually her acquiescence. In the end, however, it is she who is diminished, as she half realizes. The anchor with some weed attached and still wet from the staying of the boat is the only mark (besides the salt dried on their skin) of their action. Already a cynic, Giles comments: "There isn't ever much left when it's done." Perhaps Caroline will come to know finally that she has made nothing better; she has simply exchanged partners in a power struggle. The wind having blown from the south, now blows from the west, but the south wind will come again as it always does and, with it, more fog.

Grau writes with such compassion for characters and understanding of their situations that it often comes as a surprise that the world she creates is usually negative in its aspects—the characters being enshrouded in fog a whole lot more than they bathe in sunlight. "The Beach Party," another story set on the Northeast coast, makes the point effectively. Frieda, the youngest member of the beach party, feels out of place, not only because of her age but because she does not "know the symbols." She finds herself frustrated and annoyed, feeling "just the way she had when as a child, she found a floating bottle and a message too blurred to read." At the ocean, she is afraid. She knows that her fear has to do with the dark color and with the sound and the motion of the surf. The "unknown opaque distances of the ocean" frighten her. By the end of the story, Frieda has learned to read the symbols. A boy has drowned, but it seems no more horrible than everything else—than live lobsters steamed to death, than the evidence of dead creatures in the sea wrack all around, than the press of a male body, than the releasing of sperm and the process of ovulation that is simply a part of the movement of life toward death. But knowing the truth does not make it easier to accept. She makes her way back home grateful for the radio, "safe inside its tinny shell." In the end, the beach party in all of its aspects is a symbolic representation—a prelude for death. "The Land and the Water," another story in the collection, makes essentially the same point. Water, symbol for life, is also symbol for death. In the story, as the sky darkens overhead, the water becomes a lead-colored gray.

The two stories from which novels emerged—"The Patriarch" and "Stanley"—are among the most fascinating in the collection. *The Condor Passes*, into which "Stanley" grew, was published in 1971 and so actually preceded the publication of *The Wind Shifting West*. In the short story Grau goes back to a favorite image—the green house, an artificial environment, created to house and nourish plants not ordinarily grown in the real environment and birds not ordinarily kept in captivity. The green house provides an environment helpful to the old man in that it aids in his breathing and provides a springboard for his memory of South America where he made his fortune. There is now nothing left of the South America he knew except the old man's memory of it, for he has outlived all of his contemporaries.

The old man is clearly presented in bird images. Stanley's responsibility to rid the bird cage of dead birds every morning is tied to the old man's need to be sheltered from a recognition of his coming extinction. When the old man identifies the hawk that flies low over the green house as a condor, he foreshadows his own death, for with his death, the condor passes. There is nothing left of him but memory and that only in the minds of the people who actually knew him. When they are gone he will be extinct—as we all will be.

"The Patriarch" seems a mature reflection on and restatement of "The Black Prince" of the earlier collection. Edward Milton Henley, aged eighty-eight, is another and much more fascinating "black" prince, who could indeed be a real son of the morning, for if "truth lies beyond fulfillment of desire, in satiated appetite, then the conventional wisdom of western morality" is, indeed, the "sobbing end of shabby gentility," and paradise lost was actually gained.

Evidence for the identification of Edward Milton Henley as the patriarch is abundant. He is the "father," a mirror image of his own father, whom he sometimes thinks looked at him as through the "wrong end of a telescope." Named after John Milton, he grows up at a time when life is a preparation for paradise and death entry thereto. His father's house is gothic and its talisman is a rainbow lantern. Virtually ignored by his parents, the high point of his young life is the time he nearly dies; but he enjoys the experience—the sensation of floating in the air or swimming in water. Even in health, one of his recurring dreams is of being dead. During his illness he talks constantly—"in tongues," his mother thinks. In his desire for darkness, the covenant for him becomes not everlasting light and life but its underside—the dark side, in other terms, the irrational and hedonistic as opposed to the rational and ascetic.

As an adult Henley eschews dualities, the base of western philosophy, preferring to think of life as a stage parade where one role is exchanged for another by a simple change in costume; and what he ironically describes as perhaps "a senile astigmatism" is more a statement of his metaphysics. Along with dualities, Henley rejects "twos" in his later life, saying he is haunted "by that absurd number." Indeed, he rejects "twos" even in denying the life-sustaining role of women, creating as he does a situation as near as he can get to fathering a son without a woman. The various women in his life, including his four wives, are simply conveniences, there for his physical pleasure or objects of his mental titillation, the subjects of taunts. Nor is he bound by a need for women, a fact he proves in the four years he spends with Guido.

At the end of the story, shifting abruptly from first person to third (a feat hardly ever tried in a short story), Grau focuses on Anthony, already an old man, who is watching his father talking to his grandchildren in the grape arbor. The scene seems dramatic, unreal, reminding Anthony of an illustration of a patriarch or prophet in a book of Bible stories. And when his father raises his hand in a greeting to him: "It was, the Reverend Henley thought with a shudder, altogether like a blessing."

Given the tantalizing and complex nature of the subject matter of "The Patriarch," it is easy to see why Grau extended it to *Evidence of Love.* Indeed, in extending it, she put "the flesh on the bones and the skin on the skull."

Grau is now putting together a collection of short stories consisting of newly written pieces. At my request, she sent me "Summer Shore" and "Letting Go." It seems hardly fair to readers to comment on pieces not yet published, but the temptation is great, especially since the collection will be ready for publication, the author says, sometime this year.

"Summer Shore" seems, at first reading, a simple narrative about a couple comfortable with themselves and each other, married thirty-two years, and content in and with their family rituals. The story takes place, however, not at the beginning of a season but at its end. Image patterns of wintery blasts, approaching age, sudden death, imminent changes, and threatening transitions overpower signals of calm and sun, false in their implications. The people, regardless of how compassionately treated and understood, prove at close look to be insular, opinionated, parochial in their views, cliquish, provincial, bored—a backside presentation, what Katy sees when she looks at the aging summer crowd all facing toward the sea. Katy sees but will not allow herself to understand. She hides inside her house, her wooden shell, protected by her role as wife of the "ranking male member of a tribe" and by her family surrounding her. "How can it end," the poet Donald Davie asks, "This siege of a shore that no misgiv-

ings have steeled, / No doubts defend?" Grau uses these lines for epigraph. In Christian terms, one thinks of the apocalypse and of destruction
before the raising of the new Jerusalem. Is this why Katy thinks suddenly:
"Next year in Jerusalem"?

Lines from Emily Dickinson begin "Letting Go" as well as provide its
title: "As freezing persons recollect the snow—/first chill, then stupor,
then the letting go." In the story Mary Margaret needs to run to keep
from letting go into the "comfortable silences" provided by her parents
and their home. Although she believes she hates the pattern of the parents' lives; still, in growing up and in marrying, she patterned her own life
in basically similar ways. She has accepted the idea that regular habits and
moral behavior ward off troubling thoughts. She has conformed to expectations. At twenty-three she was secretary to a senior vice-president and
on her way to being executive assistant. At twenty-four she married, and
though her parents disapproved of the match, still she did not basically
change the pattern of her life. She worked and carefully tended the
apartment and regularly, every Wednesday, visited her parents to attend
with them the Perpetual Novena, even after her husband Edward refused
to go with her. When she and Edward decide to divorce, she wonders
whether she already has had all her parents have—apparently comfortable lives. They are so used to each other that they never quarrel; indeed
they have never showed emotion to her, not even when she was growing
up. But they do care for her; they are simply inarticulate people who
behave as they have to. Mary Margaret's acceptance of a job in Oklahoma
City is an effort to escape, to put the old patterns behind, to seek for
something else, but the temptation to stay behind is so great that she
needs to invent a fearful beast to guard the doors of her parents' house to
keep her from reentry. She does not know that crowded highways,
exhaust-filled air, and the bustle of city life form their own patterns that in
time can also, like the Perpetual Novena, provide protection—at least up
to a point.

As a short story writer, Grau's talent is immense though not revealed
by a simple surface reading; for what is beneath the surfaces and interact-
ing with them is what is characteristic of the short story genre, and Grau
has mastered the genre. Southern female writer she is, by accident of
birth and genes. Southern regionalist writer, she is not. Nor are her skills

confined to revealing and commenting on "the genuinely native particulars of a scene" in time, as Frederick J. Hoffman would have it.[2] Rather, like that of other important writers, her work transcends particulars, excellent as she is at rendering them.

NOTES

[1] See Mary Rohrberger, Samuel H. Woods, Jr., and Bernard F. Dukore, *An Introduction to Literature* (New York: Random House, 1968), 320–21.
[2] See *The Art of Southern Fiction* (Carbondale: Southern Illinois Univ. Press, 1967), 28.

Photo: Jane F. Melnick

Lisa Alther

Born in Tennessee (1944), Alther received her B.A. from Wellesley College. She has published two novels, the first, Kin-flicks, in 1976. Her articles and reviews have appeared in a number of newspapers and magazines, including the New York Times Book Review.

Lisa Alther:
The Irony of Return?

MARY ANNE FERGUSON

Lisa Alther's first two novels, *Kinflicks* (Knopf, 1976) and *Original Sins* (Knopf, 1981), follow a long-established and fruitful theme among Southern writers: home viewed from the perspective of a native who has left and returns. In both novels upper Tennessee is the Southern locale, knowledgeably depicted by Alther, born in Tennessee in 1944.

In *Kinflicks* Ginny Babcock Bliss returns from Vermont to Tennessee to be with her mother who is dying. Alther gives equal time in the novel to third-person narrative focusing on the present and first-person recapitulation of Ginny's past. Significantly, in the seven chapters dealing with the present, Alther often uses the mother as central consciousness. In fact, it is through her growing understanding of her mother that Ginny perceives as false the assumptions which had led to her leaving home in order to find herself. *Kinflicks* is a *bildungsroman* with the ironic twist that finding comes not through seeking but as a gift, after the search but not as a result of it. Through her homecoming at twenty-seven, Ginny may have grown up enough to return to Vermont to her husband and child; the Southern home of her childhood has vanished with her mother, but her newfound self-knowledge may enable her to establish a meaningful home of her own.

Original Sins ends less hopefully. When the five characters whose lives the reader has followed from childhood to about age thirty return home, it is for the funeral of one of them. The other four—three of whom have like Ginny Babcock left home for the North—seem likely to live on in the bitterness their knowledge of the world has brought them. As children they had committed the unpardonable sin of believing that they were special—invulnerable and immortal. More the sin of Milton's Satan than that of Adam and Eve, this exalted sense of their own destiny has meant

103

that their loss of innocence could result only in a sharp descent into reality. But through its cyclic structure, the novel implies that the new generation starts from a different point: the children of the original Five are very much aware of their parents' multiple sins and of themselves in relation to their parents. Without grandiose visions of ruling the world, the new generation will be content if they can somehow go beyond their parents. Through such original sin and the many other venial and mortal ones they have committed, the parents have come close to that other unpardonable sin—despair. Alther goes beyond their despair to at least the implication of hope, but her affirmation is tentative at best.

In both novels, Alther evokes a tradition beyond Southern regionalism. The cyclic structure—the departure and return home—is essentially that of the comic epic; like Odysseus, the protagonists venture out into the world in order to acquire the knowledge of reality that will, by opposing the inchoate sense of self, lead to self-consciousness. In both Western and specifically American tradition, this form has been focused primarily on the voyage out, on the world away from home. Alther instead focuses on home: the Southern world of past and present is created with great density. The two novels are of epic proportions, tracing the history of both the land and its inhabitors back to their origins. But Alther uses the Southern setting as a base for comparison with the outside world. The South, once a wilderness whose Indian inhabitants yielded it to the rifle and plow of pioneers, is now an industrial area controlled by absentee landlords—an epitome of the entire United States and, indeed, of all the capitalistic West. The destiny of Alther's characters is an exemplum of the fate of the post-modern world.

In *Kinflicks* Alther has found a technique that to a large degree controls her ambitious content. In seven chapters, she creates a first-person narrator with a keen eye for the ironies of life and even the irony of her own attitudes. This voice is almost compulsively witty about existential matters. "My family has always been into death," the narrator announces in the first sentence, and in the first chapter, entitled "The Art of Dying Well," she satirizes her parents' life through ridiculing their obsession with epitaphs, cemeteries, obituaries. In this same chapter she whets the reader's interest in her life with references to her sex life and overt promises of "more later." This technique prepares the reader for the six chapters of juicy sexual adventures which follow in the style of the picaresque novel. Ginny's self-irony as she experiments with all the forms of sex open to the young during the 1960s offers many avenues for reader identification. Ironically, these confessional chapters constitute the "skin-flicks" or soft porn on which the title puns; the home-movies the title refers to were taken by her mother. Collectively these chapters constitute not merely sexual adventures but Ginny's self-conscious efforts at education of mind as well as body. A long chapter on her college life, for example, focuses on philosophy and her anguished decision to opt for Nietzsche's and Schopenhauer's view of the world. Her experience with a group of lesbians in a commune corroborates these views as the women fight among themselves. One dies as the result of an "accident" probably caused by the local preservers of heterosexual mores, and their cabin burns to the ground as the result of a real accident—a short-circuit in a phallic vibrator. Ginny survives these and other experiences, but with little joy. Because of her sense of the meaninglessness of her own life and that of her very traditional husband, she is ambivalent about motherhood and her baby daughter.

At the time Ginny is summoned home to Tennessee, she has been caught in what looks like adultery by her husband and has been banished. Homecoming to her is like that of Frost's hired man: she has no other option. But only she realizes this truth; she has come in response to a note from a friend of her mother's who suggests casually that her mother needs her company. In alternating chapters titled with dates in the present, Alther uses third-person narration to let us see into the minds of both mother and daughter, a device symbolizing both Ginny's sense of role reversal and her growing knowledge of her mother. The reader learns more about Ginny's past in these chapters but goes beyond it to her mother's past and that of more remote ancestors. Until this homecoming Ginny has responded to such knowledge of her roots as ties of bondage. She has escaped from the world of Hullsport, Tennessee, in the hope that she would not replicate the experience of her mother and of her mother's mother who had played to the hilt the traditional role of mother/wife who gave all to husband and family. But now, she realized, "she was on her own"; the imminent death of her mother will cut the ties she had so resented.

Alther's title *Kinflicks* suggests a potential limited perspective for the book; using only the mother's home movies would have resulted in a neater novel. Alther's decision to use alternating voices is a clue to the book's central meaning: unlike her father, born "B.B. (Before the Bomb)" Ginny and her generation are obsessed with the urgency of finding some meaning in life. Alther communicates the desperation of this search through the massive detail with which she portrays the breadth and depth of Ginny's pursuit of self-knowledge. She lavishly portrays Ginny's search first at home, then in the North, at "Worthley," in Cambridge, and Vermont, through all the confusion and causes of the sixties: the anti-war movement, women's liberation, communalism, environmentalism. Ginny's lesbian lover dies a terrible death, to no purpose; the women's idealistic efforts to help "the people" are wasted. Ginny sees the futility of every avenue open to her. Not satisfied when she makes a conventional marriage and has a baby, she turns to ritual coition as access to mystical meaning. The absurdity of the limits Ginny goes to is matched by her ironic view of herself; her wit is her only recourse for distancing herself from her experience. Like the alienated male heroes in the "dark comedies" of the sixties, she can only mock herself.

Her long absence from home gives her the distance she needs to take herself more seriously. Her mother's need of her help to achieve some dignity in dying causes Ginny to add her mother's insights to her own views; this double vision gives her the strength to help her mother and to arrive at self-knowledge. Mrs. Babcock has tried to fill the empty nest after her husband's death by studying, to make up for having dropped out of college when her husband had to go off to war. Now at the point of death, she is two-thirds through reading the last volume of the family's encyclopedia. As Ginny reads with her, they both explore every possible avenue to finding meaning. Mrs. Babcock feels that her life of nurturing has been meaningless now that there is no one who needs her. Ginny tries to impress her own need for nurturing on her mother while at the same time doing all she can to nurture her mother. Mrs. Babcock refuses to pass on to Ginny the formula she has inherited from her mother and grandmother; she refuses to give Ginny any advice about how to live her life. This refusal and her sense of being totally alone take Ginny to the point of suicide, but, saved by her own ineptitude, she finally perceives that her mother's refusal was a gift to her, the gift of freedom from role-playing and from guilt. Ginny can accept the gift because she has come to see as heroic her mother's fight against death and her final willingness to die. She perceives that her mother has had a measure of autonomy even in her life of role-playing because she had always been aware of the role-playing. Only through understanding the extent to which both mother and daughter have exhausted other avenues for meaning can the reader accept this very meager promise of hope for Ginny.

The meagerness of the hope is underlined by the picture of the South we get through both Ginny's and her mother's eyes. There are no plantations and magnolias in their past; they have both long since lost touch with their coal-miner and dirt-farmer ancestors. Mrs. Babcock can remember attending her paternal grandfather's funeral when she was ten and feeling joy in the exuberance of her relatives, but she has kept this legacy entirely from Ginny, continuing her parents' quest for "improvement." The emptiness of the improvement they achieve is symbolized by Ginny's grandfather whose synthetics factory has been changed into a munitions factory by Ginny's father. In revenge for this perversion of "progress," Mr. Zed has planted all over the town the kudzu vine which threatens to consume the land which it had been intended to conserve. All the institutions of the town—its schools, churches, courting rituals—have left Ginny not only with a sense of failure to find meaning but with an anger she can contain only with her wit.

The ironic voice with which Ginny condemns her entire experience is maintained throughout *Kinflicks;* Alther's verbal wit is pervasive and sets the tone. Ginny's metaphors bring into the world of everyday life images of the violence and cheap materialism she has found in all of her relationships. Her father's fear of death is brought to life by the image of the ice pick he kept at the table in case he needed to perform an emergency tracheotomy; he has a "Cassandra complex," she tells us. His traumatic experience of being dragged behind a truck by his wedding band is dismissed as his "personal conversion" corresponding to the conversion of the synthetics plant to ammunition during the Korean War. Mrs. Babcock too has this ironic voice: she compares herself to a junky when a blood sample is taken from her earlobe, her body to that of "the Itezumi men . . . tattooed all over." It is only when she identifies with her mother as a person capable of such self-irony that Ginny can go beyond the words both of them use as defense against despair. Seeing her mother's refusal to speak as she approaches death, Ginny at last speaks seriously about herself and life: "she understood . . . [that] her mother . . . was weaning herself from her senses, trying to prepare for a dimension in which space-time limitation didn't exist"(505). Perceiving herself as now being detached—weaned—from everything she has known, Ginny first resolves to imitate her mother by dying; but finally she concludes that she is condemned to survival, being only a small component of "some infinitely larger organism" that will not allow her to die. The existence of such an organism is only a possibility, however; with a few mementoes of her past, Ginny leaves, "to go where she had no idea."

Ginny's return home has not brought happiness to her or to her homeland, as Odysseus's did for himself and Penelope; but like Tennyson's Ulysses, Ginny is setting out again. Alther has gone beyond the stereotype of woman as the one who stays home and upholds traditions to give us an anti-hero whose experiences are as alienating as those of modern male heroes but who, because of the mother-daughter bond, does not quite succumb to them. *Kinflicks* ends on a serious note; Alther does not mock the faint hope of a new start.

Though there is occasional verbal wit in *Original Sins,* Alther has abjured the witty narrator for the seriousness of the omniscient author who sees into the minds of most of her characters. Critics who found wit the main attraction of *Kinflicks* have seen *Original Sins* as only a serious version of the same story. Perhaps Alther's change of voice was influenced by the tendency of reviewers of *Kinflicks* to dwell on the "soft porn" of its sexual revelations and their almost universal failure to differentiate the irony of Alther's perspective from that of such writers as Vonnegut and Heller. In Alther's fiction alienated heroes leave home, their survival bolstered by their anger at being cheated by the corrupt world of home; like Thomas Wolfe's George Webber, they find home limited, not themselves. Alther is uncompromising in her depiction of modern society as hostile to human growth; but she views her characters' "original sins" as the cause of the system's failure. In her world the sins of the fathers are passed on; the children do not learn from their parents' experience—that is, from their parents' failures and faults, their sins. But Alther shows the parents as equally caught in the chain. In *Kinflicks* the ironic stance of mother and daughter separates them from the system and leads to a faint optimism that Ginny as an individual may profit from her mother's experience. In *Original Sins* Alther's omniscient view is appropriate to a more democratic, a more universal view. The "Five" in the novel represent the experience and attitudes of the generation now in its thirties. As the "after the Bomb" generation whose concern is human survival, they epitomize late twentieth-century America. Significantly, it is not "original sin," not innate wickedness and perversity, for which each individual is accountable, but rather "original sins," the collective experience present since the beginning.

In taking the risk of high seriousness, Alther has not merely re-written the "same story" as *Kinflicks,* minus the wit; *Original Sins* is not a brown-tone version of *Kinflicks* but a post-modern novel in the guise of an old-fashioned chronicle. It is post-modern in its refusal even to imply a unitary world view. Abandoning the myth that the modern South—or, for that matter, modern America—has a shared myth, Alther unflinchingly spells out infinitely varied perceptions of the same "facts"; she creates a world new to each perceiver, none of whom becomes able to rise above a limited view. But Alther also traces several generations of interconnected families. Though the linear sequence is obscured by Alther's interweaving of characters' thoughts, it is present, implying change and perhaps even growth. This structure is ironic because for every character change is not growth; the cyclic return at the end offers little hope that a new cycle will be different for a new generation.

In *Original Sins* the Five children learn early that their parents are ignorant. They perceive as willful the parents' inability to help them, especially with respect to sexual "knowledge." Alther as omniscient author lets us see that parents and children alike suffer from their inability to "know," from the necessity of learning through vaguely perceived social mores, of having to see through a glass darkly. Alther's god-like perspective exposes a fallen world in which human mortality is the donnée. The novel is an ironic epic; the irony is in its structure and episodes, not in its narrative voice. In *Original Sins* questers have no idea what they seek. Whether they stay home or leave and return, what they find is mortality in a world devoid of a saving grace. The only virtue left is endurance, the will to survive with meaninglessness, with little hope. This is not the world of heroes, happy or tragic; it is a world where the best of intentions causes harm. The only hope in such a world is the irony at its core: the worst may have at least good side effects.

The novel is divided into five parts, though not one part per each of the Five main characters. Parts One and Five, both entitled "The Castle

Tree," portray five children looking down on their world. Part Two traces the original Five from birth to high school graduation, a rite which sends three of them out from their home town to the North. Parts Three and Four follow the Five into adulthood, focusing on each separately. For the four who survive, home is bleak, whether they have stayed or left and returned.

In Part One the original Five view the geography of "Newland" from a totally self-referenced perspective, full of "signs" of their own importance and connection to past and future greatness; their narcissistic grandiosity is quite realistic. In Part Five, five children of the original Five are far more sophisticated than their parents as children. Seeing the town "spread out below them like a toy village," they openly tell their parents "Yall look like toy soldiers (591)," demystifying the power which the parents too have sadly learned to mistrust. These two parts are not merely a frame for the novel; they are an allegory of Alther's play with the myth of the Fall. She allows the concept of "original sin" to assume the multiple layers of meaning it has historically had by depicting many examples of the characters' self-destructive, life-denying actions and beliefs. In spelling out their sins, Alther is using the post-modernist refusal to depend upon allusion; ironically, however, the more familiar a reader is with the Bible and Milton, the more meaningful are the "sinful" episodes. In this respect Alther is very Southern, drawing on the Bible Belt common culture while apparently disavowing it. In focusing on sex as sinful, she ironically comments on a culture unable to identify other "sins": throughout one cannot be sure what "original" refers to.

In the twelve chapters of Part Two (22–226), Alther takes every advantage of the omniscient perspective in tracing the Five through adolescence. This section is technically remarkable: Alther skillfully interweaves the perceptions and experiences of parents and grandparents, of more distant ancestors' perception of the "new land" and its native inhabitants, with those of the Five protagonists to create a world as complex as that mirrored in Achilles' shield in *The Iliad.* This is epic, a depiction of a land and its people in which the characters are types. Unlike that of classic epics, however, this world has no common ethos; in this society characters cannot become autonomous but appear as stereotypes, shaped but not self-shaping. Identified by such external characteristics as race, sex, economic class, church affiliation, their parents' goals for them, they have an inner life pervaded by shallow bewilderment. One must keep remembering their callow youthfulness; they share its limited perspective with parents, teachers, preachers. The omniscient voice mercilessly exposes every subterfuge, every self-deception, every failure, as well as every institutional excuse for individual failure. Alther's miracle is to go beyond the automatons produced in such a world; she manages to make readers care for parents and children by giving readers an avenue to identification. This is a world we all recognize.

Alther's most potent device for reader identification in this section is her insistence on the multiple ways parents and children share in destroying the parent-child bond. Sally, the pretty sister obsessed with her beauty, and Emily Prince, the athletic "brain," are unlike each other and totally unlike either parent. Jed and Raymond Tatro—the jock and the misfit intellectual—mutually despise each other. Donny Tatro, son of a black veteran who committed suicide and never knew his son, hates his mother for having gone to New York and left him. Donny's mother Kathryn and her mother Ruby have worked as servants for the Princes; Ruby typifies the older generation from her perspective as Mammy to the Prince children and surrogate mother for Donny: "She just didn't understand what this world was coming to. Emily and Sally's parents weren't the people their parents were, and she didn't know what to make of these two girls"(27). Only after Kathryn returns for Donny when he graduates does Ruby have doubts about her faith in manners and her advice to conform and to succeed by manipulation. Ruby has preferred letting Donny believe his mother has deserted him to telling him that she had been forced to leave after resisting a white man's attempt to rape her. Kathryn angrily rejects Ruby's theory of parenthood, which justifies postponing teaching children the truth until "they find out for themselves." She insists, "Mama, you got to tell them from the day they're born"(101).

Ruby rationalizes withholding the truth out of a very realistic fear of its consequences for Donny; other parents' failure to communicate stems from their own personality flaws. Both Mr. and Mrs. Prince suffer from his "live-in Hamlet"(82) qualities. As a hybrid Yankee-Southerner, son of the reigning mill-owner, Mr. Prince had never felt at home in Newland; he and his wife cannot break out of the class they were born into but live according to a bleak determinism masked by Episcopalian self-congratulation. Emily has yearned for "some adult guidance, if only so that she could reject it"(56), but her mother "hadn't been able to figure out any . . . skills to pass on . . . since she didn't understand what kind of a world she was supposed to be preparing them for"(84). Realizing that "Emily had been Emily right from the womb. And Sally, Sally"(129), Mrs. Prince sees her daughters as "two aspects" of herself, neither of which she likes. Emily realizes the futility of getting adult help most vividly when she encounters a pensioner in the County Home: "Above the smiling mouth, in his eyes, Emily read misery, loneliness, lovelessness, bit-terness, resignation, fear, humiliation—and contempt for young people who understood nothing"(128). Nor can Sally find guidance; taught only that sex is sin, she cannot turn to her mother for help as she goes farther and farther in the sexual game in order to keep the attentions of Jed. Caught in the Oedipal triangle, she cannot bear to hurt her father by confiding her fears that she is pregnant at sixteen. When he finds out he reacts only with grim anger at her seducer and disappointment with her.

The Tatros are guilty of a parental flaw which has a realistic impact on many readers: they play favorites with their children, projecting all their failed hopes not on Raymond—ironically, "junior"—but on Jed. Mrs. Tatro rejects Raymond as the "boy [who] had never been anything but difficult, ever since his first month home from the hospital when he drove his daddy out of the house with his screaming"(116). But she sees Jed as "Her baby. Big and strong, but so gentle and affectionate. . . . He'd take up where his daddy gave out. . . ."(117). The Tatros continue their belief in progress, satisfied that their rise to the middle class from their back-woods origins as coal miners will be the pattern for their children.

Every social institution in Newland reenforces the Tatro's parental pat-tern. The good-looking athlete and the beauty queen—Jed and Sally—are universally approved. As long as he is fulfilling his grandmother's ideal of being an athlete and church usher, Donny is accepted as a good black. Even the intellectual Emily can win approval as long as she dates a fraternity man and intends to go to the state college; but Raymond is beyond social acceptance and remains the misfit his mother predicted. School and factory reward each of the Five according to the degree of community approval: Donny is the first black to get a job—as a sweeper; Jed is on the management ladder, and Raymond is rejected both by his radical friends in New York and by his father, who orders him out of the house. His efforts to unionize the mill ironically aid its new Northern managers in keeping the status quo.

Alther's most scathing comment is for religious sanctions of the status quo. In a chapter bitterly entitled "Hollowed Be Thy Name," the Baptist preacher recommends that Negroes be happy to suffer like Jesus and that they use the strategy of Queen Esther in cajoling their oppressors. The Methodist minister preaches to the Tatros and other lower middle class whites about duty, which he defines as debt to ancestors, parents, spouses, bosses, town, state, nation, and God—and enjoins them to expect reward only from God. The Episcopal minister tells the elite what they want to hear: there need be no "dichotomy between the spiritual and the material" and the Lord approves the paternalistic effort of industrial owners. Although none of the members of these congregations fully accepts the pronouncements of the preachers—Mrs. Tatro wants her reward now, from the town and her bosses—they do accept their doctrine as "right."

Alther's analysis of "booklearning" and of the capitalist economy—both Southern paternalism and the new franker Northern exploitation—is as ruthless as her exposé of religion. Without any hint of ideology, the picture she paints is Marxist analysis spelled out. The overwhelming impression as the details pile up is that the system is rotten and not susceptible to reform. At the end of Part Two, Sally and Jed are trapped in marriage because of their sexual transgressions; Donny and Rochelle, both once eager for education and escape, are similarly trapped. Raymond has realized that his New York friends are merely using him and that they are more concerned with their dogma than with Southern workers, but his own purer motivation is ineffectual. Emily, the high school valedictorian, has decided to go to college in the North. She knows doing so will alienate her parents and friends, though she doesn't know why she makes the decision. High school graduation has ended a stage but there is no sense that it is a new beginning.

But the characters are all alive: the wages of their sins, collective and individual, pervasive and apparently ineluctable, is not yet death. They are still young. In Parts Three and Four Alther follows them into their thirties. Though each chapter focuses on a single character, they and their old and new associates continue to interact. Gradually they all come to realize that where they are and with whom is irrelevant to their quest for meaning; the bleakness that has been shown so thoroughly for the world of Newland is inescapable. Here Alther's use of irony of situation gives credibility to each character's fate. The more Sally tries to be the perfect suburban wife, the more she drives Jed away. Jed's fight with Raymond over unionization has already been made futile by the way Mr. Prince's paternalism has played into the hands of the Northern capitalists. When Raymond seeks to live the life of his backwoods ancestors, he cannot convince even his young hillbilly cousin that there is value in the old way of life, and he compromises for the sake of comfort. Both Raymond and Emily come to realize the limitations of the ideology of their "rational" radical friends in New York and of old-fashioned Southern anecdotal wisdom, but neither can find a way to transcend them. The sexual problems of all the Five leave them little experience with joy; the three men are disgusted by female sexuality, Sally and Emily see male sexuality as an impersonal drive to dominate and possess. Emily's recourse to lesbian love seems only a rather grim alternative, although she begins to lose her own need to dominate.

A reader tires of the grim realities of these two sections. Why does Alther so relentlessly pursue her characters? I suggest that she does so in order to bring into consciousness the underlying question of the nuclear age: is survival of a few enough? The book implies no. In doing so, it suggests that only drastic, fundamental change can make survival attractive. The circular structure of the book indicates at least a faint possibility that such change is possible, but the particulars minimize hope. Living back in Tatro Cove, Raymond comes to the realization of many an alienated hero: he sees himself as "a quare turn," like some of his ancestors who had never fit into "the ordinary world of getting and spending" (491). This insight makes Raymond feel

> as though he'd been handed the template to his personality. All along everyone had thought he was a weirdo. In Newland people avoided him because of his rayon shirts and reindeer sweater vests. In New York, where everyone had prefaced remarks with "My therapist says. . . ," there was some agreed-upon state known as Normality toward which everyone worked, as though on cars with engine knock. They "managed" their relationships as though dealing with a herd of cows. . . . But actually he was a quare turn. He never fit in because it wasn't his nature to fit in! It was his nature to see what others couldn't, to blaze a trail for them into the post-industrial wilderness. . . .

But his failure to influence his cousin and to convince the community it

must fight the strip-miners who are tearing up the environment leave him
without romantic illusions. Alther does leave Raymond humanity, however: at Jed's funeral he is overcome by genuine love and grief for the
brother he had so opposed. Irony prevails.

In both *Kinflicks* and *Original Sins* a non-militant, quiet feminism
offers a less ironic suggestion of hope. In coming to love and understand
her mother through role reversal, Ginny may be able to play the role of
mother with her own daughter. Unlike all of the female characters in
Original Sins, none of whom is reconciled with her mother, Ginny experiences joy in motherhood. Mrs. Prince finds peace in doing her own
gardening; Kathryn has a sense of value through her career as a nurse.
Emily's friends have a sense of community in caring for one of their
friends who has been brutally and casually raped, and it is strongly implied that in loving women Emily may transcend the sexual mores. Alther
makes no ideological claims (she's no Yankee!), but it is clear that these
female options, open to other women, may furnish a basis for beginning a
new community. Obviously, the tradition-ridden South would be more
antagonistic to such a hope than the North; just as Alther herself has
moved away from the South to live, Emily will not be able to stay at
home.

Alther resists suggesting art as a resource or avenue of escape from
existential dilemmas. She refuses to give us a portrait of the writer as
exempt from society's claims and refuses to claim omnipotence along with
omniscience. Her totally dispassionate voice in *Original Sins* is necessary
to the structure of the novel; yet the failure to go beyond her characters'
limitations, though admirably democratic, is frustrating. The author's omniscience has left the reader no handle for entering the text, for helping to
construct it. This is not a book one wants to re-read. Perhaps in the future
work one hopes Alther will produce, she will find a new voice that will go
beyond irony.

Ellen Douglas

*Born in Mississippi (1921), Douglas attended Randolph-Macon
Woman's College in Virginia before graduating from the University of Mississippi. Her first novel,* A Family's Affairs, *1962,
was awarded the Houghton Mifflin Fellowship. She has since
published a collection of short works and four novels.*

Ellen Douglas:
Moralist and Realist

CAROL S. MANNING

Ellen Douglas is the pen name of Josephine Haxton, who grew up in Natchez and has long lived in Greenville, Mississippi. Since 1962, she has published five novels and a collection of short stories. Only in her most recent book, the highly praised *A Lifetime Burning* (1982), are the author's Southern roots not immediately felt. All the rest are set specifically in Mississippi, in places Douglas calls Homochitto, Chickasaw Ridge, and Philippi. The first two of these she locates in the hill country of southern Mississippi, somewhat north of Natchez; the latter she places, like Greenville, in the Delta. Like many Southern writers before her, Douglas writes about family ties and family tensions, about racial relations and racial guilt, about an individual's attempts to come to terms with his or her past. But she writes about much else as well. Her recurring theme, in various guises, is responsibility: the responsibility one owes or feels to some individual or group, the responsibility or burden one has to discover and tell the truth about the past.

Surprising for a work by an unknown writer, Douglas's first book, the long novel *A Family's Affairs* (1962), was reviewed by many major publications—and, justifiably, reviewed favorably. Douglas was awarded the 1961 Houghton Mifflin-Esquire Fellowship award for the manuscript. The novel follows the Anderson family of Homochitto from the courtship of Charlotte Anderson and Ralph McGovern in 1917 to the death of the matriarch of the clan, Kate, at age eighty-five, in 1948. As Frank H. Lyell observed in his review of the novel for *The New York Times Book Review* (8 July 1962), *A Family's Affairs* "concentrates on family situations" and "projects the sights, sounds and rhythms of true Mississippi life," and thus "offer[s] a mild but refreshing antidote to the run-of-the-mill Deep South Novel."

Throughout the thirty years which the novel covers, Kate remains the center of the family, and the old family home at Homochitto remains the novel's central stage. It is a stage populated most prominently by women: Kate, her three daughters Charlotte, "Sis," and Sarah D., and Charlotte and Ralph's daughter Anna. When they get together, the women talk endlessly about the family's affairs, and Anna listens, fascinated. The animated, sometimes tension-laden dialogue of the characters is one of the delights of the novel:

> Charlotte grabbed the question with both hands and everybody sat straighter. "We're anxious to meet Mr. Wheelwright, Sis," she said. "Mama and Sarah D. have been telling us what a rush he's giving you."
> Anna felt Sis's body stiffen and draw into itself, as if she would become smaller.
> "He's very pleasant," she said in the blank, courteous voice one uses with a stranger. "Someone to pass the time with."
> "Humph," Kate said.
> Sis jumped up like a shot, as if it were a signal she had been waiting for. "All right, Mama," she said. "All right, all of you. Charlotte brought him up and all of you are sitting around as solemn as if you were waiting for a baby to be born. You want me to say it, so I will. I'm in love with him. I can't think of anything else. I loved him the instant I laid eyes on him. . . . I'm going to have him if it's the last thing I ever do. Now. Put that in your pipes and smoke it."
> Ralph got up. "I think I'll take the children out to Mother's," he said. (119–20)

While Kate and her daughters all have distinct personalities—Kate is vivacious and deliberately outrageous, Sis is secretive and tense—they have this in common: they are all conventional women, Kate having "prepared her daughters for nothing but marriage, which she considered the only serious business in life"(6). Nonetheless, they are strong, capable women able to cope with whatever life hands them. Although the Andersons are considered Homochitto aristocracy, none of the women is a stereotypical frivolous Southern belle or dependent Southern lady. Widowed when her children were young, Kate had had to sell the family plantation in Louisiana and move her family into her mother's home in Homochitto. There, to make ends meet, she had, without embarrassment, begun to take in boarders. Although only "prepared for marriage," Kate's daughters all get jobs after completing high school (there is no money for college or finishing school), and Sarah D. and Sis continue working most of their lives, their incomes being essential to maintenance of the family household. The Anderson women of the next generation also work, whether as single women supporting themselves or as married women putting their husbands through school.

But, significantly, the women's jobs are never identified and apparently are seldom if ever discussed at home. Sis and Sarah D. work because they have to, not because they prefer to. They are holding down jobs, not pursuing careers. The important part of life for them takes place at home, not during the long, hard hours spent at work. Yet, ironically, they turn out to be more reliable providers for the family than do their male counterparts. Only Ralph McGovern, whom Charlotte had chosen to fall in love with precisely because she knew him to be a practical, responsible, competent, intelligent man, proves a reliable provider for his own family, and a generous contributor to Kate's household as well. In contrast, Sarah D's husband Charlie is a dreamer who goes from one career to another, always pursuing the elusive golden business opportunity; Sis's husband Alderan Wheelwright, who shortly deserts Sis for another woman, gets fired from his job because he has stolen from the company; and the checks that Will, Kate's only son, sends home from New Orleans usually bounce. Indeed, Will's wife Eunice is the financial backbone and the stabilizer in their relationship, just as Sarah D. is in her marriage. Eunice is described as "a steady worker and a hardheaded businesswoman" who "always had a good job and was ready to throw her resources into the breach" when Will gambled or drank his income away. Moreover, Eunice herself "had bought their home, and she made sure that Will did not throw it away or get his hands on the back log of savings which she had laid by for *real* emergencies"(377).

This contrast between the men and the women as providers is one reflection of what seems the novel's major theme: the individual's responsibilities to the family. While Charlie, Will, and Alderan pursue their individual impulses and dreams, the women think about the needs of the group and support one another through one crisis after another. Always, they view a crisis confronting an individual Anderson as the whole family's affair. This motif is introduced humorously in the novel's first chapter: when Ralph seems overly cautious in advancing his courtship of Charlotte, Kate conspires with her daughters to give a party intended to kindle Ralph's slow-burning flame. In subsequent chapters, the women support one another through more serious problems. When Kate fails to dissuade Sis from making what the family judges to be—and what turns out to be—

a bad marriage, the family rallies around Sis during her suffering and divorce. When Sarah D.'s husband Charlie suffers a disabling heart attack and has to come home to roost, Sis and Charlotte conspire to help Sarah D. and her daughter Charlotte over the hurdle created by Charlie's now constant presence at home. They persuade Anna, the older Charlotte's now grown daughter, to get a job near Homochitto and join Sarah D.'s household so that she can help the family financially (she will pay room and board) and so that as a respected companion to her younger cousin she can perhaps blunt Charlie's sudden inclination to play the over-protective father. And, in the last two chapters of the novel, as Kate and the old family home grow old and decrepit together, Kate's daughters not only share the financial, physical, and mental burden of caring for both home and mother but also conspire to keep Kate feeling useful, realizing that Kate "desperately needed to feel . . . that she was indispensable to her daughters' household" (312). Even Eunice, though now separated from Will, comes to Homochitto to help care for Kate after the old woman breaks her hip. While Will also usually comes home whenever his mother is ill, during all but the last of his brief visits he doesn't assume any responsibility for her care but instead plays the gay, charming guest.

This is not to suggest that the women come off looking like angels and the men like devils. As already suggested, Charlotte's husband Ralph is a paragon of responsibility. Moreover, in their concern for one another's affairs—their sense of responsibility to one another—the women sometimes offend. Kate assumes her major duty to her daughters is to see that they marry well and happily, but some of her efforts in that direction understandably strike the daughters as interference. At age seventeen, Anna has the same reaction to her parents' concern about her male friends. Furthermore, Will contributes something special to the family, not in spite of his irresponsibility but, in part, because of it: he charms and entertains them, or Kate and the children at least. To Anna he is a mysterious, wonderful legendary figure, "gay, charming, and irresponsible, a drunkard who had made a successful career for himself by sheer wit and brilliance, a free agent who lived his life as he pleased, who had dared when he was no older than she to cut himself loose, to think what he chose, and live as he pleased"(252).

Yet while acknowledging both the danger of overstepping one's responsibility and the charm to be found in the free agent, *A Family's Affairs* clearly implies that one does have obligations to others and should attempt to fulfill them. Unlike much American fiction, present and past, the novel does not romanticize individualism. In fact, Charlie and Will attain a degree of nobility through their belated efforts to assume traditional responsibilities. Some time after his heart attack, and after he has quit feeling sorry for himself, Charlie begins, at last, to put his family first. Following his death, his daughter Charlotte comments that during the last year of his life, her father, knowing he was going to die, thought only about making "Mama and Billy and me" secure. He failed—"everything's an awful mess, worse than if he hadn't tried"—but at least he tried. On the other hand, Anna, who was with Charlie near the end and heard him ask that his children not be disturbed, insisting he would be okay, knows in her heart that Charlie did finally succeed. She thinks, *"He used on dying all the courage and intelligence and self-denial that he could never find to use in his life. This one time, he was a success"*(342).

Just as Charlie makes an effort to assume his responsibilities near the end of his life, so does Will make such an effort near the end of his mother's life. After his aged mother has crushed her hip, Will comes home, troubled because his wife has left him, and hence perhaps more sensitive to the trouble of others. He tries to do too much too fast—he plans major remodeling of the family home to make it more comfortable for an invalid. His sisters and the doctor think his plans impractical. The sisters quarrel with him, yet they recognize and appreciate that now, at last, Will is turning to the family, both because he feels a duty to his mother and sisters—and guilt over his previous neglect of them—and because he finally realizes that he needs them as well:

> What the sisters [had] resented so bitterly in him, after all, was not his failure to help them, not even the suffering he had caused Kate, not those in themselves, but what they signified—that he *would* go it alone, that he did not need his family, or would not admit that he needed them, that he would not store up credit in the family fund against his own future.

The sister's moral code, learned from their mother, is a "strict sense of individual responsibility for the common good":

> They had never been willing to cut themselves off from one another, to act in the arrogance of their individuality, not even Sis, who in her deepest trouble had come home, had crawled into the den like a wounded beast, unable to conceive of doing anything else. . . . They had stubbornly loved and supported one another whether they understood one another or not. . . .(414–415)

Now, Will has come home, and as he, like Sis before him, "heave[s] and turn[s] like a dumb, suffering animal," the sisters "besti[r] themselves stiffly to make room for him"(416).

But Anna McGovern, who has served as the reader's eyes and ears through much of the novel, and has struggled over the years with her feelings for the family, deserves the last word on the family and hence on the novel's theme. At her grandmother's funeral, she thinks, *"Whatever you say about them, . . . however far you may go away, your reasons for going would never include the one that they were ignoble. . . . And what could they have given me—what could anyone give a child—more precious than the habit of moral consciousness, the conviction that one . . . must look after his own, must undertake, must dare . . ."*(438).

Three of the four pieces in Douglas's second book, *Black Cloud, White Cloud* (1963), are linked to *A Family's Affairs* through the reappearance of Anna McGovern (or Anna Glover, her married name) from the earlier work. However, though Anna's character remains consistent, these new pieces do not extend or depend on the story of *A Family's Affairs*, nor are they themselves interrelated. But the two short stories and two novellas of this collection are linked thematically. Whereas Douglas's first book portrays the relationships between members of a family and concerns the individual's responsibility to the family, her second book portrays relationships between members of two races and concerns the responsibility that conscientious Southern whites feel for the South's racial past and, in at least one story, the sense of responsibility that ignores racial lines.

In these stories there are no villains and no racial violence. As in *A Family's Affairs*, most of the scenes are domestic. The relationship portrayed is that between a well-intentioned white woman or white family and a black woman or man who is, or has been, the woman's or family's employee. Friendships between these characters are never wholly comfortable, being clouded by the unerasable effects of the Southern past and by the white characters' sense of guilt over that past. The four stories, three of which will be discussed here, offer sometimes stunning insight into the lingering, subtle effects of a history of racial discrimination in the South. Few works of fiction before *Black Cloud, White Cloud* have suggested how complicated the South's past has made personal relations between the races.

"Jesse" is two stories in one. One consists of bits and pieces of Jesse's life, revealed through his conversations with the narrator of the short story. From it emerges a disturbing picture of day-to-day life for a poor black Mississippian. When Jesse was ten and his mother died, he was left to care for himself and his two-year-old sister, his "step" having taken off after the mother's death, and his uncle's second wife being unwilling to add more children to the large brood she had married into. By having Jesse narrate this incident in his own convincing language in conversation with the white narrator (who internal evidence suggests is Anna McGovern Glover), Douglas effectively subdues social relevance to characterization:

> "I had a baby sister," he said. "Died in my arms. So little I didn't know the difference."
> I wasn't sure what he meant, although at first I thought he was saying that she was so small, so frail, he couldn't tell when the life went out of her. And I assumed that he was talking about some time recently, that his sister had been an old woman when she died.
> "What?" I said. . . .
> "I was ten years old at the time," he said. "And she was two. I was so little I didn't know she was dead."(107)

Jesse's conversations about his life are framed by a second story, the major one. It is about the first-person narrator's relationship to Jesse as that relationship is influenced by her sense of guilt over the South's history of discrimination against Jesse's race. Unconsciously, she feels responsible for Jesse's poverty and past suffering because he is black and she is white, and she tries to make amends. Thus, having hired Jesse to give her son guitar lessons, she doesn't have the heart to fire him when he turns out to be an undependable teacher and an unaccomplished player. When Jesse gives a "concert" for her family—a very bad concert—the narrator and her husband praise him enthusiastically. But if Jesse's blackness makes these well-intentioned whites uncomfortable and conditions their response to him, so does their whiteness condition Jesse's response to the narrator's husband, whom he had not met until his "concert." After performing badly on this occasion, Jesse, humiliated, shuffles his feet, bows his head, and apologizes to the white man, lapsing into a pro-nounced darkie dialect he had not used with the narrator: "I try it for you again one day soon, Bossman," he went on. "I work up a coupla pieces good"(102). As the narrator observes, "Richard had said nothing that could be interpreted as expecting or requiring [such servility]. Jesse just saw a white man and went into his act—like a firehorse at the clang of the alarm"(103).

After the narrator finally lets Jesse go—telling him that her son doesn't seem ready yet for guitar lessons after all—she has a nightmare about him. Awakening, she scribbles down two sentences that are rolling through her mind. These sentences reflect the theme of the story (and also of "Hold On," a novella in *Black Cloud, White Cloud*): "There are those of us who are willing to say, 'I am guilty,' but who is to absolve us? And do we expect by our confession miraculously to relieve the suffering of the innocent?"(115).

In "Hold On," a shorter version of which was chosen for the 1961 O. Henry collection, Anna Glover takes her two young sons and a friend of theirs on an all-day fishing trip. The story concerns Anna's perception of her relationship with Estella, a large black woman who had once worked as Anna's maid. Anna is proud of this relationship, feeling that it is one based on equality of standing and mutual respect. She has, she thinks, overcome "the universal guilt" which generally makes black-white friendships in the South uncomfortable if not impossible. This day at the lake, when she and the boys happen upon Estella, who is fishing from the pier, Anna impulsively invites Estella to join them in their boat. During their enjoyable day of fishing together, Anna is only once, she thinks, made conscious of the differences in the two women's skins and cultures: when she discovers that Estella believes in superstitions. However, Anna will eventually come to recognize as naive her image of her friendship with Estella.

As they are on the way back to shore, a storm comes up, the boat capsizes, and Estella, who cannot swim, nearly drowns both of them.

At first after the boating accident, Anna sees herself as a heroine—or tries to see herself as one. After all, she had saved Estella's life. But soon she realizes that this view of herself is a defense against admitting to herself what she fears: that she had almost caused Estella to drown. Had she, feeling Southern whites' "universal guilt" for the wrongs of the past, invited Estella along on the fishing trip *because* Estella was black? Was she trying to buy Estella's friendship and compensate for prior wrongs to blacks? An experienced boater, Anna had known that the boat should not be made to carry one more person, especially someone of Estella's weight. Moreover, she normally required all passengers to wear life jackets, yet though they had no extra jacket to offer Estella, Anna had issued the invitation anyway. Why had she ignored her better judgment in this case? Anna also has to reassess her actions in the rescue itself. She is haunted by the memory that when Estella was on the point of drowning them both, Anna had finally freed herself from Estella's weight by violently kicking Estella away, thus attempting to save her own life even if it meant sacrificing Estella's. Her eventual saving of Estella had been mainly luck, she concludes, for she had been too tired to dive for Estella again. Had Estella, unconscious and no longer fighting, not bobbed up right next to her, the black woman would have drowned.

Douglas's account of Anna and Estella's struggle in the water is an intense, frightening scene of a near-drowning. But like the title *Black Cloud, White Cloud*, it is also symbolically suggestive.

> They went down. This time they stayed under so long, deep in the softly yielding black water, that Anna thought she would not make it up. . . . She scissors-kicked again and again with all her strength, not trying to pull loose from Estella's clinging, but now more passive weight, and they came up . . . they went down again. Estella's arms rested heavily, trustingly it seemed, on her shoulders. She did not try to hug Anna or strangle her, but simply kept holding on and pushing her down.(193–94)

The black and white bodies fused together in the water, yet not operating as one, suggest the historical proximity of the races in the South and the difficulty of relations between them. In the water, Estella depends on Anna for her life, clings to her, yet Anna herself is indirectly responsible for Estella's near-drowning. Thus, Estella is a burden Anna feels she must save. The past is a weight on the Southern white's self-image, as it is on the world's image of the Southern white. The black man (woman) is a moral burden the white man (woman) must bear.

"I Just Love Carrie Lee" differs from the other stories in *Black Cloud, White Cloud* in that it is comic (ironic) and in that the major character seems a shallow bigot rather than a sympathetic character who grows in awareness of the complexity of racial relations. Narrating the story, this woman features herself as a broad-minded Southern white woman, her evidence being that she "just loves Carrie Lee," who has been her family's maid for almost fifty years. Yet she continually displays a patronizing attitude toward Carrie Lee and demonstrates that she actually considers Negroes an inferior race: "Carrie Lee is a bright Negro—both ways, I

mean, and both for the same reason, I reckon. I don't know exactly where
the white blood came from . . ."(121). As Saul Maloff said in his review of
Black Cloud, White Cloud in *The New York Times Book Review* (6 October 1963), "The method works splendidly, as the narrator, a vain, foolish,
trivial woman for whom 'love' means total ownership, is given all of the
rope she needs to hang herself."

The relationship between the narrator and Carrie Lee is not so easy to
scorn, however, as at first appears. Deceptively simple, the story offers
insights into subtleties in the relationship between a mistress and her
long-time maid. The theme of the story, as of the other stories in this
collection and of *A Family's Affairs,* is responsibility, or one's sense of
responsibility. The narrator opens the story by claiming that she feels
responsible for Carrie Lee. For the eight years that she lived away from
Homochitto, in Atlanta, she had continued to pay Carrie Lee a weekly
wage, although Carrie Lee had remained in Homochitto: "I knew Mama
would have wanted me to [Carrie is a hand-me-down from her mother],
and besides, I feel the same responsibility toward her that Mama did. You
understand that, don't you? She was our responsibility. So few people
think that way nowadays. Nobody has the feeling for Negroes they used to
have"(119). Self-serving though this remark is, it nonetheless has some
truth to it. The narrator does care for Carrie Lee and feel some responsibility for her; but, even more strongly, Carrie Lee cares for the narrator
and feels a sense of responsibility toward *her.* The narrator may be a vain,
foolish, trivial woman, even a racial bigot, yet Carrie Lee must see some
good in her. At the time she tells the story, the narrator is a middle-aged
(or older) widow whose children are busy leading their own lives, and
Carrie Lee works for the narrator's son Billy. Were it not for Carrie Lee's
Sunday afternoon visits with her, the narrator would be lonely indeed.
But on Sundays, Carrie Lee often bakes the narrator a cake and comes to
spend the afternoon with her. The two women, who have known each
other since Carrie Lee raised the narrator, sit all afternoon drinking coffee
and talking about "the old days when Mama and Bill were alive and when
the children were little. We talk about the days of the flood, about this
year's crop, about the rains in April, and in August the dry weather, about
Billy's wife, and Sarah and Billy's grown-up troubles, about the grandchildren, and 'all the days we've seen' "(140). The narrator's comment that
she would "rather visit with [Carrie Lee] than with most white folks"(141)

is obviously patronizing, but it is also true. The two women have more to
share with one another than do many friends of the same race.

That is not to say that the picture the story creates of the white woman
and her relation to Carrie Lee is, after all, largely sympathetic. The
double standard in their friendship, as well as the narrator's blindness to
that double standard, is apparent. Whereas Carrie Lee, through long
years of service to the white woman, has come to know the latter's family
as well as she knows her own, even identifying with that family (she has
pictures of all her white children on her mantel, along with pictures of her
black stepchildren), the reverse is not true. The narrator seldom even
thinks to ask Carrie about her family. For example, Carrie had taken in
and had been caring for her "crazy" stepdaughter for two years before the
narrator indirectly learned of this addition to Carrie's household. On the
other hand, when the narrator's own daughter separated from her husband and came home half crazy from despair, Carrie was there to help
out.

But while we can condemn many of the narrator's actions and attitudes,
the story nonetheless suggests that racial relations are not simple cases of
good and bad. Carrie Lee is not an ignorant woman with dog-like devo-
tion to her mistress; she is an intelligent woman who, one suspects, fully
understands the narrator yet cares for her anyway. She is an ordinary
woman caring for someone with whom she has shared much, and the
narrator, despite her prejudice, is the same. But one might well wonder
how Carrie Lee has managed to put up with the narrator's blindness and
condescensions all these years. For answer, one need only turn to Carrie
herself. On different occasions, Carrie Lee has given the narrator's children Billy and Sarah advice which might stand as the philosophy Carrie
Lee herself has lived by in her association with this white woman. When
little Billy had come home crying because the other boys in the neighborhood, all bigger than he, wouldn't let him play with them unless he ate a
mixture of coffee grounds and blackberry jam, Carrie Lee "took him on
her lap like a baby and rocked him and loved him until he quit crying,"
and then she gave him this advice:

"Honey, they bigger than you. If you wants to play, you gits on out there and
eats they pudding. If you don't like it, you holds it in your mouth and spits it
out when they ain't looking."
"But s'pose they feed me more than I can hold in my mouth?" he said.
"Honey, if they does, you got to make your mouth stretch," she said.(122–23)

When Sarah came home torn between hating her husband because he had betrayed her and loving him and wanting to return to him, Carrie Lee advised her this way: "No man never driv me crazy, nor nobody else. I tell you how I keep him from it. . . . See everything, see nothing. . . . Hear everything, hear nothing. Know everything, know nothing. Trust in the Lord and love little children. That's how to ease your heart"(139). Carrie Lee has surely had many occasions over the years to use her own advice.

She acts on the advice, in fact, on those Sunday afternoons when white folks call on the narrator while Carrie herself is there visiting, sitting in the parlor with the narrator. Evidently realizing the larger culture's attitude toward socializing between the races, Carrie Lee "goes to the door and lets them in as if she were working that day, and then she goes back to the kitchen and fixes coffee and finds an apron and serves us. Everything goes smoothly. She knows how to make things comfortable for everybody"(126). Carrie Lee cares for the narrator, feels an obligation to her, or she would not be there on her one day off. Her caring, her sense of obligation, and her insight into the situation are well revealed when she gets up and plays the black maid's role so as not to embarrass her white friend.

After beginning her career with two impressive books in two years, Douglas followed five years later with *Where the Dreams Cross* (1968), and then in the 1970s with *Apostles of Light* (1973) and *The Rock Cried Out* (1979). Whereas *A Family's Affairs* and *Black Cloud, White Cloud* excel at depicting ordinary people and daily life, their themes being fully embodied in characterization, the three subsequent novels are handicapped by a transparent manipulation of narrative design and characters for thematic purposes. In these Douglas attacks conventionality, Southern bigotry, greed, modern impersonalism, and materialism.

Where the Dreams Cross is populated by, among others, frivolous narrow-minded Southern ladies; an evil, greedy, conniving county politico who preys on an innocent, helpless old man; and the scantily dressed, beer-drinking, curvaceous heroine, whose behavior scandalizes Philippi, Mississippi, but who proves to be more responsible and caring than the local self-righteous snobs. *Apostles of Light* is a better novel, its major merit being its sensitive characterization of old people. Douglas shows them to be just like anyone else—they love, hope, enjoy, fear—

only now, their bodies and minds sometimes betray them, and those betrayals frustrate them. Aunt Martha's thoughts and feelings about being old and growing older are touching and convincing. Douglas had shown this same exceptional familiarity with the elderly in her portrayal of Kate Anderson in the last chapters of *A Family's Affairs*. And as in those chapters, she is interested here in the family's responsibility to its elderly. But whereas in the earlier novel that interest was woven into a complex characterization of the Anderson family, here it is the all-too-obvious fabric itself.

In *Apostles of Light*, the hurried, impersonal world has come to Homochitto, Mississippi, and things are changing for the worse, as the novel announces with its opening paragraphs:

> "It doesn't look any worse than most of the other houses in the neighborhood," George Clarke said. "Not as bad as some." He gestured toward the freeway that cut across the end of Clarke Street two blocks away and diverted four lanes of roaring traffic around the outskirts of Homochitto. "It's no surprise to me that this part of town has gone down."
> "But it reflects on us, you know. On us!" Newton said. "We're supposed to be looking after them [the aunts]—responsible for them."(1)

The family's sense of responsibility for its elderly is one thing that time has corroded. While Martha's relatives recognize that responsibility, they are so busy with their own families and careers that they resent the time and effort the responsibility entails. Moreover, they anticipate that maintaining Martha in the big old family home, which no one else cares about any more, will increasingly become a financial burden. But appearances must be kept up, as Newton's comment above indicates. So in walks distant-cousin Howie Snyder with a scheme for turning the old family home into a nursing home for Martha and other local elderly. Not only will this plan relieve the family of its responsibility to Martha, but also Golden Age Acres promises to be profitable. Newton foresees another profit he can reap from the project as well: when he runs for political office, he will be able to claim that he has made considerable contributions to the care of the elderly. What he and the rest of the family do not foresee, and, in fact, what most of them try not to see, is that Howie, whom they hire to run the home, will abuse his power. Howie is this novel's greedy, conniving villain, and the inhabitants of the nursing home are his innocent, helpless victims. Howie's lasciviousness and manipulative actions are all too easy to deplore.

The Rock Cried Out has a wider cast of characters and a more complex plot than the two preceding novels, but it actually suffers from the plethora of competing interests. Included among the characters are a young Southern white male who journeys North to school, then returns to his roots, determined to be a writer; his liberal, free-spirited, artsy aunt, who as a young woman had an affair with a black man and now in middle age renews that affair; a strong, independent black man who went to jail for attacking the navy satellite-tracking station (emblem of impersonal modernism, etc.), which has invaded his rural, natural world; a young hippie-type who is taking pictures and notes and interviewing quaint folks so that he can write about the real people of the South; a religious fanatic or two; and, in the background but essential to the plot, assorted bigots and Ku Klux Klaners and a beautiful young white girl who is killed while on her way to a Negro church for a Civil Rights rally.

A more serious flaw is the narrative mode. Because she has chosen to use the character Alan McLaurin as a first person narrator, Douglas has to find some way to introduce information that Alan would not know but that she wants the reader to know. She tries to solve this problem by simply having various people narrate things to Alan—and they speak for pages on end. Out of the blue, Aunt Leila decides to tell Alan and his girlfriend Miriam about her youthful affair with the black man Sam Daniels. The narration is poorly motivated. Douglas tries to justify other narrations by having Alan team up with Lindsay Lee, local-boy-turned-hippie, to record the stories and observations of country folk around the county. But the most artificial of the long narrative passages is Dallas's harangue over his truck's CB radio near the end of the novel. This twenty-five-page monologue, Dallas's confession of past misdeeds, serves to provide the whole story of how Alan's cousin Phoebe died, a puzzle that has bothered Alan for seven years. Though Dallas addresses the confession to his wife, who is listening at home on her CB, Alan is able to deliver it to the reader since he himself is listening on a CB in another truck as he chases Dallas over the backroads of Homochitto County.

A Lifetime Burning (1982) is a return to excellence for Douglas. It is set in contemporary times but does not display a self-conscious interest in contemporary issues. Narrative technique this time is wedded to characterization and is largely successful. Indeed, in terms of narrative method,

A Lifetime Burning is Douglas's most interesting and most daring work. Whereas *A Family's Affairs* represents traditional storytelling, with events being recorded in chronological order by an omniscient narrator, *A Lifetime Burning* consists of the meandering, passionate entries which sixty-two-year-old Corinne makes in a private journal over a six-month period. Corinne is not narrating a story; she is painfully tearing from her memory, bit by bit, but never in chronological order, the experiences of a thirty-five-year marriage. Tormented by her husband's infidelity, she is now trying to understand how her marriage went wrong. Sometimes addressing herself, sometimes addressing her grown children, she hedges and explains, offering first one and then another version of George's infidelity and her own behavior.

Corinne hopes that writing the journal will relieve her torment. She wants to get at the truth, but at the same time she is afraid of the truth. She delays admitting the truth by repeatedly making up stories about what happened, only to acknowledge afterwards that these are false. She is a college English professor whose imagination serves her well. The first fiction she tells is that George had begun, a few years earlier, an affair with a short, dumpy, homely younger woman. This tale is quite funny, as Corinne knows. It is a conventional version of male infidelity, George and "the Toad," as Corinne labels her, sneaking around to hop in bed together and saying silly romantic things to each other while Corinne eavesdrops. Corinne ends the tale with George and the Toad almost being discovered in the act of making love in a Sunday School room; George escapes through a church window.

But why does Corinne make up this tale about George's infidelity? What makes this fiction preferable to—or easier to face than—the truth? The answer is the tale's very conventionality. Corinne is very much aware that her body is growing old. Indeed, she thinks George quit having sex with her a few years ago because he had come to find her body repulsive. It would not be surprising, then, if he, like many an American man before him, had turned to a younger woman's body for pleasure. So, this conventional version of infidelity seems logical. Furthermore, the way Corinne tells the tale in effect ridicules the affair and makes her feel better about herself: the mistress is a "Toad," the lovers' actions are ridiculous, and Corinne is the wronged and more dignified party.

But this version of the affair serves a third purpose as well: it allows

Corinne to put off facing a more painful and distasteful truth and, simultaneously, foreshadows and makes more palatable that truth. Apparently,
George didn't have an affair with the Toad; he had an affair with "the
Musk-rat": a short, heavy, unattractive young male intern at the hospital
where George practices. Rather than suggesting to her that George was
"merely" rejecting her aging body, this truth seems to Corinne to challenge their whole married life together. She feels she has never really
known her husband. But having finally admitted, through the tale about
the Toad, that George *has* been unfaithful, she can afterwards more easily
admit the true nature of his affair.

The relation demonstrated above between the false tale and the true
tale of George's infidelity represents a pattern in Corinne's confessional.
Repeatedly in the novel, her false tales actually anticipate her true tales;
they too are truths, but deceptive truths. The mixture of false truths with
real truths makes Corinne's journal, and the novel, both funny and sad.

In her search for understanding of her own troubles, Corinne gradually
digs deeply into the present and the past, reaching even to the life of
George's grandmother, who, she has recently discovered, committed
suicide. Corinne says that the discovery of the grandmother's suicide
(through an old church record) was what inspired her to start the journal.
This relative, who was Corinne's great-aunt-in-law as well as George's
grandmother, was a legend in Corinne's family: "'Ah, she was a wonder,'
my grandmother would say. 'A real heroine. Nothing was too much for
her'"(23). Though she grew up listening to tales about the woman,
Corinne never heard that the great-aunt/grandmother committed
suicide. Did the family not know of the suicide? Did they know, but not
admit it? Or could the church record be wrong?

> So that's why I began to think about writing things down, explaining things.
> She, that old great-aunt-in-law, dead seventy years, has changed my way of
> thinking about every relationship, every character, every person in our joint
> family. Nothing is what it seemed. The facts of my life, my history, their lives
> . . . dissolve like smoke before my eyes. . . . Why should I believe anything
> about them, about anyone, if I can't believe what they said about her, whom
> they loved so passionately . . .?"(26)

The ambiguity about the great aunt's life having called into question for
her all of family history, Corinne feels a responsibility to try to understand
at least her own life and marriage, and a responsibility to leave for *her*
children a truthful account of their parents' lives together.

This novel is linked to Douglas's previous fiction in a couple of significant ways. First, like A Family's Affairs and Apostles of Light, it demonstrates Douglas's interest in and familiarity with the aging. Given our society's emphasis on youth, a sixty-two-year-old woman is an unlikely heroine. Corinne carries the weight of this novel almost alone, and does so convincingly. Moreover, Corinne is herself a keen observer of the elderly. Obsessed with the changes occurring in her own body, she notices other women's bodies:

> At the grocery store yesterday I saw an old woman (seventy-five, maybe? eighty?) staggering down the aisle pushing her shopping cart. She had very curly short yellow hair—not blond, but the color that white hair gets to be if you don't wash it often and don't put bluing on it. Bile yellow. She was skinny inside a baggy cotton housedress, her mouth distorted by ill-fitting teeth. I couldn't stop looking at her legs and arms, the muscles like roots under the wrinkled skin. . . .(17)

Secondly, like most of the earlier fiction, this novel deals thematically with responsibility. Corinne's journal is motivated by her notion that she has a responsibility, to herself and her children, to know and to report the truth about her married life. While the other works have not shared precisely this theme about responsibility, there have been characters in those works with a similar sense of responsibility "to know." For example, Anna McGovern of A Family's Affairs, who could easily be a youthful version of Corinne, had listened intensely to family tales, trying to understand everything: "I want to know, she said to herself with innocent self-confidence"(283).

After a lifetime learning, Corinne does not speak in innocence or with self-confidence. She knows that, though she must try, she cannot understand even her own life and marriage. If family tales cannot be trusted, neither can one's own observations, one's own memories. Moreover, she cannot understand the marriage without understanding George, and George won't let her understand him. Since early in their marriage, she has been painfully aware that George holds himself apart from her. He won't open up to her, won't be the perfect companion she has desired. Ironically, when Corinne had confronted George with her knowledge of his affair, George had excused the affair by explaining that the affair would not affect his relationship with her because what he was seeking through the affair was companionship. "I need the friendship of a man," he had said (92).

Perhaps the various themes about responsibility and caring which Ellen Douglas's fiction embodies can be summarized with the last words to *A Lifetime Burning*:

> "What can we do, any of us, except reach out to one another, stay within reach?"
>
> Ah, children, ah, George, here I am, then, and here is this. Waking and dreaming, I reach out to you. (212)

Doris Betts's Nancy Finch:
A *Heroine for the 1980s*

DOROTHY M. SCURA

In his review of *Heading West* (1982), John Leonard observed that "Doris Betts knows everything." The reader of the novel is inclined to agree: she knows everything about the paleontology of the Grand Canyon, epilepsy, raising dogs and wolves, the landscape of the United States from North Carolina to Arizona, and, most important, the landscape of the human heart. *Heading West* is a big book, all of a piece, tight, full of foreshadowing, suspense and mystery, written in a language glimmering and echoing with meaning on several levels at once, a profoundly serious book that is richly comic.

At mid-career with her fourth novel Betts has produced a work as American as *Huckleberry Finn* and *Moby Dick*, as old as the Greeks and the Bible, as recent as the movies and sociopathic kidnappers. It is about "mortality and time," the subjects of all her fiction according to Betts (Wolfe 171), and it presents us a heroine for the 1980s—Nancy Finch, who is sturdy, spunky, intelligent, resourceful, strong, sarcastic—and who, despite the modesty of her name, Finch, rises like a phoenix out of her own heatstroke deep in the Grand Canyon. It is perhaps surprising that Betts, who considers herself primarily a short story writer, should produce this book at all. It is her first novel set out of the rural South and the first one with a strong, single woman at the center of the action. Part of the power of *Heading West* is that Betts has adopted a feminine perspective in this novel; and the voice of Nancy Finch, which dominates the text, is convincing and, in a Faulknerian sense, uplifting.[1]

Betts's first novel, *Tall Houses in Winter* (1957), was published when she was twenty-five years old. In this apprentice novel, she seems to have attempted to write like a man. The central character, Ryan Godwin, a 48 year-old professor of English, is coming home to Stoneville after an ab-

Doris Betts

*A native of North Carolina (b. 1932), Betts received her educa-
tion at the University of North Carolina. Her first collection of
short stories,* The Gentle Insurrection, *was published in 1954.
She is the author of two other collections of stories, numerous
short stories and articles in periodicals, and four novels.*

sence of ten years to make his peace with the past. He is dying of cancer, and the odor of death hangs over the novel. The opening sentence sets the tone for the work. "[Ryan] had always said the only way he would ever come back to Stoneville would be in a pine box, one of the plain rough-hewn frontiers kind, so that people seeing it unloaded at the train station might just once, just briefly, wonder if there were other more vigorous lives being lived in other places than this one" (9).

Ryan's great love, Jessica Maple, had married his fat, boring, and platitudinous brother Avery. Both Jessica and Avery had died as the result of an automobile accident ten years earlier. The first description of Jessica in the text is as a corpse: "But she was dead, and somewhere underground perhaps that very hair had grown long and long, and lay over her in that box like a soft covering; and the rest of it—the eyes and the mouth and the flesh—whatever they had become was under all the hair and could not be seen, not ever" (15). It is not until page 221 (of 383 pages) in the novel that Ryan and Jessica's love story is recalled through Ryan's memory of the events. Significantly, this part of the book that features Jessica as the object of Ryan's affection is the most interesting and lively part of the Godwin family's story. Betts's other women characters are minor, grotesque, but excellently drawn—the materialistic, cold sister Asa; the black devoted servant Lady Malveena; the deaf cousin Miss Clara. But the weight of the narrative is borne by a middle-aged male protagonist, and Jessica's story is presented posthumously through his consciousness.

Betts's second novel is a change of pace from the first. *The Scarlet Thread* (1964) tells the story of the Allen family, but focuses primarily on the three children in that family, Thomas, Esther, and David. A historical novel, it is set in a cotton mill town in North Carolina at the turn of the century. Betts has created in Esther Allen a lively, intelligent, rebellious young girl from the ages of thirteen to fifteen. The author does a masterful job of portraying children and their family relationships, particularly in the characterizations of Esther, her cruel, materialistic brother Thomas and her artistic brother David. In this novel a female protagonist moves nearer the center of the action, but even though she is the most imaginative and lovable character in the family, she disappears midway in the book and only reappears briefly at the end. Here again, Betts does a fine job with women characters, in particular the religious mother Mildred and her demented sister Rosa. But this is a book primarily about men, Sam Allen and his sons. The novel has been called Gothic with some of the standard ingredients of that genre—madness, perversion, violence, death, and fire. In its depiction of the spiritual decline of a family, it is reminiscent of Faulkner's *The Sound and the Fury,* featuring a delightful and loving daughter who serves as catalyst for the brothers.

The River to Pickle Beach (1972), Betts's third novel, is also set in North Carolina, but she moves from a mill town in the piedmont to the coast. The time is 1968 and the violence in the country, symbolized publicly by the assassinations of Robert Kennedy and Martin Luther King, is replicated in Bebe and Jack Sellars's private lives in a violent act of senseless murder committed by an old war buddy of Jack's, Mickey McCane. Set against this chaos and violence is the genuine love of Jack and Bebe for one another. Indeed, this novel celebrates marriage. The focus switches among three characters, Bebe, Jack and Mickey. The central female character, Bebe, is simple, earthy, and sensual. The book is about violence and love—about the violence in the world and about the only comfort available, love. Here Betts comes more closely than in the earlier novels to focusing on a female protagonist; Bebe is not posthumously remembered, nor does she disappear from the text. She is very much alive and present, but she is seen in terms of her marriage, in relation to her husband, and her life is completely joined with his.

Betts's novels—one each decade since the fifties—show a steady progression. Each one is better than the one before. She has demonstrated special gifts from the beginning for describing place, for characterization, and for a rich, allusive style. And along with the maturity of her fiction has come more important roles for women in the novels. Jessica Maple Godwin is dead when her novel begins, and in the memories recounted of her, she is the victim of a thwarted love affair. Esther Allen experiences a failed love affair as a teenager and then disappears from her novel. Bebe Sellars manages to stay in her novel and at the center throughout, but she is primarily seen as one-half of a happy marriage. Not until *Heading West* and Nancy Finch does Betts focus on an autonomous female protagonist. And it is with this novel that she comes into her own as a novelist with a distinctive voice and a comic view of the world.

Nancy Finch is a worthy addition to the gallery of American heroines—
Hester Prynne, Isabel Archer, Carrie Meeber, Carol Kennicot, Lily Bart,
Catherine Barkley, Nicole Diver, Caddie Compson, Scarlett O'Hara. She
is as able as Hester and Scarlett. She is immensely more interesting than
Carrie or Carol or Catherine. And she reads better books than Isabel, is
less a victim than Lily (Nancy takes over her own kidnapping and aban-
dons prayer to take charge of her own destiny). She is saner than Nicole.
Like Caddie she is nurturing and loving to an afflicted brother, but she
does manage to occupy the center of her own novel. Significantly, she is
the only one of these women willingly to undergo a spiritual and physical
ordeal traditionally suffered by men in our literature. And she is the only
one with a sense of humor.

She needs that sense of humor. Trapped at home in Greenway, North
Carolina, taking care of an arthritic mother and epileptic brother, Nancy
Finch is a 34-year-old librarian, a spinster. She has experienced a few
tepid love affairs, and she has read a lot. Bored with her life and enraged
with her family, she is trapped in a car on a camping vacation with her
sister Faye and brother-in-law Eddie Rayburn. She'd wanted to go on a
Caribbean cruise, and she spends her time in the back seat of the car
indulging in escape fantasies. She sees herself floating down the Toe and
Little Pigeon rivers, running away to the Indians, taking up with gigolos:
"[Her] mind snaked downhill through laurel and rhododendron and
emerged somewhere into a new and freer life." (3). Later, when the
armed man steps out of the woods, Nancy knows that "part of her had
been waiting for him ever since she memorized 'The Highwayman'" (11).
The 29-year-old kidnapper introduces himself by telling her, "Call me
Dwight." Nancy intuitively realizes that this small-time criminal is "one
who had not earned his pursuers yet, whose trail sprang out of nowhere" (17). She remembers her desperate desire to meet a man, perhaps
on board a ship in the Caribbean, who would rescue her. She'd prayed for
this deliverance, promising "no longer to be choosy about the man's
habits, or income, or even intelligence." Then, to herself, she adds, "This
man was God's answer? There were divine practical jokes John Calvin had
never guessed" (25).

In Tennessee Nancy and Dwight pick up another passenger, Harvey
Jolley, a small-time judge who is burdened with guilt because of his wife's

death and who is in trouble with the law for taking bribes. Judge Jolley explains that he is "Just a transient, out studying the human condition" (34). The novel tells the story of this unlikely crew's journey across the country through Arkansas, Texas, New Mexico, and to Arizona, where Nancy descends through time into the Grand Canyon, is pursued by Dwight, confronts him, suffers a dark night of the soul and body, is rescued, recovers, falls in love, returns home.

The book closes as she is going to the airport to meet Hunt Thatcher, the son of Nancy's rescuer, Channing Thatcher. Nancy plans to marry Hunt and move west.

The summary of what happens in *Heading West* touches only a small part of what the book is about. Indeed, John Leonard suggests that there are really "three books quarreling inside this ambitious novel" (23). Beth Gutcheon puts it even more aptly: " 'Heading West' is the story of a young spinster librarian who is kidnapped from a picnic at Linville Falls, N.C., in much the same sense that Flannery O'Connor's 'A Good Man Is Hard to Find' is the story of a Southern family's vacation trip to Florida being interrupted by a gunman known as the Misfit" (12).

Consonant with the theme of a search for identity, for self, all three main characters assume different names. Nancy Finch identifies herself as Celeste Victor when she goes to a physician in Texarkana to get a prescription for birth control pills. Then, in New Mexico she tells a California pediatrician hiking with his obnoxious son that she is the widow of Randolph Macon Finch, who was killed in Vietnam. Later, Chan Thatcher can only remember that Nancy's last name is a bird's name, and Nancy is identified at the hospital as Nancy Thatcher. Dwight Anderson becomes Melrose Lee Shelton, his identity on a driver's license, and finally Ervin Childers, while the judge explains he was a foundling named Harvey Trace who was later adopted by the Jolleys.

In characterizing Dwight, Doris Betts has chosen to delineate perhaps the most enigmatic character of our time, the colorless and inarticulate man who comes from nowhere to wreak seemingly unmotivated violence and then appears on our television screens and the front pages of our newspapers—the assassins, kidnappers, Tylenol-poisoners. His literary ancestors are Faulkner's Popeye and O'Connor's misfit. And Harvey is one of those helpless, confused men without the strength or insight to find himself. Each of the three pilgrims discovers his own west: Nancy in rebirth, Dwight in death, and Harvey in madness, paranoia, religion, and the delusion that he is part Negro.

The center of meaning in the novel resides in all the suggestiveness of the title *Heading West*. And therein is embodied the book's Americanness. The historical notion was that a person headed west if he or she had nothing to lose, that travelers rarely gave up anything to go, that they often wanted to shake off an old identity and find a new one. In *All The King's Men* Jack Burden gets in his car and drives to California when he is in despair. He explains to himself the reason he "headed west" was "because when you don't like it where you are you always go west. We have always gone west." And he finally realizes that "there is innocence and a new start in the West, after all."[2]

That nineteenth-century term Manifest Destiny with all its political arrogance and religious fervor expresses the idea that providence allotted a vast territory in which Americans could seek their destiny. Much of this novel turns on double meanings, on paradox, and just as heading west signifies new life and rebirth, it also suggests death, perishing, the "Ultimate West" (where Harvey Jolley thinks of his wife as having gone). This romantic notion of abandoning an old order for a new one—freer and simpler—has formed a theme in American literature since Leatherstocking kept on the move to stay ahead of civilization and headed west. But this struggle with nature has usually been made by men—as Huck took to the river and Ishmael to the sea, so Nancy took to the Grand Canyon.

Nancy is the self-sufficient pioneer woman making her way across the country amid hardship. She begins as a victim, controlled by a man with a gun who is taking her west. But she soon modifies her role as victim and begins to take charge, deciding she may escape permanently and "never go back" (61). And she begins to make this trip her own, telling the judge that this is "*my* trip west" (63). Later she considers stealing Dwight's money in order to "go seeking her own west" (90). Finally, she redefines west and realizes that she's going to write "*my* declaration of independence, not the pursuit but the capture of happiness. Heading west to Nancy's Manifest Destiny" (140).

Nancy Finch is an earthy, direct, dark-haired woman, deeply feminine in her response to life. She is strong, intuitive, nurturing, and capable of love. In contrast to this unmarried librarian, Betts portrays Nancy's sister Faye as blonde, with fluffy curls, helpless, dependent, selfish, the very image of the falsely feminine woman our culture has encouraged. Certainly Faye lacks the intelligence and moral depth to undergo Nancy's spiritual odyssey, and Nancy's mother is quite sure Faye could never have survived the kidnapping ordeal. Perhaps Faye would not have, but Nancy is a survivor.

After being kidnapped, Nancy prays first that she won't be murdered and then that she won't be raped. But after considering the matter briefly, she decides she can survive rape: "But if it's a choice [between murder and rape], Lord? I hope you don't still consider rape a fate worse than death? If I get a vote, . . . I think I could outlast the trauma" (18). She survives a cross-country journey accompanied by an armed man who is clearly capable of violence only to endure the physically arduous journey in the Grand Canyon. What distinguishes her is not only her ability to undergo fear and physical hardship, but her capacity for self-searching and her strength in coming to terms with herself, her family, and Hunt Thatcher. If her odyssey began as an "escape from," it becomes a matter of "going to"; of breaking with her family in a morally responsible way, of marrying Hunt Thatcher, of moving west permanently.

The original escape was not only from the parasitic dependence of her family, but from her fears of becoming an old woman like Miss Boykin, the head librarian, or Evaline Sample, the dotty artist who suffered periodic breakdowns treated by electro-therapy. Nancy remembered that the tenth-grade girls thought spinsterhood had driven Evaline Sample crazy, "that older women needed 'sex juice' to stay normal." Then, Nancy thinks, "Nowadays they plugged old maids into technology. When Evaline was again as sensible as a storage battery she would sit in the county library turning photographs into sketches for the Episcopal Craft Fair. . . ." When Evaline's medication dropped too low, "she would begin to draw Mecca. Her circumsized minarets endorsed the tenth-grade view" (29).

During her westward journey, Nancy telephones Evaline Sample at the library in one of the most hilarious incidents in the book. Introducing herself as the "angel of God," she cautions Evaline not to repeat a word of the communication, and tells her to "paint electricity" (84). When Nancy returns to Greenway, she learns that Evaline is exhibiting her paintings of wiring diagrams, circuits, and solid-state things in a show entitled "Aesthetics of Technology" (355).

After returning to Greenway, Nancy visits her grandfather's old farm and decides to sell it to a developer in order to provide money for her mother and brother. She comes to terms with her past, in particular her grandfather's death, and she chooses to leave the weight of that past for a new beginning. The contrast in her past and her future is symbolized in the descriptions of two houses: her mother's, dark and narrow, is stained by the past; the other, Channing Thatcher's, is open, spacious and uncluttered. The Finch home in Greenway is "Victorian, tall, dark." There are "marble surfaces," "wing chairs with splotched armrests," and a "mirror over the mantel that made them all look yellowed by memory in its gilt frame" (330). And on the mantel is that icon of so many households, the three monkeys who neither see, hear, nor speak evil. On the other hand, Channing Thatcher's house in Arizona is long, low, and sprawling, with no paintings cluttering the walls—only a view of the mountains through an elongated window. It is in this setting so different from Greenway that Nancy meets Hunt Thatcher.

For a heroine in an American novel, Nancy Finch is a surprisingly literate woman. Betts has accounted for this by making her a librarian, and like her creator, precociously literary without the benefit—or handicap—of a college degree. Literary allusions, therefore, abound in the book quite legitimately—they grow out of Nancy's wide reading. These allusions account for some of the humor in the book, but primarily they give the text added dimension as the action reverberates against actions in the past. Nancy's childhood reading emerges in references to fairy tales (Rumpelstiltskin and Hansel and Gretel), "The Highwayman," Robin Hood, Jo March of *Little Women*, and that spunky heroine for whom she may be named, Nancy Drew. There are also allusions to Joan of Arc, to classical figures (Sisyphus, Persephone, Niobe), to British literature (Shelley, Blake, Heathcliff, Gulliver, Wordsworth), and American literature (Flannery O'Connor, Whitman, Melville). Rather than serving as ornaments for the text, the literary allusions reinforce the themes of the novel, including those having to do with time, mortality, and vision.

Ultimately, this is a book about vision, about *seeing*. Nancy's unobservant sister and her husband describe her to the police as wearing an outfit

Nancy had never owned (a blue dress, whereas she had had on red slacks). They incorrectly add that she has no identifying marks and that she bites her fingernails, a habit she had forsaken almost a decade earlier (66). In a rage over her sister's lack of observation, Nancy cunningly places her long fingernails in the plain view of a policeman at a road block.

Judge Jolley becomes so disillusioned with unseeing people that he decides that he'll never again believe that "people even noticed their temporary neighbor, much less loved him as themselves" (216). Indeed, not one of the people encountered by Dwight and Nancy sees very well. No one ever notices that he is looking at a kidnapper and kidnappee. Nancy wails to a waitress in a restaurant, "I need help!" The waitress directs her to the ladies room. Checking into a motel, Nancy and Dwight have an argument about whether or not Nancy may get a single room. The clerk is so absorbed in reading *Startling True Detective* magazine that he does not note the "crime at hand." Nancy decides that "nowhere in America was there a bellboy or waitress or gas attendant who could distinguish abduction from marriage or cared to try" (73).

Nancy wears broken sunglasses which serve to bisect the world, but she finally buries in the Canyon both those glasses and the new, unbroken ones she has purchased. And Hunt observed of Nancy after the Canyon adventure: "Although you were kidnapped and under threat for days, carried across the country, all that, much of the time you seem like a woman who stepped out for a loaf of bread and just made a wrong turn. Too calm, or maybe numb. Yet at other times you'll pull back and your eyes look at something none of us can see" (283).

Heading West operates on several levels at once. Read simply as a kidnap story, the climax comes early when Dwight steps gracefully and in slow motion over the edge of a steep cliff in the Canyon. This early climax would leave perhaps the longest denouement in American literature. But Nancy's problem has never been primarily to get away from Dwight. Her spiritual journey commences in the Canyon, and her struggle with identity as well as her struggle with her family are still to be resolved.

After Dwight's fall, Nancy dozes and awakens feeling "hungry for some rare food her stomach could retain, perhaps communion wafers" (210). She falls asleep in the water of a creek thinking "Wash me whiter than snow" (211). Feet bleeding, vision wavering, overcome with heat and thirst, she divests herself of the last of her possessions—identity cards, checks, money—and then passes out: "Then through stone she sailed off like a dust mote into endless space" (224).

In her fourth novel, Doris Betts has written a very contemporary work which echoes the past—the Bible, the theology of John Calvin, the archetypal journey used by Mark Twain and Melville, the whole cluster of meanings associated with the American notion of moving west. In a 1969 interview she talked about herself as a Southern writer and stated her reservations about that designation:

> I seem to have what people like W. J. Cash said was a Southern mystique, which is a strong sense of family, and of land, and of seasons, and the old biblical traditions, and a rather stern sense of morality, as a matter of fact. I'd like to have a deeper look at other regions of the country before I'm persuaded that that is not fundamentally American and hearkens back to the pioneer spirit, rather than just this region. (Wolfe 153)

With those words she prophesied *Heading West*, which is so fundamentally American in its pioneer spirit. What she did not foretell is that she would create for readers in Nancy Finch a heroine for the 1980s—smart, strong, intuitive, loving, funny, possessed of integrity. A heroine who could look at those three suppressed monkeys on her mother's North Carolina mantel and realize she was the fourth monkey, one "who could do evil and know it," but one who could also both hear and see reality (359).

NOTES

[1] In an interview with George Wolfe Betts quotes Faulkner's Nobel Prize speech, "'The aim of the writer is to *uplift* the heart of man . . .'" (emphasis mine), in *Kite-Flying and Other Irrational Acts*, 170.

[2] Robert Penn Warren, *All the King's Men* (1946; rpt. New York: Bantam, 1968), 309, 311.

Photo: Piroska Mihalka

Elizabeth Spencer

Born in Mississippi (1921), Spencer was graduated from Belhaven College and Vanderbilt University (M.A.). Her first novel, Fire in the Morning, was published in 1948. Spencer has published numerous short stories, articles, and reviews in such periodicals as the New Yorker, as well as six other novels and three collections of short stories.

Mermaids, Angels and Free Women:
The Heroines of Elizabeth Spencer's Fiction

PEGGY WHITMAN PRENSHAW

In 1960 Elizabeth Spencer published her fourth novel, *Light in the Piazza*, to widespread popular and critical attention. The book marked a significant departure from her earlier novels, all of which centered on male protagonists whose stories were set in Spencer's native Mississippi. In *Fire in the Morning* (1948) and *This Crooked Way* (1952), Kinloch Armstrong and Amos Dudley contend with a sense of private destiny that overshadows relations with wives and others drawn into their quest. They struggle to fulfill the identities they envision for themselves, and in doing so they come to realize the sacrifice of intimacy with others that their egoism demands. This classic theme of the humanizing of the hero is given a broader context in *The Voice at the Back Door* (1956), in which Spencer portrays a man caught in a web of racial tensions and conflicting values in a small Southern town. Spencer wrote the novel, which reviewers widely praised for the vitality of the characters and the vigor and honesty of the action, while she was in Italy on a Guggenheim Fellowship. It has so far proved to be her last novel focusing chiefly on men in Mississippi.[1]

Beginning with Margaret Johnson of *Light in the Piazza*, and continuing with Nancy Lewis of "Ship Island: The Story of a Mermaid" (1964), Martha Ingram of *Knights and Dragons* (1965), Catherine Sasser of *No Place for an Angel* (1967), and Julia Garrett of *The Snare* (1972), Spencer has created a fascinating group of female protagonists who move in a more problematic and complicated world than that in her earlier fiction. Whereas the culmination of her heroes' journeys is the recognition that one must learn to live with conflicting visions of life and acquiesce to uncertainty, it is precisely the ambiguous self that marks the starting point for the heroines. Their experience typifies the female bind much

147

written about in recent years, the difficulty for a woman of reconciling one's human needs with society's requirement of a "feminine nature" that is either less than or more than human.

In Spencer's fiction, as in myth and modern psychology, representations of female alienation or otherworldliness may take many forms, ranging from seductive but evasive mermaids to ethereal, passive angels. The alienation embodied by these images, and the conflicts that Spencer's heroines experience between inner need and outer reality, are not, however, exclusively female territory. These characters express the universal modern experience of the self torn between a private, self-conscious inner life and a compromised, shared outer life that demands the forfeiture of consciousness or separateness—the preeminent theme of twentieth-century literature. As Josephine Hendin discusses in her study of American fiction since 1945, the "sense of vulnerability distinctive to women in nineteenth-century novels is almost universally shared by current male heroes."[2] It is, nonetheless, the experience of Spencer's characters as women that most interests me here and that forms the main topic of this essay.

Like ladies imprisoned in towers, Spencer's heroines seem "enclosed" women, and indeed the words "closed," "enclosed," and "confined" often appear in the texts. In the case of Nancy Lewis and Martha Ingram, lonely isolation is initially the consequence of the circumscribed roles available to women in society. Their withdrawal is mainly reactive, an emotional numbing that seems the only response possible to expectations that they exist solely to attract, learn from, or take care of another. Similarly, Margaret Johnson's self enclosure is in part a retreat from husband Noel, as is Catherine Sasser's withdrawal from the world partly an escape from her husband. But ultimately, the stronger motive for the action of these women, especially the spiritual and psychological journey of Julia Garrett, is the discovery and assertion of the self.

As Spencer's male hero's quest seems to be the recognition of the other, the challenge for the female hero is the acknowledgment and acceptance of her separate self. Whatever her circumstance of ladyhood, whether enthroned upon a pedestal or imprisoned by fears and obsessions, the heroine moves from passive acquiescence to active choice. In pursuing selfhood, she finds her freedom. In Spencer's vision, the autonomous woman stands inevitably apart from the world—a woman enclosed, but with a difference. She frees herself from both the easily refused demands of social convention and the more compelling demands of the beloved. For these heroines, the quest that ultimately tests one's courage and integrity is not the pursuit of self denial, but of self possession.

Light in the Piazza is the story of a woman's fulfillment of a dream. Margaret Johnson's dream is wholly conventional, maternal—that her daughter Clara, who suffered a childhood accident that has left her with the mind of a ten-year-old, should have a normal life. For years, however, the dream has put her in conflict with her husband. Ever a pragmatic American, Noel Johnson has long accepted the verdict of the doctors that Clara will mentally remain a child. Margaret does not accept the diagnosis and, as her only acts of wifely disobedience through the years, has continued to try "experiments" to ease Clara into life's mainstream. Her repeated failures have almost scotched the dream, but one brilliant summer in Italy resurrects it. "Nobody with a dream should come to Italy," Margaret thinks. "No matter how dead and buried the dream is thought to be, in Italy it will rise and walk again" (61).

The novel, filtered through Margaret's limited, third person point of view, traces the development of her heroic assertion of the old dream. When Clara attracts the attention of an eligible young Italian, Margaret is at first annoyed. As Clara and Fabrizio Naccarelli grow increasingly attached to one another, she begins to allow herself a bit of idle fantasy. But as the courtship progresses, Margaret suddenly becomes frightened of the consequences, fearful of impending decisions that will inevitably be demanded by Fabrizio and his family, fearful most of all of her collaboration in a courtship that will draw the wrath of her husband. Hurriedly she and Clara leave Florence for Rome. After some weeks of anguish for Clara, who misses Fabrizio and begs to make the promised return to Florence, Margaret makes the fateful decision to return.

In the novels of Henry James, the marriage game, played out by Americans with Italians in Italy, tests every moral and social fiber of the protagonists; no less so in *Light in the Piazza*. Like James's heroines, Margaret is hopeful (but not sure) that she is right in her judgment of people, but unlike her fictional predecessors her action is rather more decisive than evasive. Armed only with courage to act, she puts obedient ladyhood behind her and becomes a woman. "What is it, to reach a decision? It is like walking down a long Florentine street where, at the very end, a dim shape is waiting until you get there. When Mrs. Johnson finally reached this street and saw what was ahead, she moved steadily forward to see it at long last up close. What was it? Well, nothing monstrous, it seemed; but human, with a face much like her own, that of a woman who loved her daughter and longed for her happiness" (86).

Many narrative and descriptive details in the novel express the risk and heroism represented by Margaret's decision to promote the marriage of Clara and Fabrizio. In the opening episodes, light imagery, like a vast spotlight focusing upon the Johnsons and the Naccarellis in the piazza, suggests an arena for testing. Nearby Cellini's Persus triumphantly holds aloft the Medusa's head. On the occasion when Margaret meets Signor Naccarelli, Fabrizio's father, they witness a holiday ceremony, complete with medieval cannons firing. Suddenly, in a burst of light almost obscured by the sun, a man falls. Not until the conclusion do Margaret and the reader discover the outcome of the accident. "He died," Signor Naccarelli replies to Margaret's inquiry, and at last we understand the full extent of risk in stumbling into Italian rituals and ceremonies. From the beginning the marriage game had been for keeps, and the stakes were Margaret's life—her daughter, her husband, and her pride. "She had played single-handed and unadvised a tricky game in a foreign country, and she had managed to realize from it the dearest wish of her heart" (107).

The action of the novel is rich in irony and allusion, not the least of which is the fact that Margaret's marriage plot, a strategy (as old as the genre) for exchanging a woman's freedom for security, actually exchanges mother and daughter's security for their freedom. Margaret finds her solitary power and uses it, and Clara is freed from hopeless dependence. It is supremely ironical that from all the evidence that Margaret can gather, the wifehood that awaits Clara is perfectly suited to a ten-year-old's mentality. The role of the Naccarelli women is extremely traditional. Above all, the bride should be sheltered and innocent. Doubtless Clara Johnson is the last twenty-six-year-old American girl to visit Italy with her "innocence" unquestionably intact. Innocence had begun to slip even in Daisy Miller's nineteenth-century Rome. As an Italian wife, Clara will remain in the home, pleasing and obedient to her husband. Her principal function will be motherhood, and with a well-to-do family like the Naccarellis to provide nurses and servants, and a mother-in-law whose arms ache to hold a baby, Clara's good physical and genetic health equips her perfectly to live happily ever afterward. She will be pampered and adored by a family clan that requires nothing beyond her cheerfulness, love, and wholehearted acceptance of their way of life. Least among Margaret's fears is that Clara will be unable to measure up to the Naccarellis' expectations. In fact, much earlier, at the point at which she decides to return to Florence and take up her plan, Margaret observes that a "warm, classic dignity" has come to Clara, that "no matter whether she could do long division or not, she was a woman" (59).

She will never be a woman in her mother's mold, however. In accomplishing Clara's chance for womanhood, Margaret engages in intricate calculation and artifice. Margaret, not her businessman husband, represents the family in the marriage negotiations with Signor Naccarelli. With wit and courage she plays the "tricky game," and though she is bested in the dowry bargaining, she wins the match for Clara. Her weapons are not maternal feelings or purity of heart, but quite the opposite. She carries the day because she devises a shrewd strategy and takes bold, solitary action. Margaret intuits that her risk will pay off not only in a better life for Clara but a chance for renewal of her own marriage. She thinks that after Noel gets beyond shock and anger at his daughter's marriage, he will "grow quiet at last, and in the quiet, even Margaret Johnson had not yet dared to imagine what sort of life, what degree of delight in it, they might not be able to discover (rediscover?) together" (109). In the end Margaret is confident that she has done "the right thing."

Light in the Piazza was Spencer's first published work set outside the South. By her own account, it represented an important change for her, a widening of horizon. In an interview with John Griffin Jones in *Mississippi Writers Talking*, she says:

> *The Light in the Piazza,* for better or worse, really did alter my vision of what I could do. It expanded me because it was so fantastically successful. The success was completely unexpected. For some reason everybody seemed to love that story. It was published in *The New Yorker,* then in book form. It was taken by a book club, it was made into a movie, . . . went through one translation after another. Reviews poured in. I thought, "Well, maybe I should take a wider scope on things. Not confine myself to the Mississippi scene." So then I went

on and wrote things that were laid in Rome. . . . I went on and did things that
challenged me in a new way. . . . The outer world seemed to interest me
more. . . . It seemed to give me a bigger horizon. (120)

Although she does not mention it, another significant change marked
by *The Light in the Piazza* is Spencer's turn to female protagonists. It
seems likely that their lives, like the world that lay beyond Mississippi,
offered her "a wider scope on things." In a series of stories and novels that
she wrote during the 1960s and 1970s, Spencer portrays characters who
are more vulnerable than Margaret Johnson, women whose efforts to
establish a self and achieve a measure of freedom are often desperate and
convoluted. Their victories are more muted than Johnson's, but then, as
women, they undertake perhaps a more ambitious challenge than hers—
action in behalf of the self. These later heroines frequently exist in a kind
of limbo, expressing through their fictional lives what Rachel M. Brownstein in *Becoming a Heroine* has called a pattern of "thinking simultaneously about what it is to be a woman and how to choose what and who
and how to be." In her discussion of the portrayal of women in novels
since the eighteenth century, Brownstein notes the centrality of questions about whether "intimacy and identity can be achieved at once, and
whether they are mutually exclusive, entirely desirable, and, indeed,
other than imaginary." Like the classic novelists Brownstein studies,
Spencer "explores the connections between the inner self and its outward
manifestations—between the personal and the social, the private and the
public—by focusing on a woman complexly connected to others, who
must depend, to distinguish herself, on the gender that delimits her life."[3]

One of Spencer's earliest portraits of a heroine adrift, one who tries to
find a mooring without sacrificing her individuality, is Nancy Lewis in
"Ship Island: The Story of a Mermaid." Originally published in the *New
Yorker* in 1964, the story contributes the title to the collection, *Ship
Island and Other Stories*, which Spencer published in 1968 and later
included in *The Stories of Elizabeth Spencer* (1981). Nancy, a young
woman who has spent two years at a "cow college in Arkansas," has
recently moved with her family to the Mississippi Gulf Coast. Although
she quickly meets and begins to date a local boy who introduces her to his
university crowd of friends, Nancy feels alien and threatened. Shortly
after moving, Nancy began the summer with the intention of studying
French, but soon she "could no longer find herself in relation to the girl

who had sought out such a good place to study, had sharpened the pencils and opened the book and sat down to bend over it" (85). What happens is that Nancy loses her grip on the "perfect girl" dream of success as the task of pleasing others and denying herself finally exhausts her. Leading to her break with the "normal" world, when she impulsively joins two strange men for a trip to New Orleans, is a series of unsettling revelations. She discovers that, of all the people around her, no one knows her, much less senses or cares to acknowledge her uniqueness.

On the beach one day Nancy is shocked by a blistering acid rain, but her report is dismissed by her mother, who "never heard of such a thing." Similarly, her alcoholic father signals his disdain with the display of a grinning china donkey bearing the message, "If you really want to look like me—Just keep right on talking." By all accounts Bob Acklen should be the perfect catch for a girl like Nancy, but "he, with his Phi Beta Kappa key and his good level head and his wonderful prospects, found everything she told about herself cute, funny, absurd" (91). An invitation to a party at Rob's friends brings the following exchange.

"What did you say?" he asked her.
"Nothing."
"You just don't want to go?"
"No, I don't much want to go."
"Well, then, we won't stay long." (96)

Rob, seemingly immune to the mosquitoes that assault Nancy, likes to make love on Ship Island or some bayou, and his snobbish friends seem to her so many human mosquitoes. "They'll sting me till I crumple up and die, she thought" (100). Like a forsaken mermaid caught in a human snare, Nancy escapes Rob's party at the Fishnet night club and retreats to the bar. Finding there a man she recognizes from her morning on the beach when the acid rain fell, she strikes up a conversation. "What's your name?" he asks. "'Nothing,' she said, by accident." The inadvertent reply expresses Nancy's desperation. Bolstered by finding someone who verifies her strange experience of the stinging rain ("he positively seemed to Nancy to be her own identity"), she goes with him and his friend when in a childlike game they propose to take her wherever in the world she wants to go. New Orleans's image of exotic strangeness has long appealed to her, perhaps it seems to her a more companionable home for her own strangeness, and so it is to New Orleans that they drive in a yellow

Cadillac. There Nancy finds her exotic element, which turns out to have its dangers too. In the French Quarter, the two men quarrel, and the friend Dennis takes Nancy as spoils. "What he had to say to her was nothing she hadn't heard before, nothing she hadn't already been given more or less to understand from mosquitoes, people, life-in-general, and the rain out of the sky. It was just that he said it in a final sort of way—that was all" (109).

If Nancy harbored romantic fantasies, she returns home without them, with big bruises on her face and body to show for her adventure. What is interesting about the conclusion of the story, however, is Nancy's response to Rob's questioning of her motive for running away. She doesn't refute his claims that he has liked her, "tried his best" to be nice to her, as have his friends, but neither does she recant her rejection of all the numbing niceness. "'I guess it's just the way I am,' Nancy murmured. 'I just run off sometimes'" (110).

In this story, composed in the early 1960s, Elizabeth Spencer has created in the compelling image of the half human mermaid a metaphor of the female condition that is explored in great richness and depth by Dorothy Dinnerstein in *The Mermaid and the Minotaur: Sexual Arrangements and Human Malaise* (1976). Dinnerstein argues that "the division of responsibility, opportunity, and privilege that prevails between male and female humans, and the patterns of psychological interdependence that are implicit in this division" have produced a "human malaise." We cast men and women into half-human roles, she writes, perhaps best signified by the images of the mermaid and the minotaur. (Our tendency to adopt such images is fed by psychological patterns stemming from the female's exclusive responsibility for child rearing, Dinnerstein maintains.) She characterizes the two controlling images as follows: "The treacherous mermaid, seductive and impenetrable female representative of the dark and magic underwater world from which our life comes and in which we cannot live, lures voyagers to their doom. The fearsome minotaur, gigantic and eternally infantile offspring of a mother's unnatural lust, male representative of mindless, greedy power, insatiably devours live human flesh."[4]

Although Dinnerstein's mermaid is no exact gloss of Spencer's Nancy Lewis, there are some instructive points of similarity between them. For all her youth and passion and curiosity, Nancy seems to herself "like a person who wasn't a person—another order of creature passing among or even through them" (105). She tries to overcome her alienation by joining Rob's circle, and by making love, but she still feels like a fish out of water. To Rob, she callously destroys their summer romance. When he confronts her with frustration and displeasure, she thinks, "He's coming down deeper and deeper, but one thing is certain—if he gets down as far as I am, he'll drown" (109). Nancy's answer to her dilemma, however, is like that of many of Spencer's later heroines. She does not deny her condition, but choses to live out her life, wide-eyed and free. Better to live one's painful condition, in harm's way, than to relinquish one's identity.

In Jones's 1981 interview of Spencer, she speaks of coming to feel at the time she was writing "Ship Island" an affinity for "waif-like women that were free. They have no particular ties, or no ties that are worth holding them, and so they become subject to all kinds of encounters, influences, choices out in the world. You know, they've got to find a foothold, they've got to find something to hold to" (122). At the end of "Ship Island," Nancy Lewis has not found the "something to hold to," other than her separate self. And in Spencer's next novella, *Knights and Dragons*, protagonist Martha Ingram similarly finds only herself at the end of her struggle, though, to be sure, a changed, cleansed, simplified self from the woman who opens the story.

As in *Light in the Piazza*, there are features of theme and technique in *Knights and Dragons* that recall the fiction of Henry James. Tissues of emotional haziness and layers of introspection and perception are evoked in this interior story of a woman imprisoned by fear and guilt. The brilliant Italian setting reflects the poles of experience pulling at the protagonist Martha Ingram. Here as elsewhere throughout her fiction, Spencer is particularly skilled in her evocative and metaphoric depictions of settings. The throbbing, sunlit landscape embodies the energy—sexual and psychological—that propels the characters, and the shadowy, labyrinthine Italian walkways mirror the masks and complexities that exhaust their energies.

Initially, Martha Ingram has come to Italy to escape the psychological tyranny of her husband Gordon, a mysterious figure who appears in the novel only through the recollections, dreams, half perceptions and vague reports of Martha and a number of other characters. Gordon Ingram is an American scholar, a philosopher beloved of his friends, and a mentor to

Martha during the ten years of their marriage. Now divorced, Martha is afflicted with the guilty feeling that she has somehow betrayed him, that in refusing to live her life for him she is destroying him. More powerful than the guilt, however, is her fear that ultimately she will not be able to resist his menacing power.

Spencer's evocation of Gordon is strikingly like that of Dinnerstein's definition of the minotaur, and indeed he is depicted in imagery as the dragon who threatens Martha. She fears that he will "rise up out of the ground and snap at her," and imagines that she can hear him across the ocean "rumbling and growling, breathing out complaining letters and worried messengers" (3). George Hartwell, her employer at the U.S. cultural office, further verifies the image of Gordon, seeing in a photograph of him a "huge figure," with "gross hands," a "shaggy head, and big, awkwardly tilted feet" (4). Imagining the former husband as a dragon makes Martha even more fascinating to George, who is attracted by her vulnerability and the flattering prospect that he may rescue her from all that threatens her. To him, she is "sequestered" in an apartment that is reached by "devious stairways, corridors."

Martha does not see herself as some mythic or medieval lady, however, but rather as "someone, not unusual, who had, with the total and deep sincerity of youth, made a mistake; now, the mistake paid for, agonizingly paid for, the only question was of finding a workable compromise with life" (29–30). The novel opens to a breaking of Martha's emotional stalemate with the arrival of a group of Americans on cultural exchange. Among these are the young couple Rita and Jim Wilbourne, an economist who eventually does play the knight's role in the release of Martha from her past. To Jim, Martha seems aloof, distracted—"enclosed," he says. He upsets her carefully wrought equilibrium with a story about Gordon's having been in an accident, a story that proves to be false but fateful. It lures Martha into imagining Gordon's destruction—that is, the removal of his influence from her life. Risking hurt, even "madness," she reaches out to Jim, taking him as a lover, using the sexual energy, as well as the imaginative energy aroused by the story of Gordon's accident, to effect her "workable compromise with life."

The erstwhile knight, George Hartwell, recognizes Martha's growing sense of selfhood, and thus his own lost chance to "rescue" her. In a fit of nostalgic remembrance he thinks of his "long lost Missouri days," when women living in shady white houses had spirits "clear to transparency," serving as they did some "trembling cross old father or invalid brother or failure of a husband or marvellously distorted and deeply loved child," always moving with the "sureness of angels." Increasingly, Martha no longer fits George's idealized vision of womanhood, and it suddenly comes to him in his daydreams that "Martha Ingram did not, any longer, exist" (79).

During the course of this novel, Spencer shows Martha to be a woman who comes fully to recognize the danger of trying to live a life defined by old tales of "ladies," "knights," and "dragons." For example, she acknowledges the coercion implicit in the good-hearted Hartwells' protectiveness: "love of the innocent, protective sort which George and Grace Hartwell offered her and which she had in the past found so necessary and comforting seemed to her now somewhat like a risk, certainly an embarrassment, almost a sort of doom" (101–02). She also comes to see that the romantic escape with a dashing, willful knight is a delusion. The waning of Jim Wilbourne's knighthood is poignantly foreshadowed in a story Martha tells him on a weekend trip they take together to the seaside. She remembers hearing once of a French farmer who dug up an Aphrodite statue and, unable to decide finally what to do with it, simply reburied the love goddess. Jim is no less perplexed than the French farmer by all the unanswerable questions looming in his life and, ill suited to the Italian weather, coughs a reply to Martha. He longs for hearth, home, his nurturing wife. Martha, who has spent ten years as girl-wife-protege of Gordon, chooses not to spend her middle age as mother-wife-nurturer of anyone, save herself. In contrast to Jim, she comes to feel at home in Italy, with its energy, elegance and toughness—its self sufficiency.

By the end of the novel, Spencer has exposed vividly the illusion of knights and dragons: they depend for their lives on some lady's dependence. For Martha the price of intimacy is too great; she withdraws to a new enclosure of her own making. At work, the reports she writes for George Hartwell reflect her completeness—they are "smooth and crisp, brilliant, unblemished. . . . There was nothing to add, nothing to take away." To George, it is "sinister" (162). But to Martha, there is a great freeing from old complexities, a shedding of old obligations of feeling. Her twisted former self is like an intricate structure "no longer habitable." Martha may not thunder her "No," but her rejection of others' definitions of what she should do/feel/want/be is no less certain. Freed of her interior prison, she gains her niche in the world. "She more and more arranged to do things alone, a curious tendency, for loneliness once had been a torment, whereas now she regarded almost everything her eyes fell on with an equal sense of companionship; her compatibility was with the world" (168). Doubtless Martha Ingram might have found a more satisfying life in a world where men could be something other than knights and dragons—or minotaurs. One imagines companionship and intimacy to be more desirable than loneliness. But on the terms that are available to her in the world that is, she opts for the freed self. In the end, Martha resembles a survivor of Stephen Crane's "The Open Boat." The novel closes, "She was of those whom life had held a captive and in freeing herself she had met dissolution, and was a friend now to any landscape, a companion to cloud and sky" (169).

In her evocation of the delicate and often ambiguous shifts of feeling in the interior lives of her protagonists, Spencer has frequently drawn the censure as well as the praise of reviewers. Writing for the *New York Times Book Review* (11 July 1965), Arthur Mizener, for example, began his review of *Knights and Dragons* by praising it as "a beautiful book." But despite his admiration for Spencer's craftsmanship, he found her style "curiously elliptical," and her narrative to be "made up largely of metaphors and symbols for qualities of experience so generalized and so remote from action and conduct that it produces an effect at once allegorical and poetically obscure" (5). Although he does not speak of a distinctly "feminine style," his words sound like those of earlier critics writing of the "elliptical" style of Eudora Welty—or Virginia Woolf. Unquestionably, Spencer's fiction since the middle 1950s has turned inward to explore the inner drama of characters, mainly women, who struggle to find a "workable compromise" between self and the outside world. In her next two novels following *Knights and Dragons* and *Ship Island and Other Stories*, Spencer creates in Catherine Sasser and Julia Garrett two women who move further than her earlier heroines in achieving such a compromise. She tells their stories by utilizing the full range of her vigorous but richly poetical style.

Set in the "grey world" of the 1950s, *No Place for an Angel* portrays a broad canvas of characters and settings. The story begins in the summer of 1958 with the artist Barry Day and his friends Irene Waddell and her businessman husband Charles. Their relationship with one another and with Catherine and Jerry Sasser, a Texas attorney turned Washington, D.C. political operative, unfolds through a complex narrative, involving abrupt shifts of scene (from Washington to Florida to Dallas to Italy, and elsewhere) and of chronology (flashbacks within flashbacks zigzagging from 1958 back to the early days of the century and forward to the new frontier of the 1960s). All the characters confront in one way or another the threatened, demoralized world of the post-war era. The peril of the atomic bomb, as well as the sadness and cynicism brought on by the war, have exacerbated the pressures human beings have always felt to make some meaning, some sense of their lives. The Waddells respond to the bad times in a very traditional way, traditional especially for Americans, Spencer suggests. They do not seek transcendence of the corrupted world; they strike a peaceful coexistence by tailoring their desires to what one can reasonably expect in such a world: pleasures of the flesh (food, sex, flashy apartments, entertaining friends, exotic travel) and satisfaction of one's desire for immortality through handsome, successful children (twin sons who are "Greek perfection"). Barry Day, who dreamed for years of being a sculptor and went to Italy to try to realize his dream in the sculpting of an angel, at last wearies of complexities and conflicts. He meets a young woman at Macy's, marries her and commences an invisible American life.

The most radical accommodation to the tainted world is that of Jerry Sasser, who comes home after the war irrevocably changed from the hopeful, eager young man he had been. Catherine fantasizes that somehow an imposter must have exchanged places with Jerry; no other explanation will satisfy the puzzle of his acquiescence to evil. At the end of the novel the reader sees a middle-aged man who is barely holding himself together. Whether his childhood with a religiously fanatical father, his war experiences, or his disillusionment with government has caused him to reject the possibility of goodness, one is uncertain. What is clear is that Jerry's terror and rejection of life are absolutely antithetical to Catherine's outlook.

Catherine Sasser, the central figure in the main cast of five, is a woman who makes a long journey from the innocence of a protected, happy childhood in a little Texas town and the hopeful naivete of the young woman-bride-mother to a disillusioning break with her husband. In the end she comes to make a modest but satisfying existence for herself "in a small Massachusetts town strong enough and old enough to envelop her" (253). Throughout her life Catherine holds to a vision of generosity and goodness, an ideal of spiritual transcendence that raises life above the material world—something other than the value-given-for-value-gotten mentality of Jerry. Through flashbacks we see her struggle to reconcile her desire for wholeness, for living what she believes, with Jerry's unrelenting pragmatism. He shapes his beliefs and actions to whatever "image" is called for; he is unfaithful; he lies and defrauds; he is, as Catherine finally admits, a man who has lost the power of human sympathy. She cannot live with him after the war, though for a time she tries. The consequence for her is madness. Like some premonition of Martha Mitchell in the latter Nixon days, Catherine has "truth serum phases" in which she speaks the unvarnished, horrifying truth to the people around her—in one instance, at a political gathering for Jerry's employer, a U.S. senator from Texas. Jerry takes her to Denver for psychological treatment, but as readily takes her out when political images must be served. Catherine's rejection of an irrational, purposeless world is, of course, the sure indication of her sanity. Even Jerry acknowledges that "if life were made up one percent of decencies, one percent of decent attitudes and right answers and good generous things to know, Catherine would never fail to understand it. It was when even that one percent was gone and not to be found that she went crazy—or crazy was what the psychiatrists were trying to say by calling it a lot of other names" (282).

It is highly ironic that such a modest expectation of decency should be viewed as "angelic." Catherine is certainly no angel, at least according to the old tradition, and Spencer goes to pains to show that she's no saint or goddess. But by contrast to the others, she is the lone exception who, Antigone-like, refuses to live under the new dispensation. "She would literally go mad rather than give up her unity" (277). Thus she divorces Jerry and renounces his world of "power." Though "angels don't belong in America," as Irene Waddell tells Barry Day on the first page of the novel, Catherine finds a spot that does recall a time when the spiritual life at least kept pace with the material—the Puritan beginning of the republic. Visited by Jerry at the end of the novel, "she was lying in a glider in late summer on the side porch of her New England house, sun on her face, hair catching the sun, freckles, no make-up, broken nails from gardening,

reading in a grey wool skirt and white blouse" (303–04). Her New England life includes her crippled son Latham, who lives nearby, pursuing
his love of nature as a biologist, and even the memory of her life with
Jerry, for she cannot expunge the lines of attachment, pity and love that
link her to him. In fact, "a thousand threads of interest and mutual sympathy, generosity, even emotion," unite her to the town and life she has
chosen. Nonetheless, Catherine is essentially alone. Like Martha Ingram
in *Knights and Dragons*, she accepts separateness as a condition for
achieving an integrated self. No angel, she accepts her human condition,
but she does so on her own terms. She will have wholeness and sanity,
decency and sympathy, even if it means living with lonely hope and
suffering.

The central figures of "Ship Island," *Knights and Dragons*, and *No
Place for an Angel* all illustrate to some degree Josephine Hendin's comment that the contemporary heroine's desire to change her life is "reactive, caused by disillusionment rather than conviction or ideology" (222).
The protagonists in these three works start out with very traditional expectations that success and happiness in life will come when they are
"chosen" by some version of prince charming, but inevitably they find
that princehood can become an oppressive power threatening one's separate identity. Julia Garrett of *The Snare*, however, presents a somewhat
different case. From the time when she comes as a child to live with her
mother's sister Isabel Devigny and her husband Maurice in New Orleans,
Julia grows up demanding more of life than the straight world of polite
society offers. In the musician Jake Springland, she finds and choses a
man who is rather like a prince of darkness. In fact, in her readiness to
explore the demonic world, the "human swamp," she resembles Jerry
Sasser rather than Catherine. Nonetheless, the Julia who opens the
novel, like Catherine, is a woman who seeks identity in her relationship
with another.

With an intricate plot and complex form that go beyond *No Place for an
Angel* in portraying the interior lives of a large cast of characters, *The
Snare* is Spencer's most ambitious literary effort and her most important
work to date. A novel of compelling symbolic power, it has a richness of
theme and technique that can only be suggested in any brief discussion of
it. Central to the novel's design is Julia's quest to experience life immediately and sensually, as befitting the vision of life passed on to her by
Maurice's father, Henri Devigny. "Old Dev," a lover of Baudelaire, a

massive dark figure who shared an Audubon Place mansion with his son and daughter-in-law, initiated Julia into the human swamp. As Julia tells her friend, the *Times-Picayune* reporter Tommy Arnold, "That's what he got me used to. If there's no way out you have to live it" (78). Rather clearly, Dev's sensuous and sexual appetites ensnared the child Julia. Both mentor and minotaur (gross body, shaggy head, lustful and power- ful), Dev is Julia's spiritual father, her natural father having abandoned her to the Devignys upon her mother's death. No wonder she grows to womanhood contemptuous of the New Orleans boys, tied as they are "to a smaller statement of life than what she wanted made to her" (97).

The novel opens *in medias res,* with Julia explaining to Tommy Arnold how she came to be involved with an accused murderer, Jake Springland. With numerous flashbacks filling in Julia's immediate and distant past, the story spirals forward. Julia has long led a double life, in her youth as a protege of the dark Dev and the genteel Isabel and Maurice, later as the respectable Tulane graduate, fiancee of wealthy Mississippian Martin Parham, until she breaks the engagement and moves to a small rundown apartment. She then takes a job with an optometrist and commences an affair with Springland, who eventually leads her into the underworld of drugs and violence. It is in the doctor's office one winter day that Jake appears incongruously with two strange misfits named Ted Marnie and Wilma Wharton. The mysterious Marnie is part hoodlum, part messiah— a "soul engineer" to Wilma and Jake. Through the bizarre machinations of Marnie, Jake is falsely accused of murdering him, though he is acquitted in a trial that brings him and Julia back together several months after their earlier encounter.

Jake represents for Julia the "something more" that she longs for be- yond the vapid facade of polite society, Dev having cultivated in her an affinity for the murky, mysterious depths of life. She is deliberate in her movement away from conventionality and security, unlike, for example, Faulkner's Temple Drake, whose descent into the underworld is essen- tially passive. Julia's idea is that "people draw life from the crooked world. There's a conversation going on with the straight world, all the time" (110). Jake provides Julia's access to this vital other world, a world she has always sensed as peculiarly embodied by New Orleans, with its black magic and jazz and swampy terrain. "To Julia, Jake had caught the city's rough corruption with its core of feeling, its peculiar tolerant knowl- edge. She had circled it for years, but now an outsider had come to discover it, claim it, experience it and give it to her whole" (118–119). She is an "orphan girl in a voodoo city," a mermaid searching for a habitable depth.

Drawn to Julia and the Marnie case, the reporter Tommy Arnold senses that to the rest of the country New Orleans represents a vital core of mysterious being. "New Orleans was the nation's true pulse beat, but the nation did not know it," he thinks. "Voodoo, jazz, sex, and food—who could go further than that toward what was really important to people in the U.S. and A." (81–82).

For a time Julia thrives on life with Jake in New Orleans, finding a joyous intimacy with her lover and exhilaration in the sense of communion she discovers among Jake and his fellow musicians. But at last, even flowers of evil fade. The Baudelairean vision of sensuality that Henri Devigny had bequeathed to Julia dims for a number of very human reasons. Ultimately, Julia cannot abandon her thinking self in the relationship with Jake. When she no longer reflects him in an image twice his natural size (to recall Virginia Woolf), he accuses her of "destroying" him. "He could make her give up everything to him but the thing that mattered most—and that was the knowledge that he knew she had, no matter what illusion he decided to believe in, that he wasn't great, that he wasn't going to get where he wanted to go" (147). Months later the reappearance of Ted Marnie and Wilma finally delivers Julia from her obsession with evil. Kidnapped, drugged, defiled in body and spirit, she dispels any lingering illusions she has about the low life. She comes to discover, as Jake says, that she wasn't "any worse than the rest."

At the end of the novel, Julia frees herself from the crooked world not so much because it is revolting and disillusioning, however, but because she is pulled by pregnancy into the ongoing, organic life of renewal. Her son, fathered by Jake, brings her into the everyday world of ordinary people, where she makes a modest life for herself and the baby. They live in a spare apartment, visited sometimes by Tommy Arnold, whom Julia refuses to marry—"by refusing marriage," Arnold thinks, "she was stopping his authority" (375). In the end, "fatherless and husbandless, she went about the world" (400).

Julia Garrett and Catherine Sasser represent women who start from two different poles of experience, the one with a deep wariness and cynicism, the other with optimism and idealism. In both novels the heroines come to a deeper knowledge and acceptance of the human condition because they are seekers, and because they are finally willing to accept separateness as the necessary condition for one's search. A striking contrast to these women is shown near the end of *The Snare*, when Isabel Devigny describes the sheltered life she had led: "I have life through you . . . that's all. For myself I'm like a piece of china, and I've existed where I was placed to exist. I've no reality, Maurice. And it's too late" (394). Whatever else Julia and Catherine may have sacrificed, they hold on to their undeniable reality.

Over the past twenty years, Elizabeth Spencer has created a memorable gallery of strong women, heroines who experience many of the strains between inner needs and outer demands that form the consciousness of contemporary women. With the exception of Martha Ingram in *Knights and Dragons*, Spencer portrays these women as native Southerners, although their stories are not tied to the culture of the South as her first three novels were. Indeed their stories involve spiritual and physical dislocation. What Spencer's heroines do not have and yearn for is a sense of place, a habitation that does not suffocate or dehumanize them. With an extraordinary richness and subtlety of technique, Spencer gives us characters who make demands of life, and in so doing accept the separateness that comes with self assertion. In the course of their lives, these women discover the cost and value of freedom. They learn that the price of autonomy is just as Lillian Hellman describes it in *The Unfinished Woman*—those who are willing to take the punishment are halfway through the battle. To the credit of her broad vision, Elizabeth Spencer does not underestimate either the punishment or the battle.

NOTES

[1] During the typesetting of this article, I read advance proofs of Elizabeth Spencer's latest novel, *The Salt Line*, published by Doubleday in 1984. Its central male protagonist and Mississippi setting mark a turn from Spencer's fiction since 1956, but in theme and technique the new novel is nearer Spencer's later fiction than to the earlier Mississippi novels.

[2] Josephine Hendin, *Vulnerable People: A View of American Fiction Since 1945* (New York: Oxford Univ. Press, 1978), 222.

[3] Rachel M. Brownstein, *Becoming a Heroine: Reading About Women in Novels* (New York: Viking Press, 1982), xix.

[4] Dorothy Dinnerstein, *The Mermaid and the Minotaur* (1976; rpt. New York: Harper Colophon, 1977), 4–5.

Mary Lee Settle's Connections:
Class and Clothes in the Beulah Quintet

NANCY CAROL JOYNER

Her literary ancestor is William Faulkner; her Yoknapatawpha is Beulah Valley, West Virginia. She tacitly acknowledges her debt to Faulkner by using his words as the epigraph for her most recent novel, *The Killing Ground:* "We are fighting, as always, the long battalioned ghosts of old wrongs and shames that each generation of us both inherits and creates." Through nine of Mary Lee Settle's ten novels, she has recorded the wrongs and shames and the battles against them in her little postage stamp of the world, which in her case is situated on two continents and spans three centuries.

Her most sustained work is what is now called the Beulah Quintet, which began in 1956 with a single novel, *O Beulah Land.*[1] The book takes place in Virginia between 1754 and 1774, dramatically recreating General Braddock's defeat in 1755 and introducing the early English and Scotch settlers. Hannah and Jeremiah Catlett, Jonathan and Sally Lacey, and Solomon McKarkle are among the most prominent of the characters whose descendants are to reappear in later volumes. *Know Nothing*, published in 1960, covers the years 1831–61, when Peregrine Catlett, grandson of both the Laceys and the Catletts of the earlier work, is master of Beulah and master of many slaves. His two sons, Jonathan and Lewis, enlist in opposing armies when the Civil War begins. *Fight Night on a Sweet Saturday*, published in 1964, originally constituted the concluding volume of "The Beulah Trilogy." Set in 1960, it records the family's reaction to the death of Johnny McKarkle, who is killed during a brawl in a jail cell by his cousin, Jake Catlett. Shortly after the presumed completion of the series, Settle explained to interviewer, Roger Shattuck, "I saw that the trilogy had not yet done what I wanted it to do. A whole part of our being American was missing, our revolutionary sense." She then pub-

Mary Lee Settle

Born in West Virginia (1918), Settle attended Sweet Briar College in Virginia. Her first novel, The Love Eaters, was published in London and New York in 1954. She is the author of ten other books, including Blood Tie which won the National Book Award.

lished *Prisons* in 1973, a novel set in seventeenth century England, in
which the narrator, Jonathan Church, is executed by Cromwell in 1649.
At age 16 Johnny Church has fathered an illegitimate child named
Jonathan Lacy, by implication the ancestor to the Virginia pioneer. In
1980 *Scapegoat* appeared, a novel involving a coalminers' strike at Beulah
in 1912. The owner of the mine, Beverly Lacey, is opposed by his cousin,
Jake Catlett, one of the miners. *The Killing Ground*, published in 1982,
might be called the sixth volume of the quintet, for it is a revision and
expansion of *Fight Night on a Sweet Saturday*. Taken as a whole, the
series is elaborately detailed, carefully constructed, and extremely complex in its connections.

Settle's saga does not end with the Beulah Quintet, however, for three
of her four other novels are set in Canona, West Virginia (presumably
Charleston), as is *The Killing Ground*, thus making a lateral connection
among those books. *The Kiss of Kin* (1955) takes place in a house close to
the Canona River, and two other novels, *The Love Eaters* (1954) and *The
Clam Shell* (1971), are set in the town of Canona and include many of the
same characters that appear in *The Killing Ground*, such as the Dodds,
the Potters, the Slingsbys, and Charlie Bland. With a single exception,
Blood Tie (1977), set almost exclusively in Turkey (and, somewhat ironically, her single winner of the National Book Award), Mary Lee Settle has
spent most of her career of nearly thirty years in creating her Canona
Saga.[2]

Critical response to Settle's work has not reflected her downright awe-
some accomplishment. Generally favorable reviews for each of her ten
novels have appeared in American and British publications, but despite
positive reactions to her individual volumes, Settle's literary reputation
remains obscure, and scholarly attention to her work has been conspicu-
ously and mysteriously absent.

George Garrett has suggested that one reason for this lack of recognition is that she has had bad luck with publishers.[3] Viking Press, who
brought out the first three Beulah books, refused to market them as a
trilogy and insisted on the cuts in *Fight Night on a Sweet Saturday* that
prompted her to revise it in 1982 and bring it out under a new title—and
a new imprint: Farrar, Straus, Giroux. Furthermore, *Scapegoat*, which
was published by Random House two years after she received the National Book Award, received more featured book reviews than her earlier

books, but the publisher nevertheless chose not to advertise it beyond two lines in trade ads, without even a mention of her recent prestigious award.[4]

Critical attention is, however, gradually burgeoning. Both Roger Shattuck and Granville Hicks have written introductions for the Ballantine editions of the Beulah series.[5] (Coincidentally, Hicks, in the first critical overview of Settle's work, reports that her novels were brought to his attention by Malcolm Cowley, the man whose critical edition of Faulkner's work, in the Viking Portable edition of 1946, helped to rescue the novelist from obscurity.) George Garrett has championed her cause in more than one publication, but essays that do something other than provide a general introduction to her work or assess individual volumes are rare.[6]

In fact, a minor backlash appears to have occurred before there was much of a forward motion in criticism of the Beulah Quintet. When *The Killing Ground* appeared in the summer of 1982, Aaron Latham went on record on the front page of the *New York Times Book Review* to say he found Settle's powers diminishing over the last twenty years and feared he would find "a stripped mine" in her latest book, only to discover "ore worth mining." Nonetheless, he thought Settle could profitably "remove the slag" from the five novels in the series and compress them into a single volume ("The End" 21). In a recent article in the *Appalachian Journal* on the Quintet, William J. Schafer announces at the outset that he sees Settle as "an ambitious, accomplished, and impressive writer" (78) but goes on to compare her technique pejoratively with that of E. M. Forster, Stephen Crane, and Tolstoy, and concludes that she lacks a panoramic view of history. Commonly one sees such negative criticism in response to inflated praise or extreme popularity, two literary situations that Settle has never enjoyed. Surely her work merits more critical analyses than it has so far received.

The critics who have dealt with the Beulah Quintet inevitably attempt to find common threads within the five novels that link them to one another. Even Schafer, after he has examined the series and found it wanting, identifies four such threads: recurring prison imagery, the presence of war, "the inextricable complexities of family structure," and changes in the land (84–85). While these elements are not in each novel, they occur in four of the five and are legitimate linking devices. But these four categories are not exhaustive; other linking elements occur. The Biblical source for the name Beulah (Isaiah 62:4) or a quotation from the nineteenth century hymn "O Beulah Land" appears in each of the five novels. Classical allusion, such as the Narcissus myth, abounds throughout, with particularly heavy emphasis on the Antigone legend, which Settle told an interviewer was the controlling myth for the series (Shattuck 44). At least one prominent historical figure appears in each of the novels, from Oliver Cromwell to J. F. Kennedy. Some objects that are first discussed in *O Beulah Land*, a silver handle of a riding crop and a deep red stone found by Hannah Bridewell in the wilderness and variously referred to as a ruby and a garnet, are traced through subsequent novels until they are held as family heirlooms in *The Killing Ground*. Aside from the requisite family connections in the five Beulah novels, then, Settle consciously and conscientiously has included many other kinds of links in the series.

Settle uses these linking devices to reinforce one of her major themes in the Quintet, class consciousness and the resultant conflict such awareness engenders. She does this through a cluster of images relating to dress and the decoration of houses, as well as through statements concerning status and wealth. Because critics have heretofore tended to ignore this particular set of connections, an examination of some of the instances in which these images and attitudes are present should be useful in determining the quality of Settle's art.

In *Prisons* Johnny Church's earliest memory is of the Christmas of 1634, when he goes to visit the estate of his Royalist uncle, Valentine Lacy. His mother dresses him in a black velvet suit to indicate his family's Puritan predilections. The five year old Johnny is especially impressed with the yule log and the silver punch bowl from which he is offered a drink of wassail. When Sir Valentine pays attention to the "Little preacher," Johnny reports "I sat upon his lap and saw, for the first time, my new black clothes against the soft white satin sash he wore" (24). The distinctions between the two adjoining estates are more profound than habits of dress, of course, but the description of dress symbolizes those differences in religious belief, political affiliation, and social prominence. Johnny studies with his cousin Peregrine's tutor until they both go to Oxford, an exhilarating experience. Johnny says of it:

What comes back first to me from Oxford, why, it makes me laugh to think it—
that I longed for an ostrich plume to put into my hat! They cost a year's living
for honest men and were smuggled over for the court all the way from France.
The lordly boys from Lauds and Magdalen flaunted them, though some of them
were so poor they had to go to their beds until their shirts were washed. (59)

When Johnny argues with his father and goes off to fight in the Civil War
with Cromwell, he stops by Lacy House, where he has an illicit tryst with
his aunt. She asks to see what provisions he has for his journey, and they
have the following conversation:

> "No money. . . . These saints that make themselves God in their houses and
> will not let their children free. Now hark it, my Johnny, money is freedom."
> "Freedom's more than that." I did not like to hear such words from her lips.
> "Aie, money's the oil of it, though." (70–71)

Because *Prisons* is primarily about Johnny at war, relatively little is mentioned about clothes, decoration of houses, or money. Nevertheless, the
themes are included.

Class distinctions are more domestically presented in *O Beulah Land.*
Hannah Bridewell, a convicted thief transported from London, is found
after wandering in the wilderness for forty days following her escape from
the Indians. Her benefactor is Jeremiah Catlett, an indentured servant
who had run away into the wilderness after having found religion and
having escaped his master. When he stumbles upon the unconscious
Hannah he first notes "a gray shred of linsey" and sees the "ludicrous
remains of her clothing" (28). He takes her home to his small, one-
roomed, dirt-floored hut, dominated by a rock fireplace on one end and
his hog, Hagar, on the other. The clothes he first provides the woman
who eventually becomes his wife consist of deer skins and a panther fur.

In sharp contrast to the Catletts are the founders of the Beulah community, Jonathan and Sally Lacey, who have moved there from the eastern
shore of Virginia. When Jonathan brings Sally to the house he has built for
her, the arduous trip is marked chiefly by the accident in which all but
one of her "blue and white Cheeny plates, all sent from England," are
lost (210). The remaining plate becomes a symbol for prosperity and
culture thereafter, being displayed on the chimney ledge. When Sally
invites the other women in for hot chocolate (which none knows how to
drink), she allows each to hold the plate briefly and tells them that once
she had five others:

"Ye niver had six of thim!" Mary Martha was shocked.
"I did too. I'll swear." Sal was firm.
"Well, I'll be a cockeyed son of a bitch." Maggie Cutwright's sister-in-law . . .
passed her leathery finger over and over the plate's surface. (227)

Jonathan is dismayed beyond anger at Sally's behavior and tries to
explain her new position in life: "Now listen to me, ye poor leetle gel.
There's a mighty lot ye've got to leave behind ye, over the mountains. . . .
Tomorrow morning ye're goin to take a hoe over your shoulder, and ye're
goin down to the stockade field and ye're goin to work all day like a
Negrew to show ye're one with the rest of us" (223). The other women,
however, save her from that fate, for they convince Jonathan that her
hands are far too delicate for such strenuous work. Thus we see that in the
frontier society members of the lower class actively maintain class distinctions.

Because Jonathan's land holdings exceed those of his neighbors, he is
considered the wealthiest and most powerful of the settlers, and Sally
rigidly maintains her position as the society leader in the community she
insists upon calling "Cicero" instead of Beulah. She is so unsatisfied with
her house, the finest in the settlement, that she encourages everyone who
passes by the river bank to bring home one rock so the outside might
eventually boast a stone veneer. When her daughter marries beneath
her, as inevitably she must, Sally is unable to cope with the strain. On the
day of the wedding she tells her husband, "All them Cohees, common as
dirt, entertained like they was quality. To think a daughter of mine should
fetch up with such dirt as that" (299). One reason for her dismay is that the
groom, Ezekial Catlett, comes dressed for his wedding in a buckskin
outfit Hannah has made for him "that had taken nearly the winter to make
fine enough" (295). In the description of the wedding, then, Settle dramatically presents the conflicting social norms present in the frontier
society.

Sally, with all her airs, is presented as a comic figure, made ironic in
light of the Laceys' actual financial and social background. As Jonathan
explains to a friend, "I sometimes think I done her a great wrong, bringin
her from what she was used to. But there was nothin there—there was
nothin left for us. I've made here what she wanted, but she don't see
it" (303). Earlier in the novel there are indications that Sally's family had
lost its social and financial status. When she goes west with her husband

she apparently does so because she has nothing left of the comfortable situation in which she grew up except a few household furnishings—and two slaves.

In *Know Nothing*, the novel that begins in the 1830s, slaves play an important role, as do the Catletts, the current first family of Beulah. In the first scene another Sally Lacey, from the eastern branch but in financial straits, is on her way to see her western cousins. Her husband, Brandon Lacey, calls them their "backwoods Catlett kin" but Sally admonishes him: "they are Virginians even if they are transmontane" (13). When they arrive they admire the new three story brick house and the furnishings in the parlor—the red plush sofa, the table with the velvet covering whose fringe lay "gracefully abandoned on the flowered carpet, like a woman's skirts" (57). Sally is gushingly enthusiastic: "Oh Brandon! . . . *Le dernier cri!* They've got flock paper! Why can't we have it? . . . oh, our little old furniture we've just had for generations!" (58). The backwoods kin are as conscious of fashion as their Tidewater relatives, and, by the mid-nineteenth century, their position as members of the upper class has become as substantial as the Victorian elegance of their house.

Know Nothing might be considered a sort of Appalachian *Gone With the Wind*, with its deliberately romantic scenes of match-making and sociability. The middle and longest section of the book is set primarily at Egeria Springs, where the family vacations in hopes of finding suitable husbands for the marriageable girls. On the day the trip begins, Peregrine stops his horse to watch them: "Far way down the path toward the carriage, the three bell-shaped women swayed, the heads of the girls up and expectant, as if in the first excitement of going they were practicing their gliding strut, working out like two fillies down the course of the walk" (127).

Proper clothes and wearing clothes properly play an important part at Egeria Springs. Sally Lacey is there, for instance, passing judgment on visitors from other sections. The South Carolinians, she whispers, "wear their *rings* at *breakfast*," a sin she considers not so heinous as that of the Northerners, who wear silk then (143). Melinda is sent off to practice wearing a hoop before she is allowed to do so in public, but the girl has her own ideas about proper apparel. In one scene she is frantically cutting off the ruffles from the top of her dress and having her slave sew them on her petticoat: "She closed her eyes and tried to recall the exact shape of the Northern ladies' Paris dresses, how they looked like they had risen out of clear water and not like a big gob of soapsuds" (166). She is accused of looking "half-naked" (169) when she appears dressed to go to the ball, in sharp contrast to her cousin Lydia, who wears "a tent of sprigged, tucked, starched, faintly pink mousseline from Cincinnati, for all the world . . . like a little grown-up poor lamb for the slaughter" (167).

But it is Melinda in her outlandish outfit who succeeds in making the most financially advantageous match. The need for money to maintain the life style of these upper class Catletts and Laceys is an important motif of *Know Nothing.* Peregrine Catlett is reduced to selling some of his slaves because of his financial difficulties, and Brandon Lacey, in dire straits, presumably commits suicide: he "took the only way out a gentleman could take under the circumstances, gone through with everything, even his people and Sally's jewels knocked down to his creditors" (142). Sally is desperate to make a good match for her regrettably plain daughter and does her best to train her properly. At one point she says, "Don't talk about money, Sara. It ain't genteel. My stars, nobody talks about money but Yankees" (153). Sara, "having heard her mother talk about nothing else since her father's death," does not demur (153). In *Know Nothing,* the false gentility of the women reflects the increasingly frantic attempts to disguise a weakening economy.

While the Catletts and the Laceys are on more or less equal footing in society in *Know Nothing,* such is not the case in Settle's post-Civil War novel, *The Scapegoat,* for in 1912 Jake Catlett, Peregrine's grandson, lives west of Beulah at Lacey Creek, where he is employed by his distant cousin, Beverly Lacey, owner of the Seven Stars Coal Mine. On the same day that Beverly entertains men who have come in their private train to discuss the threat of unionization, Jake entertains Mother Jones, who has come by coach to help organize. Jake's wife, Essie, is the Laceys' cook, for Ann Eldridge Lacey will have none of the black Laceys inside her house. Although the house is not described in detail, the reader knows that it is sufficiently elegant to boast a tower room ("Mother calls the cupola her sanctum sanctorum," Mary Rose tells us; "it's where she takes her naps," 21); a library with a large plaster copy of Victory of Samothrace; a wine cellar (which Beverly will allow no one but himself to enter because he doesn't want anybody to see how poorly stocked it is); and a large front porch. Of particular interest when the book opens is the Gatling gun that has just been installed on the porch. Jake's house, in contrast, is actually the cabin his father Lewis built on property he claimed through squatter's rights. The furniture is cast-off from the Lacey house. When the novel opens, a tent city has been established in his front yard, a refuge for coal miners who have been evicted.

Clothes in this novel are important symbols of status. Essie wears her hat instead of her poke bonnet every day when she goes to the Laceys "to help out" because "it showed every one of them that she wasn't no servant" (48). The men who have been brought in to guard the mine dress in black, as does Mother Jones.[7] In contrast, Beverly Lacey has taken to wearing an old ill-fitting white suit, because "it made him feel rich again" (27). His daughters were also in white. The middle daughter, Althea, reports "Papa insisted, by the calendar, that his girls greet the May, as he called it, in white dresses. He made a little ceremony out of it" (145). When the eldest daughter, Lily, leaves suddenly for New York, her mother gives her the dress she had been saving for her birthday: "Look at your new dress. Crepe de chine, with gold fringe. It's all the rage. *Vogue* says so. . . . You might have need of it. Besides, you have to look rich. It's a great protection in this world" (244). Many other references to clothes appear in the novel, but these examples should be sufficient to show the variety of symbolic purposes with which choice of dress is imbued. The preceding brief examples, however, do not do justice to Settle's stylistic mastery in description of clothes. The following passage illustrates her ability to create a complex of moods while she is indicating another set of symbols emanating from the description. Althea, the most iconoclastic of the daughters, remembers the events in 1912 from the vantage point of a day in 1927:

> Oh I was the loveliest thing when I was a girl. Mother had bought me a hat in the Via Condotti in Rome. It was the loveliest thing you ever saw and it cost the earth, pale gray clouds of georgette with pink rosebuds faint behind them. I can still smell that smell of a costly hat before the Great War, smell of tissue paper, silk, and straw and hear the sound of the weightless lifting of it, a rustle and a falling breeze of tissue paper, and it had no weight at all and I moored it to my head with my best hatpin, filigreed gold, oh absolutely lovely, and I sallied out to meet my dear one who had followed us all the way from Lausanne. We were madly in love.
>
> Shit. I don't even remember his name. But I do remember the black trees,

and the old, old shade, and I remember the hat, perched on the grass like a gray dove and I lost my cherry in the Borghese Gardens. (150)

In this case the hat does much more than indicate class consciousness; it symbolizes Althea's lost youth, lost wealth, and lost innocence.

Althea figures prominently in the final volume of the Quintet, for, as Hannah McKarkle's oldest living relative, she is one of the agents by which the protagonist searches for the secrets of her family's past which will help her discover her own identity, the principal theme of *The Killing Ground.* The most experimental of all of Settle's books, this one presents the fictitious Hannah, twelve years younger than Settle herself, as the author of the other Beulah novels. The book begins in 1978, when the distinguished author, Hannah, returns to her home town to deliver a speech. While she is lecturing news of Charlie Bland's suicide reaches the audience, and when Hannah hears of it she is vividly reminded of the accidental death of her brother Johnny, which brought her back to Canona in 1960. She retraces the events surrounding his death and her search for her own roots at the time (the subject of *Fight Night on a Sweet Saturday,* the original fifth volume of the Quintet that *The Killing Ground* supercedes). The book ends with an epilogue, set in 1980, when Hannah returns for her Aunt Althea's funeral and finally straightens out the tangled threads of her background—Hannah's connections with the past.

In Hannah's search she visits many houses that were important to her. She remembers, as a child, sneaking into the abandoned Neill house in Beulah, where her mother had grown up; as an adult she visits the house again, now restored by strangers, whose excessive use of the strawberry motif in the kitchen makes her cry. She returns to the high mountains of her father's home place, a farm operated by her Uncle Ephraim McKarkle, the place where she feels, more than any other, "the sense of ensconcement, of taproots down" (127). She visits her cousin, Jake Catlett, to tell him his son Jake is in jail on a manslaughter charge for killing her brother Johnny: "The Catletts' cabin squatted at the side of the dirt road beyond an orchard and the long neat furrows of the fall garden. A pickup truck jutted halfway out of a corrugated-iron shack. . . . Neatly in front of the house two old tires from the truck had been whitewashed and filled with geraniums" (280). In Canona she sees "the identical Tudor houses that Hannah's parents and her sister Melinda had built" (48) in the area, new in 1939, where English houses had sprung up "like expensive mushrooms" (183). The houses of Hannah's past are impressively diverse in style and social prominence.

As in the earlier novels, clothes play a significant role, but in *The Killing Ground* the emphasis is on the dress of the upper class. Hannah remembers Johnny in his rented morning suit at their sister's wedding, in his black tails during the first grown-up dance she attends, in the habitual white dinner jacket for the boring dances at the country club. She remembers her own exaltation and dismay when she wore her white organdy for Melinda's wedding and the green taffeta with the torn ruffles at her first dance.

All of the McKarkles dress properly. Melinda worries that the black outfit she has to wear to the funeral might be inappropriate, since it is a designer dress. She borrows for Hannah a black dress "with a small waist and a big acceptable Republican skirt" (259). Hannah recalls that she had on a stylish scarlet shift on the day Johnny died: "I see a slight, thin, easy-striding girl . . . among the women in the last little waists and big skirts of the Eisenhower years, and I smooth my smooth hair with the checking, secretive dandyism we were trained to have" (243). When she returns in 1978 she is conscious of wearing "a linen dress that cost a hundred dollars" (93).

But it is money—the awareness of having it, of having had it and lost it—that most informs the book. When the women of Hannah's country club set take her to her lecture in the essential luxury of a Cadillac Seville, one of the women thinks, "there was . . . nearly ten million dollars riding in the car, and a fat lot of good it did any of them" (23). Hannah herself grew up in an affluent household, untroubled by money or the lack of it, but her mother, having come from a family in which the fortune was lost, is overly conscious of both possessions and appearances. At one point Althea reminisces about her sister-in-law, Hannah's mother:

> "My God, I thought those girls, Sally Brandon and your Aunt Annie Neill from Beulah, were the goddamned cat's pajamas. . . . How was I to know they'd tripped and fallen lower than we ever did and that it was all pride and one-dress poorhouse Tory? Your mother never did know except with her mind . . . that they were poor. Broke we were, poor we were not she used to say like that kind of fooling people was something to take pride in." (72–73)

Sally Brandon, for her part, has never recovered from her father's losing their property in Beulah. Once she tells Hannah: "We were haunted by money. Money money money! The drains said money, don't run out of money. Money makes the mare go, don't marry for money but marry where money is; pride and patches and no money. That's what I lived with. I would climb up the pear tree and think about money when I wanted to be thinking of higher things" (121).

This fixation with money and the position it confers is partially responsible for making Sally Brandon McKarkle, as Gail Godwin calls her in *New Republic,* "a monster of Southern respectability" (31). She is that and more, for, when Hannah refuses to come back to Canona to fill the vacuum left by Johnny's death, Sally disinherits her.

When Sally McKarkle wonders to Hannah "Do you think . . . they'll put it in the paper? All that business about Jake Catlett being a distant relative? After all, everybody has a less fortunate branch of the family . . ." (337), and when she later snubs Jake Catlett at Johnny's funeral, she is echoing the behavior of the Sally Laceys of *O Beulah Land* and *Know Nothing.* In doing so she confirms Hannah's thoughts about her own disinheritance: "I would, through the years, have a genetic inheritance more powerful than money; slave, slave owner, slave in turn. I would trace the tap of my mother's bare foot back to poor little genteel Sal who carried with her over the mountains, imitation of an oppressor she did not know, a camouflage" (340). Hannah also realizes that she has inherited an impulse to rebel as well as the impulse to conform. But, she goes on to say, "most of all I would carry that itch for balance between them, a quality that quarrels with itself, poised between democrat and slave owner" (340).

The Killing Ground represents a deliberate attempt to connect the Beulah Quintet, to make coherent the diverse styles and stories of the other novels. Because the book is a gloss on the other novels, it is impossible to appreciate without having read the entire series. And because the final novel explicitly states the comprehensive theme and draws connections among the preceding books, it is at times unfortunately self-conscious and redundant, especially in light of the connections of images, of which dress and decoration of houses are only two of many; and implicit themes, of which attitudes about money, class consciousness and family connections are only three of many, are already present. Nevertheless, the Beulah Quintet is a stunning achievement. With it, Mary Lee Settle has made a major contribution to American fiction.

NOTES

[1] Page references in text for *O Beulah Land* (1956) and *Know Nothing* (1960) are to the 1981 Ballantine editions.

[2] Settle has also written several short stories and journal articles, as well as two non-fiction works: *All the Brave Promises* (1966), a memoir of her experiences with the WAAF in 1942, and *The Scopes Trial* (c. 1972).

[3] See "Mary Lee Settle," *Dictionary of Literary Biography: American Novelists Since World War II*. Second Series (1980).

[4] See "Settle may write 'Gone with Wind' sequel," *The Charleston Gazette,* 24 Jan. 1981, 11. (This article refers to an interview by Cynthia Amorese in the January 1981, issue of *Commonwealth: the Magazine of Virginia.*)

[5] The introduction by Granville Hicks is in the Ballantine edition of the Beulah Trilogy, published in 1965. When the edition of the Beulah Quintet appeared in 1981, the introduction by Hicks was replaced by an introduction by Roger Shattuck.

[6] Other appreciative articles by George Garrett have appeared in *Rediscoveries,* ed. David Madden, 171–78, and in *Blue Ridge Review,* 1 (1978), 18–24.

[7] According to an interview, the description of Mother Jones is accurate, based on an eye-witness account by Settle's mother: Mother Jones, who "looked like Queen Victoria. . . , had been a seamstress who cared about her clothes. She dressed in black bombazine, with a little lace at her throat." (Taormina, "On Time with Mary Lee Settle," 14–15.)

The Androgynous, Bi-racial Vision of Berry Morgan

MARGARET JONES BOLSTERLI

Writers are such prisoners of experience that it seems to me vain to expect them to have the androgynous vision that Virginia Woolf told us to look for in *A Room of One's Own*, especially since her own prime example, Shakespeare, occasionally falls so short of the mark. And I am such a prisoner of my own experience as a Southerner that I least expected to find it in a Southern woman. When I learned that Berry Morgan is a white woman from Port Gibson, Mississippi, I was astonished. Because she writes so convincingly in the voices of a poor, black woman and a white male planter, for years I had marvelled at the versatility of what I took to be a black man's gift. I assumed that the author was a man because of what seemed to be a masculine name and because the characterization of Ned Ingles, the protagonist in *Pursuit*, indicated an intimate knowledge of running a plantation, knowledge usually available only to men. The knowledge traditionally allowed planters' wives and daughters is different, a fact evident from a glance at the women in Eudora Welty's *Delta Wedding*. It was remarkable, I thought, that this black man was able to get inside the head of a white planter even in those situations where the Southern black man was not likely to have spent much time, *inside* the Big House. And only a black person, it seemed to me, could get inside the head of Roxie Stoner, the simple-minded protagonist and narrator of the stories in *The Mystical Adventures of Roxie Stoner,* and organize the world in such a convincing black idiom. The deep South does not offer particularly fertile soil for sprouting an androgynous vision, particularly one that can also cross the color line at will. Let us look first at the reasons why this is so and then celebrate Berry Morgan's achievement.

In the first place, to attain an androgynous vision a writer must be close enough to the experiences of both sexes to give the imagination material

179

Berry Morgan (left) and daughter Frances.
Photo: Margaret Bolsterli

Berry Morgan

Born in Mississippi (1919), Morgan attended Loyola and
Tulane Universities in New Orleans. She was awarded a
Houghton Mifflin Literary Fellowship for a planned series of
books, the first of which, Pursuit, *was published in 1966. Her*
short stories appear frequently in the New Yorker.

with which to build. In the South, the chasm between the men's and women's cultures is so wide that crossing from one side to the other is difficult and rare. The things that little boys and little girls are encouraged to aspire to have traditionally been further apart in the South than in other parts of the country for a number of reasons, with fear of miscegenation involving white women and black men being perhaps the most important factor. To keep white women pure and consequently white men's honor intact, women have had to be kept caged, protected from accessibility to black men. Thus they have been encouraged to confine their interests to house and garden and to aim at only a remote control of the outside world, a control that is practiced by manipulating men. This is especially true in the planter class, that cream of Southern society to which all aspire to rise. The social contract that orders these arrangements between men and women is spelled out in *Delta Wedding* by the poor outsider, Robbie Reid.

> She had never thought it strange in her life before, having no land or possessions herself—Reids and Swansons had never become planters—but now she did. It was as if the women had exacted the place, the land, for something—for something they had had to give. Then, so as to be all gracious and noble, they had let it out of their hands—with a play of the reins—to the men. . . .[1]

The "something" that the Fairchild women have to give is their autonomy. They agree to stay locked up in the women's culture and in exchange receive everything the men have which they then let them manage at the end of their manipulative tethers. In the same novel, Aunt Tempe's notion of the positions of men and women in the natural scheme of things sums up a fantasy of expectations for men. Tempe's vision, the result of her upbringing as a wealthy planter's daughter and her sustenance as the wife of another one, is of course not *Welty's* vision of the way things should be, or in fact are. She makes it clear that the fantasy has little to do with reality, though it is a believable view for Tempe, who has never had to grow up and has retained the idea that the function of men is to be protectors of women. Women, in turn, are supposed to relish that protection. "It was laziness on men's part, the difficulties that came up in this world. A paradise, in which men, sweating under their hats like field hands, chopped out difficulties like the green grass and made room for the ladies to flower out and flourish like cotton, floated vaguely in Tempe's mind, and she gave her head a toss" (*DW* 187–88).

Eudora Welty's grasp of the women's culture is wide and deep. Her novels are particularly valuable because each illuminates a different area of the experience of Southern women. However, hers is as far from being an androgynous vision as that of William Faulkner covering the same territory from the male point of view. His world of the male Sutpens, Sartorises, and Compsons is the obverse of this coin; they are privy to a knowledge of the world from which women are excluded except during emergencies like war and sudden poverty. Women go to the fields in Faulkner's novels only when they have to and none are brought up aspiring to be planters, rather than planters' wives. The brave Drusilla who goes to fight alongside Colonel Sartoris is prevailed upon after the war to marry him, wear a skirt, and confine herself to the occupations of the house and garden while he fulfills his dream of empire.

Even tomboys who are privy as children to the world of young males are usually pruned by necessity into belledom before achieving an adult vision of the male world. The aspirations for a future planter's wife must, by nature, be different from those of a future planter and the process of pruning a tomboy into a belle who can fulfill her destiny by attracting the right kind of husband is perhaps most persuasive in the case of that mythic mother of Southern womanhood, Scarlett O'Hara, who was shaped so capably by two mistresses of the art, Ellen and Mammy.

> To Mammy's indignation, her preferred playmates were not her demure sisters or the well-brought up Wilkes girls but the negro children on the plantation and the boys of the neighborhood, and she could climb a tree or throw a rock as well as any of them. Mammy was greatly perturbed that Ellen's daughter should display such traits and frequently adjured her to "ack lak a lil lady." But Ellen took a more tolerant and long-sighted view of the matter. She knew that from childhood playmates grew beaux in later years, and the first duty of a girl was to get married. She told herself that the child was merely full of life and there was still time in which to teach her the arts and graces of being attractive to men.
>
> To this end, Ellen and Mammy bent their efforts, and as Scarlett grew older she became an apt pupil in this subject, even though she learned little else. . . . her education was sketchy, but no girl in the County danced more gracefully than she. She knew how to smile so that her dimples leaped, how to walk pigeon-toed so that her wide hoops swayed entrancingly, how to look up into a man's face and then drop her eyes and bat the lids rapidly so that she seemed a-tremble with gentle emotion. Most of all she learned how to conceal from men a sharp intelligence beneath a face as sweet and bland as a baby's.[2]

In order to visualize the relationship between the different spheres assigned white women and white men in Southern culture, it is useful to imagine them as separate transparent bubbles which occasionally combine and then separate again into discrete entities. The integrity of neither sphere is altered by its momentary merging with the other. Most of the time men and women are in separate spheres that are almost mutually exclusive, but at times they come together in a common bubble, or culture. This model may be expanded to illustrate the complications of race in the question of literary vision in the South by adding two more spheres, one for black men and another for black women. Now there are four separate spheres floating around, occasionally colliding and combining and then separating. The two which meet with least frequency and combine most seldom are those of the cultures of white women and black men. The spheres containing white and black women, however, cross the color line fairly frequently. Because of the presence of black women as domestic help in the houses of whites, the intimacy between black women and white children of both sexes is expected; it is further to be expected that white women who listen to the black women who work in their houses have an opportunity to learn about black culture. For the most part, however, all the spheres are discrete and the inhabitants of each rarely get more than a glimpse of the cultural differences between them, with the result that individual men and women, black and white, see the other three groups as "other" and the otherness frequently becomes the point of a creative vision.

Because the spheres come together for such limited periods of time in such a limited number of possible situations, it is extremely difficult to develop a vision of any sphere besides one's own that is comprehensive enough to sustain a credible voice. Perhaps this is why Caddy Compson is not allowed to speak and Dilsey is seen from the outside. Welty's optimist is dead; it is his daughter whose problems are explored. The black cooks in novels by white writers like Faulkner and Welty are vastly different from Old Nanny in Zora Neale Hurston's *Their Eyes Were Watching God*. In "An Odor of Verbena," Faulkner is reflecting the "otherness" of the black Ringo when he has him suggest a solution that white men like Bayard Sartoris would consider dishonorable, "We could bushwhack him," he said, "like we done Grumby that day. But I reckon that wouldn't suit the white skin you walks around in." He notes a different kind of "otherness" in *Absalom! Absalom!* when he has Mr. Compson tell Quentin "Years ago we in the South made our women into ladies. Then the War came and made the ladies into ghosts. So what else can we do, being gentlemen, but listen to them being ghosts?"[3]

It is a rare white who enters deeply enough into the sphere of blacks to write convincingly in a black's voice, and yet the necessity for doing so is a challenge accepted by many Southern writers who know that it is not possible to see life in the South clearly and whole without the black vision. William Styron has characterized his attempt to reconstruct the workings of Nat Turner's mind as a partial fulfillment of the mandate felt by every white Southerner: ". . . to break down the old law, to come to *know* the Negro, has become the moral imperative for every white Southerner."[4] The complexities of gender and race in Southern culture are enough to boggle the creative mind and render it helpless or else to force it into a way of seeing that finds new channels of expression when the old ones are blocked. And this is what Berry Morgan accomplishes by using the point of view of a black woman and a white man. She knows their spheres so well that she does not write of them as "other." The phenomenon brings to mind some lines from Adrienne Rich's "Snapshots of a Daughter-in-law," ". . . are you edged more keen/ to prise the secrets of the vault? has Nature shown/ her household books to you, daughter-in-law, that her sons never saw?"[5]

Berry Morgan had a peculiarly advantageous childhood for developing the ability to prise secrets out of Nature about the spheres of black women and white male planters. She was born on a plantation near Port Gibson, Mississippi, in 1919 and because her mother was an invalid, spent her waking hours in the company of black people from birth until the age of seven. As she tells it, "I listened to the wisdom of the Negroes, a considerable wisdom that I still feel is my own by osmosis and love if not by heritage."[6] This was her entry to the thought processes and word patterns of women like Roxie Stoner. Moreover, at the age of eleven she became her grandfather's chauffeur and until the age of fourteen, drove him around to inspect his various holdings, an activity which allowed her ample opportunity to learn the problems and routines of running a plantation. In fact, this is the traditional way in which little boys are taught to be planters but rare experience indeed for little girls. In this case it provided a fertile imagination with material for an androgynous vision, for she is able to make Ned Ingles a believable man because she knows what he could have seen and heard as a boy.

Berry Morgan received Houghton Mifflin Fellowships in 1966 for the novel *Pursuit* and in 1974 for a collection of stories, *The Mystical Adventures of Roxie Stoner.* These books compose the first two volumes of a proposed trilogy to be collectively entitled *Certain Shadows.* Stories now appearing serially will be collected for the third volume to be called *The Mississippian.* The title "Certain Shadows" is explained by a passage in *Pursuit* that defines the habit of the protagonist, Ned Ingles, of looking past the real for more abstract and transcendent meanings in life.

> He found a pleasure these days in letting his mind go beyond reason and chase certain shadows whose shape constantly changed just as these hills below Natchez moved with the angle of the sun. This way you could never find anything out for sure, but you dissociated yourself from the facts and lived a wholly different life, watered by the spirit. Facts and details supplied themselves, when they were needed, like manna, but this other spooky research gave a different sense of life, making it mysterious and unaccountable. (144)

Ned is a jaded plantation owner who returns to Ingleside, his 4,000 acre plantation in King County after quitting his job as instructor at a university in New Orleans. Ingleside is the end of Ned's rope; he has no aim in life and nothing to live for but he loves Ingleside and returns in the hope that family traditions will give him a purpose in life and make him into "somebody." The epigraph "Now of that long pursuit" is taken from the last stanza of Francis Thompson's poem "The Hound of Heaven."

> Now of that long pursuit
> Comes on at hand the bruit;
> That Voice is round me like a bursting sea
> "And is thy earth so marred,
> Shattered in shard on shard?
> Lo, all things fly thee, for thou fliest me!

The gist of the poem's message is that the speaker who has been pursued by the Hound of Heaven is finally told that the only way he can receive love is by returning to God: "Ah, fondest, blindest, weakest,/ I am He whom thou seekest!/ Thou dravest love from thee, who dravest Me." Ned Ingles, an alcoholic, neurotic fallen-away Catholic who loves nobody and has secretly at one time even thought of murdering his illegitimate son Laurance now desperately tries to force the child to love him and take his place in the line of heirs to Ingleside. For Ned so loves the earth and house and traditions that compose "the place," that when he comes back to it on September 3, 1937, for lack of anything better to do, he decides to "civilize" the seventeen-year-old son. Laurance, who has been ignored at Ingleside all his life, understandably does not want now to be bothered with a father he has gotten along quite well without. It becomes an obsession with Ned to turn Laurance into the willing heir who will in turn pass the family name and traditions to his own son. All Laurance wants to do is become a priest. Ned picks out a girl for Laurance to marry—a distant cousin named Annabella—and arranges for her mother Anna to tutor Laurance as a way to throw the children together so the inevitable can happen. What actually does happen is that Laurance falls for the mother and Ned ends up marrying the girl himself so he can respectably move mother and daughter to Ingleside, where he continues to hope that in the future Laurance will fall in love with Annabella, marry her, produce sons and live happily ever after. In a state of drunkenness, however, Ned impregnates Annabella, producing a son named Dana; later Laurance contracts Hodgkin's disease and dies. Ned is then committed to an insane asylum after trying to commit suicide. He escapes and returns to Ingleside where Anna is raising Dana.

Into this novel of the decline and fall of yet another aristocratic Southern family wanders the saintly figure of Roxie Stoner, a simple-minded black woman who is a bit player in Ned's life but whose testimony in her own book is necessary to complete the picture of life in King County, or at least that portion of it concerning these two characters and the cultures, sometimes separate, sometimes common, in which they move. Because she is saintly and harmless, Roxie Stoner is allowed to wander around the neighborhood, in and out of houses, both black and white, reflecting the life around her in a black mirror. Like Benjy Compson, she does not comprehend, she simply reflects. By using a white male planter and a poor black woman as her central characters, Morgan is able to show the simultaneous proximity and distance between the white ruling class and black people. Ned Ingles is of the class of doers, Roxie Stoner is of the class that is done to. The trick that Morgan performs so successfully is showing the life these two groups have made in their accommodation to the way things are and to each other. The lives of blacks and whites are so inextricably woven together in King County that it would be impossible to give an adequate picture of one without the other. Even when their spheres are separate, the field of influence around each drastically affects the other. As Ralph Ellison has remarked, "Southern whites cannot walk, talk, sing, conceive of laws or justice, think of sex, love, the family, or freedom without responding to the presence of Negroes."[7] Blacks, of course, are equally affected by the presence of whites. Ned Ingles, driving back from New Orleans one day reflects on the difference between the reality of things and the whites' delusions about them.

> When he finally reached the state line, he found himself drawing a breath of relief to be this far. There was the familiar billboard announcing that you were in the state of Mississippi, with a picture of its pale flower, the magnolia. Its very sickly whiteness was supposed to imply to the traveler that the dark half of the state wasn't there. Meanwhile the Negroes went their usual way, attending church, eating, begetting, hoping and fearing, officially unadmitted to. (P 144)

But the reality of things is quite different from the implications of the state flower. Ned's father's best friend was Wheeler, the black overseer; Ned's best friend is Wheeler's son Roosevelt, the current overseer. And Laurance, Ned's son, abandoned by his parents at Ingleside as a baby, was raised by the blacks on the place and feels himself one of them. At one point Ned, angry at his wife, goes to the cemetery to sulk and amuses himself by making a list of everybody he likes better than her; they all turn out to be black. The whites in this family are absolutely dependent on the blacks and yet, aware of this though he is, Ned's attitude is still that of the ruling class—the man in charge. His is the same attitude that made his father refuse to let Wheeler name his son after him—and choose Roosevelt instead as a name for the baby. The separate accounts by Ned and Roxie of the same incidents show the extent to which their lives are intertwined as well as their different attitudes toward this fact. Roxie and her invalid mother have always lived on Ingleside and been Laurance's friends; the summer Dana is born, Laurance, already sick with Hodgkin's disease, spends his time playing with the baby and inviting all his black friends to come admire it.

> The most frequent caller, although she could never stay long on account of her sick mother, was Roxie Stoner.
> At first Ned was embarrassed to see Roxie because he knew she had once been afraid of him. They had been the same age, growing up here and he had been attracted by her radiant woodswild manner and had inadvertently frightened her with a white man's smile. For twenty years afterwards, until Laurance

sent for her to come see him, she had not set foot on Ingleside but had used the Fornika Creek road to walk with her baskets of vegetables into King's Town. (*P* 116)

Roxie's reference to the incident that changed the route she took to town for twenty years illustrates the resignation and passivity of the oppressed, and the saintly, in this case. Laurance is dying and does not want to see Ned, who is trying desperately to establish connections with him. Roxie is called in, forced to leave her mother alone, to help with the household and keep Ned occupied and away from his son: "The first day, I fixed Mama up as good as I could with her Vicks and her new medicines on a chair by her bed and made it across the ridge early. Mr. Ned was already up and sitting on his back steps and it looked like he'd been crying. I was wondering—he used to be a little bit frisky with lady people—but now he stood up just as humble to let me by and told me thanks for coming" (*RS* 30). The story in which Roxie mentions this incident, "Passing," is about Roxie's guilt at being at the Ingles' house helping with Laurance's dying while her own mother died alone. But she had no choice; she had to go.

> I tried to tell Miss Anna that I had sick of my own to tend and I couldn't be gone but a little while from Mama, but she held up her hand for me to stop. Just listen another minute, she said, before I made my mind up. We had been using this family's tenant house and their land and everything else we could help ourselves to lo these many years and hadn't done a thing to pay it back. If Lilly—that's what she called Mama—saw fit to die right during this jam, there was nothing we could do. She's made a good thing out of my waiting on her all these years and she didn't believe she would. I've heard people say those Merediths would send a king around to the back, and that's the way she acted. (*RS* 31)

When Roxie finds her mother dead one day on returning from the Ingles' her response is the one required by God in "The Hound of Heaven," the one impossible for Ned Ingles to make in *Pursuit.*

> I tried to hear her voice in my remembrance—Mama's I mean—but all I could think was what she said her father said, the Reverend Isaac Stoner: Bless God. Whatever happens, bless God. Then do your studying out. I took this order then and got down on my knees and blessed Him over and over. This gave me enough space in my head to know that she had risen. Dying means more life (Whose voice was telling that?), closer to our Father. (*RS* 36)

By contrast, Ned is too tied to the material aspects of life to accept this higher vision of death for Laurance. He is never successful in getting

Laurance to love him and never, in turn, receives God himself. The pursuit does not end. When Laurance dies, Ned tries to commit suicide by butting his head against a piece of marble from the dresser in the sickroom and succeeds only in breaking his wrist and knocking himself out. He was trying to kill himself, not so that he and Laurance would be together in heaven, but so they could be buried together. To the end, Ned sees the dead as remaining in the cemetery; Roxie sees her mother in heaven and consequently always at her elbow offering counsel. Ned is obsessed; Roxie is saintly—and she is loved. Ned, who has driven out God, is not loved by anyone. He is unlovable. The Thompson poem quoted in the epigraph fits him perfectly, "Thou dravest love from thee, who dravest me."

The effect of Morgan's telling about the life in King County from both sides of the color line provides not so much a contrast as a completion. For one thing, the testimony of the blacks is necessary to show the effect of the whites' actions on their lives. It shows what life is like for these people who, as Ned remarks in his soliloquy on the significance of the magnolia as the state flower, go on with their lives while the whites are denying their very existence. Life in their sphere is complete in itself and only a voice from within could tell about it. The whites see only from the outside, and yet their actions produce shock waves of disaster for the blacks. For example, there is an old black woman on the place called Sweetbit by the whites and Miss Sweet by Roxie Stoner. Sweetbit was brought up by the Ingles family in the big house as a sort of pet until puberty, as she tells it, ". . . they 'let me sit to the table, play cards, carry on all the foolishness I wanted. Naturally when I got up to a size to change into a lady it created a lot of puzzlement to them'" (RS 63).

The family then put her in a little house to watch a dangerous gully and call for help during rains when the chance of erosion looked especially threatening. She planted flowers around the gully until she had the most beautiful garden in King County, and for a little money served as nurse for the blacks on the place. When the blacks all moved away and she was left without income, she turned to the novel profession of killing unwanted animals. She became known as the "killing lady," and when pets had to be put away, would charge a dollar for drowning cats and shooting dogs, and throwing their bodies out the window to the bottom of the gully where the buzzards would take care of them in short order. This grisly business was combined with kindness in Sweetbit's character; it was she who cooked chicken and dressing for the poor, abandoned Laurance every Sunday for years.

In *Pursuit* Ned Ingles goes to visit her because he is lonesome and she knows all the gossip, and also because he thinks of her in the old paternalistic way that whites think of "their" blacks. But it is interesting that in *his* story her killing business is never mentioned. Roxie has to tell us that. We must also go to Roxie to find out what eventually happens to Miss Sweet, who tells Ned in *Pursuit* that she knows that the minute she is dead they will shove her house into the gully with the pictures still on the walls, which indeed they do because Ned, while drunk, sells the property her house stands on and the new owners bulldoze it to make way for a housing development. Sweetbit herself was said to have died of a heart attack, as Roxie tells some years later, "He had bulldozed Miss Sweet's off into the gully just like she said they would, with all her boastful pictures still hanging on the walls. Some said she died of a heart attack but there was an axe mark on her head" (*RS* 146).

Both Ned Ingles and Roxie Stoner are committed, at different times, to the state mental hospital, Ned because he really is crazy, Roxie because she is in the way of the new owners who want to take possession of the land she lives on. Morgan uses Roxie's stay in the hospital as a technique for letting her tell the stories of other blacks. Since she is not crazy and likes to work, she is given keys and put to cleaning wards. At one point she is sent to work in the ward where violent adolescent boys are kept and is so taken with the pitiful story of the most violent one that she lets him out to help his family. He had been committed for threatening to kill the finance man who took his family's property when they did not pay for a house full of furniture bought on time. To quiet the boys in the ward, she tells them that she will let him out.

> Then the boy that's father lost the land could go on home and get his business straight and raise himself a family like he ought to. But I would *not* have a killing, now or ever.
> My boy broke down and started in to crying. It wouldn't do him any good to try to raise a family. The law had had him spaded. (*RS* 99)

Of course there is no comment on this terrible practice of sterilizing mental patients, for Roxie merely holds a mirror up to life and reflects what she sees. While we know from their remarks that whites like Ned and Dana know that things like this happen to blacks in Mississippi, and although they care, they are distanced from such treatment. For the full impact, such testimony must come from a black person. It is appalling that the things that Roxie tells happen to people, even more appalling that they can be related in such a matter-of-fact way. Through the technique of letting Roxie tell what she sees, Berry Morgan shows *another side of life* in the Magnolia State. In all, she shows that life does go on in each sphere in a complete and more or less acceptable way. Blacks and whites have made an accommodation that makes life possible.

The androgynous vision is apparent in Morgan's depiction of Ned Ingles, the planter. For Ned's vision of what life ought to be is that of a person brought up to think of himself in relation to larger tracts of land than a flower bed. It is the crops in the fields and the cows in the pastures that interest him and not garden clubs and azaleas. His quest, moreover, is that most male quest of all, the continuation of the male line. His vision of family is dynastic in the same way that Thomas Sutpen's is. He wants to reclaim Laurance as a son, not for love of the child, but as a carrier of the male line who will inherit Ingleside and pass it on down in turn to *his* son. Ned's love for the place and all it entails is believable because his character as a male is built on a solid understanding by the author that it takes a boy to grow into a man and her knowledge of what a boy like Ned would know is one of the surprising pleasures of this work. One instance of this comes at a point in *Pursuit* where the adult Ned is recalling an incident that happened in his childhood, some twenty-seven years earlier. The ten-year-old Ned had been riding by the house of a black couple, Ira and Udell, when Ira, coming home early, caught Udell in bed with another man and stabbed her with an ice pick. Ned took Ira up on the horse behind him and rode to the fencing crew where Wheeler, the black foreman, was in charge and where Ira had been working when he caught a chill and had to go home early. Ira, of course, was terrified that Wheeler would call the police. Instead, this is what followed:

> Wheeler had caught sight of them now and they rode up close so that Ned could slip off the horse and confront him, "Excuse me, but he killed Udell."
> Wheeler had not shown any extraordinary interest. Instead he turned and addressed himself to the men, giving them more directions for stretching the fence. Finally he turned to Ira. "Why didn't you get *him?*"
> Ira was sobbing now, looking huge and ridiculous on the horse. "He blazed out of there so fast—"

The hands started to laugh but Wheeler turned toward them and they fell silent, quickening their work and stepping as noiselessly as Indians so as to not miss a word.

"Do you see that stob yonder?"

Ira jumped off the horse and came to attention. "Yes, Sir."

"Well then. Take ahold of my wire and run thataway with it till you hit that next stob."

Ira hitched up his pants by the belt and dropped the ice pick into them, where it slid until it hit the hilt. "All right, mens," he said, a lilt in his voice. "Let's go." The relief in his tone, his brisk enthusiasm for the work, carried across the years now, so near his vanished cabin. (*P* 110–11)

It is unusual for a woman to have the information that this passage presupposes, to know what Ira would say, for example, and how that ice pick would look sliding into his belt, not to mention what a fencing crew would be doing and what the foreman's instructions would be. But without such information Morgan could not have fully characterized the boyhood or manhood of Ned. Her information comes from the androgynous experience that leads to an androgynous vision. As the roles for men and women change and the male and female cultures merge, the androgynous literary vision will doubtless become more common. For now, it is still a rare circumstance, worth celebrating when it occurs in Southern or any other culture.

Rare, too, is a vision that extends across the color line with such keenness as Berry Morgan's. There is a question, however, of how much longer the cultural color line will be as distinctive as it was when Morgan was carried across it as a child by the black people who took care of her. Black culture is under siege as never before. As long as there was a state-supported segregated school system, the perpetuation of black culture in the South was guaranteed. Black teachers taught black children, most of whom were never around whites enough to have their cultural patterns changed. Cultural flow, ironically, tended to go the other way with more black influence on white culture than the other way round because it was blacks who raised white children of the planter class. Integration of the schools may have sounded the death knell of black culture as Southern blacks become drawn into the mainstream of American life along with white Southerners. But up to this point in American history there has always been a separate black culture in the South and Berry Morgan is one of the few whites who has been able to write about it from a convincing point of view.

Having said all this in good faith, I still doubt that a completely androgynous, color-blind vision is possible. There are areas of experience which members of the opposite sex cannot penetrate; there are areas of black experience in the South where whites have never entered. Chances are that life will never be the same for both races. To claim acquaintance with those areas of experience one has not shared would be as foolish and short of the truth as the claims by men that they comprehend the pain of childbirth because they have been in the delivery room when women were giving birth to babies. Berry Morgan's overwhelming achievement is that she comes so close.

NOTES

[1] Eudora Welty, *Delta Wedding* (New York: Harcourt, Brace and World, 1946), 145.

[2] Margaret Mitchell, *Gone With The Wind* (New York: MacMillan, 1936), 58.

[3] William Faulkner, "An Odor of Verbena," in *The Unvanquished* (New York: Random 1938), 251; William Faulkner, *Absalom! Absalom!* (New York: Random 1936), 12.

[4] William Styron, "This Quiet Dust," *Harper's Magazine*, April 1965, 138.

[5] Adrienne Rich, "Snapshots of a Daughter-in-law," in *Snapshots of a Daughter-in-law* (New York: Norton, 1967), 23.

[6] This information was given me by Berry Morgan in March 1983.

[7] Quoted in Styron, "This Quiet Dust," 135.

Photo: Robert Llewelyn

Rita Mae Brown

Born in Pennsylvania (1944), Brown spent her childhood in Florida. She has a B.A. from New York University and a Ph.D. from the Institute for Policy Studies, Washington, D.C. Her first published collection of poetry, The Hand That Cradles the Rock, *appeared in 1971. She is the author of one other collection of poetry, five novels, and a volume of collected essays.*

Rita Mae Brown:
Feminist Theorist and Southern Novelist

MARTHA CHEW

Rita Mae Brown is known both for her political writing, which consists of the essays that came out of her activism as a lesbian feminist in the late sixties and early seventies and were collected in *A Plain Brown Rapper* (1976); and for her fiction, which to date consists of five novels, *Rubyfruit Jungle* (1973), *In Her Day* (1976), *Six of One* (1978), *Southern Discomfort* (1982), and *Sudden Death* (1983). Although the two bodies of work overlap chronologically, they come out of essentially different periods in Brown's life, and the novels have been increasingly directed toward a mainstream audience.

The movement of the novels away from the political focus of the essays is reflected in the way the two types of writing diverge in their publishing histories. Brown's essays originally appeared in lesbian and feminist publications; the collected edition, *A Plain Brown Rapper,* was published by Diana Press, a west coast lesbian-feminist press (which also published her second collection of poems, *Songs to a Handsome Woman,* in 1973 and reissued in 1974 her first collection, *The Hand That Cradles the Rock*). Her first two novels, *Rubyfruit Jungle* and *In Her Day,* were published by Daughters, Inc., a Vermont feminist publishing house (co-founded by another Southern woman writer, North Carolina novelist June Arnold). When *Rubyfruit Jungle* became an underground best seller (selling 80,000 copies in hardcover), it was reissued by Bantam,[1] a subsidiary of Harper and Row, and Harper and Row simultaneously contracted for her third novel, *Six of One.* Her next two novels, *Southern Discomfort* and *Sudden Death,* were published by Harper and Row and by Bantam, respectively.

Brown had evidently anticipated and planned these two publishing tracks with a clear sense of the different audiences that her political essays

195

and her novels would eventually have. In 1976, a year before Bantam reissued *Rubyfruit Jungle,* she responded to a questionnaire on publishing policies sent to lesbian and feminist authors, "I see my political writing going to the feminist press while in time my fiction will go to establishment presses" (Clausen, "Politics" 101).

The widening gap between Brown's essays and her fiction is marked by the disappearance from the novels of the lesbian feminist political vision that is set forth with revolutionary fervor in the early writings. This apparent shift in her ideological stance is underlined by the change in her lifestyle from that of political activist and street-level organizer to that of Hollywood scriptwriter, celebrity novelist, and member of Charlottesville's polo-playing set. This change has, predictably, been noted with favor in some camps and disfavor in others. Jan Clausen, writing in *A Movement of Poets* about the relationship of poets to the contemporary American feminist movement, notes that "it is a sobering experience . . . to read early 'underground heroine' Rita Mae Brown's musings on the joys of owning a Rolls Royce in a recent issue of *Savvy*" (14). The mainstream press, on the other hand, feels that Brown has "broken through" and that her success with standard publishers marks "the difference between being famous as a lesbian writer . . . and being a writer of greater substance and vision who is perhaps breaking new literary ground" (Holt 17, 16).

Brown, who points out that she gives ten percent of her after-tax earnings to women's political causes (Shister, 12), talks about her feminist politics as having evolved, rather than changed. In her 1976 introduction to the essays in *A Plain Brown Rapper,* she explained that, although her vision of a feminist revolution remained "unchanged," she had come to see that revolution as "the slow, steady push of people over decades" (13). And in a 1978 interview upon the publication of *Six of One,* after pointing out that fiction made her politics "more palatable," she added, "I still feel I'm part of the movement, but the form of my expression has changed" (Holt 17).

Although the distance between the political viewpoint in Brown's essays and that in her fiction clearly signals more than a change in form, the essays and fiction are linked by Brown's concern with some of the same issues. We can begin to see that link, and to define the extent to which Brown's themes in her fiction reflect her early politics, if we look first at

the account her essays provide of the development of her political thinking in the early sixties and late seventies.

> There is a growing movement of Lesbians dedicated to our
> freedom, to your freedom, to ending all man-made oppres-
> sions. You will be part of that surge forward and you will leave
> your fingerprints on the shape of things to come.
> —Brown, "The Shape of Things to Come," 1972

Brown's political essays and speeches, which appeared from 1969 to
1975 in *The Ladder, Women: A Journal of Liberation, The Furies, Quest:
A Journal of Feminist Liberation,* and other lesbian and feminist publications, chart the development of her vision of a feminist revolution. Looking back on that period in her 1976 introduction to her essays in *A Plain
Brown Rapper,* Brown said, "In those days I ate, breathed and slept
feminism. Nothing else mattered to me. We would bring about a revolution in this nation and we would do it now" (13).

After making the Southern writer's archetypal journey to New York,
she began to move from one political group to another. She helped found
the New York University Homophile League, then left it because, as she
explains in her 1972 essay, "Take a Lesbian to Lunch," "the homosexual
movement" was "male-dominated" (86). She joined the National Organi-
zation for Women (and was appointed national administrative coor-
dinator), then quit, reportedly blasting the leaders as "sexist, racist,
reformist clubwomen" (Alexander 112) because of their reaction to the
issue of lesbianism.[2] She joined Redstockings (a New York radical feminist
group that used consciousness-raising groups as a way of organizing
women); found they reacted as negatively to her lebianism as had NOW;
joined and then left Gay Liberation. She eventually became part of Radicalesbians, the New York collective that in 1970 issued the now-classic
essay "The Woman-Identified Woman." In its definition of lesbianism as a
political act, the Radicalesbians essay moves beyond "the traditional
definition of women toward a concept of women defining themselves," as
Brown explained in a later essay, "Living with Other Women" (76).

What Brown has called the "burning intensity" (*PBR,* Intro. 13) of her
commitment to a feminist revolution led her in 1971 to help organize the
Furies, a Washington, D.C., collective of lesbian feminist separatists. The
impact that the collective's newsletter, *The Furies,* had on *Feminary,* a

Southern feminist publication, is described by M. Segrest in her article on writing by Southern lesbians in *Southern Exposure.* "The Furies collective was a religion to us in Chapel Hill between 1971 and 1974," Segrest quotes a former *Feminary* collective member as saying (59). After Brown was purged from the Furies, she went on to become one of the founding editors of *Quest,* a journal of feminist ideology and research.

Brown's movement from one group to another was typical of the experiences of other lesbian feminist activists at the time. In *Dreamers and Dealers,* Leah Fritz's account of the second wave of the women's movement, Fritz recalls that "Lesbians began to defect from one women's group after another, to move around in search of a place where they would feel at home, a place which would serve both the totality of their needs as women and their specific needs as lesbians" (32). In documenting Brown's political odyssey during that period, the essays in *Plain Brown Rapper* are, as Brown says in the introduction, "as much a chronicle of the decade as of my own development" (22).

The essays are also important, not just as history and personal biography, but as ideology. The collection—twenty previously published essays, plus an introduction, conclusion, and a new essay—is uneven. Often the essays fire movement rhetoric at the reader in a machine-gun style that makes one piece sound very like another. And some of Brown's prescriptions for bringing about the revolution are simplistic, just as some of her predictions seem amazingly naive—"Within five years we will have our party" (117).

Yet many of the essays offer perceptive insights into class divisions and other artificial categories dividing human beings. Brown feels strongly that "Separation is what the ruling rich, white male wants: female vs. male; black vs. white; gay vs. straight; poor vs. rich" (95). Her essays attack the tendency of society to put everyone into one category or another, and she points out the ways in which these categories are restricted by what she calls "the male culture's vulgar conceptual limitations." For example, her review essay "The Last Picture Show" offers a paradigm for analyzing films that depict only "the white, middle class, heterosexual version of life" (154). A later essay, "I Am a Woman," offers an equally useful analysis, not just of the limitations of "the male concept of the female," but also of the limitations of a heterosexual view of women that ignores the fact that "even the most blatantly heterosexual woman has a relationship with her mother, her sisters, her girlfriends, aunts, grandmothers, office workers" (176).

Perhaps the best writing in the collection has to do with class, which has always been an issue of great personal significance to Brown. She identifies herself as coming from a working class background: her mother was a bakery and mill worker, and her father was a butcher. Her interviews and essays repeatedly point to lack of class consciousness in the women's movement (along with lack of consciousness about lesbianism) as the source of her problems with the different groups that she joined and then left. In a 1978 interview she recalled the New York women's groups as hostile to "lower class" issues: "the early years of the movement were bitter years, especially for me because I was from poor origins and therefore 'lower class.' Let's face it, the Women's Movement is still a white middle-class movement: I was always bringing up the basic issues that faced the poor—food, shelter and clothing. But nobody wanted to hear that. . . . With NOW and the others it was bad enough that I was a lesbian and said so, but to call into question the very process by which we were organizing ourselves—in other words the unspoken assumptions of class privilege—well, you couldn't have asked to become a more unwanted person" (Holt 16–17). Writing in the introduction to A Plain Brown Rapper about her experiences with the Furies, Brown says that, although the collective had tried to deal with class issues, "we ignored the psychology of class differences" and "in the end, it was this issue and the issue of identity which destroyed our collective" (16).

In "The Last Straw," perhaps her most important essay on class differences, Brown attacks two middle class assumptions: the idea that acquiring middle class income or status "removes the entire experience of our childhood and youth—working class life" (100) and also the belief in "downward mobility" embraced by some middle class revolutionaries. She points out that "for those of us who grew up without material advantages downward mobility is infuriating—here are women rejecting what we never had and can't get!" (104).

Brown's concern in her essays with class divisions is at times characterized by an ambivalence that foreshadows the movement of her novels away from her early political stance. For example, in "The Last Straw" her attack on "downward mobility" reveals an emotional defensiveness about capitalism, even though her official line in this and other essays is clearly a socialist one. Brown is not, of course, the first working class revolutionary to find her intellectual commitment to socialism in conflict with her need to protect herself by acquiring material possessions. In this defensiveness about capitalism in "The Last Straw" we can see the same conflicting feelings that turn up later in the ambivalence with which she portrays upper and middle class characters in her fiction.

On one level Brown's novels can be seen as a working and reworking of the interlocking problems of the oppressiveness of class and other artificial divisions of human beings and the isolation imposed by these divisions. As we might expect, in her essays Brown brings the expediency of the activist and the organizer to her analysis of society's readiness to put everyone in one category or another. Nonetheless, the essays reveal the intellectual basis of Brown's concern with the problems of class, race, and gender categories that her fiction explores in the lives of Southern women and in the context of the Southern environment in which Brown herself grew up.

> "I'm not saying it's easy but maybe that's just what we have to
> do, Adele, go back where we came from and fight this out."
> —Brown, *In Her Day*

Although Brown's political essays were an important influence on the Southern women putting out *Feminary* in Chapel Hill, it is her novels that identify her as a Southern writer for the majority of her reading public. On promotional tours for her novels Brown has repeatedly emphasized her Southern background and indicated that she wants to be identified as a Southern writer. For example, in a Boston interview she effusively expressed her pleasure in the enthusiastic reception to her appearances in the South: "I just love the South and I'm pleased to say it loves me right back. Everytime I speak there I'm just overwhelmed by love. I think Southerners are happy and proud when one of their own makes it" (White). And she clearly wanted the *New York* interviewer to see her in the tradition of Southern writers when she called *Six of One* a Southern novel and described the South as a good environment for writers. "Actually I think the book is rather southern. The South allows itself eccentrics, and, of course, if you're going to be a writer it's fabulous to grow up with that, which I did in a way" (Turner 60). In a recent interview in Philadelphia she was equally eager to identify herself as a

Southern writer: "I pretty much dislike Yankees. They're no fun. They don't have a wild streak in them. They're too rational. Art is intensely emotive, and at least in the South you are allowed your emotions" (Shister 12).

Each of Brown's first four novels can be seen as a different stage in her attempt to go back to her Southern roots, either in her choice of settings or in her focus on Southern characters. Most of the first half of *Rubyfruit Jungle* is set in Fort Lauderdale; *Six of One* is set in a Pennsylvania-Maryland town on the middle of the Mason-Dixon line; and *Southern Discomfort* is set in Montgomery, Alabama. *In Her Day* takes place in New York, but a central scene, and the only flashback, focuses on Carole's trip back home to Virginia to visit her family. (Brown's fifth novel, *Sudden Death*, which is about the world of women's professional tennis and depicts a love affair that has obvious parallels to Brown's relationship with tennis star Martina Navratilova, breaks the pattern of her increasing focus on the South in her fiction. Brown wrote the novel because of a promise to a dying friend, a sports writer, and she labels it an "interruption" in her writing plans: "I was all set to go on to my next novel about the War Between the States, and this came as an interruption." The biographical note at the end of *Sudden Death* is clearly intended to alert readers to Brown's intention to return to her focus on the South: "Rita Mae Brown is currently retracing Stonewall Jackson's steps during the War Between the States in preparation for her next novel.")

Brown's first four novels go back not only to the South but to specific events and places in Brown's own life. She was born in a small Pennsylvania town and moved at an early age to Fort Lauderdale. Her adoptive parents were working class. Her biological father was French—although Brown has said that she was "without knowledge of my ethnic origins"[3]— and her biological mother at one time employed the woman who adopted her (Alexander 111). After being expelled from the University of Florida for her lesbianism and civil rights activism, Brown put herself through New York University. In the late seventies she returned to the South to live, settling in Charlottesville, Virginia, which she says is "home" now: "It's the source of my power" (Shister 12).

Different aspects of these experiences are reenacted by the various heroes of her four Southern novels. Molly in *Rubyfruit Jungle*, Carole in *In Her Day*, and Nickle in *Six of One* grow up poor in the South and leave. Brown's circuitous route from Pennsylvania to New York is specifically paralleled in Molly's move from Pennsylvania to Fort Lauderdale, her expulsion from the state university, and her flight to New York, where she puts herself through film school. Brown's move back to the South has parallels in two of the novels: at the end of *In Her Day*, Carole and her Southern friend Adele consider going back to the South to live; and in *Six of One*, Nickel returns to Pennsylvania after publishing a successful book, buys her grandmother's house, and prepares to settle down. Although *Southern Discomfort* does not for the most part have these literal autobiographical parallels, Catherine like Brown, is adopted (as are Molly and Nickel in the two earlier novels⁴) and, like Brown, has a non-Anglo biological father. (Catherine's father is black, and there is speculation that Molly's father and Nickel's father are black, although both are identified as French.) Catherine's biological mother employs her adoptive mother, just as Brown's biological mother once employed her adoptive mother.

Brown's novels are autobiographical not only in their portrayal of these experiences but, more importantly, in their exploration of the issue that concerned her both personally and politically during her activist years. All four of the Southern novels depict people who defy society's division of human beings into artificial categories and who struggle to come to terms with the isolation imposed by those categories, and they develop this theme in more depth and with more complexity than either the scope or the purpose of her political essays permitted. In exploring this theme in autobiographical novels about Southern women, Brown is using her fiction to do what Carole in *In Her Day* tells Adele (who is also a transplanted Southerner) that they must do about the oppression they face as lesbians, "go back where we came from and fight this out."

Brown treats the problem of class and other societal categories on two levels in the novels: a realistic, or literal, level, and a symbolic level. On the literal level, she shows women running head-on into the barriers imposed by class, race, and gender categories. Locked into some categories and locked out of others, her characters have varying degrees of success in breaking through the barriers and making contact with people in other categories.

On the symbolic level, Brown suggests a bridging of these divisions through the identification of the main character with two very different types of characters, an upper or middle class character (the "aristocratic" character) and a black character. The significance of the roles of these two types of characters as the doubles of the main character is underlined by the fact that in the first, second, and fourth novels the main character is adopted. (In the third novel, *In Her Day*, Brown offers a variation on the adoption motif in that Carole's parents are dead and she has adopted a friend to replace her dead biological sister.) Although the situation of the main characters as adopted children can be emblematic of the essential loneliness of the human condition, it also functions in a more specific way to underline the extent to which societal categories cut people off from one another. As Molly puts it in *Rubyfruit Jungle*, "I had never thought I had much in common with anybody. I had no mother, no father, no roots, no biological similarities called sisters and brothers" (88).

This double-barrelled approach is evident in Brown's first novel, *Rubyfruit Jungle. Rubyfruit Jungle* became an underground best seller because of its reputation as a novel about "growing up gay in America" (as ads and reviews described it when it was reissued by Bantam in 1977),[5] but Molly Bolt is, as her name suggests, in rebellion against the restrictions imposed on her by race and class as well as gender. When her family moves from Pennsylvania to Fort Lauderdale, her father tries to explain to her that racial segregation is more obvious in Florida: "Down South things are a little different than up in York. Here the whites and the coloreds don't mix and you're not to mess with those people, although you are to be mannerly should you ever have to talk to one" (58). Her mother puts it more bluntly: "If I ever see you mixing with the wrong kind, I'm gonna wring your neck, brat" (59). Her family is poor—in her grandmother's words, "God knows with all of us working we can't make hardly enough to keep going" (23)—but it is not until they move to Florida that Molly really becomes aware of class distinctions: "Back in the Hollow we were all the same. . . . Here it was a distinct line drawn between two camps and I was certain I didn't want to be on the side with the greasy boys that leered at me and talked filthy" (61). Molly also comes up against the restrictions of gender roles. Early on her mother complains that "she don't act natural" because she "climbs trees" and "takes cars apart" instead of learning "the things she has to know to get a husband" (39), and when Molly says she wants a "candy apple red Bonneville Triumph, her cousin Leroy echoes her mother's criticism: "you ain't natural. . . . It's time you started worrying about your hair and doing those things that girls are supposed to do" (63).

Molly's reactions to the restrictions imposed on her by societal categories are in keeping with her strong sense of herself. Her reaction to racial segregation is to ignore it: "I ain't staying away from people because they look different" (59). She tackles the problem of class like the survivor she is: "It took me all of seventh grade to figure out how I would take care of myself in this new situation, but I did figure it out" (61). Her solution is to combine the traditional methods of "passing" (high grades, correct grammar, and a few good clothes) with humor: "I decided to become the funniest person in the whole school. If someone makes you laugh you have to like her" (62). Although Molly opts for "passing" in high school, later on in New York she becomes more class conscious and insists on identifying her working class background, so much so, in fact, that her friend Holly accuses her of "wearing your poverty like a badge of purity" (176). She takes an even more defiant line when faced with gender roles. When her cousin Leroy labels her interest in motorcycles unfeminine, she retorts, "I'll buy an army tank if I want to and run over anyone who tells me I can't have it" (63).

The success of Molly's defiance depends, of course, on her position in relation to the dominant culture. As white, she is a member of the dominant culture and can cross racial lines in a way that blacks cannot. As female, lesbian, and poor, she is in a more difficult position. She is able to gain the respect and liking of some people and survive the insults and attacks of others, but she can go only so far. Near the end of the novel, when she is by-passed for jobs in spite of her *summa cum laude* degree and her demonstrated talents and skills as a filmmaker, she says, "I kept hoping against hope that I'd be the bright exception, the talented token that smashed sex and class barriers" (245). The novel's closing passage records her awareness of the power of barriers erected to maintain the power of the dominant culture: "Damn, I wished the world would let me be myself. But I knew better on all counts" (246).

Molly's defiance of societal conventions concerning race, class, and sex is paralleled by the novel's symbolic identification of her with characters from different social worlds. Two of the women with whom she becomes romantically involved in New York, Holly, a beautiful black woman from a wealthy family, and Polina, an older white woman who is a medieval scholar, function as Molly's doubles, roles that are underlined by the similarity of the names of the three. Holly's role as Molly's black double is reinforced by Molly's childhood speculations about her own parents: "Since I don't know who my real folks are maybe they're colored" (59). Her other double, Polina, a medieval scholar, represents aristocratic values to Molly; she needs Polina because of "the conversations, the theater, and her stories of Europe where she grew up" (207). Although both relationships are short-lived, Holly's and Polina's roles as Molly's doubles identify her with women whose class and race are different from her own and, in doing so, foreshadow the more significant roles of the black and "aristocratic" characters in the later novels.

Brown's second novel, *In Her Day*, focuses on Carole Hanratty, a forty-four-year-old medieval art historian in New York. The break-up of her love affair with Ilse, a twenty-two-year-old lesbian feminist revolutionary from a Boston Brahmin family, is balanced against the stability of her friendship with Adele, her black friend. The novel has been described as "an embarrassing attempt to write a Lesbian-feminist novel of ideas," (Kleindeinst 3) and, with the exception of a few reviews in lesbian feminist publications, it is generally agreed to be a failure, an assessment with which Brown herself agrees.[6] Nonetheless, the novel develops the rebellion theme in *Rubyfruit Jungle* on both literal and symbolic levels. Although Carole is stately, reserved, and distrustful of Ilse's political enthusiasms, she has bucked the system in some of the same ways that Molly Bolt has. Carole's friendship with Adele in the fifties was, as Ilse reminds her, a form of "breaking the code," for "when you two became friends white and Black women weren't seen together" (93). Like Molly, Carole has fought her way up from poverty: "I worked for everything I have. I didn't come from money. Honey, I grew up in the Depression in Richmond, Virginia. . . . We lived in the Fan. It was a slum pretty much, although we didn't call it that ourselves" (76). As female and a lesbian she has rebelled against the restrictions of gender roles, first as a child ("I knew as a kid that boys got all the breaks but it made me mad—just made me fight that much harder"); then as a student at Vassar opting for a career at a time when "there wasn't a women's movement except in the direction of Yale" (26); and finally as a university professor in a department where "I would have been head . . . if I weren't a woman" (54). Carole is, as Ilse somewhat patronizingly describes her, "a proto-feminist" (26).

On the symbolic level of the novel, Adele functions as Carole's black double in a development of Holly's role in *Rubyfruit Jungle*. A beautiful black woman from a wealthy family, Adele is Carole's age and, like her, a Southerner. Her role as Carole's double is underlined by Carole's adoption of her as her sister. When Carole's biological sister is killed in an automobile accident, Adele comforts her, riding partway to Richmond with her on the train and meeting her returning train: "the hours, like a magic circle, closed around them and strengthened the bond of friendship already between them. As Carol boarded the train, finally, she turned to Adele and said, 'You're my sister now'" (62). Their identification is made even more explicit in the last scene, in which they talk about their need as Southerners to go back to their "roots" and the impossibility of their going unless they go together. "I love you more than anyone on earth" (194), Carole tells Adele.

Ilse, Carole's "aristocratic" double, attended the same college, Vassar, that Carole had attended twenty years earlier, and she looks like "white America's dream of femininity," as Carole had at her age. Ilse's role as Carole's double is underlined by Carole's internalization of upper class values. Carole acknowledges that, like Molly Bolt, she had tried to overcome class barriers by "passing": "I spent close to a decade trying to pretend I was an aristocrat" (134). Ilse remarks upon this ambivalence: "At first I thought she was some kind of aristocrat" (166). As Adele puts it in explaining Carole's attraction to Ilse, "Carole has always been fascinated and repelled by people who had it easy" (103). Although the relationship between them fails, they are, as Bernice Mennis notes in her review of the novel in *Conditions: One*, "two parts of a dialectic" and "by the end of the novel and of their relationship, each incorporates a small part of the other's vision" (119, 120). Ilse's role as Carole's "aristocratic" double builds on Polina's role in *Rubyfruit Jungle*, just as Adele's role builds on Holly's role, and the two characters prefigure the roles of the doubles in the novels that follow.

Brown's third novel, *Six of One*, portrays the women in two families in a small town in southern Pennsylvania between 1909 and 1980. The novel focuses on the lively feuding between two sisters, Juts and Louise, from their childhood (shown in flashbacks) to their old age (described by the first-person narrator, Juts's adopted daughter, Nickel). Nickel had been a "bullheaded" child, "ready to get into trouble" (284), and she had grown up to be an adult who "left the church, left the town, left [her mother] . . . writes books that disgrace the whole family" (2), and sleeps with women. She and her mother, Juts, whose "hell-raising bent" (135) she has inherited, are both reincarnations of Molly Bolt. Another hell-raiser in the novel is Celeste Chalfonte, the wealthy Southern white woman who employs Nickel's grandmother, Cora. (Cora was, Brown tells us, modeled on Brown's own grandmother and her "favorite character in the whole book").[7] Celeste defies convention by openly living with her female lover, but she cannot completely break through the class barrier. Her statement to her lover Ramelle reveals the power of the social structure in her life: "If I could choose a sister I would choose Cora. Our tragedy was to be born at opposite ends of the social spectrum. This [their employer-servant relationship] is the only way we can be part of one another's lives short of revolution" (210).

The novel symbolically bridges this class division, however, through the identification of Nickel with Celeste, her "aristocratic" double. While a black double is absent in this novel, the speculation that Nickel's biological father may have been black identifies her to some extent with blacks, much as Molly's speculation about whether her parents were black functions in *Rubyfruit Jungle*. For example, when Cora decides to adopt Nickel, her sister warns her, "For all you know, the father could be black as spades" (248), and one of the strike-breakers hired by the local munitions factory taunts Nickel, "I hear tell your father was a nigger" (291).

Celeste and Nickel are repeatedly identified with one another throughout the novel, although the two never see each other. Nickel is born on Celeste's sixty-seventh birthday, and Celeste's unexpected death the night before ushers in the birth. Celeste's thoughts on the evening of her death suggest an identification with Nickel that has undertones of reincarnation: "Celeste found herself strangely excited about the baby. She hoped it would come forth tomorrow. . . . Celebrating earthly renewal with a new person might be fun" (251). This identification of the two is continued by reminders of Nickel's resemblance to Celeste. For example, when Nickel says, "I hope I grow up to be like Celeste," her grandmother Cora replies, "I do, too" (296). When Nickel's mother tells her, "Sometimes you remind me of Celeste Chalfonte with an engine on your back," Nickel replies that one of Celeste's Vassar friends "told me . . . that I reminded her a bit of Celeste" (226). Celeste is further connected to

Nickel through a bequest in her will that provides for Nickel to attend Celeste's alma mater, Vassar. The bequest links Nickel not only to Celeste but also to Celeste's social world.

The identification of Nickel with Celeste is underlined by the elaborate parallels between Celeste's two worlds. On the one hand there is her "aristocratic" world—her biological family, her lover, and her Vassar friends (who, significantly, were known as "the Furies" in college). On the other hand there is her working class family—her servant Cora, Cora's daughters Juts and Louise, and Cora's granddaughter, Nickel. When Celeste's lover becomes pregnant (by Celeste's brother), Celeste assumes the role of "a mother or mother number two" (108) to Ramelle's child. Celeste is also a second mother to Cora's daughter Juts, a relationship suggested in part through the presence of Cora's daughters in Celeste's house when their mother is working there and in part through Celeste's love for Cora. (The bond between Celeste and Cora is put in physical, although not sexual, terms when Celeste, frightened and seeking comfort in Ramelle's absence, goes to Cora's house in the middle of the night and sleeps in the same bed with her.)

The parallels between Celeste's two "daughters," her daughter by her lover Ramelle, and her daughter by her servant Cora, are continued in the implied comparison of Cora's two "granddaughters," Ramelle's granddaughter and Cora's granddaughter Nickel. Significantly, the passage in which Ramelle and Cora compare their two granddaughters ends with Cora's summing up their similarity with the phrase from which the novel takes its title, "Six of one, half dozen of the other" (284). Although attempts to break through class barriers are only partially successful on the literal level of the novel, on a symbolic level the two classes are brought together through the identification of Nickel with her "aristocratic" double, Celeste, an identification that is underlined by the complex paralleling of Celeste's two families.

Brown's recent novel, *Southern Discomfort*, takes place in Montgomery, Alabama, and is set in two periods ten years apart, 1918 and 1928. The first half of the novel focuses on the secret love affair between white society leader Hortensia Reedmuller Banastre (whose imposing demeanor recalls both Carole Hanratty in *In Her Day* and Celeste Chalfonte in *Six of One*) and Hercules Jinks, a black fifteen-year-old boxer. Their affair, which ends when Hercules is killed in a railway yard accident, leaves Hortensia pregnant with their daughter Catherine. Hortensia arranges for Catherine to be brought up by her black servant, and the second half of the novel focuses on Catherine's gradual discovery of her real heritage.

Hortensia rebels against race barriers in her love affair with Hercules, and against class barriers in her friendship with Blue Rhonda, a white prostitute. In a passage that recalls Celeste Chalfonte's envy of the "zest" and "immediacy" (124) of Cora's family in *Six of One*, Lila, Hortensia's mother, acknowledges to herself that the hope for the upper class is to break out of their rigid mold: "Half of her longed to usher her daughter into the human race and the other half of her fought to preserve the stultifying social order over which she, Lila, presided" (10).

In the end, the social order is preserved. In spite of Hortensia's love for Hercules, she is "not yet prepared to run away" (98) with him, although she does not fully realize the significance of her reluctance until ten years later.

Brown suggests a possible transcending of class barriers in a key conversation in the second half of the novel between Hortensia and Blue Rhonda. Blue Rhonda makes a fumbling speech in which she calls societal categories "God's joke" because "God put beautiful spirits into these bodies, all kinds of bodies" and "we dumb humans are confused by the outside." She ends by saying, in a tone of finality, "We are one" (131), a phrase picked up by Hortensia in their parting exchange:

> "How odd that we live so close to one another . . ."
> Rhonda finished her thought for her. "Same town, different worlds."
> Hortensia's smile caught the moonlight. "Ah, but we are one." (132)

But this transcending of categories is clearly only momentary. For example, when Hortensia gets Blue Rhonda and two other prostitutes invitations to a society wedding, she sees their presence there as a joke, in spite of the debt she owes them and the bond forged by that debt in their private meetings.

Rebellion against gender roles is equally short-lived. After Blue Rhonda's death, she is revealed in the epilogue to the novel to be a man who has masqueraded as a woman. The letter she leaves behind for her friends echoes her reference to "God's joke" in her conversation with Hortensia, but her statement this time, "God played a joke on me and put me in a

man's body" (248–49), puts the emphasis on the power of societal categories, not their artificiality.

By virtue of her mixed heritage, Catherine defies both race and class
barriers. Her feelings of isolation are movingly suggested in several
scenes. When she realizes that she cannot join Hortensia's friends for
drinks after a polo match, the ensuing dialogue between her and her
mother reveals her sense of not fitting into any societal category:

> "It's because I'm piebald, isn't it?" Catherine flatly stated. . . .
> "What?" Hortensia inquired.
> "Piebald, pinto—half black and half white. I don't fit anywhere, do I?" (174)

The reaction of one of Hortensia's otherwise obtuse friends links
Catherine's isolation to the "discomfort" of the novel's title: "Sugar Guer-
rant felt her heart sink. For one flutter of an eyelash she had a sense of the
child's displacement, and worse, an insight into what Southerners used to
call 'our special problem'" (174–75).

Hortensia's acknowledgment of Catherine as her daughter does not
really change Catherine's sense of not belonging, as the closing of the
novel's last chapter suggests:

> "I don't feel like I belong to anybody but myself."
> Tears filled Hortensia's eyes. "You can belong to me if you want to."
> "I don't know," Catherine said thoughtfully.
> "As long as you like yourself, then if you do belong only to yourself perhaps
> you're ahead of the game."
> "I like myself." Catherine smiled, kissed Hortensia and then lay down and
> went right to sleep. (246)

This last scene is inconclusive. The only time the novel suggests that
these rigid divisions could be done away with permanently comes when
Hortensia observes, "Still, if we wanted to, if we truly, truly wanted to, I
think we could change the world" (176). Although Hortensia believes in
the possibility of change, she is nonetheless resigned to accepting the
"stultifying social order" in much the same way that Celeste is when she
says that, although she loves Cora like a sister, there is no way "short of
revolution" that she and Cora can step out of their roles as employer and
servant.

Although class and race lines ultimately prevail in *Southern Discomfort,* the symbolic bridging of these divisions in the novel is more complete than it is in Brown's earlier novels. The identification of the adopted

character with a black character and/or a middle or upper class character (an "aristocratic" character) in the other works is brought to the forefront of the novel here in the casting of Catherine's father as her black double and her mother as her "aristocratic" double. Her father Hercules is a variation on Molly's black double, Holly, in *Rubyfruit Jungle,* and on Carole's black double, Adele, in *In Her Day.* (Hercules also recalls the biological fathers of both Molly in *Rubyfruit Jungle* and Nickel in *Six of One* in that both men are French but are suspected of being black.) Catherine's mother Hortensia is a development of the roles of the "aristocratic" doubles in the earlier novels, Polina in *Rubyfruit Jungle,* Ilse in *In Her Day,* and Celeste in *Six of One.*

The symbolic union of Catherine with both her "aristocratic" double and her black double is climactically brought about through Hortensia's murder of the younger of her two sons, Paris. Like Celeste Chalfonte in *Six of One* with her two families, Hortensia has children in two different worlds—Paris, her beautiful and immoral son by her white husband, and Catherine, her daughter by her black lover. Paris represents the shallow side of Hortensia that she must kill in order to accept the part of her that is Catherine. This process of becoming whole began earlier when Hortensia recognized the evil in Paris and when she saw Catherine's anguish at being rejected by the white children of Montgomery: "When Paris fully revealed his twisted self, and then recently when Catherine was unmasked at the Great Witch Hunt, she was pushed into herself" (234). When Paris physically attacks Hortensia and Catherine, Hortensia kills him (in a more dramatic version of the killing or displacing of siblings than in Brown's earlier novels). The murder of Paris not only allows Hortensia to accept the part of herself that is Catherine but also brings Catherine into a fuller sense of herself. The act literally establishes Catherine in her rightful place as Hortensia's daughter and is followed by Hortensia's acknowledgment to Catherine that she is her mother. The murder also completes the union of Catherine with her black father, a process that began when Catherine had been given a picture of him and then was tutored by his mother. When the sheriff decides to report the murder as a suicide, he explains to Hortensia, "I owe Catherine's father one" (245).

Catherine and Hortensia, like Brown's heroes in her three earlier novels, rebel against a system of values that infringes on their sense of themselves. In so doing, all these characters embody the definition of "the woman-identified woman" in the essay that Brown wrote with other members of the Radicalesbians: "She is the woman who, often beginning at an extremely early age, acts in accordance with her inner compulsion to be a more complete and freer human being than her society . . . cares to allow her. These needs and actions, over a period of years, bring her into painful conflict with people, situations, the accepted ways of thinking, feeling and behaving. . . ." While the Radicalesbians essay defines the "woman-identified woman" as one who rebels against "the limitations and oppression laid on her by the most basic role of her society—the female role" ("Woman-Identified" 87), Brown's heroes rebel against all roles that reflect society's "conceptual limitations." On the literal level, this rebellion has become progressively less open in Brown's novels, moving from Molly Bolt's free-swinging defiance of everyone who gets in her way in *Rubyfruit Jungle* to Hortensia's acceptance of the social order in *Southern Discomfort*. (Anne Gottlieb, in her review of *Southern Discomfort* in the *New York Times Book Review*, sees Brown as having become aware in this novel that no one can break "*all* the rules" and that "every freedom must be understood within the bounds of a shared social structure that can, if stretched, yield painful renewal; if shattered, tragedy," 10.) At the same time, the symbolic bridging of class and race divisions has intensified, reaching its height in *Southern Discomfort* in the biological identification of the adopted character with both a black character and an "aristocratic" one.

Jill Johnston, in writing about Brown's portrayal of herself in Molly in *Rubyfruit Jungle*, says, "What I admire most is her own early, or prepolitical, refusal to compromise her identity by permitting anybody to either closet or contain her."[8] Molly Bolt is the most openly rebellious of Brown's heroes. But although the women characters in Brown's other novels do not rebel against societal categories in the same defiant way that Molly does, their rejection of the limitations that society attempts to place on them through class, race, and gender divisions is the essence of their being. It is in Brown's portrayal of the rebelliousness of her heroes that we can see how her concerns as a lesbian feminist underlie and inform her portrayal of Southern women and link her early political vision with her imaginative vision as a Southern novelist.

NOTES

[1] Page references are to the Bantam edition.

[2] Brown also discusses the NOW experience in her 1972 essay, "Take a Lesbian to Lunch," *Plain Brown Rapper*, 87–91.

[3] In "Take a Lesbian to Lunch" Brown says of NOW's attempt to co-opt her: "They got a real bargain with me. Not only was I a Lesbian, but I was poor, I was an orphan (adopted) without knowledge of my ethnic origins," *Plain Brown Rapper*, 89.

[4] Judith Winn, book review editor for *Sojourner*, first pointed out to me the adoption motif in these two novels.

[5] See, for example, the ad and review in *The Village Voice*, 12 Sept. 1977, 4.

[6] See Kleindeinst's review in *Gay Community News*, 3, and Turner in *New York*, 60.

[7] See Turner, 60.

[8] Quoted by Alexander, 110.

Toni Cade Bambara

Born in New York City, Bambara received her B.A. from Queens College in 1959 and, after study abroad, her M.A. from City College of New York. Her first collection of short stories, Gorilla, My Love, *was published in 1972. She has since published another collection of short stories and a novel, which appeared after she moved to Atlanta.*

Youth in Toni Cade Bambara's *Gorilla, My Love*

NANCY D. HARGROVE

In reading Toni Cade Bambara's collection of short stories, *Gorilla, My Love* (1972), one is immediately struck by her portrayal of black life and by her faithful reproduction of black dialect. Her first-person narrators speak conversationally and authentically: "So Hunca Bubba in the back with the pecans and Baby Jason, and he in love. . . . there's a movie house . . . which I ax about. Cause I am a movie freak from way back, even though it do get me in trouble sometime" (14). What Twain's narrator Huck Finn did for the dialect of middle America in the mid-nineteenth century, Bambara's narrators do for contemporary black dialect. Indeed, in the words of one reviewer, Caren Dybek, Bambara "possesses one of the finest ears for the nuances of black English" ("Black Literature" 66). In portraying black life, she presents a wide range of black characters,[1] and she uses as settings Brooklyn, Harlem, or unnamed black sections of New York City, except for three stories which take place in rural areas. Finally, the situations are typical of black urban experience: two policemen confront a black man shooting basketball in a New York park at night; young black activists gather the community members at a Black Power rally; a group of black children from the slums visit F.A.O. Schwartz and are amazed at the prices of toys. Bambara's stories communicate with shattering force and directness both the grim reality of the black world—its violence, poverty, and harshness—and its strength and beauty—strong family ties, individual determination, and a sense of cultural traditions. Lucille Clifton has said of her work, "She has captured it all, how we really talk, how we really are,"[2] and the *Saturday Review* has called *Gorilla, My Love* "among the best portraits of black life to have appeared in some time" (97).

Although her work teems with the life and language of black people,

what is equally striking about it, and about this collection particularly, is
the universality of its themes.[3] Her fiction reveals the pain and the joy of
the human experience in general, of what it means to be human, and most
often of what it means to be *young* and human. One of Bambara's special
gifts as a writer of fiction is her ability to portray with sensitivity and
compassion the experiences of children from their point of view. In the
fifteen stories that compose *Gorilla, My Love,* all the main characters are
female, thirteen of them are first-person narrators, and ten of them are
young, either teenagers or children. They are wonderful creations, especially the young ones, many of whom show similar traits of character; they
are intelligent, imaginative, sensitive, proud and arrogant, witty, tough,
but also poignantly vulnerable. Through these young central characters,
Bambara expresses the fragility, the pain, and occasionally the promise of
the experience of growing up, of coming to terms with a world that is
hostile, chaotic, violent. Disillusionment, loss, and loneliness, as well as
unselfishness, love, and endurance, are elements of that process of maturation which her young protagonists undergo.

   "Happy Birthday" focuses on the experience of loneliness and isolation
as seen through the eyes of a young black girl. One of only two stories in
the volume with a third-person narrator, it describes an especially lonely
Saturday in the life of Ollie, an orphan who lives with her grandfather.
The story begins in the morning with Ollie attempting to find some
companionship, but she finds her grandfather drunk, the building super-
intendent busy, and her friend Wilma gone. In the early afternoon, she
continues her search, at one point trying to talk to some older boys
drowsing on the roof of an apartment building. A simile comparing the
boys to "dummies in a window" implies that they offer her nothing in the
way of human contact. From the roof Ollie looks down into the park, but
sees no one there; indeed, "There was hardly anyone on the block. . . .
Everything below was gray as if the chimney had snowed on the whole
block." Desperate for some one, any one, she mounts a fire hydrant in
front of the Mount Zion A.M.E. Church, flapping her arms and yelling,
"This time I'm going to fly off and kill myself." She attracts only the
attention of a woman who scowls at her and the minister who orders her
to play elsewhere. Thus even the church, the enduring sanctuary of the
outcast and lonely, offers Ollie no solace. In agony, she whispers to and
then yells at the pigeons, revealing to the reader the intense poignancy

and pain of her loneliness on this particular day: "Better wish me happy birthday . . . or somebody around here is gonna get wasted."

At last a human figure seems to come to her aid as a neighbor leans from her window to inquire about Ollie's distress. Ollie yells at her, "You should never have a birthday in the summertime, cause nobody's around to wish you happy birthday or give you a party." Miss Hazel's reply is meant to be mildly consoling, but only reveals her insensitivity and lack of understanding: "Well, don't cry, sugar. When you get as old as me, you'll be glad to forget all about—" As Ollie sobs in the street, the woman closes her window "so she could hear the television good." Ollie really is all alone.

Throughout the story Bambara uses a number of subtle devices to reinforce the theme of isolation. The word "Empty" appears twice as a separate sentence, and negatives are found in abundance, "no one," "nothing," "none." The absence of people is stressed through references not only to individual characters who are away, such as Wilma and a neighbor named Mrs. Robinson, but also to large groups, as in the sweeping sentence, "Everyone was either at camp or at work or was sleeping like the boys on the roof or dead or just plain gone off." Elements of the setting are actually empty, like the park and the block, or are symbolic of emptiness and depression, like the gray cinders from the chimney and the ruins of the burned down bar-b-que place. Even the church rejects Ollie, as the grumpy minister literally chases her from its doors. Further, she is addressed several times as "little girl" rather than by her name, suggesting a lack or loss of identity, her nothingness in relation to other people. None of this is lost on Ollie, who realizes that "sometimes [the building superintendent] *wouldn't even remember her,*" that the big boy Ferman "had just yelled at her as if he had *forgotten her name or didn't know her any more,*" and that Reverend Hall calls her by her name only when she is with her grandfather: "How come you always calling me *little girl,* but you sure know my name when I'm walking with my grandfather?" (italics mine).

Finally, small touches of irony are apparent not only in the title but also throughout the story. For example, although we are told from the opening sentence that "Ollie spent the whole morning waiting," it is not until the closing passages, which describe the end of the long, lonely day, that we discover what she is waiting for—someone who will remember what day it is and wish her "Happy Birthday." Further, a subtly ironic contrast to Ollie's perception of the day as sad and bleak is suggested when Miss Hazel's great-grandmother, disturbed by the child's loud sobbing in the street, comes to the window "to see who was dying and with so much noise and *on such a lovely day*" (italics mine).

While the loneliness of a child is the main thematic element of "Happy Birthday," the disillusionment which is an inevitable part of growing up is dominant in the lives of the young girls who are the narrators and main characters in "Gorilla, My Love," "The Lesson," and "Sweet Town."

With great sensitivity Bambara portrays through Hazel in "Gorilla, My Love" the feelings of pain and betrayal experienced by a child in a situation that adults would generally consider trivial or ridiculous. When Hazel was very young, her favorite uncle, Hunca Bubba, promised to marry her when she grew up, a promise which he gave lightly but which she took seriously. The story centers on her discovery that he has not only dropped the affectionate name Hunca Bubba, but also intends to marry someone else. For Hazel this bitter betrayal reveals to her that even adults who are "family" cannot be trusted to keep their promises. Her disillusionment is intense and painful; as she says," I ain't playin. I'm hurtin. . . . ," speaking the words of the original title of the story.

Hazel's realization and subsequent disillusionment are skillfully prepared for from the opening lines, where the idea of unpleasant changes is introduced through her first-person narration: "That was the year Hunca Bubba changed his name. Not a change up, but a change back, since Jefferson Winston Vale was the name in the first place. Which was news to me cause he'd been my Hunca Bubba my whole lifetime, since I couldn't manage Uncle to save my life." Further foreshadowing follows. From Hazel the reader learns that she, her grandfather, Hunca Bubba, and her younger brother are in a car driving to an undisclosed destination when Hunca Bubba begins talking about the woman he loves. Hazel affects boredom with the subject and criticizes a photograph of the woman, responses indicative of her true dismay, although at this point the reader has no clue as to the cause of her antagonism: "And we got to hear all this stuff about this woman he in love with and all. Which really ain't enough to keep the mind alive, though Baby Jason got no better sense than to give his undivided attention and keep grabbin at the photograph which is just a picture of some skinny woman in a countrified dress with her hand shot up to her face like she shame fore cameras."

There follow five pages (a large section in a story of only seven and a half pages) that appear at first to contain a long and puzzling digression on a memory from the previous Easter. In fact, the episode furnishes the key to our understanding of the enormous, shattering impact that Hunca Bubba's "betrayal" has on Hazel. The remembered incident seems initially to reveal only an occasion on which Hazel got into trouble as a result of her "toughness"; however, as we discover, Hazel is both sensitive and vulnerable beneath her tough exterior.

The episode concerns a movie which Hazel, Baby Jason, and Big Brood went to see. Although the marquee advertised that "Gorilla, My Love" was playing, the actual movie was about Jesus. The three were disappointed and angry: "I am ready to kill, not cause I got anything gainst Jesus. Just that when you fixed to watch a gorilla picture you don't wanna get messed around with Sunday School stuff. So I am mad." After "yellin, booin, stompin, and carrying on" to show their displeasure, they watched the feature, hoping that "Gorilla, My Love" would follow. When it did not, as Hazel so bluntly puts it, "we know we been had. No gorilla no nuthin." She daringly went to complain to the manager and to ask that their money be refunded. Getting no satisfaction from him, she took some matches from his office and set fire to the candy stand. She later explained to her father that she expected people (and marquees) to keep their word: "Cause if you say Gorilla, My Love, you suppose to mean it. Just like when you say you goin to give me a party on my birthday, you gotta mean it. . . . I mean even gangsters in the movies say My word is my bond. So don't nobody get away with nothin far as I'm concerned."

Clearly, Hunca Bubba's breaking his promise to marry her is far more devastating to Hazel than the false advertising of the movie theater. Since a person whom she has every reason to trust has betrayed her, the entire adult world becomes suspect. Indeed, throughout the story, Hazel makes numerous comments on the conflict between children and adults. When her grandfather and Hunca Bubba make a weak attempt to justify what has occurred ("'Look here, Precious, it was Hunca Bubba what told you them things. This here, Jefferson Winston Vale.' And Hunca Bubba say, 'That's right. That was somebody else. I'm a new somebody'"), Hazel is not buying and turns to her little brother for solace, bitterly condemning the perfidy of adults: "I'm crying and crumplin down in the seat. . . . And Baby Jason cryin too. Cause he is my blood brother and understands that we must stick together or be forever lost, what with grownups playin change-up and turnin you round every which way so bad. And don't even say they sorry."

A second painful experience of disillusionment appears in what is perhaps the best of the fifteen stories, "The Lesson." Again, the story centers on and owes much of its vitality to its first-person narrator, a young girl named Sylvia. Arrogant, sassy, and tough, with a vocabulary that might shock a sailor, Sylvia is also witty, bright, and vulnerable. In the course of the story she learns a lesson which disillusions her about the world in which she lives, about the society of which she is a part. Against her will, she is forced to realize the unfairness of life and, as a black girl, her often low position in the scheme of things. Although she fights against this realization and indeed refuses adamantly even to acknowledge it, it is clear to the reader that the young girl is irrevocably affected by the events of the day.

In the opening paragraph, Sylvia sets the stage for the action to follow by introducing her antagonist, Miss Moore, while revealing some facets of her own personality as well as the kind of environment in which she lives. Having a college degree, Miss Moore has taken upon herself "responsibility for the young ones' education." Accordingly, from time to time she takes them on "field trips," during which they learn a great deal about life. Sylvia clearly does not like Miss Moore or her lessons: "And quite naturally we laughed at her. . . . And we kinda hated her too. . . . [She] was always planning these boring-ass things for us to do." In describing Miss Moore, Sylvia reveals her own toughness, which she communicates largely through strong language ("sorry-ass horse," "goddamn gas mask," "some ole dumb shit foolishness"), as well as her own pride and sense of superiority ("[M]e and Sugar were the only ones just right"), both of which will be seriously damaged in the course of the story. Finally, she indirectly indicates the type of urban environment in which she lives: "And we kinda hated [Miss Moore] . . . the way we did the winos who cluttered up our parks and pissed on our handball walls and stank up our hallways and stairs so you couldn't halfway play hide-and-seek without a goddamn gas mask." She also reveals that she and her cousin live with their aunt, who is "saddled" with them while "our mothers [are] in a la-de-da apartment up the block having a good ole time."

The action begins on a hot summer day when Miss Moore "rounds us all up at the mailbox" for one of her outings. This one will be on the subject of money, although the implications are much wider by the story's end: ". . . Miss Moore asking us do we know what money is, like we a bunch of retards." Even though Sylvia affects boredom with the subject, it is clear that the mention of their condition of poverty is unpleasant to her, apparently because it causes her to feel inferior: "So we heading down the street and she's boring us silly about what things cost and what our parents make and how much goes for rent and how money ain't divided up right in this country. And then she gets to the part about *we all poor and live in the slums, which I don't feature*" (italics mine).

To illustrate her point in a striking manner, Miss Moore takes the children to an expensive store on Fifth Avenue where they can see for themselves the extravagant prices and then realize the difference between their lives and those of the very wealthy. A skillful teacher who provides the opportunity for the children to have their own flashes of insight, Miss Moore simply leads them from window to window, casually asking or answering questions. They are amazed at a $300 microscope, at a $480 paperweight (an object with which they are not even familiar), and finally at a $1,195 toy sailboat. Even Sylvia, as superior and untouched as she has tried to be, is astonished at the latter, whose price seems beyond all reason: "'Unbelievable,' I hear myself say and am really stunned." Although she herself does not realize the cause of her anger ("*For some reason* this pisses me off"), the reader understands that it lies in the injustice of things in general, but more specifically in Sylvia's frustration at being unable to purchase and possess even one of the toys displayed tantalizingly before her.

Another unpleasant, and in this case unfamiliar, emotion overcomes her as Miss Moore tells the children to go into the store. Ordinarily aggressive and daring, Sylvia now hangs back: "Not that I'm scared, what's there to be afraid of, just a toy store. But I feel funny, shame. But what I got to be shamed about? Got as much right to go in as anybody. But somehow I can't seem to get hold of the door. . . ." Her shame arises from her sense of inferiority, of not belonging in such an expensive store, communicated indirectly and subtly by her comparison of the children's chaotic entrance to "a glued-together jigsaw done all wrong." Once inside, her painful feelings become intense: "Then Sugar run a finger over the whole boat. And I'm jealous and want to hit her. Maybe not her, but I sure want to punch somebody in the mouth." Angry not only at her own deprivation but also at Miss Moore for making her aware of it, Sylvia bitterly lashes out at the older woman: "Watcha bring us here for, Miss Moore?" Attempting to help Sylvia acknowledge her anger, Miss Moore responds, "You sound angry, Sylvia. Are you mad about something?"

Although too proud to admit her emotions to Miss Moore, Sylvia on the way home reveals her longing for one of the toys, her realization that what it costs would buy many items desperately needed by her family, and her anguish at the injustice endured by the poor:

> Thirty-five dollars could buy new bunk beds for Junior and Gretchen's boy. Thirty-five dollars and the whole household could go visit Granddaddy Nelson in the country. Thirty-five dollars would pay for the rent and the piano bill too. Who are these people that spend that much for performing clowns and $1,000 for toy sailboats? What kind of work they do and how they live and how come we ain't in on it?

When she seems toughly to dismiss the painful lessons of the day, "Messin up my day with this shit," the reader is aware that they have in truth touched her deeply, messing up far more than that one day. When she returns home, the overwhelming effects of her disillusionment are confirmed through her description of time (she seems years older than she had been that morning) and her revelation that she has a headache: "Miss Moore lines us up in front of the mailbox where we started from, seem like years ago, and I got a headache for thinkin so hard."

Her only protection against further pain and humiliation seems to be in not acknowledging formally, aloud, what has been so powerfully demonstrated to her. Yet, when Miss Moore urges the children to express what they have learned, her cousin Sugar blurts out the harsh facts in what is to Sylvia a bitter betrayal, an admission of the injustice, inferiority, imperfection of her world. Responding to Miss Moore's question, "Well, what do you think of F.A.O. Schwartz?" Sugar surprises Sylvia by saying, "You know, Miss Moore, I don't think all of us here put together eat in a year what that sailboat costs." The older woman urges her on to further exploration of the subject by commenting, "Imagine for a minute what kind of society it is in which some people can spend on a toy what it would cost to feed a family of six or seven. What do you think?" (This is a rather blunt and heavy-handed statement of the theme). When Sugar, rejecting Sylvia's desperate attempts to silence her, asserts, "I think . . . that this is not much of a democracy if you ask me," Sylvia is "disgusted with Sugar's treachery." However, as the story ends, she is going "to think this day through," even though she still appears determined to maintain her former arrogance and superiority: "But ain't nobody gonna beat me at nuthin."

"The Lesson" is especially fine in its sensitive portrayal of Sylvia, in its realistic use of black dialect, and in the view of American society it offers from the vantage point of the poor. While this story describes a young girl's disillusionment with the society in which she lives and is therefore a kind of social and political commentary, another story, "Sweet Town," centers on a more personal, yet enduringly human and universal experience of disillusionment: the failure or disappointment of young love. Again, the narrator is a memorable young girl; but while Ollie's loneliness and Hazel's and Sylvia's toughness seem their impressive qualities, it is Kit's joie de vivre and her delightful romanticism that make her such a moving character. Her narration is light and lilting, breathless, swift, and largely free of the tough language used by Hazel and Sylvia as she recalls the ecstasy and sorrow of the spring and summer of her fifteenth year.

In the introductory section Kit's character and her situation are established as much by her narrative style as by the revelation of incidents. To illustrate the crazy, magical quality of her "youth in the sweet town playground of the sunny city," she describes in a breezy, grandiose style appropriate to her intensely romantic nature a series of absurd, loving notes she exchanged with her mother:

> And then one day, having romped my soul through the spectrum of sunny colors, I dashed up to her apartment to escape the heat and found a letter from her which eternally elated my heart to the point of bursture and generally endeared her to me forever. Written on the kitchen table in cake frosting was the message, "My dear, mad, perverse young girl, kindly take care and paint the fire escape in your leisure. . . ."

Her exuberance and romanticism are conveyed by the length of the first sentence and by her extravagant diction—a style far different from that of the blunt young narrator of the previous story. Kit quickly endears herself to the reader, whereas Sylvia grows on the reader rather more slowly.

Kit's natural exuberance and tendency to craziness are compounded by her awakening sexuality, which has coincided with the season of spring: "With Penelope splintering through the landscape and the pores secreting animal champagne, I bent my youth to the season's tempo and proceeded to lose my mind." In the midst of "this sweet and drugged madness," she meets the handsome B. J. and his less attractive friend Eddie. (Not one for modesty, Kit recalls with refreshing frankness, "It was on the beach that we met, me looking great in a pair of cut-off dungarees.") Through the seemingly endless summer, they share such delightfully crazy and innocently romantic "we-experiences" as "a two-strawed mocha, duo-jaywalking summons, twosome whistling scenes." Their craziness transforms the city into a kaleidoscope of magical colors and designs and B. J. into the fertility god Pan: "Hand in hand, me and Pan, and Eddie too, whizzed through the cement kaleidoscope making our own crazy patterns, singing our own song."

But suddenly, abruptly, the ecstasy ends. Awakened from a nightmare by pebbles thrown through her open window, Kit learns that B. J. and Eddie are leaving, the latter having stolen money from his grandmother. That the harsh reality has shattered her romantic idyll is reflected in Kit's juxtaposition of a romantic setting of casement window, garden, and balcony to her grim urban setting with its stoop and milkbox: "It wasn't a casement window and there was no garden underneath. . . . I went to the window to see who I was going to share my balcony scene with, and there below, standing on the milkbox, was B. J. I climbed out and joined him on the stoop." Her Romeo has come to bid her an unromantic farewell: "We're cutting out." Although Kit yearns to convince him to stay by expressing romantic, noble sentiments, she says instead, "I don't know why the hell you want to hang around with that nothing. . . . Eddie is a shithead."

Yet, in the midst of the pain and shock of the abandonment, her romantic nature briefly takes over as she imagines herself, in an amusing and curious mixture of Western movies, popular love ballads, and romantic novels, on a long, arduous quest somewhere out West in search of the two boys: "And in every town I'll ask for them as the hotel keeper feeds the dusty, weary traveler that I'll be. 'Have you seen two guys, one great, the other acned? If you see 'em, tell 'em Kit's looking for them.' And I'd bandage up my cactus-torn feet and sling the knapsack into place and be off." However, she then dismisses whatever may happen in that imagined future as not mattering after all, for she has been betrayed, the magical spell of youth has been broken, and its sweet fruit has begun to rot: "No matter. Days other than the here and now, I told myself, will be dry and sane and sticky with the rotten apricots oozing slowly in the sweet time of my betrayed youth."

Bambara uses a number of devices to reinforce her theme of the disillusionment of young romantic love. The brevity of that love is suggested by the story's own brevity; a scant five pages, it is the shortest of the fifteen works collected in the volume.[4] Further, the description of the ecstatic portion of her love affair with B. J. is limited to one single page (the first two pages cover introductory material and the last two, B. J.'s departure and Kit's reaction). The story is also filled with words suggesting speed. From the opening passage, "It is hard to believe that I *so quickly squandered* my youth," to Kit's last view of B. J. and Eddie "*dashing* down the night street" (italics mine), Bambara employs such words as "romped," "dashed," "tempo," "race," "jumped," "ran," "flying," "pace," and "whizzed."

The pleasure and joy of young love, which make its loss so difficult to bear, are conveyed through the title as well as through references to sweetness, to intensity (everything seems about to explode: "bursture," "orange explosure"), to craziness, and to music (trumpets, whistling, singing). Finally, several classical references also serve to reinforce these magical qualities. A somewhat ambiguous allusion to Penelope is presumably meant to evoke the faithful wife of Ulysses, though she seems a bit too old and sedate for this story; one wonders if perhaps Persephone, with her associations of mad passion and springtime, would not have been more appropriate. However, the comparisons of B. J. to Pan (lust and spring) and to Apollo (male beauty and perfection) clearly convey what he means to Kit and what, at the end of the story, she has lost.

Another theme which centers on young girls and which runs throughout a number of the stories is that of the value of human solidarity, of love for family or one's fellowman: a sense of unity and comradeship with a former enemy in "The Hammer Man"; a very special bond between a young girl and an old woman in "Maggie of the Green Bottles"; and a sister's love for her retarded brother in "Raymond's Run." In each case the bond is shown to be a very positive and sustaining one, whether it is brief or long-lived.

The youngster who narrates "The Hammer Man" is the sole *unnamed* narrator in the fifteen stories. However, she is similar to her young counterparts in being tough, sensitive, and imaginative, though she is not as tough as Sylvia, as sensitive as Hazel, or as imaginative as Kit. In general, her character does not seem to be drawn with as much complexity as theirs. Yet her story is a very moving one, even though its central incident clearly does not have a lasting effect on her. It revolves around her relationship with Manny, an older boy, perhaps even a young man, who is mentally disturbed. As the story opens, the reader learns that they have had an altercation, caused by the narrator's taking away his hammer and insulting him. He camps out on her doorstep for days or weeks, waiting to retaliate: "Manny told [my father] right off that he was going to kill me first chance he got." Meanwhile, she feigns yellow fever in order to stay in the safety of her home. During this time period, several relatives and friends become involved in their fray, including her father, who has a violent confrontation with Manny's older brother and is subsequently threatened by their uncle, and Miss Rose, who several times fights in the streets with Manny's mother. Thus, the antagonism is deep, long-lasting, and widespread.

However, when Manny falls off a roof and is too disabled to be danger-ous, the protagonist immediately recovers from her illness and returns to the outside world. Because "Manny stayed indoors for a long time, . . . [she] almost forgot about him," becoming involved with new kids on the block, with activities at a recently opened neighborhood center (where she reads her folder and discovers that "I was from a deviant family in a deviant neighborhood"), and with attempts to abandon her tomboyish ways and be more feminine.

Suddenly one night Manny re-enters her life, and just as suddenly she and her former enemy become strangely and briefly joined in a bond of solidarity; indeed, she becomes in a sense his defender and protector. Walking by a park near midnight, she sees him practicing basketball in the dark. In his mentally disturbed condition, he is replaying, over and over, the last seconds of an important game in his past in which he had missed the final winning basket. With sudden sympathy and sensitivity, the young girl realizes what anguish he endures as he tries to reclaim and change the past, now making the basket successfully time after time: "He went back to the lay-ups, always from the same spot with his arms crooked in the same way, over and over. . . . He never missed. But he cursed himself away. It was torture."

When two policemen appear to investigate their presence in the park, she takes Manny's side against them. Heroically, she stands up to the policemen, defending Manny's right to be in the park, insisting on the innocence of his activities, and urging them to give him his basketball. Although she speaks to them sharply, she is careful to "keep her cool," being well aware of the hammer in Manny's pocket and the potentially explosive nature of the situation.

With the ball again in his possession, Manny returns to shooting lay-ups. Looking at him with eyes made more sensitive by her newly acquired relationship with him, the young girl sees him as "some kind of beautiful bird" and his movements as "about the most beautiful thing a man can do and not be a fag." Thus the sudden decision by the police to take him in after all is shocking, disillusioning, and terrifying to her. She is also certain that the episode, which has now erupted into pushing and yelling, will end in her being shot and killed along with Manny. Her terrified imagination is so intense that, in the space of a few seconds, she sees a kaleidoscopic rush of scenes in which she is shot in the stomach and bleeds to death, her confirmation picture is in the obituary section of the newspaper, and her distraught relatives mourn in various attitudes of sorrow or anger.

However, the outcome is not this melodramatic nightmare, for Manny quietly enters the squad car, they drive away, and the young girl goes home. Unlike most of the other stories discussed, this episode, as intense and as striking as it is, apparently has no enduring effect on her. A brief, transitory moment of unity in which two former enemies join together against a sudden threatening force, it is only one of the myriad elements in the experience of growing up. As the final sentences of the story indicate, it recedes quickly into the past as the former tomboy turns her attention to becoming a young woman: "And then it was spring finally, and me and Violet was in this very boss fashion show at the center. And Miss Rose bought me my first corsage—yellow roses to match my shoes."

The story is positive in its portrayal of the capacity of human beings, a young one in this case, to be compassionate, unselfish, and even heroic in their concern for others. The protagonist is clearly presented as admirable in her desire to protect Manny against what seem to her powerful forces of injustice and cruelty. The experience, the story suggests, is valuable not only in itself but also as an integral part of the process of maturation, in which the young individual learns to see others sympathetically and to join with them against (or even defend them from) threatening forces.

In "Maggie of the Green Bottles" Bambara perceptively traces the very special relationship between a young girl and an old woman, apparently her great-grandmother. As in several other stories, although the narrator is grown and is recalling an episode from her childhood, she narrates it from the child's point of view, as the child that she was experienced it. In this particular story, the child-narrator is an innocent eye, for she does not understand fully the meanings of many of the things she describes. While to the other characters in the story—and, to some extent, to the reader—Maggie is a crazy old woman, a free-loading relative, and an alcoholic, to Peaches (who has the same nickname and some of the same family members as the narrator of "Gorilla, My Love") she is a kind of fairy godmother endowed with many special qualities. She is magical and enchanted, possessing wisdom and knowledge about astrology, the planets, destiny; her room is a "sanctuary of heaven charts and incense pots and dream books and magic stuffs." She is strong-willed and tough, with Aries as her astrological sign. She wins Peaches's awed admiration by taking on the child's powerful father, variously described by the child as a giant, a monster, a Neanderthal, in titanic verbal battles. In describing these encounters, Peaches appropriately compares the pugnacious Maggie to David pitted against Goliath. In fact, Maggie will do battle with anyone: "[S]he'd tackle the lot of them right there in the yard, blood kin or by marriage, and neighbors or no." Finally, she is not ordinary; according to Peaches, she is "truly inspired," wanting to rise above the level to which she is bound, aspiring to greatness of some kind. She wears lace, writes with lavender ink, and generally scorns those who are satisfied with the mundane:

> . . . Margaret Cooper Williams wanted something she could not have. And it was the sorrow of her life that all her children and theirs were uncooperative—worse, squeamish. Too busy taking in laundry, buckling at the knees, putting their faith in Jesus, mute and sullen in their sorrow, too squeamish to band together and take the world by storm, make history, or even to appreciate the calling of Maggie the Ram, or the Aries that came after.

Her relationship with her great-granddaughter is a very special one, for from the day of the baby's christening Maggie is determined to endow her with a sense of a capacity for greatness, for rising above her circumstances. At her christening Maggie, like the gift-giving godmothers of fairy tales, begins a book to inspire her great-granddaughter. And the little girl grows up feeling that she is indeed a very gifted creature with the ability and the obligation to achieve the extraordinary: "I was destined for greatness. She assured me. And I was certain of my success, as I was certain that my parents were not my parents, that I was descended, anointed and ready to gobble up the world from urgent, noble Olympiads."

Because of the bond between the two and because Peaches is very young and naive, she does not recognize Maggie's weaknesses as such; indeed, she often perceives them instead as further evidence of her extraordinary nature. Peaches does not see Maggie as a "freeloading" relative, nor does she seem concerned about her bizarre treatment of their dog. Rather, she sees Maggie's verbal battles with her father as signs of her greatness, and her green bottles, containing the liquor to which she is apparently addicted, as enchanted and full of magical charms: "Whenever I saw them piled in the garbage out back I was tempted to touch them and make a wish, knowing all the while that the charm was all used up and that that was why they were in the garbage in the first place. But there was no doubt that they were special." Although she describes Maggie's drunken stupors, she does not seem to know what they are nor does she realize that Maggie dies of alcoholism, with herself as an unwitting accomplice at the very end.

After the funeral (which the child neither attends nor describes), when asked what she would like as a keepsake, she requests the bottles, still seeing them as magical. Ironically, the adults, not understanding that she means the empty green liquor bottles, give her another set of bottles: "I had meant the green bottles. I was going to tell them and then I didn't. I was too small for so much enchantment anyway. I went to bed feeling much too small. And it seemed a shame that the hope of the Aries line should have to sleep with a light on still, and blame it on Jason and cry with balled fists in the eyes just like an ordinary, mortal, everyday-type baby." These lines make clear the value of what Maggie has given to Peaches and suggest that the effect of her death may be to reduce the child to a view of herself as small, ordinary, and mortal. But the ending is ambiguous. Although she has lost Maggie and the magic bottles, and feels very small, she still describes herself as "the hope of the Aries line" and says only that she is crying "just like" an ordinary child, implying that she is not one.

Bambara makes extensive use of imagery, comparisons, and symbols from the literature of magic, myth, and fairy tale to reflect and even recreate the enchanted world shared by Maggie and Peaches. Maggie herself is likened obliquely to a fairy godmother who bestows a gift on a child at her christening, as in "Sleeping Beauty." She is also called "Maggie the Ram," a reference to Aries, the first sign of the zodiac, which represents the creative impulse and the thunderbolt. Peaches is compared to a descendant of the gods of Olympus, particularly to Athena, and she is associated twice with Alexander the Great through her zodiacal sign Aries, which she shares with Maggie. In most myths and fairy tales, a sinister figure is set in opposition to the hero/heroine, and Bambara's story contains such a figure. Peaches's father, an enormous, pugnacious man "whom Grandma Williams used to say was just the sort of size man put on this earth for the 'spress purpose of clubbing us all to death,'" is described as a monster, a giant, a wolf man, the phantom of the opera, and a "gross Neanderthal."

Finally, the narrator's use of religious terminology in connection with Maggie reinforces her perception of her great-grandmother as sacred and suggests her feelings of reverence and awe. Maggie's room is called a "sanctuary," and in her encounters with Peaches's father she is a Biblical David to his Goliath. Just prior to her death, Peaches notes that "she was humming one of those weird songs of hers which always made her seem *holier* and blacker than she could've been" (italics mine). And Peaches's worshipful attitude toward her is revealed in the metaphorical positions she adopts in praising the old woman's "guts": "It is to Maggie's guts that I bow forehead to the floor and kiss her hand" and "I must genuflect and kiss her ring."

"Raymond's Run," another story of initiation, centers on Hazel Elizabeth Deborah Parker, perhaps the most appealing and lovable of Bambara's young narrators, and concerns two discoveries she makes on the way to growing up. One has to do with her retarded older brother, for whose care she is responsible, and the other with her rival in the May Day races. As in the two previous stories, both discoveries reveal the value of human solidarity, of love for family and friends.

Hazel is a totally engaging character. In a narrative style entirely free of the strong language used by most of the other young narrators, she reveals a refreshing honesty as well as a dedication to hard work and a dislike of phonies. She clearly knows who and what she is. Her life centers on two things: caring for Raymond and running. At the story's beginning she indicates that the former is a large and consuming task, but one which she accepts stoically and with love: "All I have to do in life is mind my brother Raymond, which is enough. . . . He needs looking after cause he's not quite right. And a lot of smart mouths got lots to say about that too. . . . But now, if anybody has anything to say to Raymond, anything to say about his big head, they have to come by me."

If Raymond has her heart, running has her soul. She tells us honestly, but not arrogantly, "I'm the fastest thing on two feet. There is no track meet that I don't win the first place medal." She works hard to improve her skill, and she illustrates her disgust with those who pretend they never practice by describing Cynthia Procter, who always says, after winning the spelling bee, "'I completely forgot about [it].' And she'll clutch the lace on her blouse like it was a narrow escape. Oh, brother."

She is also determined to be herself, rather than what others want her to be. Rebelling against her mother's desire for her to "act like a girl for a change" and participate in the May Pole dance instead of the fifty-yard dash, she insists that "you should be trying to be yourself, whatever that is, which is, as far as I am concerned, a poor Black girl who really can't afford to buy shoes and a new dress you only wear once a lifetime cause it won't fit next year." Although when she was younger she had once been a "strawberry in a Hansel and Gretel pageant," she now asserts, "I am not a strawberry. I do not dance on my toes. I run. That is what I am all about."

The May Day race, the central episode of the story, is thus of tremendous importance to Hazel. She is determined to win again, especially because she has a new challenger in Gretchen, who has recently moved into the neighborhood. Her descriptions of her feelings before and during the race are superb in their realism, revealing her great intensity and concentration. Yet, as she is running, she notices that Raymond is running his own race outside the fence. Suddenly she realizes that she could teach Raymond to run and thereby make his life more meaningful; thus, whether or not she herself has won the race now becomes secondary: "And I'm smiling to beat the band cause if I've lost this race, or if me and Gretchen tied, or even if I've won, I can always retire as a runner and begin a whole new career as a coach with Raymond as my champion. . . . I've got a roomful of ribbons and medals and awards. But what has Raymond got to call his own?" Her sincere love for her brother and her excitement at discovering something that he can learn to do well are so intense that "by the time he comes over I'm jumping up and down so glad to see him—my brother Raymond, a great runner in the family tradition."

Ironically, everyone assumes that she is elated because she has again won first place.

Almost simultaneously she realizes that, far from disliking her rival or feeling superior to her, she admires her for her obvious skill in and dedication to running: "And I smile [at Gretchen]. Cause she's good, no doubt about it. Maybe she'd like to help me coach Raymond; she obviously is serious about running, as any fool can see." The story ends with the two girls smiling at each other with sincere appreciation for what the other is.

Hazel represents the best of youthful humanity in her unselfish desire to make her brother's life more significant, in her determination to be herself, and in her honest admiration of the abilities of a rival. But it is perhaps her wise understanding of what is most to be valued in "being people" that makes her such an appealing character. "Raymond's Run" is a story rare in this collection, and in modern literature, in that everyone wins in one way or another, and yet it is neither sentimental nor unrealistic, but sincere and believable.

Thus, with compassion, understanding, and a warm sense of humor, Bambara portrays in many of the stories in *Gorilla, My Love* an integral part of the human experience, the problems and joys of youth. Told from the viewpoint of young black girls, they capture how it feels as a child to undergo the various experiences of loneliness, disillusionment, and close relationships with others. Bambara's short fiction thus belongs to the ranks of other literary works portraying youth, such as Twain's *The Adventures of Huckleberry Finn*, Joyce's *A Portrait of the Artist as a Young Man*, and Salinger's *The Catcher in the Rye*. Furthermore, because her protagonists are female, black, and generally pre-adolescent, these stories, like the works of several other contemporary black female writers, contribute a new viewpoint to the genre.

NOTES

[1] The only white characters are Neil in "Mississippi Ham Rider," Miss Ruby in "Playin with Punjab," the two men filming a documentary in "Blues Ain't No Mockin Bird," and the two policemen in "The Hammer Man."

[2] As quoted on the book jacket of *Gorilla, My Love.*

[3] C. D. B. Bryan in his review of *Gorilla, My Love, The New York Times Book Review,* 15 Oct. 1972, 31, commented that the affection in Bambara's volume "is so genuinely genus homo sapiens that her stories are not *only* black stories."

[4] "Happy Birthday" is a close second, containing only a few more lines than "Sweet Town."

The Miracle of Realism:
The Bid for Self-Knowledge in the Fiction of Ellen Gilchrist

JEANIE THOMPSON
and
ANITA MILLER GARNER

Few writers can achieve with a first collection of short stories published by a university press the kind of instant popular success and critical acclaim Ellen Gilchrist won with *In the Land of Dreamy Dreams* (University of Arkansas Press, 1981). Not only did it immediately sell out its first printing, the collection was literally the talk of New Orleans, selling many copies by word of mouth and winning for its author a substantial contract with a notable publisher for a novel and another collection of stories. Gilchrist's regional success has been explained in much the same way the regional success of writers like Walker Percy, Eudora Welty and, more recently, John Kennedy Toole has been explained: that is, readers in the South cannot resist the descriptions of settings, landscapes, dialects and societies which, love them or not, are easily recognizable as home. Yet, like these writers, Gilchrist writes fiction that is more than regional. Indeed, if it is regional, it is so in the sense that the works of Dostoyevsky and Flaubert are regional, which is to say that it represents not regionalism so much as the successful capturing of a social milieu. Gilchrist captures the flavor and essence of her region without drowning in its idiom. She does not diminish her work by parroting already established Southern voices or depending upon stereotypes of landscapes and character. The view that Gilchrist gives us of the world is a very straight and narrow path of realism, traditional fiction peopled with characters whom life doesn't pass by, characters who lust and kill and manipulate, and most importantly, dream.

The focus of Gilchrist's realism in *In the Land of Dreamy Dreams*, as well as in her novel, *The Annunciation* (Little, Brown and Company,

233

Photo: Andrew Kilgore

Ellen Gilchrist

A native of Mississippi, Gilchrist received her degree in philosophy from Millsaps College. Her first collection of poetry, The Land Surveyor's Daughter, *was published in 1979. She has since published a collection of short stories and a novel.*

1983) is the female psyche, for Gilchrist puts us deeply inside a female point of view in eleven of the fourteen stories as well as in much of the novel. Even in "Rich," "The President of the Louisiana Live Oak Society," and "Suicides," stories in which she employs a more nearly omniscient point of view, her narrators still manage to sound as if they are characters in her stories. (Gilchrist similarly manipulates the point of view in *The Annunciation*, making us privy to the minds of various characters as well as the protagonist, Amanda McCamey.) In "The President of the Louisiana Live Oak Society," the narrator's eye and voice are those of a woman confiding to her friend in a beauty salon, much like Flannery O'Connor's omniscient narrators who often sound like the "Georgia crackers" who people her stories. The result of an intense focus on the female point of view and a shortage of three-dimensional male characters will undoubtedly result in charges by some of Gilchrist's lack of range. Fortunately, the placement of "Rich" as the first story in the collection presents Tom Wilson, perhaps the only fully rounded male character in the book. The glimpses we are given of his coming to terms with a hatred of his difficult daughter Helen are some of the most poignant and human scenes in the collection. Yet, when we put all the stories together, add up all the views the reader gets of the female mind, the composite suggests that Gilchrist's treatment of women is very traditional and in several areas resembles that of her predecessors.

Like at least two Grandes Dames of Southern fiction, Eudora Welty and Flannery O'Connor, Gilchrist evidences a type of Romantic Calvinism in her view of women. On one hand, she seems delighted with the idea of innate depravity, while on the other she seems convinced that a woman's life is often like an extended downhill sled ride, starting out with much promise for excitement and speed, but troubled by ill-placed obstacles, icy spots, and a fizzle at the end. For example, Gilchrist likes to show her young protagonists as simultaneously wonderful and horrible. In "Traveler," LeLe prefers telling lies to telling the truth, concocting wild tales to tell her summer companions about her social success back in Indiana, when in fact she has just lost a bid for cheerleader. When her cousin Baby Gwen Barksdale greets LeLe at the train station, LeLe tells her that "practically the whole football team" saw her off at the station back home, and then she creates a melodramatic tale about a college boy she supposedly dates who is dying of cancer. LeLe's sloth is shown through her failure to face up to the real cause of her obesity. She does not feel guilty for all of the lies she tells. In fact, the only emotion akin to guilt she feels is the remorse she experiences for eating vanilla ice cream directly out of the carton while the freezer door stands open, something she is sure Sirena the maid knows about and holds against her. Yet for all of LeLe's exaggerations and lies, the reader cannot fail to be charmed by her sheer spunk when she swims the five miles across the lake with Fielding, her summer crush, and exuberantly realizes that she has created an identity for herself. "I was dazzling. I was LeLe Arnold, the wildest girl in the Mississippi Delta, the girl who swam Lake Jefferson without a boat or a life vest. I was LeLe, the girl who would do anything" (151). LeLe's exaggerations sound as if she has listened too often to Scarlett O'Hara's lines in *Gone with the Wind*, but her gutsy actions are more reminiscent of Katherine Anne Porter's Miranda stories, stories in which the female characters gain more than petty desires and whims by their actions. What LeLe gains by swimming the lake has much in common with what Miranda's idol, Aunt Amy, gains by riding off to Mexico astride a horse in "Old Mortality." Just as Miranda's dull life is reshaped by this socially rebellious event, LeLe cannot forget when she returns to hum-drum Indiana how "the water turned into diamonds in [her] hands" that day (153).

In "Revenge," Gilchrist uses the same pattern with success. Rhoda is only ten years old when she is sent with all of her brothers and male cousins, five in all, to spend the summer with their grandmother during World War II. Rhoda's language is spicy and her thoughts are full of how sweet it would be to get even with the hateful boys who constantly ignore and diminish her abilities. Rhoda is particularly angry about the fact that the boys will not allow her to participate in the building of the Broad Jump Pit, and she calls vicious remarks to them from the distance at which they keep her. Secretly she begins to pray that the Japanese will win the war so that they will come and torture her tormentors. She puts herself to sleep at night imagining their five tiny wheelchairs lined up in a row while she rides around by her father's side in his Packard. In short, Rhoda's spirit is eaten alive with envy and bitterness, hate and anger. Yet she gets her revenge and a miraculous boost for her self-image when she sneaks away from her cousin Lauralee's wedding festivities to strip off her plaid formal and vault over the barrier pole at the Broad Jump Pit. Rhoda imagines "half the wedding" is calling her name and climbing over the fence to get her when she runs down the path in the light of the moon to sail victoriously over the barrier. The Romantic vision of this early success is amplified by Rhoda's last thought: "Sometimes I think whatever has happened since has been of no real interest to me" (124). This line does a great deal to separate Rhoda from other depraved and naughty young female protagonists such as Carson McCullers's Frankie Addams in A *Member of the Wedding* or Flannery O'Connor's child protagonist in "A Temple of the Holy Ghost."

Indeed, in story after story Gilchrist's grown-up female protagonists are living life after the Fall. She in fact reworks the pattern in *The Annunciation*, though with a different result. In "There's a Garden of Eden," Alisha Terrebone decides that although she has always been a renowned beauty, her preeminence is drawing to a close. Alisha perceives herself to be "soft and brave and sad, like an old actress" (43). Like many of Gilchrist's characters, she becomes to others what she perceives herself to be. She is painfully aware of the folly of her life, nonetheless, knowing that inevitably her present lover will leave her. She thinks, *"And that is what I get for devoting my life to love instead of wisdom"* (47).

In their downhill journey through life, the protagonists of these stories run into obstacle after obstacle to mar their gorgeous, effortless journeys. In "1957, a Romance," Rhoda fears another pregnancy and cannot face what she perceives as the ugliness of her body. In the title story, La-Grande McGruder finds her obstacle in the form of "That goddamn little new-rich Yankee bitch," a crippled, social-climbing Jewish woman who forces LaGrande to cheat if she wants to win in a game of tennis, the only thing important in LaGrande's life other than her integrity and pride at being at least a third-generation member of the New Orleans Lawn Tennis Club. In "The President of the Louisiana Live Oak Society," Lelia McLaurin's life tumbles into chaos as the trappings of the social revolution of the sixties—blacklights, marijuana, and pushers—trickle down into her adolescent son Robert's life and then into her own carefully ordered home. Lelia's buffer from such madness and social unrest is to visit her hairdresser, who shares Lelia's psychiatrist and who creates for Lelia a hairdo that resembles a helmet.

Thus in gathering for the reader a whole cast of female characters in various stages of life, with the character Rhoda appearing by name in four of the stories, Gilchrist achieves a kind of coherence of style and voice that is absent from many first collections of short fiction. She invites us to compare these women with each other and determine whether or not the sum of their experiences adds up to more than just their individual lives. The result is a type of social commentary that pervades the work, full of sadness and futility. By dividing the collection into sections, Gilchrist emphasizes how "place" has affected these females' lives, and how what has been true in the past may exist nowhere other than in dreams in the future. The rural and genteel Mississippi in which Matille and the very young Rhoda summer seems to offer little preparation for the life in which Rhoda finds herself in 1957, in North Carolina with a husband and two small sons and the fear of a third child on the way. Clearly nothing in LaGrande McGruder's life has prepared her for the disruption of a society she has always known, nor for the encroachment of dissolution upon her territory. Similarly, Lelia McLaurin's only plan for escape is a weekend spent with her husband on the Mississippi Gulf Coast, just as they used to do in the old days, driving to Biloxi with a shaker full of martinis.

With the creation of Amanda McCamey, the female protagonist in her new novel, *The Annunciation*, Gilchrist may be reversing the trend set by Rhoda, LeLe, Matille, even LaGrande McGruder and Lelia McLaurin. Amanda is possibly Gilchrist's first female protagonist who may be elevated to the class of *hero*. Although Amanda has in common with her "sisters" a penchant for the downhill slide, a heavy cargo of guilt, and a similar Mississippi Delta/New Orleans background, she redeems herself with an honest attempt to flee "the world of guilt and sorrow," to borrow a phrase from Flannery O'Connor, by literally asserting her will against the forces that would slow her down in her bid for a self-directed, meaningful life.

Amanda is the central focus of the novel, most of which is narrated in a close third person through her perceptions, though occasionally Gilchrist, like O'Connor, dips into the consciousnesses of other characters for a balancing effect. Still, it is Amanda's story, her quest to know who she is and how to live her life that is the main theme of the novel.

The Annunciation is divided into three sections: "Cargo," "Exile," and "The Annunciation," the latter being about four times as long as the second, which is twice as long as the first. This structure invites questions: What is Amanda's "cargo"? From what or whom and to where is she exiled? Is "the annunciation" intended as a scriptural parallel? If not, is it used ironically?

Amanda's "cargo" we learn is in part her guilt over a child born out of wedlock and given up for adoption when Amanda is just fourteen. In the second section of the novel, it is revealed that her daughter, adopted by a wealthy New Orleans family, the Allains, has married and is living on State Street only blocks from Amanda. Eventually their paths cross: Amanda and Barrett Allain Clare pass each other on the way to the ladies room at Antoine's one evening, and later when Amanda sees Barrett fighting with her husband Charles she almost intervenes. Still later, they are even introduced to one another by a mutual friend. Though their relationship is profound, mother and daughter can't and don't recognize one another.

Growing up in the same small Mississippi county, Issaquena, which figured prominently in at least three of the short stories, Amanda is drawn from an early age to her athletic, darkly handsome first cousin Guy. They seem to be the pride of the stock on Esperanza plantation, and as children they develop an intense loyalty that later blossoms into sexual attraction when they are adolescents.[1] When Guy is eighteen and a football sensation in Rolling Fork, Mississippi, and Amanda a precocious fourteen year old, she seduces Guy. Though she desires him physically, she also feels a spiritual need to keep him near. As they make love for the first time she thinks, "Guy is ours. . . . Guy belongs to us" (14). She dreads the thought of his leaving for college because it will mark the end of their childhood together and the relationship they have had. It also heralds, ultimately, the close of their direct ties with the place they were reared, the Mississippi Delta. Unfortunately, Amanda becomes pregnant and is sent to a Catholic home for unwed mothers in New Orleans. This is the beginning of "what she must carry with her always. Her cargo" (15). From then on she is irretrievably split from Guy, and, for a good part of her life, from herself. The fact that the baby girl she delivers by Caesarian section is taken from her, remembered as a slick, slippery thing with eyes squeezed shut, haunts her throughout the novel.

"Now you can be a girl again," Sister Celestine tells Amanda as she prepares to leave New Orleans for Virginia Seminary (20). But, of course, Amanda has been initiated into the adult world, though she only dimly perceives it through her obsessions with pleasures of the body and her own vanity; there is to be no return to girlhood. Although later Guy drives to meet her at school, it is clear that a continued relationship with him is out of the question. Amanda's cargo, then, also is loss—loss of her home place, her closest friend and lover, Guy, and her first child.

Amanda's period of "exile" takes place in New Orleans, the land of dreamy dreams, where she enters Uptown society by marrying Malcolm Ashe, a wealthy Jewish management lawyer. Their childless marriage is further marred by Amanda's alcoholism—a state that existed prior to their union. In the "Exile" chapters, Gilchrist covers some of the same territory traversed in the New Orleans society exposé stories of *In the Land of Dreamy Dreams:* the Junior League women, the politically corrupt men, materialism of the rankest sort, "good" schools, worried children, class consciousness, racism, and sterility. Amanda eventually sobers up, awakening to realize that these people either hate each other or themselves. "What am I doing here?" (69), she wonders but, until she stops drinking, she can't find her way out of the maze.

Amanda's ticket out of town is the interest that she develops in language translation while pursuing a degree at Tulane University. Chiefly with the support of her black maid, her friend and "ally" Lavertis, Amanda is able to stop drinking and find the encouragement to go to school. Also at this time, Amanda and Guy have a brief reunion at their grandmother's funeral at Esperanza, which they will jointly inherit. They are drawn together again through grief and "the old desire"; they even leave the post-funeral gathering in Guy's car and end up making love in the rain. But when they discuss the daughter that neither of them knows, it is obvious that Guy is obsessed with locating the girl and is no happier than Amanda.

Amanda's exile is both literal and metaphorical. Exiled from her home territory, the family plantation, Esperanza, in Mississippi, she has not yet found her second home, Fayetteville, Arkansas. On a figurative level, she is exiled from herself through her drinking and also in her lack of knowledge as to who she is and what she should do with her life. Childless, without a career, the wife of a rich man, living with guilt over her daughter, Amanda is in despair most of the time. Yet one of the main themes of *The Annunciation* is Amanda's bid for freedom through self-knowledge. During their time alone at their grandmother's funeral, Guy offers to leave his wife and take Amanda some place where they can be happy. Amanda, who is waking up from a dream of happy-endings, refuses his offer, saying, "all I'm really trying to do is find out what I'm good at. So I can be a useful person, so I can have some purpose" (60). When Guy says he can give her anything "that goddamn ingratiating Jew" can give her, she replies that she's not interested in money. "I want something else," she tells Guy. "Something I don't know the name of yet" (59).

Eventually, Amanda gets a chance to name her desire. She becomes involved in translating a manuscript smuggled out of the Vatican and put into the hands of Marshall Jordon, a seventy plus year old translation scholar from the writing program at the University of Arkansas in Fayette-ville. Ironically, Amanda will translate a manuscript of poems in middle French by a poet named Helene Renoir, who also had an illegitimate child, was sent away to live with nuns, and who chose to hang herself at age twenty-one. It is Amanda's involvement with this project, her separa-tion and eventual divorce from Malcolm, and her move to Fayetteville to start a new life as a single, working woman that constitute her deliverance from exile. Thus the stage is set for her "annunciation."

Arriving in Fayetteville with all the best intentions of living alone, Amanda starts out well, and her new ally, Katie Dunbar, an extremely strong, positive female counter-psyche for Amanda, stands by her throughout her emergence into wholeness. The theme of freedom is highlighted when on the first night alone in her new home, after the guests have gone, Amanda must bravely face exactly what it was she wanted: solitude. A poignant moment occurs in which we see Amanda summoning her power for courage:

> This is it, she thought. This is what I dreamed of. The old sugar maples outside
> the window moved in the wind, sending shadows onto the wall behind her.
> That doesn't scare me, she thought. Nothing scares me. That's only the wind
> I'm watching. That wind has traveled around the world a million times to be
> with me. That wind was alive when Helene Renoir walked the earth. (147)

But Amanda is still Amanda, and soon she is restless, bored and lonely. Though she has learned that freedom is necessary for her work, the isolation of freedom is hard to take. Before long she becomes involved with Will Lyons, a twenty-five year old local guitar player who gives her pure joy and lets her believe she wants to love again. The night after she first goes to bed with him, she menstruates for the first time in months, and believes Will has "touched the part of [her] that wants to live" (164). Once again Amanda's nameless desire seems close to articulation.

The tug between real, joyous, even stormy love and the need to accomplish her work is a fierce struggle for Amanda, and it is further complicated by money: her abundance of it and Will's complete lack of it. Not surprisingly, her translations play second fiddle when her young lover comes "breezing in and put[s] his hands on her hair" (191). Later, when they are swimming in a local river, she is unafraid to show off her older woman's body. She strips and swims alone in the water. Will, impatient, young, is soon ready to leave, but Amanda dives far and deep, as if away from him and all the world, perhaps even herself. Their relationship is fraught with paradoxes.

On a spring white water canoe trip down the Buffalo in Arkansas, Amanda and Will make love on a rocky beach in the middle of the night. Earlier in the day, Amanda had felt a "sharp pain low on her left side"— "the old quirky pain of ovulation." On their way home after their night on the beach, Amanda and Will wait out a thunder storm and later, when Amanda grows "bored with the river" and fails to pay attention, she accidentally turns over the canoe. She and Will are spilled out into treacherous white water. In a bluntly brutal yet lyric passage, Amanda encounters Death. Her own mortality seems about to sweep her away, and she appears willing to surrender to it—presumably just as she has conceived for the first time in thirty years! The passages of conception and the nearness of death are surprisingly similar and bear comparison, foreshadowing as they do the nearly simultaneous birth of the child and the death of Will in the last pages of the novel. In each, lyricism heightens the narrative:

> Amanda woke in the night. There was mist all over the water and the little rock peninsula. She stirred in Will's arms, moving her body against his until she woke him. Then, half asleep on the hard bed of the earth they made love as softly as ever they could in the world. Love me, Amanda's body sang. Dance with me, his body answered. Dance with me, dance with me, dance with me.
>
> *Now,* the darkness demanded. And Amanda surrendered herself to the darkness and the river and the stars. (243)

A very similar demand darkly presents itself to Amanda when the canoe overturns less than twenty-four hours later:

> Everything in the world was cold green water, so cold, so very cold. The whole world was singing in a higher key. She could not breathe, the pressure of the water against her chest was so deep, so hard and dark and cold and full. I am

here forever, she thought. This is what it is to die, this pressure, this powerless-ness. Then Amanda let go of fear, surrendered, gave in to the water, gave in to her death. (246)

Amanda does not give in, however; something impels her to save herself. One can perhaps conclude that the life inside her has done this; at any rate, Amanda is destined to survive, unlike Helene Renoir, her role model from another life.

Soon after their bittersweet canoe trip, Will strikes out to solve his money troubles by working on an off-shore oil rig. Some time later, Amanda learns that she is pregnant and writes to Will, telling him of her pregnancy, and also that she has learned her daughter's name and where-abouts from Guy. On his way back to Fayetteville to see his child, Will (who dreams of literally giving children to Amanda) stops in New Orleans to tell Barrett Clare that her mother is alive and well and loves her. Though Will never makes it home, this gift, given impulsively as befits his youthfulness, surely immortalizes him for Amanda.

Gilchrist's choice of *The Annunciation* as a title for her novel about a woman who, after giving up one child at age fourteen, gives birth to a son thirty years later on Christmas Eve leads one to question how closely the novelist intends to parallel the biblical annunciation. Perhaps the author is playing with this motif, suggesting a modern version of "miracle." If one goes to what is considered by many to be the loveliest of the four gospels, St. Luke, and reads the disciple's account of Mary's annunciation, some parallels can be seen to Gilchrist's novel. However, a word of warning is in order at the outset: while this approach sheds interesting light on Gilchrist's structure and helps clarify certain details in *The Annunciation*, the main character's hardline stand against organized Christianity, and the Roman Catholic church in particular, makes the possibility of the author's intention to render a strict biblical reference or allegory highly unlikely. Neither is Gilchrist satirizing Christianity; rather, she takes what she needs to shape her narrative. Still, what she appears to need of the New Testament is quite revealing.

To begin with, Amanda is told of her pregnancy by a masseuse who has looked into her eye and seen "a little configuration." This "unwashed hippie doctor of the hills with his gorgeous tan," is, coincidentally, named Luke. After learning her amazing news, Amanda plays briefly with the idea that Luke is "the angel of the Annunciation." Somewhat comically, she imagines that he has almost struck a classical pose of the annunciation angel: "His hands were folded at his chest. He might have dropped to one knee" (279). In addition, she notices that she is wearing the Virgin's colors, "blue shorts, white T-shirt," and calls herself "Maria Amanda Luisa, the gray-blue virgin of the middleweights." Luke's words, *"a special case. A very special child,"* ring for her, and she wonders whether her young lover Will is her "Joseph leading the donkey." But Amanda puts her feet back on the earth when she admits that "he is not here. . . . I have not even heard from him and there is no donkey" (279). Amanda, the High Blasphemer, decides that "it's time to think straight," and so for the moment she ends her flirtation with outright scriptural comparisons.[2]

A fiction writer might be understandably attracted to the gospel of Luke, the "storyteller," who is interested above all in people and especially women. It is in Luke's gospel that human beings speak most eloquently and dramatically, often breaking into songs. As Mary Ellen Chase points out in *The Bible and the Common Reader,* Luke alone includes in his Gospel the Magnificat of Mary. In addition, Luke is known to biblical scholars and readers as a setter of scenes and a chronicler of homely details.[3]

Like the Virgin Mary, Amanda has a close relationship with a female companion, Katie Dunbar. For Mary it is the mother of John, Elisabeth (who also experienced a miracle), and it is in her presence that Mary sings of the angel's visitation and her joy. Though there isn't a strict parallel to this in *The Annunciation,* Amanda is comforted repeatedly by the "experienced" and wise Katie at the potter's home. Finally, one notes that St. Luke refers to Judea as "hill country" and Gilchrist sets her final portion of the book, "The Annunciation," in the hills of northwest Arkansas.

Perhaps a more productive comparison to make, however, is the fact that Mary's news comes to her as a disturbing revelation, and Amanda is likewise extremely troubled by her unexpected pregnancy. She is unmarried, forty-four years old, presumably has experienced an early menopause, and is about to embark upon a possibly auspicious career as a translator of middle French and as a writer. The prospect of having a baby and the ensuing duties of motherhood appear to stand directly in her path toward self-determination. Gilchrist deals with a sharply realistic situation: a woman who perhaps must choose between a career and motherhood, options which until this point have both been closed to Amanda. She struggles with the conflict, and even goes to Tulsa for an abortion, but then she changes her mind, gets drunk to celebrate and has to be taken care of by the Good Samaritan Katie. At this point Amanda seems to have reached a low point, but like Mary, she comes to believe that nothing is impossible and so decides to have the child.

As if sensing that this birth will help ease the guilt with which she has lived for thirty years, Amanda joyfully prepares for labor in her go-for-broke style, "training like she was going out for the Olympics," Katie observes (344).[4] Finally, although the word "obey" seems an odd one for Amanda McCamey, she does in some sense obey a law of nature by not having the abortion. Like Mary, she acquiesces to motherhood. Though what Amanda does may not be said to have strictly to do with grace in the Christian sense, she does redeem herself by being able to give life, through her son, and therefore forgive herself of her sins. Here, then, is the novel's central theme: Amanda's life-long search for love and acceptance and peace.

Amanda achieves a form of heroism by overcoming her alcoholism and to a certain extent, her materialism, and by giving of herself through her late-life motherhood. The favor that she seeks through learning how to live her life is won through hard circumstances, and will be won anew through even harder days to come as she learns of Will's death and as she seeks her daughter, an event that will surely take place given Will's visit to State Street and Amanda's nearly simultaneous resolve to meet the young woman, Barrett Clare.

As parents of Barrett Clare, Amanda and Guy must face what proves "desperately hard": their act of incest (they were first cousins) and their ultimate responsibility to identify and subsequently love their child, a responsibility from which they can no longer run or hide.[5] The question remains whether Guy and Amanda ever achieve true, lasting heroism. For Guy, it is not so clear cut. With a great deal of money and power within his reach, the first step toward facing his daughter is easily taken when he asks a rich New Orleans politico to find out about the girl's fate. When handed the information, however, Guy asks to have it summarized for him; he can't bear to read it. Later, he visits the New Orleans Lawn Tennis Club and watches his daughter play a match "as if she were a tennis-playing machine." He sees his grandson, a "wild fat little red-headed boy" and feels deeply the need to know this child also. Yet Guy can't approach Barrett alone; he needs Amanda. By the novel's end, Guy hasn't yet contacted his daughter.

Amanda, on the other hand, vows to find her daughter after her son is born, though she had earlier refused to go with Guy to see their child. In the final pages, the possibility for her heroism is strongly hinted; we can believe that, buoyed by the strength which she has already gained from loving her baby son, she will have the courage to seek and acknowledge her first born.

As the novel closes, Amanda drifts to sleep shortly after delivering her son, "dreaming of herself in a white silk suit holding her beautiful daughter in her arms." She at last has the courage to imagine the reunion a happy one, though formerly she had always dreamt of the meeting in nightmare. Perhaps at this point Amanda goes beyond courage to hubris, as she continues: "My life leading to my lands forever and ever and ever, hallowed be my name, goddammit, my kingdom come, my will be done, amen, so be it, Amanda" (353). In her blasphemy of the Lord's Prayer, Amanda McCamey gropes toward self-respect, forgiveness and love. There is nothing irreverent in Amanda's creation of her own liturgy as she accepts motherhood and acknowledges a degree of selflessness shortly before she goes into labor:

> This is my body which is not broken by you. This is my flesh and blood. This is myself. I am going to stop being alone in the world. Already I am not alone. Already a miracle is inside of me. Already a miracle has occurred. My child, my ally, are you listening. I love you so much. I can not tell you how I love you. Be well, be whole, stay well. (325)

Later, when the child lies peacefully in his mother's arms, in Gilchrist's contemporary nativity, Amanda speaks to him in words that are surely holy for the love and forgiveness they embody:

> "Flesh of my flesh," she whispered. "Bone of my bone, blood of my blood. You are kin to me," she whispered, touching his soft hair. Kin to me, kin to me, kin to me. And the memory of the other child was there with them, but it was softer now, paler. (347–48)

Guided often in her life by lust, hunger, greed, and curiosity, Amanda finally, at age forty-four, begins to direct her own life with loving intelligence: "My life on my terms, my daughter, my son" (353). The lyricism of the ending of *The Annunciation* is a hymn to self-determination, from which we can only wonder at the reserves of Amanda McCamey's imagination and strength.

In her two works of fiction to date, Ellen Gilchrist portrays the workings of a complex female psyche through a variety of women of all ages. Rhoda, Matille, Alisha Terrebone, and Amanda McCamey, to name a few, are all mined from the lode of a larger consciousness which Gilchrist is working with amazing confidence. It is encouraging to see that with *The Annunciation* a possibility for redemption appears on the horizon for Gilchrist's anguished but tenacious women. The writer has struck one element that may lead to a greater wealth for her characters: courage to face the truth about themselves. With this discovery, Gilchrist's women may go further in future works to develop a realism that not only entertains but enobles.

NOTES

[1] This treatment of children's sexual awakenings is similar to the children's sex games in "Summer, an Elegy," in which Matille and Shelby discover sex while in bed recovering from typhoid vaccinations. Later, when Shelby dies while under anesthesia, Matille feels she has been freed from guilt and the fear that he will tell of their game, though clearly a part of her has also died, as he was her first lover.

[2] Gilchrist also toys with the notion of immaculate conception. Shortly before the birth scene, Katie Dunbar's boyfriend Clinton asks, "What about the father?" Katie replies that "she willed it into being, all by herself out of light and air" (315). Though this is meant light-heartedly, Amanda uses the word "miracle" to describe her child only pages later.

[3] See Chase's comments (New York: Macmillan, 1960), 284–89, on Mary in Luke's gospel.

[4] Amanda is essentially a life-affirmer and is powered by the will to live. One should note here that her lover's name "Will" invites a supposition that when he dies, practically at the moment she is giving birth to their son, a transference of "will" takes place.

[5] That their daughter Barrett Clare has suffered from feelings of neglect, isolation, abandonment, and despair—despite, or perhaps because of, her adoption by a wealthy New Orleans family—is made painfully apparent: she has a terrible relationship with her husband (he represents the "heartless" New Orleans society that threatened to consume Amanda) and is out of touch with herself and trying desperately to gain self-respect by playing ferocious tennis and writing anemic confessional poetry. Her links to humanity are through her psychiatrist, Gustave (an obviously one-sided infatuation based on narcissism: she believes he loves her but his job is to be interested in her) and through her love for her hyperactive son.

Lee Smith

A native of Virginia (b. 1944), Smith was educated at Hollins College. Her first novel, The Last Day the Dogbushes Bloomed, *was published in 1968. She has since published a number of stories in periodicals, a short story collection, and four novels.*

The World of Lee Smith

ANNE GOODWYN JONES

It's real hard—as Lee might put it—to write about somebody you know is an actual human being. Mostly you write about either dead people or people so famous that they might as well be—they'll never read it anyway. You can be clever and abstract, and wield a sharp pen that demonstrates the formidable powers of intellectual analysis. But Lee is a friend of mine. Reading her stories, almost weeping with laughter, I could just hear her telling them. How can that be rendered in criticism?

Even more unnerving, the meaning of her stories challenges, well, *critical discourse* itself. Take the diction, the tone of a chapter title in *Oral History:* "Richard Burlage Discourses Upon the Circumstances Concerning His Collection of Appalachian Photographs, c. 1934." Richard's "discourse" had once been the wordlessness of love and the incoherence of immediacy; his "circumstances" had included passion and betrayal and madness and death, had included another real human being, Dory Cantrell. So his present diction betrays his betrayal of his own past. So does criticism inevitably betray the fiction it analyzes.

Intellectuals in fact do not fare well in Lee Smith's prose. Take Paul, in the short story "Saint Paul." He's been in love with Billie Jean all his life; he's collected her little lost things—a red velvet bow, an ankle chain—like saint's relics and put them in a box labeled BJL. But when Billie Jean finds out, comes to his house (where he is of course writing a book), and gives him a big hug and an invitation to make love, he tells her she's got it all wrong: "It wasn't you, it wasn't ever really you, it was the *idea* of you, which made possible the necessary—" betraying her by making her a symbol. Yet Smith refuses the sentimental easy cry: it's not Billie Jean who is damaged by these words. She finds another man to love, and winds up pitying professor Paul, whose hair turns white, whose pants ride up funny, and who starts to talk to himself in public.

249

That's the point, too, of "Mrs. Darcy Meets the Blue-Eyed Stranger at the Beach," like "Saint Paul" a story from *Cakewalk.* Mrs. Darcy's lifestyle has changed since her husband's death. She's taken to eating frozen pizza, leaving the dust where it falls, and putting on rubber flip-flops instead of spectator heels. And she has a vision at the beach of a longhaired whiterobed blueeyed man coming out of a rainbow. This bothers her psychologist daughter Maria and managerial daughter Trixie, who are with her at the beach: Maria analyzes her mother's "symptoms," and Trixie prescribes a "cure." But Ginny, the youngest daughter, who unlike her sisters says what she feels, will not put up with their intellectualizing. And Ginny's vindicated: Mrs. Darcy's "problem" turns out to be the gift of healing, a gift that challenges all rational thought.

In fact, Lee Smith's eye for, ear for, love for what either of the Saint Pauls might have called the "gross world" is entirely compelling. You just can't live very well for very long in abstractions, if you are one of Lee Smith's characters, even though you might have some very good reasons to want to. The epigraph to *Oral History* says it in eight lines of a song:

> Come all you fair and tender ladies
> Be careful how you court young men.
> They're like a star in a summer's morning,
> First appear and then they're gone.
>
> If I'd a-knowed afore I courted
> That love, it was such a killin' crime,
> I'd a-locked my heart in a box of golden
> and tied it up with a silver line.

Those who do lock up their hearts in Lee Smith's stories paradoxically lose themselves, or make other people miserable, or live, parasitically, in other people's stories. And those who embrace the gross world, who court young men and learn about killin' love, do indeed suffer. But they have stories of their own to tell.

A good case in point is "Cakewalk," the volume's title story. Stella and Florrie Ludington—sisters who grew up, the crème de la crème, in the big house on the corner of Lambert and Pine—both love art. Stella, like a star above it all, is transported by transcendence; she loves the chandelier over her makeup counter in Belk's, its thousands of crystal lights unmoved by even the strongest winds outside. Like the makeup she sells, art is (Stella believes) superior to life; like the social class she sustains,

Stella's art is for the "superior" few, the rich. She does not sell Cover Girl, and she ignores a woman who asks for it. Yet Stella has married a man who originally loved, and unbeknownst to her, still loves, her sister Florrie.

Florrie's art is for all and for each. In a great mess of a kitchen, at all hours, she makes cakes—from scratch, not a mix. She will make a cake for anyone, but it will suit that person uniquely: for a secretary, a giant typewriter with Necco wafers as keys; for a golfer, a nine-hole course with a tiny sugar pellet ball and little mirrors for water hazards. Stella's makeup, sold only to a few, is nevertheless the same for all, a homogenizing veneer. Florrie's life is as messy, as organic, and as productive as her name suggests. Her husband Earl Mingo is a nocount wanderer whom she marries, pregnant, for love. They keep on having children past all reason; then he leaves her for a friend of his daughter. Florrie grieves, and Stella frets; it is all, she feels, so unnecessary. Claude would never have done such a thing, she thinks, unaware of the irony. For like Smith's other survivors and real artists, it is Florrie whose life and cakes create meaning for others: for Claude, who runs his boat in circles thinking of Florrie, and who's been sleeping with her for years, and—in the story's ultimate irony—for Stella, whose own story is filled with Florrie's, and whose effort to deny time through her art of makeup is countered with Florrie's celebration of change in her last cake, an autumn leaf.

Clearly a literary critic might think twice about the abstractions of formalism or deconstruction or post-structuralism, might hesitate before writing, say, "Smith privileges the speakerly over the writerly text." Even though it's true: she likes words in people's mouths better than on a page. It's all part of that instinct for the gross world, for—beyond the meaning—the meaning makers.

Lee Smith has been making up stories all her life. She wrote her first novel as a senior at Hollins College in 1967; *The Last Day the Dogbushes Bloomed* (1968) won a Book of the Month Club Fellowship. *Something in the Wind* appeared in 1971, and *Fancy Strut* in 1973. Smith's fourth novel, *Black Mountain Breakdown,* appeared in 1980. Meanwhile, two of her stories won the O. Henry award, and in 1981 she published a collection of stories, *Cakewalk.* Her latest novel (1983) is *Oral History.* She grew up in the mountains in Grundy, Virginia, and now teaches at North Carolina State University in Raleigh.

Typically, Lee Smith's stories choose cakes over chandeliers, choose shaping life over transcending it. Often as not, the metaphor for art in her stories comes out of women's culture; not only does it shape life but it is useful as well, like cakes or quilts or hairstyles. Her tendency to prefer traditionally female immanent art to traditionally male transcendent art parallels her preference for the spoken to the written word. Spoken words have a human context more concrete than that of written prose; at least before tape recorders, oral narratives implied a voice and a set of ears, two bodies, rather than one pair of eyes and a piece of paper. It's hard to think of a writer with as good an ear for the spoken word as Lee Smith's. She reveals character, distinguishes social class, creates irony, and laughs affectionately at her people as they speak out and in speaking become themselves. Stella, in "Cakewalk," describes her social class as "aloft . . . on the top rung of the social crust," and complains about Florrie's wild grandchildren, "not a thing like Stella's own . . . who unfortunately live so far away." Smith's stories are written to be told by first person narrators or by special third person narrators who are either very close to one character or are voices of the communities they tell us of. "I have an awful time with omniscience," she says. *Oral History* expresses Smith's commitment to oral over literary traditions, individuals over omniscience, in an intricate and quite self-conscious way. It compiles the narratives of people from and in the Virginia mountains, from the late nineteenth century to the present. Writerly texts get into trouble at the very start. Jennifer's diary, which she keeps, ironically, for a course in oral history, is filled with the pomposities of freshman prose. But the oral narratives—such as that of Granny Younger and Rose Hibbitts—have a coherence and genuineness like that of the epigraph song, which are missing in the rhetorical prose of the educated outsider Richard Burlage. His text unravels and disintegrates as human voices get loud and clear. He finally forsakes all punctuation, all grammar as he waits in the schoolhouse with his lover, the mountain girl, golden Dory, the door coming down, her kinfolk yelling outside. Such is the power of oral over written language, of lived sexual and emotional experience over the control of the mannered Richmond way.

In another variation of these closely woven themes, assertion of various kinds—sexual, violent, linguistic, religious—is explored as an alternative to voiceless passivity. The issue is particularly acute for Smith's women, who find it all too easy to center themselves outside themselves. Finding a true voice is connected with locating a self within that can hate as well as love, can do bodily harm as well as feel bodily pleasure, can experience spirituality as well as sensuality. Brooke Kincaid in *Something in the Wind* learns to express the truth of her body as she learns to speak a true language of words. But Crystal Spangler, in *Black Mountain Breakdown*, finds her voice (especially in teaching), then silences it. Crystal takes the issue of a woman's passivity through one more twist: except for her teaching, she consumes assertion instead of creating it. She feels "real" only when a man has shown sexual interest in her to which she responds, or when God enters her. When she sees a human vegetable in the mental hospital, she holds his hand, recognizing, she thinks, herself—just as she had lain back and endured the pain of Uncle Devere's rape, instead of fighting him off.

Lee Smith is exact and devastating in her portrayals of women, usually married, caught in a cycle of guilt, self-deprecation, entrapment, rebellion, and again guilt that screens them from themselves. The men in their lives—Crystal's Roger Lee Combs, Debbi's Bobby (in "Gulfport"), Martha's Jerry (in "Dear Phil Donahue") may be earnest and loving or violent and aggressive. But in either case, they can neither comprehend nor help the woman; most often they contribute to her problem by imposing a fantasy screen of womanhood and refusing or failing to hear the messages from the interior. An interesting exception is Mack Stiltner, Crystal's wrong-side-of-the-tracks high school lover, who writes a perceptive song about Crystal and goes on to become a Nashville recording star, one of the relatively few male artists in Smith's fiction. Shut up both by their men, and by their self-hatred, then, the women's true voices seem to them alien. And so they hear voices that sound "strange" coming from beyond the pale, beginning with Eugene's in *Dogbushes*, voices so far outside conventional norms of class or sanity as to suggest the extremity of the problem, the isolation and unreality of these women's lives.

Smith experiments too with the Southern fantasy of masculinity. Whereas women help men to perpetuate Southern womanhood despite its damage to themselves, it is mostly only men who perpetuate the macho good old boy norm. (When women support this fantasy, it is an aspect of their self-betrayal.) Michael's father in "Not Pictured" wants his son to be a man, not a sissy who prefers making pictures to playing baseball. Again in *Fancy Strut* Bevo Cartwright feels a conflict between his authentic (and artistic) self and the demands of Southern manhood; he resolves it by perpetuating the pattern of masculinity as physical and sexual dominance. By contrast, in "Not Pictured" it is easier for Michael to find an asserting self; he has seen his father cry, something Bevo could not imagine. But, he, too, does so at the cost of a woman. As he joins hands with his father, for the first time grinning and yelling and loving the ferris wheel, Michael's Aunt Lily—the catalyst—has been shut up in a mental hospital.

So far, then, Smith's characters, particularly women, find a kind of health in assertion centered in the self, in the body. (Men's aggression is a different matter.) Those who fail, who prefer intellectualizing to feeling, moralizing to sensuality, religiosity to spirituality, inevitably reveal in their diction and their taletelling their own unacknowledged rages and desires. No one escapes the body.

Finally, the possibility of assertion is often associated with class structure. Smith is never mealy-mouthed about the Southern class system; there are aristocrats, nouveau riche, bourgeoisie, coalminers, holler people, "lowlife." The further the class from Southern gentility, the more likely it will offer some hope (perhaps illusory) for genuine feeling. Often suburban women will yearn for the liberation they imagine to be found in a lover from a lower class. But Smith does not sentimentalize or generalize. In "Gulfport," for instance, the focus is on "lowlife," but the story's irony cuts two ways: just as the suburban housewife yearns for the freedom she sees in Debbi's life with Bobby at the Beachview Motel, so Debbi yearns for the clarity and tranquillity and beauty of a clean yellow suburban kitchen with "plants and spice racks all over the place." Moreover, Lee Smith consistently distinguishes the deracination of "lowlife" from the rootedness of mountain folk culture; what may be an illusion in the one can be genuine in the other.

Lee Smith's first novel, *The Last Day the Dogbushes Bloomed*, tells the story of Susan Tobey's ninth summer, the summer when her mother leaves with a lover, when Frank the gardener dies, when her sister Betty gets engaged, and when pale thin little Eugene arrives from the city to create a club that acts out his disturbed fantasies. Susan's story is not so much of the events as of her changing perception of events, revealed through her evolving imagination and diction. Thus it is a novel, like all of Smith's, about language. Susan's rather conventional upper middle class family find it impossible to speak about feelings or to utter the least honest word about what is happening to them. Susan fills in the blank with her own words: Queen for mother, Princess for sister, Baron for her mother's lover, dogbushes for a secret hiding place. Susan's namings explain her experience (her mother's coldness is royal prerogative), protect her from painful knowledge (she struggles to believe her Wading House animal "friends" are safe despite a flood), and allow the magical, the numinous into her world.

Eugene's voice may be strange but its darker tones are more potent than Susan's efforts to invent an innocent world. Little Arthur, his invisible friend with cape and boots and gun, is immediately accepted as the club's leader. Eugene has his power precisely because the children in the club still believe in tooth fairies and mountain dogs and Queens; but Eugene's fantasies have to do with violence and sexuality, merging and confusing the two.

Hearing little plain talk from the grownup world, Susan nevertheless finds their art. Her father's paintings show his unvoiced feelings, and the cook Elsie's stories teach Susan indirectly about love. Eugene, too, uses art as his mediator; but for him, paintings are didactic and prurient and actual: he gets the kids to punch a picture of a naked woman. Susan's final words move out of story and art, as they must, into plain talk. She says at the end of the novel, "Mother had left us and Betty was engaged and Frank had died." When Susan names her world directly and clearly, it is an act of courage. Does that mean the imagination is to be abandoned? By no means, as the conclusion to *Dogbushes* (and Lee Smith's later fictions) will show. At one point, Susan disconsolately thinks, "Everything was human"; her sense of myth and mystery has been so challenged that she believes "nothing is real unless it is happening to you." But at the end, Susan insists that Robert's father is lying when he says he has killed Little Arthur. She is not clinging to an evasive fantasy, but has accepted a reality through symbol. Little Arthur now means to Susan both her own capacity for violence—it was she who thought of pulling up Mrs. Tate's roses—and her vulnerability to violence—she agreed to be the "patient" in Eugene's Iron Lung/rape "game." Keeping Little Arthur is keeping her new knowledge. Similarly, the vision of the circle of dogs that comes down in the moonlight to look at Susan and disappear is never demythologized in the text.

The possibilities raised in *Dogbushes* inform Smith's later fictions. She continues to nibble at the limits of empiricism, offering, like Toni Morrison and Gabriel Garcia Marquez, instances of magic in the realistic novel, and like them locating the magic within the roots of an oral culture. She continues, too, to seek an image of art that satisfies. When Susan compares her summer to flowers under a glass bell, she reveals an art that preserves at the cost of life. Similarly, Susan tries to deal with the complexities of her summer by placing her "topics" in boxes, which she believes she can choose when, and whether, to open. But boxes, like glass bells, may instead suffocate what is in them. Art in these images is closer to suppression than to formed expression; one remembers the "box of golden" in *Oral History's* epigraph, in which the singer wishes she'd locked her heart.

Lee Smith's second novel also uses a first person point of view. Brooke Kincaid, seventeen, begins her story when she comes home (outside Richmond) from boarding school for her friend Charles Hughes's funeral; she ends it when she comes home from college for her brother Carter's wedding. Brooke's own story, framed by these rituals that presumably integrate public and private worlds, has to do with her coming to terms with her own two worlds, the private, authentic self and the public Southern lady. And Brooke's struggle for an original self takes place in terms of diction and within relationships, mainly with young men: Houston, who satisfies her need for (as it were) rhetoric, and Bentley, who speaks the language of her heart.

Thus *Something in the Wind* (the title comes from surely the least known quotation from Shakespeare: "There is something in the wind," *The Comedy of Errors*), like *Dogbushes*, connects its protagonist's struggle for authenticity with her manipulation of language. Charles Hughes, who saw Brooke as like him, "different," "made her mind," she feels. Bereft of this later and more benevolent Eugene, Brooke can't grieve: the language of the public world—the preacher's "This is no time for mourning," her father's "I think you know how to act"—seems to shape a world that denies originality and genuine feeling. Brooke identifies that world as "Southern" and her prescribed role in it as "lady." She feels alone in her difference now and creates a "life plan" that will let her fit in by imitation.

But, simultaneously and intuitively rejecting that choice, Brooke divides herself into two people, as Susan made her boxes; they are the "real" Brooke and "Brooke Proper," a third person character or persona she creates to get through the Southern world of ritual and denial. At the university, she succeeds: she is pinned to a Beta, has joined a sorority, and has for a best friend Diana, the ideal coed. It can't last. Again, language is the clue. Brooke can't wear the rhetoric with the pin. "I wore the jeweled Beta pin on the tip of my breast and felt safe," she begins conventionally enough, but then can't help but add, "like somebody wearing garlic to ward off witches in the night" (73). The two people who speak to her "real" self before she meets Bentley play word games, Elizabeth with hink pink, and David Golden with his crossword puzzles. And in a pivotal scene, Brooke, out in the snow, pulling down his zipper, plainly and directly demands sex from Houston: "'Come on,' I said. 'Come on, come on, come on.' There were better words but I couldn't think of them" (99). Nice Southern boy that he is, Houston can't handle this encounter, though he has had no problems being the sexual aggressor himself. He gets back his pin. And when Brooke returns to the dorm without a blouse, Diana finds another roommate.

Brooke moves into an apartment with Elizabeth, who is easier to imitate because her styles and friends are so various. It is only when Brooke meets Bentley—who introduces himself with "Let's screw"—that Brooke feels she can talk without having to think what to say. Bentley, son of a revival preacher, is struggling himself with the need to emerge from a defining past (he has been a religious "star" as a boy, with visions) and the guilt and anger he feels at the process. Living together in the "pit," a dank basement apartment, Brooke and Bentley together struggle with their deepening love and sexuality, and with their accompanying capacities for hatred and violence. The victory goes to their worst views of themselves. Bentley sees himself as a destroyer; Brooke sees herself still as two separate selves. She lets Bentley continue to believe he was her first lover, thereby feeding his belief that he destroys. The sight of children dancing in a circle is an image of innocence too painful for both. Brooke begins to read Bentley's Bible; both begin to hear and see apparitions, noises, ghosts. Brooke struggles to work it through: "I thought it all out in my head," she says, "but I didn't say it out loud" (226). Thus it is with unconscious irony that she tells us, when she finally moves out, that there was "nothing left to say." In fact, not enough has been said.

At Carter's wedding Brooke resolves not to choose his way—conscious accommodation to the Southern norms—but to take "new directions." Presumably they will lead away from rotten diction and silence, away from the mannered South, away from the "lady." Late in the novel, the type of woman she once imitated appears as a grotesque: "She had high, round breasts like pincushions, that never budged as she danced, doing the same little step over and over, occasionally smiling a fake red smile that scoured the room without settling on any of us" (224). And at a good moment with Bentley, Brooke imagines making up a "whole new language," for telling the truth.

During the novel, Brooke buys for herself an object that satisfies her "real" self unequivocally, if temporarily. It is a large chunky glass paperweight; inside is an entire village, three mountain peaks, and a church. When Brooke turns it upside down, it snows. Brooke "makes a blizzard" in "my town" when she is caught in situations that make her feel powerless. This village in the mountains, of which she is sole proprietor, I connect with her desire to write a "whole new language." But she discards that village, giving it at the end to her landlady for her bricabrac collection, apparently believing she has outlived its usefulness. Perhaps it is a bit too perfect, though those three peaks and those houses in a holler reappear in Lee Smith's fiction, if not in Brooke Kincaid's life, but as the geography of *Oral History.*

The shift from a corsage under a glass bell to a glass enclosed town marks, at the very least, the move from Susan's preoccupation with the natural world to Brooke's with the social. Smith introduced the image of the kaleidoscope in *Wind;* twice Brooke feels dizzy, sees the world as a series of kaleidoscopic images. In another geometric image, Brooke, alone among her class at St. Dominique's, can understand the intricate geometry of the graduation formation. Another geometric image, even more abstract, becomes the central metaphor for art in *Fancy Strut.* In its abstraction, it marks a departure in tone and point of view from the first two novels.[1]

In *Fancy Strut* an entire community's story is told; it's Speed, Alabama, celebrating its Sesquicentennial. Fancy Strut is the "most prestigious category of them all" at the Susan Arch Finlay Memorial Marching Contest for majorettes. To see that as a paradox is to see the parodic possibilities of the novel. Everyone's involved in some fancy strut—the town planning the pageant, run by a hired Hollywood hack; a rich black student wishing to have a bathroom of his own; the bullying mayor; the self-styled champion of truth beset by delusions. Smith connects individual stories with the story of the town; the working out of the plot, despite the rich humor, suggests a point of view closest to that of the cynical idealist Lloyd Warner, the lawyer who sees too much and can do too little.

About two-thirds of the way through *Fancy Strut*, the narrator directs the reader to "visualize an isosceles triangle, superimposed on the town. . . . the lines . . . are straight and black, outlining the . . . excitement" of the Sesquicentennial (214). The points are the office of the Speed Messenger, where Boy Scoutish editor Manly Neighbors reads threat letters directed at the "Sesqui"; the football field and junior high gym, where Buck Fire, the White Company agent hired to stage the celebration, directs the pageant; and the coffeeshop of the El Rondo Motel, "central to the political and business life of Speed." Here Lomas Cartwright, Super Good Old Boy, tries to form a vigilante group to protect the women against the Communists, who he believes lie behind the threat letters. With the triangle, the narrator of *Fancy Strut* puts us at a distance from characters, emphasizing patterns and connections that characters cannot see. (Speed Junior College coeds, for instance, "do not know, or care, about the isosceles triangle." The novel thus carries easily the tone of parody that Smith uses widely for the first time here. Naming, for instance, is parodic: slow Speed, the "Ivory Towers" apartments where a black student wants to live. The humor is mostly ironic because the overriding theme of the novel is hypocrisy, the split between appearance and reality. Only when Buck Fire "changes his real laugh to a deep fakey chuckle" do the "girls relax" (38). A good old boy uses a story about attempted rape—"This breather tried to have his way with her but she hopped right up and kicked him you know where and he ran all doubled up out the door" to show how "we've got to protect our women" (221). Frances Pitt "looked around through lowered lids during the prayer, to see who was really praying and who was just looking around" (303).

As the triangle connects the separate foci of public life, so the theme of isolation connects the several characters whose interior lives are available to us through the narrator. Appropriately, their aloneness derives from their distance from themselves, a distance maintained by their self-delusions or fancy struts. Monica Neighbors, who could be an older Brooke, has married Manly to "take care of her" and in "gratitude" after she has slept with several men in Europe. Now she despises the black woman who takes care of the house, but can deal neither with her nor with Manly directly; she is too distant from her own sexuality and aggression to do anything direct. Instead, she fancies an affair with Buck Fire, whom she sees as a sleazy transient. Though the affair transforms her understanding of sexuality, she chooses to retreat from Buck Fire into the "permanence and guilt" that she has always really wanted. She fires the maid Suetta and resolves to have a baby, but our hopes are not high for her growth.

Buck Fire distances himself by the ease with which he manipulates the desires of small town genteel women. He genuinely falls for Monica, however, and so is vulnerable when she dumps him for security. Ruthie denies her need for affection and companionship by seeing herself as, well, not quite a whore; she gets what she wants, Ron the Mouth, a man unlike her first husband who likes to talk to women, and does so with a vengeance. Bob Pitt, who thinks he wants to succeed, gets his real wish when he brings his reputation crashing around him when he exposes his affair with Sandy DuBois; Sandy, who wants both the security of her husband and the adventure of a lover, sees her fancy strut collapse as well. Lloyd Warner, the Southern liberal cynical lawyer with a suicide father and an unexplained attachment to the big old family house and to his mother ("Faulkner shit," he calls all this), loses his strut when he tries to kill himself at the pageant, and fails. Bevo, the repressed adolescent, overcomes his fear of fire by setting the stage aflame after his strut—the bugle call—fails. Like the town's pageant that collapsed into flames and gunshots and looting, nobody's strut wins.

Fancy Strut picks up themes that permeate Smith's fictions. Miss Iona, the ancient society page editor and keeper of the Old South flame, whose commitment to Art overrides both human beings and accuracy (she adds bougainvillaea to her society news stories at will) suggests both the seductiveness and the illusion of the dream of the Old South, a dream of character over money, wood over plastic, care over speed. Both illusions—that the Old South really meant that character prevailed, and that the New South means free market democratic capitalism—are mocked by the choice of the Queen. In one of the novel's finest ironies, Anne de Coligny does not win because of her economic skill any more than her predecessor (and cousin) won the Centennial Queen because of her character. Both are Queens because they represent one unchanging reality in Speed: the dominant white moneyed blueveined class. Plus ça change. Thus perhaps the final irony comes with the recognition that Smith's narrator has broken the boundary of class, crossed that distance, connected those foci, by giving us access to Speed folk of almost every class.

Fancy Strut is a transitional novel. It is funny, poignant, and occasionally uneven and uncertain in tone. The treatment of Miss Iona is a good example. Her behavior in sections adjacent to Monica's (who abhors her) is silly and even despicable; her behavior in sections involving Sandra and Frances (whom we abhor) seems almost fine. And the shift in tone doesn't seem explicable by shifts in point of view. Secondly, there is that question of distance. Certain sections of the novel seem too consciously crafted—Bevo and his fires, for example, or the various ominous forebodings of disaster at the pageant. But if these are problems, they are temporary. In *Fancy Strut* Lee Smith explored a voice that is richer and stronger for its capacity for parody, wit, humor, play. And, I suspect, such growth required distance from both characters and community.

The technical problems Smith set herself in *Black Mountain Breakdown* take advantage of this growth. She could have written Crystal Spangler's story from the straight first person point of view, as she had done in *Wind* and *Dogbushes*. She could have distanced Crystal's story entirely, by giving it to the voice of another narrator—as she did, in fact, in the novel's first writing as "Paralyzed: A True Story," which a much less sympathetic Agnes tells. Neither choice would have allowed her the vision of a community that, she has said, she wanted to be the final voice of the novel. Yet the isosceles triangle method, the omniscient American narrator, was too far from the community for her purposes. In *Black Mountain Breakdown*, then, Lee Smith worked out a narrator who speaks with the diction of the mountains where Crystal and Agnes grow up. No longer do we hear the detached ironic tone of *Fancy Strut;* yet we have gone beyond the implications of first person narration.

Her technical achievement reflects a growing conviction in Smith's fiction that character and time and place are inextricable. Crystal Spangler's pale-haired, fineboned ethereal beauty, her surface, that part of her seen most by others and least by herself, works against her from the moment she's born. Her mother Lorene plans to make her into everything she couldn't be, which is everything that American culture in the 1950s wanted of its "girls." And that is precisely what her almost entirely withdrawn father fears. So Crystal Renée, with the "prettiest name" her mother could think of, wins beauty contests and the football hero, Roger Lee Combs. Even when Crystal trusts the sensual and spiritual voices inside her, voices that lead her, as they did Brooke, away from convention, Crystal perceives it as a response to someone outside who can supply her need to feel real. Later, when she sleeps with almost anyone, it's because it's only when she is with boys that she feels "pretty, or popular, or fun." Thus the interiority that Brooke Kincaid had perceived as her "real self," Crystal sees as outside, a power, like a man or God's spirit, entering her. Her perception of her essential passivity is confirmed when she is raped by her retarded uncle Devere. That she forgets it immediately, until the end, explaining her pain as only a virus, is a clue to her desire (itself passive) to avoid confronting her own passivity.

Besides sex and God, however, Crystal finds a third source of reality: teaching. The scenes in her classroom show an incredibly different Crystal: she speaks, thinks, chooses, enacts, and has probably more *words* here than in the rest of the novel. Nor should this be a surprise, after all. As a high school student, Crystal loved to go to the blackboard and diagram compound-complex sentences. Patterns, again, and a voice: this is as close as Crystal will come to becoming a Lee Smith artist.

Crystal's decision to "paralyze" herself comes as a consequence of other choices she has made, or, more accurately, that she has allowed to be made for her. Crystal loves her father with a romantic intensity that he encourages with his *One Hundred and One Famous Poems.* The morning after she is raped, she walks into the front room where he has lived for years and finds him on his sofa dead. Her response is understandably hysterical and enraged; as a consequence, she is drugged to sleep. Later, in her twenties, having found as a teacher the only real voice we hear from her in the novel, she again feels twice bereft: her mother leaves home after marrying Odell, and Crystal, seeking connection, spends the night with her aunts—where she was raped, and where now her mind "whirls." After this repetition, and with Roger Lee Combs waiting for her with a promise to take care of her, the temptation to return to passivity is nearly irresistible. And yet Crystal might have resisted it—she is capable of anger, for instance—had the feeling that she has always followed not reappeared. The sense of her own reality that accompanies a feeling of inner sexual response, something she has never felt for Roger before, compels her now and makes her following *his* words inevitable. Victim to her own interpretations of her sensuality and of her bereavement, believing she needs Roger on both counts, she says she will like "Whatever you think." Then "some part of her is screaming, or almost screaming, and then it breaks off and is still. . . . It's so comforting, really, to have somebody again to tell her what to do" (200, 202).

Another way to see Crystal's predicament is through her diction. Agnes says Crystal is missing some "hard thing inside her that Agnes and Babe were born with." Brooke Kincaid had that hard thing, which was evident in her incapacity to let conventional rhetoric slip past her lips for long. But someone else, not Crystal, says "This is a lot of shit" about the Richmond beauty pageant. Crystal's words are to the radio announcer: "It's a memory I will always cherish . . . Everyone there was so sweet." Certainly her search in the family history, the region's history, through the oral histories of her father and great aunts fails to provide her with the connection she needs, or the hard thing, or the words. And thus Crystal the English teacher seems finally beyond the healing capacity of language.

Cakewalk, a collection of stories written since 1970, includes several already discussed: "Saint Paul," "Mrs. Darcy," "Gulfport," and the title story. As in "Cakewalk," contrasts between working class and elitist art shape "Artists." A prissy, "sensitive" child, pet of her aristocratic grandmother, Jennifer stands amazed when her grandfather's mistress comes to help him die. The grandmother has refused to share this most intimate of mortal experiences; tellingly, she is in another room, working at her art. But the mistress Mollie Crews's art is of and for the world; she is a beautician. Ultimately, like Miss Iona in *Fancy Strut,* Grandmother retreats into a psychosis that saves her idea of art by denying reality. "I'm watching art," she says, as she watches a stock car race on TV. Jennifer chooses; she packs away the art supplies she inherits from her grandmother, goes to get a haircut, and then finds Scott, a "good kisser." She never becomes an artist, she says (though she tells this story); she gives her grandmother's figurines to her children, who make them into patterns in their play, the patterns that, in all Lee Smith's fictions, suggest art.

"Between the Lines" and "All the Days of Our Lives" are *tours de force*

of point of view. Joline B. Newhouse tells in plain English what's between
the lines of the heavily Victorian rhetoric of her column by that name.

> I write, for instance: "Mrs. Alma Goodnight is enjoying a pleasant recuperation
> period in the lovely, modern Walker Mountain Community Hospital while she
> is sorely missed by her loved ones at home. Get well soon, Alma!" I do not
> write that Alma Goodnight is in the hospital because her husband hit her up the
> side with a rake and left a straight line of bloody little holes going from her waist
> to her armpit after she yelled at him, which Lord knows she did all the time,
> once too often. (*CW* 12)

She is easy to laugh at, to see as a parody figure. She's unabashed about
mentioning what she sees as her good points, and she is entirely innocent
as a writer. She signs her column, "Peace be with you from Mrs. Joline B.
Newhouse" because she likes a line that "has a ring to it," which this one
patently lacks. She "reveals" to a dying man that she made up her characters, Mr. and Mrs. Cardinal, and then feels bad about her "meanness."
But only fools would only laugh at Joline. Between the lines of her narration is a strong woman who loves and affirms life. When Joline analyzes
others, she'll tell you the bad first—"Sally is loud and excitable"—then
she'll say, "But she has a good heart." Religious as she is, she will not
trade her sin—adultery with a revival preacher—for anything. It is a sin,
she is right, of "loving pure and simple." Joline's voice is so real, so rich,
so complex that it subsumes (but does not deny) its parodic possibilities.

The third person narration of "All the Days of Our Lives" gives us
Smith's now familiar narrator who speaks the language of the characters:
"It's been a real bad week for Helen," the story begins. Helen is losing
control of her life. She's run off with a man who's run off from her, and
now she's living with the consequences: divorce, a job at Aesthetic Print-
ers, and three kids to raise. Her incapacity to act is suggested by her
unwillingness to cook, despite plenty of recipes dutifully reproduced in
the text. Helen fools herself, like the soap opera victims she watches, into
believing that all will be better tomorrow—not because of what she can
do for herself, but because of what she can get a man to do for her.
Marriage still might be a "beautiful pastel country," she thinks (her
daughter: "My father is a turkey"). And because of the complex tone of the
narration, we feel both irritated at her and sympathetic with her, as she
sees in the backyard sprinkler a "shimmering pastel rainbow. . . . promising everything."

and Snowman—has a powerful character derived partly from its nature (geology, weather and plants) and partly from its culture (the fabric of myth and story that creates and perpetuates the sense of its meaning). And among the people who live in the hollers and on the sides of the mountains, nature and culture are likewise inseparable. In their consciousness, history and legend, fact and fiction, world and imagination, body and mind are one. In earlier work Lee Smith has largely skirted this locus for her fictional imagination. In *Dogbushes*, the mountains fringed the novel; but except for the stunning dog vision and the compelling life of Elsie's stories from the holler, their reality doesn't impend in the novel. *Something in the Wind*, with its mainly social tasks, moves into Tidewater Virginia and Piedmont North Carolina where gentility is the issue. When the dark cave of the pit fills with ghosts, destroying the emotional life there, and when Brooke tries to assert control over her experience by making blizzards in her little world, the possibilities of the mountain world touch the novel. *Fancy Strut*, set in Alabama, has no mountains and, except for Bevo's, no ghosts; its tone is parody, its mode detached from the symbolic or lyrical. Crystal, though, begins to look actively to the mountains and to the past, in stories; these are among her relatively few self-generated actions. Her father told stories *(Listen, he would say. Listen.)* of a lost silver mine and a man in a hollow tree. They echo in Crystal's mind, and she'd like to track them down. She asks everyone to tell the stories of the family, again and again. And she finds and treasures the journal of Emma Turlington Field. But Roger burns her journal, Little Emma Mining Camp goes the way of the New South, and her father dies, leaving her only the memory that "There's a silver mine out there somewhere." In *Oral History*, Lee Smith mines the mind/mine that Grant Spangler drank away and that Crystal inherited but silenced.

At the center of *Oral History* are a place and a family story that sustain place through time. The place is Hoot Owl Holler, located in the middle of the three mountains. The time is framed by the present but returns to one hundred years earlier by means of the oral histories within. A college student, Jennifer, returns to her dead mother's mountain home for her oral history project. She is filled with academic illusions, infatuated with her professor and prone to freshman diction. But she tries, earnestly, to get to know her strange and sullen "grandmother," her garrulous "grandfather," and her cousins with their TV and their trailer with shag rug walls. At the end, the frame story leaves us with tawdriness, too; the young Almarine Cantrell is exploiting his heritage by making the Cantrell homeplace into a theme park called Ghostland. But he reveals his sense of the realities he and Jennifer are denying in his diction at the end. First he begins to tell Jennifer the truth about her mother, then he lies: "You can't take all that too serious-like. . . . You come back sometime and see us again. And drive careful, now, you hear?" But his last message is a kiss that is like a rape, "so hard that stars smash in front of her eyes. Al sticks his tongue inside her mouth" (284). That kiss, like his warnings and his true words about her mother, comes from the Almarine that has been made by the mountains.

The devolution of the contemporary South, given in inimitable Lee Smith detail, is not a new theme for her. In *Fancy Strut,* both the turquoise plastic El Rondo chairs and the mahogany at Mrs. Warner's are empty of solidity and sufficiency; Miss Iona, who loves the past, is no more trustworthy than Buck Fire, who lives in the present. But in *Oral History,* there is a real, authentic past, whose loss is grievous. So the tawdriness of Ghostland means more than the absurdities of the Sesquicentennial; it marks the loss of a reality, not an illusion, and *Oral History* is an elegy, not a parody.

As Almarine's kiss suggests, however, Lee Smith refuses to sentimentalize the loss, to offer a simplistic image of organic mountain life to counter the polyester present. For one thing, that "organic life" is filled with brutality, tragedy, and loss, with illness and death and betrayal, and with just plain petty meanness and lies. But there is also love of almost unbearable intensity and clarity—the first Almarine's for Red Emmy, Dory Cantrell's for Richard Burlage. And there is the barely utterable beauty of the natural world.

Fictions abound in the mountains; they keep the mountains standing and the families alive. Manhood and womanhood are harshly defined fictions. Young Jink Cantrell, like Bevo and Michael, must become a man by rejecting a love of living things and a sensitivity to complex feelings: he sings, finally, filthy songs with the men, and eats cracklins while looking at the hog's head. Fictions are invented for all kinds of motives, and believed for as many. Red Emmy, for instance, may be a wild mountain woman of breathtaking beauty; she may be a mean witch; she may be a supernatural creature torn between her love for Almarine and her immortality. We really don't know, as readers, whose story to credit; there is an absence at the heart of *Oral History* that is the absence of absolute and objective truth. All that we have is stories, Smith the post-modernist implies; we'll never see the thing in and for itself.

Lee Smith's ability to invent full and fully distinct human voices lets her tell *Oral History* as she does, giving us so various a group of narrators. Again, she prefers the spoken voice to the written one. And in this novel, she explores the implications of oral and written language. A kind of authenticity comes from the diction and tone of speakers like Granny Younger. It is in part the dignity and authority of the unself-conscious lyricism of the mountains, of a hymn like "Bright morning stars are rising/ Day is breaking in my soul." Matter of factly, as she tells everything, Granny Younger calls Hoot Owl Holler a "play pretty cotched in the hand of God"; again, in the course of her plain and simple narration, she will pause with a sentence like "she growed up with ravens, in caves" (33, 46). Even Rose Hibbitts has lyrical possibilities; she describes her astonishment at her own lies: "These words come out of my mouth just as smooth as glass and I like to have died when I heard it" (87). The authenticity comes in part from the social implications of telling a story as opposed to writing one, that is, from the presumption of a concrete human audience rather than an abstract mental one.

Though we hear many of the narratives, we merely read the narrative of the outsider Richard Burlage. Like his granddaughter Jennifer, who keeps a diary, Richard brings to the mountains a set of abstract expectations. Unlike her, he learns to love in the mountains, with the golden Dory Cantrell from Hoot Owl Holler. Retreating from the mountains, he betrays Dory and loses (ironically) the meaning of the mountains he told himself he had come to seek, a meaning Jennifer never allows herself to find.

Smith connects the self-consciousness that characterizes most of Burlage's prose with modernism. In his language and his brother Victor's ideas, we watch stiff, Latinate, educated Victorian male minds experience essentially abstract and intellectual, white, masculine, post-World War I angst. But this shift from the dominant Victorian to the dominant modern consciousness takes place, rightly, on the fringe of this novel's plot and setting, in Richmond. Thus the comment on the limits of conventional academic readings of modern history is clear. Richard hopes to prove his

"disembodied" brother wrong, to disprove the "nothing at the core." Like
so many modernists he leaves "civilization" on a self-conscious "pilgrim-
age . . . to a simpler era . . . to the very roots of consciousness and
belief" (97). Richard is sensitive and intelligent and honest and earnest
enough to find something more real in the Freewill Followers than he had
in the Episcopal Church, and to be seduced out of his diction and out of
his mind by Dory Cantrell, in a passion in which, he writes, "our vastly
different manners of speech seemed to melt and blend together into some
single tongue we share" (129). In that sentence, Richard moves toward
lyric rather than self-consciously abstract language; of course, he connects
the move with orality. Yet an indication of how different their tongues
really are can be seen in the lyric poetry they choose. Where Richard
finds that Christopher Marlowe's highly stylized and civilized "The Passionate Shepherd to His Love" expresses his feelings for Dory exactly,
surely the novel's epigraph, with its "box of golden," is Dory's poem. For
she courts Richard, and she learns how killing love can be.

Richard can't for long relinquish words, written words, reason. He
writes down a list of pros and cons for staying with Dory (number 6 on the
con list is: "Her father and her brothers would kill me"). When he decides
to leave, taking Dory with him, he sends the written message to her by
hand, by "one of the loafers below," he thinks. But such abstracting, like
writing itself, can be deadly. It is the hand of cold and envious Ora Mae
Cantrell that holds the message; she destroys the note, Richard never
knows Dory does not get it, and Dory never knows he sent it. So it is
written language that is limited and fragile: divested of sound, separated
from its body, rendered merely visible, reified into ink on paper, it can be
manipulated or lost or silenced or misinterpreted almost at will. The
power of the written word in this oral culture is attenuated and almost
inhuman. The honest plainness of Richard's silence, of the journal sections that lose all conventional coherence, of the capacity for lyricism that
grew as he grew, disappear with Dory. Richard goes home to Richmond,
to the self-consciousness of the literary tradition, and to marry a wife who
is the daughter of an Episcopal bishop.

Near the end of the novel in the section called "Richard Burlage Discourses Upon the Circumstances Concerning His Collection of Appalachian Photographs, c. 1934," he tells of developing a photograph that he
thought showed merely the Smith Hotel, but that in developing he finds

to show two smiling women leaning out the window. This intrusion of the human gives him "quite a shock"; but, without pause, Richard denies the impact by using the image to validate both his aesthetic theory and his "settled life." He calls the photograph "Whorehouse, c. Hard Times," and we remember *Something in the Wind's* Brooke Kincaid in art class, thinking that the professor has forgotten that those Etruscan tombs had real human beings buried in them, and we remember Saint Paul, who said he cared only about the idea of Billie Jean, and we know Richard's "circumstances" were actual human beings, and his "discourse" once the incoherence of love.

The horrific failure of what we traditionally call modernism is its erasure of human experience in the name of an idea; it is a failure that invades the mountains in this novel, with Ghostland. In a sense a victim to both modernism and literacy, Dory dies, years after Richard leaves her, after her marriage to Little Luther Wade, after her children by both men are nearly grown, haunted still by the life of the past in her imagination. A train on a spur line cuts off her head.

The tension between oral and written cultures appears also in two characters who are moving in opposite directions. Young Jink Cantrell has been profoundly moved by his teacher, Richard Burlage. How deeply so is evident in his narrative, which never names Richard but intimately calls him "he," and in his speech, as he stammeringly revises mountain talk into standard English ("I knowed—knew"; "it weren't—wasn't"). Nor should this be taken as simply the unwelcome and disruptive impact of self-consciousness upon coherent speech: Lee Smith's vision is never simple. For with literacy, Jink has learned ideas—like justice and brotherhood—that he sifts through his experience as he sifts standard English into his grammar. And his initiation into mountain manhood is as horrifying in its denial of humanity as abstractions can be to the literate. The reverse process is shown in the aging Methodist minister Aldous Rife, who came from the University with his notes fifty years before Richard, preaches dry, somber sermons, *writes* a history of the area, and yet sustains a long and vital sexual relationship with Justine Poole. Most tellingly, his speech slips into the vernacular—to what avail is uncertain.

The ultimate affirmation of the novel is that it renders in written prose the possibilities of both spoken and written language. To call a *written fiction Oral History* is Lee Smith's latest, best joke. Ironically, too, the structure and implications of *Oral History* reflect no less modernist a sensibility than Richard Burlage's. But if we look for the modernist tradition out of which this novel has grown—or at least to which it has affinities—we will find the experimental but fundamentally life-affirming heritage of women writers like Katherine Mansfield and Virginia Woolf, a heritage that differs fundamentally in tone from the standard "masculinist modernists" yet employs similar techniques.[2]

It's easy to read Lee Smith's fictions. They are funny, poignant, entertaining, and they eschew certain of the more distancing techniques common to postmodernist fiction. That's probably why they get published in *Redbook* and *McCalls*. But in fact what keeps Smith's best fiction unsentimental despite its popular appeal (and I wonder about the implications of "despite") is that she turns quarrels with others into quarrels within. Thus it is Susan Tobey who thinks of tearing up the roses, not Eugene. Brooke's simplifying people into real and unreal is challenged by Diana's and by John Howard's self-revelations; in refusing to acknowledge their reality (and it would be unrealistic to expect her to do otherwise), Brooke cuts off a part of her self; likewise, she contributes to the end of the relationship with Bentley when she does not say what she feels. When Crystal projects her sexual power onto Roger, the quarrel is still within her; Richard Burlage's diary is a transcription of a war within.

Technical virtuosities in Lee Smith's work serve her human meaning; vision always takes priority over technique. Yet the implications of her technical virtuosity call into question critical clichés about modernist and postmodernist fictions. The values implicit in her fiction—unlike those in popular fiction, at least as conventionally interpreted—call into question the sustaining pieties of class and gender that continue to define for so many the meaning of human experience in the South. Smith's fiction is never programmatic or didactic on anything, including class and gender issues. The point of Smith's stories is not their *points* any more (or any less) than the point of Florrie's cakes is to feed someone. Rather, she writes from and about an extremely rigid traditional system that pervades Southern experience, and she tells us what she hears. What she hears is the sometimes heroic, sometimes comic, sometimes sneaky and petty ways in which Southern women and men try to salvage a sense of self within a system that tries to define that self for them.

The Career of Joan Williams:
Problems in Assessment

JUDITH BRYANT WITTENBERG

What we have come to think of as the shape of a writer's career—its peaks and valleys, its topography, if you will—is often more readily discerned when that career is completed than when it is *in mediis rebus*. While some writers conceptualize a large design such as a Yoknapatawpha saga, a Wessex chronicle, or a *comedie humaine* and carefully strive toward its completion, sometimes even preparing maps and genealogies as they progress, most others work along serendipitously, seizing gratefully at a chance idea or a publisher's request, then being amazed when they can retrospectively see any satisfying pattern. To be sure, the "shapely" career is to some degree a projective creation of the critic, who needs to impose order and structure on the chaos that marks the lives of nearly all human beings, including those of many novelists. Although there are thus problems inherent in efforts to discuss the precise nature of any writer's development, they are especially thorny in the case of Joan Williams. While some of these problems are a product of circumstance and others the result of her own tendencies, and while they don't sort into categories as neatly as one would like, I will attempt to clarify some of the particular challenges in assessing Williams's career.

The first of these is the very nature of her corpus, which is rather small and marked by some striking hiatuses. Born in Memphis in 1928, Joan Williams published a short story, "Rain Later," in 1949, while still a student at Bard College. It won first prize in the *Mademoiselle* College Fiction Contest and was given honorable mention in *Best American Short Stories 1949*. Four years later, another Williams short story, "The Morning and the Evening," was published in the *Atlantic Monthly* as an Atlantic First. That story would become the opening chapter of a novel by the same name, but it was eight more years until the novel was completed and published. *The Morning and the Evening* (1961) is a sensitive story of a gentle retarded man, Jake Darby, attempting to cope with the death of his mother and with a group of well-meaning but uncomprehending

Joan Williams

Born in Tennessee (1928), Williams attended Southwestern at Memphis before graduating from Bard College in New York. Her first novel, The Morning and the Evening, *1961, won the John P. Marquand Award. Her later publications include short stories and articles in periodicals, as well as three novels and a collection of short stories.*

townspeople. Adroit in its handling of dialogue and tone, and effective in its sympathetic characterization of a series of individuals struggling with the limitations imposed by poverty, isolation, or bad luck, *The Morning and the Evening* was highly praised by reviewers, including Robert Penn Warren and Granville Hicks. It won the John P. Marquand Award for the best first novel of the year, which conferred both prestige and a cash stipend of $10,000.

Williams's career thus began auspiciously, yet despite the exhilaration, she took five years to complete her next work, *Old Powder Man* (1966). Somewhat of a departure from her previous work in its scope, Williams's second novel chronicles both the entire life of a dynamite salesman and the development of levee building along the Mississippi River. Its protagonist, Frank Wynn, bears numerous similarities to the author's father, P. H. Williams, to whom the novel is dedicated, and the work achieves special poignancy near its close, as Wynn's daughter, a young mother as was Williams herself at the time she began writing the book, tries with limited success to arrive at some sort of understanding and acceptance of her father before his death from emphysema. *Old Powder Man* was, like Williams's first novel, widely reviewed, mostly favorably. The fact that it was a fictionalized biography more than a dramatically conceived novel drew criticism from the *New York Times Book Review* (Scholes 40), but Robert Penn Warren felt that what he called her "anti-technique" had, by the end of the novel, "the dignity of a method." Warren praised *Old Powder Man* in a *Life* review entitled "Death of a Salesman—Southern Style," in which he compared it to *An American Tragedy* (10, 18).

Four years later, in 1971, appeared *The Wintering*, the story of a young woman's romance with a famous writer, which is extremely autobiographical. Amy Howard, a student when she meets the famous Jeffrey Almoner, attempts over the next few years both to find herself as a writer and to attain some sort of emotional equilibrium in her relationship with the older man, about whose desire for her she is highly ambivalent. Perhaps because of the novel's uneasy relationship to historical fact and its intimate portrait of one of America's most honored authors, it received fewer reviews than Williams's previous novels, none of them in the mass-circulation periodicals and most of them negative.

Affected at some level by the knowledge that public interest in her work was now negligible, Williams, always a slow writer, began to work at a snail's pace. It took her more than a decade to complete *County Woman*, a novel about the feminist awakening of a middle-aged Mississippi woman, Allie McCall, whose story is juxtaposed with the racial turmoil of the early 1960s; it appears in 1982. The next year, however, Williams's new publisher also produced a collection of her short stories entitled *Pariah*, which includes all of her previously published short fiction and one story which was purchased by *Mademoiselle* but never appeared in the magazine.

Although most of her fiction has been favorably reviewed, much of it by such writers as Robert Penn Warren, Joyce Carol Oates, Anne Tyler, and Doris Betts, who themselves enjoy distinguished reputations, sales of Williams's work have been relatively small. Moreover, she has received virtually no attention from the academic critics, presumably because her work is relatively traditional, both artistically and socio-culturally. The early and later novels which bracket Williams's career are in some ways more successful than the heavily autobiographical middle works; this suggests the merit, in her case, of staying away from material which is intensely personal. Nevertheless, all of her work draws liberally on her own life experiences and those of members of her family.

Some of the fallow periods in Joan Williams's career are undoubtedly attributable to the demands of a complicated personal life, which has included three marriages, two divorces and an annulment, the raising of two children, and moves between the Northeast and the South. The gaps are also a result of the fact that she writes rather slowly and tends to work effectively only when inspired. As she said in a recent interview, speaking of her early years as a writer, "No one ever talked to me about discipline, that to be a writer you sat down and worked every day, so [after my first short story, "Rain Later"] I just kept waiting for the muse to strike, and it didn't strike me again for four years." Long periods without publication also require, she feels, that she essentially begin anew with each work, that without any impelling momentum it is "as though I am starting over" every time.[1] Despite the hiatuses and qualitative inconsistencies in her work, which are perceptible both to Williams and to her reader, one sees in it suggestions of the potential for a largely-conceived, coherent oeuvre. Nearly all of her fiction is set in and around Memphis, where she grew up and which is usually called "Delton" in her work, and in the nearby north Mississippi town of Arkabutla, which Williams calls "Marigold" or "Itna

Homa," where her maternal grandmother lived and where she spent a good deal of time in her early years. One also sees recurrent characters like the spinsters Ruth Edna May and Hattie McGaha and the storekeeper Miss Loma, and recurrent thematic patterns such as change and loss, generational differences, racial tensions, or sound and silence. Williams has done less than she might have with such inter-textual resonances, but the possibilities are evident.

If certain problematic variations create some difficulties for her critics, other challenges are posed by the nature of her tutelage, the looming figure of her mentor William Faulkner, who influenced and in some ways over-shadowed her career almost from its inception. A figure omnipresently *there* for any contemporary Southern writer—Eudora Welty compared him to a mountain always in the background—Faulkner was far more important to Williams than to most comparable writers, for he played a role in her life alternately of father, Pygmalion, and ardent lover. He offered her valuable advice and inspiration, but in some imaginative way created a trap from which she has had difficulty escaping. Williams first discovered her writing ability while doing high school essay assignments. As a college junior, she transferred to Bard College a few years later along with a friend, Louise Fitzhugh, because the writer Peter Taylor told them it was a good place to study writing. She began her career as a writer of fiction when a Bard professor, Joseph Summers, suggested she enter a short story contest and she astonishingly produced her prize-winning "Rain Later." She feels that at that point the major influence on her work was the short fiction of Eudora Welty. She particularly remembers reading the 1941 collection of Welty's, *A Curtain of Green,* before beginning her own fiction writing. One can see significant traces of such Welty stories as "Lily Daw and the Three Ladies" and "Clytie" in Williams's first novel, and one can imagine that "Death of a Traveling Salesman" might have inspired the conception of Williams's second novel. The direction of her literary career changed drastically, however, in the summer of 1949 when she read *The Sound and the Fury* and met its renowned author, who was shortly to win the Nobel Prize.[2] The rapport was almost instantaneous, though the relationship was fraught with complications from the outset, including an age difference of thirty-one years, the fact that Faulkner was married, and Williams's reluctance to become involved. Matters were settled officially, if not emotionally, only with her 1954 marriage to writer Ezra Bowen, himself the son of the famous non-fiction writer, Catherine Drinker Bowen.

For Williams the relationship with Faulkner was also complicated artistically, because he began reading and advising her on her work. He was enthusiastic about the story she wrote before she met him, eloquently praising it as "moving and true, made me want to cry a little for all the sad frustrations of solitude, isolation, aloneness in which every human being lives, who for all the blood kinship and everything else, cant really communicate, touch."[3] He soon was reading her subsequent fiction in draft, offering both criticism and encouragement. Letters from Faulkner to Williams published in L. D. Brodsky's recent book detail specific suggestions on both the short story "The Morning and the Evening" and the later novel by the same name, as well as his rather surprising advice, given his instinct for privacy, that she write a novel about their affair. Faulkner was very ambitious for Joan. He wrote to Saxe Commins of his fear that she was "not demon-driven enough for art,"[4] and he repeatedly exhorted Joan to "write another," to "keep your sights high,"[5] and, as early as late 1951, almost ten years before her first novel was published, asserted that "I intend for you to win that [$10,000] prize," which, of course, she went on to do.[6]

The Faulknerian strains in Williams's work are obvious: the small town Mississippi setting with its gallery of grotesques, the protagonist who is a moaning idiot and falls in love with a cow, a combination of Benjy Compson and Ike Snopes, and the compassion for all the narrow and frustrated lives a sensitive observer discerns in a confining community. Like Faulkner, she also shows great concern for the interior lives of her characters, and her moments of macabre humor seem distinctly Faulknerian. The protagonist of her third novel is, moreover, closely modeled on Faulkner himself. Jeffrey Almoner of *The Wintering* shares with his real-life counterpart a sense of being an alien in the small Mississippi town where he lives and works, a propensity for self-destructive alcoholic binges, and a desire for a relationship with his young protégée that is compounded of emotional intimacy and professional guidance. He goes so far as to give her the manuscript of his favorite novel, just as Faulkner gave Joan Williams the manuscript of *The Sound and the Fury*.

Although Williams's fictional depiction of their complicated affair may have been cathartic in a personal sense, even now, more than twenty

years after his death and nearly thirty years since the end of their romance, his impress on her work is evident, from the fact that she dedicated *Pariah* to him to the Faulknerian flavor of many of the stories,
particularly the early ones in the volume, written while he was still alive.
The others, more concerned with issues of recent decades such as the
racial integration of lunch counters and high schools in the South, the
efforts of civil-rights workers to find better jobs for black sharecroppers,
or a mother's problem with a marijuana-smoking child, reveal less distinctively the Faulknerian stamp. Reviewers of *Pariah* have repeatedly in-
voked the comparison of Williams's work with that of Faulkner, and
indeed the book's dedication and jacket copy actively invite such a comparison. But possibly it is time to recognize the fact that the recurrent
stress on the commonality of their technical approaches and character
types fails to take into account significant ways in which Williams differs
from her mentor. Not only her reviewers but perhaps Williams herself
have been excessively concerned with the Faulknerian parallels.

Just as the Faulknerian presence, both personal and artistic, has provided what is for Williams at once an inspiration and a sort of psychic
bondage, the same has been true of her Southernness. She essentially left
the South in 1947, when she spent a year at a Washington, D.C. junior
college before going on to Bard, and she has lived in the Northeast almost
constantly since, primarily in a suburb of New York City. Yet her work has
been almost exclusively about the South, especially the South of her
childhood, and the literary predecessors she found influential include,
beside Faulkner and Welty, Katherine Anne Porter and Carson McCullers. It is the memories of the sounds of Southern conversation, of the
character configurations of small-town society, and of the heat, dust, and
smells of a Southern summer that provide the largest impetus to her
work. She says that remembering the empathy she felt for the retarded
man in Arkabutla she knew as a child gave rise to *The Morning and the
Evening,* even as the tales she heard of her father's life in levee camps
along the Mississippi are behind *Old Powder Man,* and her visits to black
sharecroppers during the civil rights turbulence of the early 1960s provided the background for *County Woman* and material for several short
stories. As effectively as Williams has transformed much of this Southern
experience into fiction, she now feels that the fact that she "wanted to
write just about the South" has been in some sense a "mistake," limiting

both the audience for her fiction and the material available to her imagination. At the same time, paradoxically, she believes that leaving the South more or less permanently in the late 1940s detached her from the source of regular inspiration. As she put it, "[If I had lived there full time], I would have written a lot more because all that Southern flavor would have kept turning me on as I was exposed to it." She finally returned in 1982, spending nearly a year in Memphis, only to discover that "the kinds of things I was writing about are [now] gone," that the contemporary South is "much like anyplace else" (Williams interview). Thus her ambivalence about the South, her sense that it was once both hauntingly unique and a place too limiting to live in, is ironically offset by a nostalgic feeling of loss for a now vanished way of life.

Williams's complicated struggle with her Southernness, evident both in her fiction and in her public comments on the subject, is paralleled by her efforts to come to terms with what she now realizes is an increasingly feminist-oriented aspect to her work. This awareness may have led her to say recently that Welty, Porter, and McCullers were greater influences on her work than Faulkner because "as females there are things and themes they wrote about that were closer to what was going to come out of me than the things he wrote" (Williams interview). Even her first two novels, though centered around males, show a special sympathy for the plight of women living in the confining and patriarchal Southern society that Williams knew as a young person. Ruth Edna May, the lonely spinster of *The Morning and the Evening,* complains that men "have all the advantages in this world. They can hide their flaws, and they can marry if and when they choose" (86). Ruth Edna expresses the frustrations of long years spent caring for members of her family by secretly drinking paregoric and by making efforts to find a job. Another character in the same novel, Frances, seeks to surmount her frustrations with an intense extra-marital affair and thinks about "the advantage men had over women—their work. They could always worry about it instead of something they couldn't do anything about" (115). Although Frank Wynn dominates *Old Powder Man,* his mother Cally is memorable for her strong-willed restlessness and the hypochondria that is perhaps a response to unacknowledged frustrations inherent in her situation as a woman, and Frank's two wives respond to his workaholism and his lack of interest in their lives, the first by carrying on an adulterous affair, the second by drinking heavily. Other women in Williams's fiction similarly enact their secret rebellions by recourse to drugs, alcohol, or infidelity, including Almoner's wife in *The Wintering*, and various characters in the short stories, most memorably the protagonist of "Pariah," who is forced to recognize the havoc wreaked on her family by her uncontrolled drinking.

While Williams's sympathy for any character confronting the difficulties of a "rebellious heart" in a limiting environment extends to her male characters, whether black or white, the embryonic feminism revealed in her previous work comes effectively to fruition in the 1982 novel, *County Woman*, in the character of Allie McCall. Constricted both by the girdles she wears and by half a lifetime of having to care for her husband and invalid father, the fifty-year-old protagonist gradually breaks free. She is filled with terror when we first meet her "because all her life she had fought against a feeling of nothingness, and in middle age she had the terrible fear that she was losing that battle" (10). In some sense, Allie's plight is a general one; "women her age were beginning to discuss how tired they were of catering to men, feeling they had served their sentences" (21). Moreover, her situation is echoed by that of the blacks, who are attempting to change things with their courageous efforts to integrate the University at Oxford. Allie thinks of James Meredith "making a mark on history" and "long[s] more deeply to make some mark of her own" (46). Her first actions are symbolic and potentially self-destructive—a trip to Oxford, made despite male admonitions that the racial turmoil there made it too dangerous for a woman, and also a wanton sexual encounter with a filling station attendant. This encounter, faintly implausible to the reader, is recognized by Allie as having moments of male "domineering" that reveal "men did not very much like women" (129).

Unlike most of Williams's previous female characters, Allie learns to act constructively and politically; she evolves from a frustrated housewife to a public figure. With the Oxford riots in the background serving as an emblematic amplification of Allie's private turbulence, she manages to solve the long-standing mystery of her mother's death and exonerate a wrongfully accused black in the process, to expose a hit-and-run killer, and to agitate for the construction of a new bridge. Already acting like a community spokesperson, she becomes one by running for constable, an office previously held only by men, specifically by "good old boys." Not only is Allie's "liberation" successful, it galvanizes at least a few of the other women of the town in crucial ways. The book is over-plotted in some respects, an occasional problem in Williams's work as she seeks to compensate for her tendency to concentrate on thought processes and the slow pace of daily life. Its portrait of the political and racial awakening of a woman at an age when so many females are thought to be past the possibility for growth and change, however, is one many readers will find cheering. To be sure, the ending of *County Woman* finds honor and truth more triumphant than they usually are in real life, a product of Williams's publicly expressed desire for "moral resolution" in her fiction (Williams interview). Yet Allie's emergent feminism is a new and essentially promising sort of fictional vein for Williams and one she is likely to continue to mine in her new work, which she has said will deal in some way with the challenges she now faces in her mid-fifties and living alone for virtually the first time in her life.

The career of Joan Williams is thus still very much in progress, so the urge to precisely define its shape is as likely to run into difficulties as it would in the case of many writers still actively tangling with their muses or demons. I have tried to delineate some of the challenges in assessing the corpus of this particular writer, haunted by a powerful male mentor, struggling to keep working through the difficulties of a somewhat turbulent personal life, and attempting desperately to come to terms with her Southernness in the North where she lives and with her femaleness in what has been for her largely a male-dominated world. Her problems are not unique, perhaps, but because her fiction both records and attempts to work them out, her situation cannot but compel us as readers and as human beings.

NOTES

[1] Personal interview with Joan Williams, 12 Aug. 1983. Hereafter cited parenthetically as Williams interview.

[2] For details of her meeting and subsequent friendship with Faulkner, see Williams, "Twenty Will Not Come Again" 58–65.

[3] Joseph Blotner, ed., *Selected Letters of William Faulkner* (New York: Random, 1977), 297.

[4] Letter of 4 Mar. 1954, in Louis Daniel Brodsky and Robert W. Hamblin, eds., *Faulkner: A Comprehensive Guide to the Brodsky Collection. Volume II: The Letters* (Jackson: Univ. Press of Mississippi, 1984), item 992.

[5] Letter of 4 Jan., probably 1960, in Brodsky and Hamblin, item S-79.

[6] Letter of 31 Dec. 1951, quoted in Joseph Blotner, *Faulkner: A Biography* (New York: Random, 1974), 1406.

Stopping Places:
Bobbie Ann Mason's Short Stories

MAUREEN RYAN

Bobbie Ann Mason's short stories, published in 1982 in the award-winning collection *Shiloh and Other Stories*, are set in western Kentucky in a contemporary South marked by change.[1] Small towns and farmhouses have made way for subdivisions with "new brick ranch houses of FHA-approved designs" and "mobile homes that have appeared like fungi."[2] New shopping centers and industrial parks have displaced "the farmers who used to gather around the courthouse square on Saturday afternoons to play checkers and spit tobacco juice ("Shiloh"4). But the old farmers are barely missed; in the new TV-infested South they have been replaced by Johnny Carson and Phil Donahue as the oracles of humor and truth.

Mason's characters stumble through their lives in this protean world, puzzled by intimidating new mores. In "The Climber," Dolores, apprehensively awaiting an appointment with a doctor who will diagnose the lump in her breast, hears "the Oak Ridge Boys . . . singing 'Elvira' on the radio. The Oak Ridge Boys used to be a gospel quartet when Dolores was a child. Now, inexplicably, they are a group of young men with blow-dried hair, singing country-rock songs about love" (115). The New South is in many aspects a more liberal, expanded world; a middle-aged grandfather asks who bought the "toes," no longer referring to " 'nigger toes,' the old names for the chocolate-covered creams" ("Drawing Names" 95). Yet it is as well a plastic, superficial world of television, Sara Lee cheesecake, and Star Wars toys.

Against the backdrop of this modernized society, Mason's characters, most of them in early to late middle age, grapple with the vicissitudes of life and their own personal upheavals—marriage and divorce, illness and aging, family relationships. Their ambivalent attitudes—and Mason's—toward the events in their own lives parallel their uncertain reactions to the complexities of the world around them.

283

Bobbie Ann Mason

A native of Kentucky (b. 1940), Mason received her B.A. from the University of Kentucky, her M.A. from the University of New York at Binghamton, and a Ph.D. from the University of Connecticut. Her work has appeared in various periodicals, and she is the author of two nonfiction books. Her first collection of short stories, Shiloh and Other Stories, *appeared in 1982.*

In Mason's South, middle-aged men recognize, hesitantly and be-latedly, that they have missed out on much of life. In "The Ocean," Bill Crittendon has sold his farm and invested in a deluxe camper, and he and his wife have set off to see the Atlantic Ocean because "he had once promised Imogene that they would see the world, but they never had. He always knew it was a failure of courage. After the war he had rushed back home. He hated himself for the way he had stayed at home all that time" (159).

In "A New-Wave Format," twice-divorced Edwin Creech is forty-three and living with a twenty-year-old woman when it occurs to him that his life is unfulfilled. Drifting from woman to woman, job to job, "he used to think of himself as an adventurer, but now he believes he has gone through life rather blindly, without much pain or sense of loss" (216). Edwin is a bus driver who transports mentally retarded adults to and from their training classes. He complements the music he plays on the tape deck with disc jockey patter; the passengers like the mellow rock of the sixties, and "it makes Edwin sad to think how history passes them by, but sometimes he feels the same way about his own life" (222). Feeling "that he is growing and changing for the first time in years," Edwin begins to alter his musical selections; "he plays music he did not understand fifteen years ago, music that now seems full of possibility: the Grateful Dead, the Jefferson Airplane, groups with vision," and "the passengers on his bus fill him with a compassion he has never felt before" (222). Invigorated by his fresh perceptions and unconsciously trying to keep up with his young lover, Sabrina, Edwin begins to play new wave music and believes that "the passengers understood what was happening. The frantic beat was a perfect expression of their aimlessness and frustration. Edwin had the impression that his passengers were growing, expanding, like . . . his own awareness" (228). The retarded passengers become over-excited by the driving music, and after two days of the B-52's and The Humans one has a seizure while the others scream in a frenzied chorus. Edwin has forgotten what he has been told about "the developmentally disabled"—that they "need a world that is slowed down; they can't keep up with today's fast pace" (217). Edwin does not see that *he* cannot keep up with the contem-porary world; he knows only, at the story's end, as he practices CPR on his girlfriend, that she too will leave him. "Bend over like this," he tells her. "Just pretend you have the biggest pain, right here, . . . right in your heart" (231).

Leroy Moffitt, the protagonist of the title story, is a disabled truck driver who has been unemployed for four months and whose suddenly sedentary life has inspired new perceptions. Having recently "grown to appreciate how things are put together," Leroy decides to build his wife Norma Jean a log cabin, because, as he recognizes, "the house they live in is small and nondescript" (2). He begins to notice the rampant suburbanization of the once-rural community, but more threatening is his observation that Norma Jean has become stronger and more independent in his absence. When on a long-planned trip to the Civil War battleground in Shiloh, Tennessee, she announces that she is leaving him, Leroy reflects on the past. But he "knows he is leaving out a lot. He is leaving out the insides of history. History was always just names and dates to him. It occurs to him that building a house out of logs is similarly empty—too simple. And the real inner workings of a marriage, like most of history, have escaped him" (16).

These confused men share an emotional impotence and ineffectuality that are manifested most obviously in their relationships with women. Edwin, who has never been able to keep a woman happy, is insecure about Sabrina; "if I say the wrong things, I want you to tell me," he pleads. "It's just that I'm so crazy about you I can't think sometimes. But if I can do anything better, I will. I promise. Just tell me" (214).

Mickey Hargrove, in "Private Lies," seems to resent the fact that "marriage to Tina was like riding a bus. She was the driver and he was a passenger. She made all the decisions—food, furniture, Kelly's braces, his socks. If he weren't married to Tina, he might be alone in a rented room, living on canned soup and Tang. Tina rescued him. With her, life had a regularity that was almost dogmatic."[3] Yet he admires strong women and is attracted to his ex-wife because she has changed, has become "different, prettier and more assured" (64). He is excited by the new Donna who has flown over Mount St. Helens ("He admired a woman who would charter a plane") and who has "learned all new techniques" of love-making (65).

In "The Rookers," it is not Mary Lou Skaggs but her husband Mack who is suffering from the empty nest syndrome now that his youngest child has gone off to college. Mack does his carpentry work at home and becomes distressed if he must be away from the house for too long.

> Mary Lou has tried to be patient with Mack, thinking that he will grow out of his current phase. Sooner or later, she and Mack will have to face growing older

together. Mack says that having a daughter in college makes him feel he has missed something, but Mary Lou has tried to make him see that they could still enjoy life. . . . She suggested bowling, camping, a trip to Opryland. But Mack said he'd rather improve his mind. He has been reading *Shōgun*. He made excuses about the traffic. (20–21)

Mack is afraid of Mary Lou and her insistence upon living; "You're always wanting to run around . . . You might get ideas" (25). He is content to stay at home with his television and his *Old Farmer's Almanac*, reading about the weather. Not until the story's end does Mary Lou recognize the motivation for her husband's fascination with the weather:

Mary Lou suddenly realizes that Mack calls the temperature number because he is afraid to talk on the telephone, and by listening to a recording, he doesn't have to reply. It's his way of pretending that he's involved. He wants it to snow so he won't have to go outside. He is afraid of what might happen. But it occurs to her that what he must really be afraid of is women. Then Mary Lou feels so sick and heavy with her power over him that she wants to cry. She sees the way her husband is standing there, in a frozen pose. Mack looks as though he could stand there all night with the telephone receiver against his ear. (33)

If many of Mason's female characters are stronger, more in control than their husbands and lovers, their assertiveness is as new and tentative as the men's awareness. Like Mason's men, her women are assessing their marriages and their lives.

Norma Jean Moffitt, pregnant and married at eighteen, has at thirty-four endured the death of a child, the incessant advice of a meddling mother, a husband on the road, and a job at the Rexall drugstore. No longer the child whom Leroy married, she is at his return taking a body-building class and later graduates to adult-ed composition at Paducah Community College. She gives up the electric organ and *The Sixties Songbook*, begins to cook "unusual foods—tacos, lasagna, Bombay chicken" (11). And Leroy is not surprised when Norma Jean announces that she is leaving him, with the explanation that "in some ways a woman prefers a man who wanders" (15).

Georgeann Pickett, in "The Retreat," grows increasingly discontent with her marriage to a good but shallow minister who must supplement his modest salary with part time work as an electrician. Distressed because low attendance is about to force the closing of his small church, Shelby looks forward with eagerness to the annual church retreat and workshops like "The Changing Role of the Country Pastor." Georgeann, however, attends reluctantly. At a workshop on Christian marriage, she asks the participants—mostly other ministers' wives—"What do you do if the man you're married to—this is just a hypothetical question—say he's the cream of creation and all, and he's sweet as can be, but he turns out to be the wrong one for you? What do you do if you're just simply mismatched?" But "everyone looks at her" (143).

When she stumbles upon a video game in the lodge basement, Georgeann finds a refuge. Playing the game, Galaxian, she feels that "the situation is dangerous and thrilling, but Georgeann feels in control. She isn't running away; she is chasing the aliens" (145). She cannot explain the attractions of the game to her bewildered husband, when he finds her much later. "You forget everything but who you are," she tries to tell him. "Your mind leaves your body. . . . I was happy when I was playing that game" (146). When they return home to the children and Shelby's reassignment letter and the reality that they will have to move, Georgeann announces to her husband that she will not go with him.

Georgeann's inability to articulate to Shelby her feelings about the video game illustrates the failure to communicate that plagues Mason's marriages. Leroy, recognizing that his marriage is in jeopardy, wants to make a fresh start with his wife; he "has the sudden impulse to tell Norma Jean about himself, as if he had just met her. They have known each other so long they have forgotten a lot about each other. They could become reacquainted. But when the oven timer goes off and she runs to the kitchen he forgets why he wants to do this" (9).

In her letters to her husband Tom, who has gone to Texas to play "born-again cowboy," Louise Milsap, in "Still Life with Watermelon," is more "expressive" than she ever was during their four-year marriage. She recognizes that the incident that precipitated Tom's departure, in which she threw "a Corning Ware Petite Pan" at him, was merely an attempt to get his attention (63). Linda will not return to her husband, in "Old Things," because, as she tells her mother, "I don't feel like hanging around the same house with somebody that can go for three hours without saying a word. He might as well not be there" (79).

Most of Mason's stories are concerned with marriage and male-female relationships that reflect, in their instability and disquietude, the fluidity of this society. Mason recognizes, however, that in complicated times close and lasting relationships become—if more difficult—more imperative as well. In brief, often poignant scenes she offers glimpses of durable, satisfying marriages.

After Imogene, in "The Ocean," expresses the hidden resentment she has long felt at having cared for her husband's invalid mother and, inadvertently, her own fears about growing old, Bill comforts her. Later, watching her sleep, he remembers when, just after their marriage and his induction into the service, he "watched her sleep for a full hour, wanting to remember her face while he was overseas. . . . Now Imogene's face was fat and lined, but he could still see her young face clearly" (161). A recently separated Kay Stone returns home in "Gooseberry Winter" and, after a day's outing with her mother, in which the older woman tells her daughter about her unhappy childhood, watches as her parents plant flowers. "For awhile she watches the relaxed way they work together, her father patiently digging holes, following her mother's directions. For all Mama's fears, she is comfortable with her husband, as though he were a refuge even now from her loveless past" (147).

For Mason such scenes, however rare and transitory, demonstrate that marriage—indeed, any human relationship—can offer a permanence seldom found in a mutable world. As Kay notes, "she had thought that marriage was so much simpler than the intricacies of blood ties, so easy that it could be canceled, forgotten. But her parents make marriage seem as permanent as having children" (147).

Having children may be more enduring than marriage in Mason's fictional world, but it is no less problematical. Many of her stories deal with aging parents and grandparents, and unhappy adult children returning home. The interaction among generations further illustrates the unrest that characterizes their society.

Although widowed Cleo Watkins cannot understand why her daughter would leave her faithful husband, Linda and her two children have moved in and overtaken Cleo's house. The grandmother is unable to adjust to the constant noise of the television, dishwasher, and telephone that the children create, and she "has forgotten to move effortlessly through the clutter children make" (84). Neither can Cleo comprehend why her daughter buys new clothes and goes out without her children, nor can Linda accept her mother's refusal to create a new life for herself. When Cleo argues that "people can't just have everything they want all the time," Linda responds, ". . . people don't have to do what they don't want to as much now as they used to." "I should know that," Cleo says. "It's all over television. You make me feel awful" (88).

The generation gap is dramatized too in "Graveyard Day." Waldeen Murdock, recently divorced, does not understand her ten-year-old daughter. "Her daughter insists that she is a vegetarian. If Holly had said Rosicrucian, it would have sounded just as strange to Waldeen" (165). Holly is precocious and unhappy, and Waldeen wonders whether she misses her father, who has moved to Arizona. Joe McClain wants to marry Waldeen, but she knows that marriage is complicated. She loves Joe, she admits, but proclaims that "that's the easy part. Love is easy" (169). She tries to explain to Joe that "you can't just do something by itself. Everything else drags along. It's all *involved*" (172). Considering the effect of her remarriage on Holly, Waldeen sees that "Holly would have a stepfather—something like a sugar substitute" (165–66). But "she hates the thought of a string of husbands, and the idea of a stepfather is like a substitute host on a talk show. It makes her think of Johnny Carson's many substitute hosts" (173). Waldeen and Holly disagree about everything from the relative benefits of plastic vs. real flowers to whether the cat was neutered or nurtured, and after one of her spats with her very contemporary daughter, Waldeen "suddenly feels miserable about the way she treats Holly. Everything Waldeen does is so roundabout, so devious" (174).

Devious is the word for Sandra's interaction with her grandmother in "Offerings." Sandra's husband has gone to Louisville to work at a K Mart, and Sandra, a country girl, has stayed behind. Her mother and grandmother come from Paducah to visit, and "they aren't going to tell Grandmother about the separation. Mama insisted about that. Mama has never told Grandmother about her own hysterectomy. She will not even smoke in front of Grandmother Stamper. For twenty-five years, Mama has sneaked smokes whenever her mother-in-law is around" (54). Neither can Kay Stone tell her father about her separation from her husband, whom she has left because he will not accept the responsibility of dealing with his son from a former marriage. Only at the end of the story (again, after her mother's disclosure of a loveless childhood with an aunt and uncle) does Kay understand her reluctance to confide in her father.

> Kay realizes that although it is cowardly of her, she is not going to tell her father about the separation. She will let her mother tell him. She reasons that she wants to save him the embarrassment of letting her see his pain, but she knows she wants to avoid her own embarrassment at admitting to him her failure. . . .

because he is her father and expects her to be happy, for her he has an authority that is . . . absolute . . . and so she cannot tell him what she feels. . . . Now, for the first time, Kay has an idea that her feeling of dread around her father is something like Gary's fear of dealing with his child, and she feels ashamed that she left Gary for having that kind of weakness. (147)

Family ties are close in Mason's Kentucky, but the insecurities and anxieties of her characters are evident in their interactions with loved ones. If neither marriage nor familial relationships provide an answer for many of Mason's characters, some seek constancy in a return to the past.

Kay's epiphanic comprehension of her parents' marriage and her relationship with her husband and father is a result of her return home and a visit to her reluctant mother's birthplace. Picnicking in the pasture near the decaying house, Kay "tries to imagine being a girl in this place. . . . It could be fifty years ago. This landscape could be the whole world. In it, marriage, like death, could seem absolute and permanent. A storm would be like the breath of God" (143).

Nancy Culpepper, in the story of the same name, returns to Kentucky from her home in Pennsylvania to help her parents move her aged grandmother to a nursing home. The familiar environment evokes the memory of her 1967 wedding. Married in Massachusetts, Nancy insisted that her parents not travel that long distance, but throughout the 1960s wedding and reception, with its Beatles music, and wine and 7 Up punch, she finds herself thinking about her parents and the past. Dancing with her new husband to the continuous music "in a slow two-step that was all wrong for the music," Nancy expresses her nostalgic longing for a distant time. "'There aren't any stopping places,' Nancy said. She was crying. 'Songs used to have stopping places in between'" (182).

Nancy's interest in her heritage was stimulated years later (and several years before the time of the story) when, on a visit with her grandmother to the Culpepper family graveyard, she had stumbled across a headstone marked "NANCY CULPEPPER, 1833–1905." She has since been entranced with the idea of an ancestor who shared her name—which she has subsequently re-adopted, eschewing her husband's surname—and now that Granny's belongings are to be moved, she hopes to find a photograph of the original Nancy Culpepper, who was, Granny says, Nancy's grandfather's aunt. Nancy does find a photo, a wedding portrait, forgotten in a closet "crammed with the accumulation of decades—yellowed newspapers, boxes of greeting cards, bags of string, and worn-out stockings"

(193–94), and Granny identifies the tiny woman in the picture as Nancy Hollins Culpepper. The final scene, like those of most of Mason's stories, is open-ended:

> Nancy sits down in the rocking chair, and as she rocks back and forth she searches the photograph, exploring the features of the young woman, who is wearing an embroidered white dress, and the young man, in a curly beard that starts below his chin, framing his face like a ruffle. The woman looks frightened—of the camera perhaps—but nevertheless her deep eyes sparkle like shards of glass. This young woman would be glad to dance to "Lucy in the Sky with Diamonds" on her wedding day, Nancy thinks. The man seems bewildered, as if he did not know what to expect, marrying a woman who has her eyes fixed on something so far away. (195)

"Old Things" demonstrates most poignantly the authority of the past in Mason's world. Cleo Watkins is perplexed by the modern predilection for antiques, for she "has spent years trying to get rid of things she has collected. . . . She doesn't want to live in the past" (76). Cleo does not perceive that her avoidance of life, her discontent with contemporary society, anchor her in a past that no longer exists. "Kids never seem to care about anything anymore," she reflects bitterly when her grandchildren act oblivious to their cluttered surroundings, and "she has put a chain on the door, because young people are going wild, breaking in on defenseless older women" (78, 80). Cleo envies a friend who has just taken a trip out West but maintains that she could not "take off like that" because "now there are too many maniacs on the road" (82-3).

Although she declares that "there's no use trying to hang on to anything. You just lose it all in the end. You might as well not care," the story's denouement teaches Cleo that some of the past cannot—and should not—be forgotten. At a flea market, amidst the Depression glass and rusty farm tools, she spots a familiar object, a miniature what-not in which her husband used to keep his stamps and receipts. At the sight of the small box, with its drawers that form a scene of a train running through the meadow, Cleo's "blood is rushing to her head and her stomach is churning" (92). As the story ends, she pays three dollars (too much) for the piece and, looking at the train, imagines that her happy family is aboard, crossing the valley, heading West: "Cleo is following unafraid in the caboose, as the train passes through the golden meadow and they all wave at the future and smile perfect smiles" (93).

Although the past offers quiet solace from the hectic pace of modern life, Mason is aware of the dangers of ignoring the inexorable changes of society. Cleo, with her refusal to adapt to contemporary culture, personifies another Mason theme—the inordinate fear of life in this strange new world. At fifty-two Cleo feels and acts like an old woman; "everything seems to distress her, she notices" (81). Mack Skaggs is also relatively young (in his late forties), but his agoraphobia and his ineffectual attempts to keep up with his college-student daughter (he struggles with *The Encyclopedia of Philosophy* only to discover that she is studying physics) are the pathetic actions and attitudes of a man completely overwhelmed by the world around him. In "Still Life with Watermelon," Louise's husband goes off to Texas without her because, he claims, she is "afraid to try new things" (63). She is initially angry at his accusations and his wanderlust, but at his return her feelings change. "Something about the conflicting impulses of men and women has gotten twisted around, she feels. She had preached the idea of staying home, but it occurs to her now that perhaps the meaning of home grows out of the fear of open spaces. In some people that fear is so intense that it is a disease, Louise has read" (73).

Mary, in "Residents and Transients," has, unlike most of these characters, experimented with various lifestyles, but she has returned to her roots in Kentucky. Now, although her husband has been transferred and has moved to the city to work and find them a home, she stays behind because, she says, "I do not want to go anywhere" (121). Mary loves her parents' old farmhouse and worries about a world that sends her mother off to live in a mobile home in Florida. She knows that her mother, who loved her canning kitchen, would be appalled to find that her daughter has taken a lover and spends her afternoons with him drinking Bloody Marys made with the old woman's canned tomato juice. An obviously more educated and sophisticated woman than many of her neighbors in these stories, Mary too is torn between the serene seductions of an obsolete lifestyle and the intimidating uncertainties of a variable present and future. Eventually she recognizes the dangers of stasis: "I am nearly thirty years old," she proclaims. "I have two men, eight cats, no cavities. One day I was counting the cats and I absent-mindedly counted myself" (127). Near the end of the story Mary relates to her lover the perception that will ultimately send her—however reluctantly—to Louisville and a new life with her husband:

"In the wild, there are two kinds of cat populations . . . Residents and transients. Some stay put, in their fixed home ranges, and others are on the move. They don't have real homes. Everybody always thought that the ones who establish the territories are the most successful. . . . They are the strongest, while the transients are the bums, the losers . . . The thing is—this is what the scientists are wondering about now—it may be that the transients are the superior ones after all, with the greatest curiosity and most intelligence. They can't decide. . . . When certain Indians got tired of living in a place— when they used up the soil, or the garbage pile got too high—they moved on to the next place." (128–29)

Bobbie Ann Mason's Kentucky is paradigmatic of the contemporary South, and to an extent of modern America. Overwhelmed by rapid and frightening changes in their lives, her characters and her readers must confront contradictory impulses, the temptation to withdraw into the security of home and the past, and the alternative prospect of taking to the road in search of something better. There are no easy answers, Mason tells us, a fact that makes her stories all the more satisfying. They are small stopping places, brief, refreshing respites from a complex world.

NOTES

[1] *Shiloh and Other Stories* won the PEN/Hemingway Award for First Fiction; and was a finalist for the PEN/Faulkner Award, the American Book Award, and the National Book Critics Circle Award.

[2] Bobbie Ann Mason, "Gooseberry Winter," *Redbook*, November 1982, 28–147.

[3] Bobbie Ann Mason, "Private Lies," *Atlantic Monthly*, March 1983, 62–67.

Why There Are No Southern Writers

DAPHNE ATHAS

To enter the South at the end of the thirties from New England was to experience that dead air space between the legend of the Fall from Glory and the New Era about to begin. The South I saw was the raw, ignoble South of small patch farms and spinning mills. North Carolina rivers were brown or muddy red. The Gastonia strikes had happened the decade before. There was no trace of Tara or magnolias.

To come from the outside as I did was to notice, but such was the degree of my unfamiliarity that it was, in fact, to define. The only given was the name: *The South.*

The first thing I heard was the music. I was thirteen years old. The civics teacher said: "Turn to page one hundred and fifty-fo." There was a blonde boy from Alabama named Richard Lewis, and when he opened his mouth in high school I could see his lips move and hear a voice, but I could not understand a word he said. After I got used to the pronunciation of words, it was the repetitions that struck me.

"Maybe he's gone on up there and entered college."
"Maybe he has. Education."
"Yeh, education. . . ."
"Where is the great I Am, the Almighty God? Listen now while us gi' you the call. Eigh, Lord come with the 'sponse—"

> I call my people—hanh,
> I said my people—hanh
> I mean my people—hanh
> Eigh, Lord!

"That's right. Sing him ou'n the bushes," said the first guard.
"Sing him back from college," said the second.
"Sing."

> I call my friends—hanh,

I said my friends—hanh,
I mean my friends—hanh,
Eigh, Lord!

These lines come from the story, *I Call My Jesus,* by Paul Green. Here is the first sentence:

In the bright glare of a fierce August day six striped convicts were digging on a blazing road, swinging their picks aloft and bringing them down.

Compare this to the last section of Carson McCullers's *The Ballad of the Sad Cafe.*

The Forks Falls highway is three miles from the town, and it is here the chain gang has been working. . . . The gang is made up of twelve men, all wearing black and white striped prison suits, and chained at the ankles. There is a guard, with a gun, his eyes drawn to red slits by the glare. The gang works all day long, arriving huddled in the prison cart soon after daybreak, and being driven off again in the gray August twilight. All day there is the sound of the picks striking into the clay earth, hard sunlight, the smell of sweat. And every day there is music. One dark voice will start a phrase, half sung, and like a question. And after a moment another voice will join in, soon the whole gang will be singing. . . . The music will swell until at last it seems that the sound does not come from the twelve men on the gang, but from the earth itself, or the wide sky.

And what kind of gang is this that can make such music? Just twelve mortal men, seven of them black and five of them white boys from this county. Just twelve mortal men who are together.

If there is any truth to Robert A. Lively's observation that stories of Northern life are focused on the abilities and characters of single heroes or heroines, individuals whose society is the hostile setting for their lonely struggles and ambitions, while Southern stories operate on a social, rather than personal scene, families and communities in a time and geography heavy with past and future, then this particular South was the socially conscious, New Deal, WPA, TVA-dominated, post-Depression, pre-World War II Rooseveltian wave of the future.

The place was Chapel Hill, seat of the University of North Carolina, a school of three thousand students in a piedmont area where rednecks left farms to become lintheads in mills, where the blending of liberal academia, cosmopolitanism, historical tradition—the charter and buildings of the University dated back to the beginning of the eighteen hundreds, with legends of Yankees and horses—combined to make a ferment which belonged to the New Deal. Sociologists made studies of *pellagra.*

Playwrights specialized in words like *mule, mountain,* and *Moon Pie.*
People drank R.C. Cola in response to tattered signs on tobacco barns. No
one used the word *prison.* They said "penitentiary," leaving out the "i" as
if they were raising a *tent* on top of a *pen,* so that the word climbed up in a
long, increasingly lonely scale, with the "ary" trailing away like smoke
upon the universe. "O Lost and by the Wind Grieved, Ghost come back
again." Snopes was not yet in the vocabulary. Thomas Wolfe was.

The sociologists and the playwrights were in the ascendancy. Howard W. Odum translated the sociology of the South to Washington, D.C.,
which did something about it, and abolished pellagra; and Frederick H.
Koch inspired down-at-heel mountain students to repeat the music of
"what they knew." This South was self-conscious. North Carolina, the
poor white state sandwiched in between aristocratic Virginia and plantation South Carolina had little to lose and was therefore progressive. This
South trembled with ideals, Jeffersonian ones, presided over by President of the University Frank Graham, later governor of North Carolina
and official of the United Nations.

My goal, as I saw it in high school, was to fit the music with what I saw.
Since I had known I would be a writer from age seven, it was amazing to
find myself in a place where there were writers that wrote, a place which
made no separation beween music and event, or music and being. The act
and the expression of the act took on reality then as part of the same thing.

But it is important to recognize that this was the Southern version of a
national movement. Such a novelist as Betty Smith of *A Tree Grows in
Brooklyn* repeatedly made the statement that if Thomas Wolfe had gone
to Brooklyn to write about North Carolina, she had come to North
Carolina to write about Brooklyn. Wolfe's protagonists identified with
"America" like latter-day Whitmans. The cadences of Richard Wright and
Paul Green came together when they collaborated on the play version of
Native Son, distinguishably Southern, but a form of the self-consciously
proletarian rhythms of the Group Theater. A plebian rhythm. Heavy
metaphor. Barbara Stanwyck slaps Robert Ryan's face in the movie version of Clifford Odets's *Clash by Night.* He snarls back with a smile:
"Peace on earth." Every word, every line means more than its literal
meaning. In Southern writing that ramification reached out beyond the
region to America, and the substratum of the prose predicated the hardship, nobility, and oppression of the Common Man and the Black Man as

he dreamed the promise of America and suffered. The Southern scions of the time were Richard Wright, Tennessee Williams, and Carson McCullers, and they found themselves together in a boarding house in Brooklyn forging the new social South. Faulkner still occupied an unrecognized position there like a backdrop which future generations of critics could discover, probably wrongly, to have been the dominating influence on all the younger Southern writers. Of the half generation even younger, Truman Capote, Calder Willingham, Speed Lamkin, and the half generation beyond, William Styron and Gore Vidal: some drop away as names, and most fade into the national landscape of writers as Southern particularities gave way and writing became issue rather than region oriented.

This forties generation of Southern writers, born of the Depression, one might say, enspirited the beginning of recognized Black writing, although, inasmuch as such generalities are false, this one, too, is false. It did not, however, enspirit the idea of women as writers. I had brought to Chapel Hill with me a firm tradition of woman as writer, stemming from the Brontës and George Eliot in England, and Louisa May Alcott, Margaret Fuller, and that first Southern woman writer, Harriet Beecher Stowe from New England. I had no notion of Southern women writers per se at the time, and it took twenty five years, until the sixties, for me to hear the claim that Ellen Glasgow and Willa Cather, Southern writers, were without peer the serious American women writers. It took an even longer time, as it did with Gertrude Stein, for me to read and appreciate them.

But it was easy in Chapel Hill in the forties, when *Native Son,* a fait accompli, was being translated into a play, when *The Glass Menagerie* was so classic as to seem cliché, and *Streetcar* was starting out the Southern-Jewish competition with *Death of a Salesman,* and when *The Member of the Wedding* was seen to be a partial and popularized replay of the more complete and multidimensional *The Heart Is a Lonely Hunter*—it was easy to know that the boundaries of race and sex had been broken down and that we were in a modern age. Among artists these boundaries are always open, and so analysis of what history does to literature or literature does to history is ambiguous. Those forces which made Faulkner are presumed to have made Tennessee Williams, Carson McCullers, Eudora Welty, and Reynolds Price. And didn't Richard Wright spawn his assassin, James Baldwin, who in turn spawned his own, as the written vision of injustices turned to civil rights and then to civil laws? America has always been a country which has written down what it ought to be and then tried to be it. And that includes TV commercials as well as the Constitution and the Bill of Rights as is apparent in the blasphemous similarity between the two.

At the time, however, of the two directions in Southern writing, social consciousness and gothic vision, social consciousness dominated the writing coming out of Chapel Hill, and the gothic was linked with the aristocratic part of the South and also with the feminine, probably because of its inception in *Jane Eyre* with the governess, the madwoman in the attic, and the female writer. Both strands existed in Faulkner and in McCullers. One thinks of Tennessee Williams as gothic but the two viewpoints are submerged in the moral framework, the lost-magic-gone-decadent always at battle with the amoral, brutal plebian force. In these writers and consummated in their last, sterile offspring, *To Kill a Mockingbird*, the ideals are held by the aristocratic mind, and the plebians are the renegades, except for dignified Negroes.

It was Truman Capote in the forties who finished off the seriousness of the gothic and left the field free for women writers with new heroines and for the absurdists of junk. He turned those environmental talismans, with which any writer of today under fifty grew up in small towns, into humor—creepy if not amoral. The embroidered, the painful and the lunatic, the decrepit and scary house of spinsters and transvestites he made acceptable by crossing the border and having gone over, stopped. In the decade of the fifties land-poor families literally abandoned those houses for trailers, and with that move the gothic was literarily swallowed up in juxtaposition and absurdity. The new junk landscape was left to be explored by Southern men and women alike: Harry Crews, James Dickey, Doris Betts, and Fred Chappell among many.

The idea of beauty was a historical antecedent of Southern gothic, "the beauty," the "Southern belle," the victim of the sheltered life. She was basic to the work of Ellen Glasgow, and Willa Cather also wrote of her. She was a tenet and symbol of the set, genteel society until World War I. By World War II the conception was passé, and by the sixties the word "beauty" had been flattened out to banality by Kurt Vonnegut and overuse, its adjectival qualities rendered cliché in such expressions as "beautiful experience" and "beautiful human being." It is interesting to notice

that in the forties women writers did not deal with the Beauty. It was left
to the men writers and in a point in time as far from Eva Birdsong as Miss
Havisham. Decayed, brittle, caricatured, pathetic rather than tragic,
neurasthenic, irritating, the historical nuisance with echoes of nostalgia,
the Beauty became the bailiwick of Tennessee Williams. She was aging if
not old, and neutered but sexually active, endowed with furies and male
force, a vision of incipient camp.

Women writers had gone on even then to something different. One
might paradoxically look at *Gone With the Wind,* that historical romance
of the heyday of the "belle" to find the modern prototype. Scarlett, the
Beauty, was irresistible because of her ability to eat radishes and hire
convict labor. The only reason people can go on wallowing in nostalgia is
that there is an indomitable if uncertain present. There has never been
enough serious attention given to the ethics of Scarlet's undervaluing her
own penchant for action or better still, survival. Scarlett is so unaware,
that after the whole book goes by and she tells Ashley at Melanie's death
regarding her lifelong love: "Suddenly it doesn't matter any more,"
dumping him out like a baby with the bathwater—more like a rubber
duck—the moment is not to be believed. Why hasn't someone pointed
out how unintentionally funny it is? Well, Scarlett may be disappointed
with herself, but the contemporary Southern woman writer isn't. The
point is that the Beauty lives, but her vitality is in the scrapping, spunk,
schemes, determination, marrying, working, and even in the slapping of
other women who fail to have her guts. Certainly a plebian model. One
that forms the basis of these contemporary characters of Sylvia Wilkinson,
Doris Betts, Lisa Alther, Rita Mae Brown, Bertha Harris, Shirley Ann
Grau, Lee Smith, and Gail Godwin. No boasting of aristocratic heritage.
Many are strictly from the farm, the mill, the new city, some from the
university. Their names are as often Vicki or Elizabeth as Ora Mae or
Norma Rae. This character is sexy rather than a beauty, gets on with the
job, sees through things but also sees things through.

There is another corollary to this. If it is the backside of the Southern
Lady, it may also be a transformation or development from that sensitive
girl-adolescent of winsome pain, part, perhaps, of a backlash against
McCullers. This Southern young woman character often has an involuted,
magpie brilliance, cousin to Jenny the crookback dollmaker of Dickens or
to McCullers's Miss Amelia, but the defect is now banished. By some

transmutation of the ethical system the magpie brilliance has plus value. Innate courage is given the freedom of ambition. The character may be divorced thrice, a librarian, a lesbian, a movie star, an adventuress, an investigative reporter, an executive, or an eyewitness, but she is not a lost child nor is she a lost low-class Southern waitress. That particular pain syndrome played itself out with William Inge and is now a revival classic in movies, played by the real-life, ever-living suicide, Marilyn Monroe. Self-conscious pain has moved its center from adolescence to characters aged about thirty. It is part of the Southern contribution to women's writing by writers like Gail Godwin, Kate Millett, and Alice Adams. The brilliance analyzes the pain, and the characters do not have physical defects and do not consider themselves ugly, deformed, or crazy. In line with the national movement they see that as having been put upon them by men.

I use these modern prototypes because it seems easier to talk about Southern women characters than Southern women writers. But perhaps it's an off-the-top-of-the-head clue to what may be the human precondition for the modern Southern woman writer. In high school when I heard the music, I was casting around for what it fit *for me*. I was all different from it, yet it was my environment from that time on. It made me aware first of the English language, and then of the Bible which had not been a vivid feature of my high-minded bringing up, and then of every writer I had ever loved or was to love in the future. I at once catalogued everything that struck me as Southern, the paraphernalia of the environment unfamiliar to me. I have those lists now, and I used them in my novel *Entering Ephesus*. Broom grass. Tin roofs. Railroad tracks. Red dirt. Sweeping dirt yards with brooms. Lumber mills and sawdust piles. "Thank you, you must wear it sometime." Plug tobacco. My daddy. Your daddy. Snuff. Ah thank for I think. Railroad ties. White fountains versus colored fountains. Chinaberry trees. Co Cola leaving out the ca. This is not very profound, but it is what *was*. Objects. Artifacts. Strangely enough, it is probably not as passé as it sounds, but literarily it is historical. And setting it down makes it a matter of style.

When I was in high school the second thing I brought down from the North, after my notion of women writers, was undisguised or frank ambition. People even wrote it in my high school annual: "She has ambition." Although I prided myself on it, it was one of the attitudes which prevented me from being allowed to be a Southerner. Not the ambition, merely the undisguised nature of it. Yet it is the quality of ambition connected with the actuality of freedom which made the forties the turning point for women and, I suppose, created this new female character from *Becky Sharpe*, way before the women's movement. And yet, even now, in a disguise less from literal convention than from an old habit to do with the South rather than with sex—the Southern belle and the Southern gentlemen both had it—it is good form to speak of ambition at most in a subordinate clause preferably in a phrase. It is that quality that caused Northern liberals watching Sam Erwin operating on the Watergate Committee to discover: "He's not dumb, he's shrewd!" and which gave them an exaltation and liberation watching the TV coverage of Martin Luther King's funeral.

My ambition was not to write things as they are, but to write them as I saw them, and if I noticed to define, it was by the music that I learned. But the music expressed the difference. Little did I suspect, and little did the possessors in elementary and high schools all over the South suspect, that this same ambition was imbedded in them too, these girls who would later be the Southern women writers. It occurs to me now that the music of the important in subsidiary clauses is the music of the aristocrat with an overweening sense of noblesse oblige. At the same time it is the music of the underling who has to hide the real thing. Where did the Southern accent come from? I used to let that question squirrel around in my brain and always arrived at the cliché that it was from African rhythms taught by the broken-Englished Negro nannies. Be that as it may, it feels to me now as if that subtle way of talking and writing expresses more truth than straight telling. Straight telling is a vision of one in an omniscient voice, and as such, from the Southern point of view, arrogant. And so, after the fact, if the ambition, which spawned these heroines created by Southern women writers rather than lady writers, were there all along, it is a joke that time has played, to mix up our notion of the aristocrat and the plebian as well as of men and women.

The reason I am stressing style is that it is the one constant from which to mine new interpretation. If Southern literature still exists as something distinguishable in contemporary writing, it is in the implications of the prose rather than the content. It is *under* the prose though, rather than *in* it, because the corporate and the standard have changed the environment

Christian on every count, and the writers doing it are both men and women, among them Doris Betts, Reynolds Price, and Walker Percy. Many of them are doing it in perhaps the only way it can be done in the present day, affirming by elimination of the negatives. It is as if the century's destiny has caught up with Flannery O'Connor's physical imperative which made her say what she had to say with no trucking around, because she had to say it faster. Her intolerance for lip-service and her seriousness about Roman Catholicism had Protestant fervor, and her gothic details were transmuted with rowdy, grotesque humor to serve with frightening economy the harsh, religious view. Reynolds Price has been edging in this direction with essays and translations of the New Testament as if stepping into a New World demands a change of form. In his last novel, he presented a picture of Southern women that I have seen nowhere else, an essentially humorless one which is historical, of women in nightgowns who spend a lot of time in bed, analyzing husbands and sons with ferocious neutrality while demanding, if not obeisance, homage to their woman's pain, namely the horror of childbirth. As unpopular as it was with the women's movement, it ought to be heeded, for I think it has something universal to say about the psychological imperatives of the later religious direction. The words "earn" and "pay" travel through *The Surface of Earth,* and so do the words "peace" and "kindness," gestures to the difference between the Old and New Testaments. But I see them as naked emblems underlying this whole direction. They are understood and named in Doris Betts's later work too, where Old Testament fatality merges with stoic, logical rationalism in an uncompromising indictment of the easy gratification of the fat and the mindless, who both cause and suffer the seemingly coincidental violence of contemporary life. So far these two streams of thought seem to hint at the only source of rebirth, but they are at odds in a netherworld which the rational world refuses to let be born. In *Lancelot,* Walker Percy cleverly demolishes the garbage veneer of the present day with intellectual rather than Biblical prose. It is a dialogue in monologue form. The addressee is the unbelieving, priest-like liberal whose answers and attitudes the reader provides quite easily. The speaker is the sane man who has violated what amounts to the insane world. The unspeakable crime is tolerance for the dead emblems of modern insanity, and there is no panacea in the last generation's forms of nobility, which now look like sheer romance. Such is the cleverness of the form of the novel that it leads to a Yea-saying answer without speaking either of God or the protestant ideas of paying or earning.

None of this amounts to a movement. It is the work of a scattering of Southern writers who find themselves up front in responding to a nation-wide automatism and standardization which seems more flagrant in the South because landscape which had rotted since Reconstruction became radicalized in the fifties. I find myself wondering about the plebian and aristocratic strands in these writers. I find moral compulsion plebian. Despite the Catholicism of two of them, only Walker Percy has the feel of the aristocrat. He dares to hate out loud. But he so thoroughly rejects any hope that the enlightened aristocratic generation of rational judges and lawyers in the Faulknerian canon who prevailed through dignity can do anything now against the triumphant, tamed evil wrought by the unde-moned post-Snopeses, so rejects even that pattern of social structure, except as Hollywoodized, that the effect is of an entirely new game. Throughout *Lancelot* he has segments of self-conscious Southern dia-logue, mock music, as if even Southernism is dead while the forms remain and are spoken without knowing. Flannery O'Connor is too demonic to be anything ultimately but plebian, despite her unerring sense of every social attitude. Reynolds Price seems to me to be plebian in attitude, while his prose gives off an aristocratic stance, and Doris Betts, despite the complexities of her subordinate clauses, seems to me to be unre-servedly plebian.

Ultimately it strikes me that the women writers of Southern origin or experience are responding to plebian urges. One cannot be a woman writer now without being part of, or in some way acknowledging or responding to, what has happened since the sixties to the consciousness of women. Gail Godwin, Alice Adams, Kate Millett, and Anne Tyler have dealt with it directly. Interesting to note, though, the peculiarly aristo-cratic impulse in the prose of Alice Adams, who uses the South as a gone-by state of being, overlaid by cosmopolitanism. She uses that style of omission and of taking away from the main clause by the subordinate to separate the aristocrats of *taste* from the dogs of vulgarity. There is noth-ing more elite, lethal, sophisticated and Southern.

A far cry from that hot, social sing-song of the people, prayer and response, that I first noted in Chapel Hill in high school. Hardly any white man is writing of the penitentiary, and if he does, it is called "prison" and is a metaphor. Women are analytical now and in content devoid of disguise. If you are to find the South in them, you must look for it in style. It is there. It is simply the reverse of what I heard in Chapel Hill as Southern music. Now it is style gone subtly aristocratic to serve the defiantly plebian.

It makes sense, this paradox, in the case of women writers since it is the natural course to take. But all serious writing has a selfconsciousness that it didn't use to have, and if Southerness was once an obvious characteristic of writers, it is now mere evidence, detectable in style, waiting perhaps to be recognized.

Checklist of Sources

CHERYL MCALLISTER SAUNDERS

The following is a selected checklist of material by and about the contemporary writers discussed in the preceding essays.

Works by each author appear first and are listed by category—novels, collected short stories, collected poems, nonfiction, edited works, articles, and essays.

Works about each author include secondary material cited by the essayists as well as material for further reference. This section is intended to supplement biographical and bibliographical information found in the following reference works: *Contemporary Authors; American Women Writers: A Critical Reference Guide from Colonial Times to the Present,* Ed. Lina Mainiero (Unger, 1979–82); *Dictionary of Literary Biography: American Novelists Since World War II* (Gale Research, 1978–80); *Southern Writers; A Biographical Dictionary,* Eds. Robert Bain, Joseph M. Flora, and Louis D. Rubin, Jr. (Louisiana State University Press, 1979). Abbreviations for the last three works appear in the checklist as *AWW, DLB,* and *SWBD* and are listed first.

LISA ALTHER

By Lisa Alther

NOVELS (Published by Knopf, New York):
Kinflicks. 1976; rpt. New York: New American Library, 1977.
Original Sins. 1981.

NONFICTION:
"Introduction," *A Good Man Is Hard to Find.* By Flannery O'Connor. London: The Women's Press, 1980.

About Lisa Alther

Smith, Marilynn J. "Condemned to Survival: The Comic Unsuccessful Suicide."
Comparative Literature Studies, 17 (March 1980), 26–32 (includes discussion of

Kinflicks); Waage, Frederick G. "Alther and Dillard: The Appalachian Universe." In *Appalachia/America: Proceedings of the 1980 Appalachian Studies Conference*. Ed. Wilson Somerville. [Johnson City, TN]: Appalachian Consortium, 1981, 200–08. REVIEWS: Rumens, Carol. "Staying Cool." Rev. of *Original Sins. Times Literary Supplement*, 26 Jan. 1981, 730.

DAPHNE ATHAS

By Daphne Athas

NOVELS:
The Weather of the Heart. New York: Appleton Century, 1947.
The Fourth World. New York: Putnam's, 1956.
Entering Ephesus. New York: Viking, 1971.
Cora. New York: Viking, 1978.

PLAYS:
Sit on the Earth (co-author). In *The Observer Plays*. London: Faber, 1957, 77–156.

NONFICTION:
Greece by Prejudice (memoir). New York: Lippincott, 1963.

ARTICLES/ESSAYS:
"Greece by Prejudice." *Botteghe Oscure* [Rome] (Spring 1958), 282–308.
"How Much Power?" *Grid* [London] (Autumn 1958), 23–35.
"The Art of Storytelling." *South Atlantic Quarterly*, 73 (Spring 1974), 256–60.
"It's a War—And Young Men Went Laughing." *Charlotte Observer*, 21 Sept. 1974, 11-A.
"Goddesses, Heroines, and Women Writers." *St. Andrews Review* (Fall–Winter 1975), 5–13.
"Tolstoy's and Dostoevsky's Houses." *St. Andrews Review* (Fall–Winter 1978), 29–34.
"Cyclops in Steam, A View of Russia." *Shenandoah*, 31:1 (1979), 3–34.
"'The Beauty' in *The Sheltered Life*—A Moral Concept." *South Atlantic Quarterly*, 80 (Spring 1981), 206–21.
"Why There Are No Southern Writers." *Southern Review*, 18 (Oct. 1982), 755–66.

About Daphne Athas
REVIEWS: Haynes, Muriel. Rev. of *Entering Ephesus. Saturday Review*, 9 Oct. 1971, 38–39; Raper, Jack. Rev. of *Cora. Carolina Quarterly*, 31 (Winter 1979), 92–93; Rev. of *Entering Ephesus. New York Times Book Review*, 3 Oct. 1971, 35.

TONI CADE BAMBARA

By Toni Cade Bambara

NOVELS:
The Salt Eaters. New York: Random, 1980. Rpt. New York: Vintage, 1981.

COLLECTED SHORT STORIES:
Gorilla, My Love. New York: Random, 1972. Rpt. New York: Vintage, 1981.
The Sea Birds Are Still Alive: Collected Stories. New York: Random, 1977.

WORKS EDITED (as Toni Cade):
The Black Woman (also contributor). New York: New American Library, 1970.
Tales and Stories for Black Folks (also contributor). Garden City, NY: Doubleday, 1971.

About Toni Cade Bambara

Shockley, Ann Allen and Sue P. Chandler. *Living Black American Authors: A Biographical Directory.* New York: Bowker, 1973, 9; Dybek, Caren. "Black Literature for Adolescents," *English Journal,* 63 (Jan. 1974), 64–67; Salaam, Kalamu ya, "Searching for the Mother's Tongue" (Interview), *First World,* 2:4 (1980), 48–53; REVIEWS: Bryan, C.D.B. Rev. of *Gorilla, My Love. New York Times Book Review,* 15 Oct. 1972, 31; Rev. of *Gorilla, My Love, Saturday Review,* 18 Nov. 1972, 97; Traylor, Eleanor. "*The Salt Eaters:* My Soul Looks Back in Wonder," *First World,* 2:4 (1980), 44–47, 64; Wideman, John. "The Healing of Velma Henry." Rev. of *The Salt Eaters. New York Times Book Review,* 1 June 1980, 14, 28.

DORIS BETTS

By Doris Betts

NOVELS:
Tall Houses in Winter. New York: Putnam's, 1957. Rpt. London: Cassell, 1958.
The Scarlet Thread. New York: Harper & Row, 1964.
The River to Pickle Beach. New York: Harper & Row, 1972.
Heading West. New York: Knopf, 1981.

COLLECTED SHORT STORIES:
The Gentle Insurrection. New York: Putnam's, 1954
The Astronomer and Other Stories. New York: Harper & Row, 1965.
Beasts of the Southern Wild and Other Stories. New York: Harper & Row, 1973.

About Doris Betts

AWW, Vol. 1, 151–52; DLB *Yearbook: 1982.* Ed. Richard Ziegfeld. Detroit: Gale Research, 1983, 219–27; SWBD; *Contemporary Literary Criticism.* Ed. Carolyn Riley. Vol. 3. Detroit: Gale Research, 1975, 73; Evans, Elizabeth. "Another Mule in the Yard: Doris Betts' Durable Humor." *Notes on Contemporary Literature,* 11 (Mar. 1981), 5–6; Evans, Elizabeth. "Negro Characters in the Fiction of Doris Betts." *Critique,* 17:2 (1975), 59–76; Holman, David Marion. "Faith and the Unanswerable Questions: The Fiction of Doris Betts." *Southern Literary Journal,* 15 (Fall 1982), 15–22; Wolfe, George. "The Unique Voice." In *Kite-Flying and Other Irrational Acts: Conversations with Twelve Southern Writers.* Ed. John Carr. Baton Rouge: Louisiana State University Press, 1972. REVIEWS: Gutcheon, Beth. "Willing Victim." Rev. of *Heading West. New York Times Book Review,* 17 Jan. 1982, 12, 28; Leonard, John. "Books of the Times." Rev. of *Heading West. New York Times,* 17 Dec. 1981, Sec. 3, 23.

RITA MAE BROWN

By Rita Mae Brown

NOVELS:

Rubyfruit Jungle. Plainfield, VT: Daughters, Inc., 1973. Rpt. New York: Bantam, 1977.

In Her Day. Plainfield, VT: Daughters, Inc., 1976.

Six of One. New York: Harper & Row, 1978. Rpt. New York: Bantam, 1979.

Southern Discomfort. New York: Harper & Row, 1982.

Sudden Death. New York: Bantam, 1983.

COLLECTED POEMS:

The Hand that Cradles the Rock. New York: New York University Press, 1971. Rpt. Oakland, CA: Diana Press, 1974.

Songs to a Handsome Woman. Baltimore: Diana Press, 1973.

ARTICLES/ESSAYS:

A Plain Brown Rapper (collected essays). Oakland, CA: Diana Press, 1976.

"Rita Mae Brown." In *Ariadne's Thread: A Collection of Contemporary Women's Journals.* Ed. Lyn Lifshin. New York: Harper & Row, 1982, 307–09.

New York Radicalesbians (collective essays). "The Woman-Identified Woman." In *Lesbians Speak Out.* Oakland, CA: Women's Press Collective, 1974.

About Rita Mae Brown

AWW, Vol. 1, 257–59; Alexander, Delores. "People: Rita Mae Brown—'The Issue for the Future is Power.'" *Ms.,* 3 (Sept. 1974), 110–13; Clausen, Jan. *A Movement of Poets: Thoughts on Poetry and Feminism.* New York: Long Haul Press, 1982; Clausen, Jan. "The Politics of Publishing and the Lesbian Community." *Sinister Wisdom,* 1 (Fall 1976), 94–115. Fritz, Leah. *Dreamers and Dealers: An Intimate Appraisal of the Women's Movement.* Boston: Beacon Press, 1979; Holt, Patricia. "PW Interviews: Rita Mae Brown," *Publishers Weekly,* 2 Oct. 1978, 16–17; Segrest, M. "'Lines I Dare to Write': Lesbian Writing in the South." *Southern Exposure,* 9 (Summer 1981), 53–62; Shister, Gail. "Rita Mae Brown: A Nice Southern Girl Makes Good as a Chronicler of Unconventional Love." *Philadelphia Inquirer,* 12 May 1983, 12, D; Turner, Alice K. "Rita Mae

Brown." *New York*, 18 Sept. 1978, 60; White, Diane. "At Large: Brown Denies Categorization." *Boston Globe*, 21 Nov. 1978. REVIEWS: Gottlieb, Annie. "Passion and Punishment." Rev. of *Southern Discomfort. New York Times Book Review*, 21 Mar. 1982, 10, 29; Kleindeinst, Kris. "Art Imitates Life? *Sudden Death.*" *Book Review: Gay Community News*, June 1983, 3; Mennis, Bernice, "*In Her Day* by Rita Mae Brown." *Conditions: One* (April 1977), 119–22; Rev. of *Rubyfruit Jungle. The Village Voice*, 12 Sept. 1977, 4.

ELLEN DOUGLAS

By Ellen Douglas

NOVELS:
A Family's Affairs. Boston: Houghton Mifflin, 1962.
Where the Dreams Cross. Boston: Houghton Mifflin, 1968.
Apostles of Light. Boston: Houghton Mifflin, 1973.
The Rock Cried Out. New York: Harcourt Brace Jovanovich, 1979.
A Lifetime Burning. New York: Random House, 1982.

COLLECTED SHORT STORIES:
Black Cloud, White Cloud (two novellas, two short stores). Boston: Houghton Mifflin, 1963.

NONFICTION:
Commentary on Walker Percy's The Last Gentleman. Religious Dimensions in Literature Series, 11. New York: Seabury Press, 1969.

About Ellen Douglas

SWBD; Dean, Michael P. "Ellen Douglas's Small Towns: Fictional Anchors." *Southern Quarterly*, 19 (Fall 1980), 161–71; Jones, John Griffin. "Ellen Douglas." In *Mississippi Writers Talking II*. Jackson: University Press of Mississippi, 1983 (interview). REVIEWS: Isaacs, Susan. "Not Going Gentle at All." Rev. of *A Lifetime Burning. New York Times Book Review*, 31 Oct. 1982, 11; Lyell, Frank H. Rev. of *Family's Affairs. New York Times Book Review*, 8 July 1962, 18; Maloff, Saul. Rev. of *Black Cloud, White Cloud. New York Times Book Review*, 6 Oct. 1963, 5.

ELLEN GILCHRIST

By Ellen Gilchrist

NOVELS:
The Annunciation. Boston and Toronto: Little, Brown, 1983.

COLLECTED SHORT STORIES:
In the Land of Dreamy Dreams. Fayetteville: University of Arkansas Press, 1981.

COLLECTED POEMS:
The Land Surveyor's Daughter. San Francisco: Lost Roads, 1979.

GAIL GODWIN

By Gail Godwin

NOVELS:
The Perfectionists. New York: Harper & Row, 1970. Rpt. New York: Warner Books, 1979.
The Glass People. New York: Knopf, 1972. Rpt. New York: Warner Books, 1979.
The Odd Woman. New York: Knopf, 1974. Rpt. New York: Warner Books, 1979.
Violet Clay. New York: Knopf, 1978. Rpt. New York: Warner Books, 1979.
A Mother and Two Daughters. New York: Viking, 1982.

COLLECTED SHORT STORIES:
Dream Children. New York: Knopf, 1976.

ARTICLES/ESSAYS:
"Becoming a Writer." In *The Writer on Her Work: Contemporary Women Writers Reflect on Their Art and Situation.* Ed. Janet Sternburg. New York: Norton, 1980.
"Keeping Track." In *Ariadne's Thread: A Collection of Contemporary Women's Journals.* Ed. Lyn Lifshin. New York: Harper & Row, 1982, 75–85.
"The Southern Belle," *Ms.,* July 1975, 45–52, 84–85.
"Towards a Fully Human Heroine: Some Worknotes." *Harvard Advocate,* 106 (Winter 1973), 26–28.

About Gail Godwin

AWW, Vol. 2, 148–50; *DLB,* Vol. 6, 105–09; Gardiner, Judith K. "'A Sorrowful Woman': Gail Godwin's Feminist Parable." *Studies in Short Fiction,* 12 (Summer 1975), 286–90; Gaston, Karen C. "'Beauty and the Beast' in Gail Godwin's *Glass People.*" *Critique,* 21:2 (1980), 94–102; Smith, Marilynn J. "The Role of the South in the Novels of Gail Godwin." *Critique,* 21:3 (1980), 103–10. REVIEWS: Hendin, Josephine. "Renovated Lives." Rev. of *A Mother and Two Daughters. New York Times Book Review,* 10 Jan. 1982, 3, 14.

SHIRLEY ANN GRAU

By Shirley Ann Grau

NOVELS (Published by Knopf, New York):
The Hard Blue Sky. 1958.
The House on Coliseum Street. 1961.
The Keepers of the House. 1964; rpt. New York: Fawcett, 1965.

The Condor Passes. 1971.
Evidence of Love. 1977.

COLLECTED SHORT STORIES:
The Black Prince and Other Stories. New York: Knopf, 1955.
The Wind Shifting West. New York: Knopf, 1973.

About Shirley Ann Grau

AWW, Vol. 2, 171–74; *DLB*, Vol. 2, 208–14; Lepper, Gary M. *A Bibliographical Introduction to Seventy-Five Modern American Authors.* Berkeley, CA: Serendipity Books, 1977 (includes Grau); Montgomery, Marion. "Southern Letters in the Twentieth Century: The Articulation of a Tradition." *Modern Age*, 24 (Spring 1980), 121–33; Rohrberger, Mary. "Conversations with Shirley Ann Grau and James Feibleman." *Cimarron Review*, 43 (April 1978), 35–45; Schleuter, Paul. *Shirley Ann Grau.* Boston: Twayne, 1981.

BEVERLY LOWRY

By Beverly Lowry

NOVELS:
Come Back, Lolly Ray. New York: Doubleday, 1977.
Emma Blue. Garden City, NY: Doubleday, 1978.
Daddy's Girl. New York: Viking, 1981.

About Beverly Lowry

REVIEWS: DeMott, Benjamin. "The Three Faces of Sue." Rev. of *Daddy's Girl. New York Times Book Review*, 25 Oct. 1981, 15, 45; Jonathan Yardley. Rev. of *Emma Blue. New York Times Book Review*, 12 Nov. 1978, 34.

BOBBIE ANN MASON

By Bobbie Ann Mason

COLLECTED SHORT STORIES:
Shiloh and Other Stories. New York: Harper & Row, 1982.

NONFICTION:
Nabokov's Garden: A Nature Guide to Ada. Ann Arbor: Ardis, 1974.
The Girl Sleuth: A Feminist Guide to the Bobbsey Twins, Nancy Drew, and Their Sisters. Old Westbury, NY: Feminist Press, 1975.

About Bobbie Ann Mason

Polack, Marilyn Lewis. "Kentucky on Her Mind." *Philadelphia Inquirer Magazine*, 25 Dec. 1983, 5–6 (interview). REVIEWS: Broyard, Anatole. "Books of the

Times." Rev. of *Shiloh and Other Stories. New York Times*, 23 Nov. 1982, C-14;
Grumbach, Doris. "No Longer Is the Story All." Rev. of *Shiloh and Other
Stories* (included with two other reviews). Quammen, David. "Plain Folk and
Puzzling Changes." Rev. of *Shiloh and Other Stories. New York Times Book
Review*, 21 Nov. 1982, 7, 33; Tyler, Anne. "Kentucky Cameos." Rev. of *Shiloh
and Other Stories. New Republic*, 1 Nov. 1982, 36, 38.

BERRY MORGAN

By Berry Morgan

NOVELS:
Pursuit. Boston: Houghton Mifflin, 1966. London: Heinemann, 1967.

COLLECTED SHORT STORIES:
The Mystic Adventures of Roxie Stoner (connected stories). Boston: Houghton
Mifflin, 1974.

About Berry Morgan

DLB, Vol. 6, 241–43; *SWBD; Contemporary Literary Criticism* (lists reviews),
Vol. 6, 339–41.

MARY LEE SETTLE

By Mary Lee Settle

NOVELS:
The Love Eaters. New York: Harper, 1954; London: Heinemann, 1954.
The Kiss of Kin. New York: Harper, 1955; London: Heinemann, 1955.
O Beulah Land. New York: Viking, 1956; London: Heinemann, 1956. Rpt. New
York: Ballantine, 1981.
Know Nothing. New York: Viking, 1960; London: Heinemann, 1961. [Republished
as *Pride's Promise.* New York: Pinnacle, 1976.] Rpt. New York: Ballantine,
1981.
Fight Night on a Sweet Saturday. New York: Viking, 1964; London: Heinemann,
1965.
The Clam Shell. New York: Delacorte, 1971; London: Bodley Head, 1972.
Prisons. New York: Putnam's, 1973. [Republished as *The Long Road to Paradise.*
London: Constable, 1974.] Rpt. New York: Ballantine, 1981.
Blood Tie. Boston: Houghton Mifflin, 1977.
The Scapegoat. New York: Random, 1980. Rpt. (large print) Thorndike Press,
1980.
The Killing Ground. New York: Farrar, Straus & Giroux, 1982.

NONFICTION:

All the Brave Promises. New York: Delacorte, 1966. Rpt. New York: Ballantine, 1980.

The Story of Flight [Juvenilia]. New York: Random, 1967.

The Scopes Trial: The State of Tennessee v. John Thomas Scopes. New York: Franklin Watts, 1972.

About Mary Lee Settle

DLB, Vol. 6, 281–89; *SWBD; Contemporary Literary Criticism.* Ed. Sharon R. Gunton. Vol. 19. Detroit: Gale Research, 1981, 408–12; Amorese, Cynthia [Interview]. *Commonwealth: The Magazine of Virginia,* Jan. 1981; Garrett, "An Invitation to the Dance: A Few Words on the Art of Mary Lee Settle," *Blue Ridge Review,* 1 (1978), 18–24; Garrett, George. "Mary Lee Settle's Beulah Land Triology." In *Rediscoveries.* Ed. David Madden. New York: Crown, 1971, 171–78; "Settle May Write 'Gone With Wind' Sequel." *Charleston Gazette,* 24 Jan. 1981, 11; Schafer, William J. "Mary Lee Settle's Beulah Quintet: History Darkly, Through a Single-Lens Reflex." *Appalachian Journal,* 10 (Autumn 1982), 77–86; Shattuck, Roger "A Talk with Mary Lee Settle" (interview). *New York Times Book Review,* 26 Oct. 1980, 43; Taormina, C. A. "On Time with Mary Lee Settle" (interview). *Blue Ridge Review,* 1 (1978), 8–17. REVIEWS: Doctorow, E. L. "Mother Jones Had Some Advice." Rev. of *The Scapegoat. New York Times Book Review,* 26 Oct. 1980, 1, 40–42; Godwin, Gail. "An Epic of West Virginia." Rev. of *The Killing Ground. New Republic,* 16 June 1982, 30–32; Latham, Aaron. "The End of the Beulah Quintet." Rev. of *The Killing Ground. New York Times Book Review,* 11 July 1982, 1, 20–21; Steel, Edward M., Jr. "Review Essay: Fact or Fiction." Rev. of *The Scapegoat. West Virginia History,* 42 (Spring–Summer 1981), 314–15.

LEE SMITH

By Lee Smith

NOVELS:

The Last Day the Dogbushes Bloomed. New York: Harper & Row, 1968. Rpt. New York: Ballantine, 1969.

Something in the Wind. New York: Harper & Row, 1971.

Fancy Strut. New York: Harper & Row, 1973.

Black Mountain Breakdown. New York: Putnam's, 1980. Rpt. New York: Ballantine, 1982.

Oral History. New York: Putnam's, 1983.

COLLECTED SHORT STORIES:

Cakewalk. New York: Putnam's, 1981.

About Lee Smith

MacKethan, Lucinda H. "Artists and Beauticians: Balance in Lee Smith's Fiction." *Southern Literary Journal*, 15 (Fall 1982), 3–14. REVIEWS: Coggeshall, Rosanne. Rev. of *Black Mountain Breakdown*. *Hollins Critic*, 18 (April 1981), 15; Coggeshall, Rosanne. Rev. of *Cakewalk*. *Hollins Critic*, 18 (Dec. 1981), 17; Pollitt, Katha. "Southern Stories." Rev. of *Cakewalk*. *New York Times Book Review*, 22 Nov. 1981, 10.

ELIZABETH SPENCER

By Elizabeth Spencer

NOVELS:

Fire in the Morning. New York: Dodd, Mead, 1948, Rpt. New York: McGraw-Hill, 1968.

This Crooked Way. New York: Dodd, Mead, 1952; London: Victor Gollancz, 1952. Rpt. New York: McGraw-Hill, 1968.

The Voice at the Back Door. New York: McGraw-Hill, 1956; London: Victor Gollancz, 1957. Rpt. New York: Time Incorporated, 1965.

The Light in the Piazza. New York: McGraw-Hill, 1960; London: Heinemann, 1961. Rpt. New York: McGraw-Hill, 1971.

Knights and Dragons. New York: McGraw-Hill, 1965; London: Heinemann, 1966.

No Place for an Angel. New York: McGraw-Hill, 1967; London: Weidenfeld and Nicholson, 1968.

The Snare. New York: McGraw-Hill, 1972.

The Salt Line. Toronto and Garden City, NY: Doubleday, 1984.

COLLECTED SHORT STORIES:

Ship Island and Other Stories. New York: McGraw-Hill, 1968; London: Weidenfeld and Nicholson, 1969.

Marilee: Three Stories by Elizabeth Spencer. Jackson: University Press of Mississippi, 1981.

The Stories of Elizabeth Spencer. Garden City, NY: Doubleday, 1981.

About Elizabeth Spencer

AWW, Vol. 4, 139–40; *DLB*, Vol. 6, 320–27; *SWBD*; Anderson, Hilton. "Elizabeth Spencer's Tale of a Mermaid." *Mississippi Folklore Register*, 12 (Spring 1978), 32–34; Anderson, Hilton. "Elizabeth Spencer's Two Italian Novellas." *Notes on Mississippi Writers*, 13:1 (1981), 18–35; Barge, Laura. "An Elizabeth Spencer Checklist, 1948 to 1976." *Mississippi Quarterly*, 29 (Fall 1976), 569–90; Broadwell, Elizabeth Pell and Ronald Wesley Hoag. "A Conversation with Elizabeth Spencer." *Southern Review*, 18 (Winter 1982), 111–30; Jones, John Griffin. "Elizabeth Spencer." In *Mississippi Writers Talking I*. Jackson: University Press of Mississippi, 1982, 95–129 (interview). REVIEWS: Park, Clara Claiborne. "A Personal Road." *Hudson Review*, 34 (Winter 1981–82), 601–05; Price, Reynolds. "The Art of American Short Stories." Rev. of *The Stories of Elizabeth Spencer*. *New York Times Book Review*, 1 Mar. 1981, 1, 20.

ANNE TYLER

By Anne Tyler

NOVELS (Published by Knopf, New York):
If Morning Ever Comes. 1964; rpt. New York: Popular Library, 1977.
The Tin Can Tree. 1965; rpt. New York: Popular Library, 1977.
A Slipping Down Life. 1970; rpt. New York: Popular Library, 1977.
The Clock Winder. 1972; rpt. New York: Popular Library, 1977.
Celestial Navigation. 1974; rpt. New York: Popular Library, 1980.
Searching for Caleb. 1976; rpt. New York: Popular Library, 1977.
Earthly Possessions. 1977; rpt. New York: Popular Library, 1977.
Morgan's Passing. 1980; rpt. (large print) Boston: G. K. Hall, 1980; rpt. New York: Playboy Paperbacks, 1981.
Dinner at the Homesick Restaurant. 1982.

ARTICLES/ESSAYS:
"Still Just Writing." In *The Writer on Her Work: Contemporary Women Writers Reflect on Their Art and Situation.* Ed. Janet Sternburg. New York: Norton, 1980, 3–16.

About Anne Tyler

AWW, Vol. 3, 275–76; *DLB,* Vol. 6, 336–45; Nesanovich, Stella. "An Anne Tyler Checklist, 1959–1980." *Bulletin of Bibliography,* 38 (Apr.–June 1981), 53–64; Nesanovich, Stella. "The Individual in the Family: A Critical Introduction to the Novels of Anne Tyler." Diss. Louisiana State University 1979. REVIEWS: DeMott, Benjamin. "Funny, Wise and True." Rev. of *Dinner at the Homesick Restaurant. New York Times Book Review,* 14 Mar. 1982, 1, 14. Nesanovich, Stella. "Anne Tyler's *Morgan's Passing.*" *Southern Review,* 17 (Summer 1981), 619–21.

ALICE WALKER

By Alice Walker

NOVELS (Published by Harcourt Brace Jovanovich, New York):
The Third Life of Grange Copeland. 1970; rpt. New York: Harcourt Brace Jovanovich, 1977.
Meridian. 1976; rpt. New York: Washington Square Press, 1981.
The Color Purple. 1982.

COLLECTED SHORT STORIES:
In Love and Trouble: Stories of Black Women. New York: Harcourt Brace Jovanovich, 1973. Rpt. New York: Harcourt Brace Jovanovich, 1974.
You Can't Keep a Good Woman Down: Stories by Alice Walker. New York: Harcourt Brace Jovanovich, 1981.

COLLECTED POEMS:

Once: Poems. New York: Harcourt Brace Jovanovich, 1968. Rpt. New York: Harcourt Brace Jovanovich, 1976.

Revolutionary Petunias and Other Poems. New York: Harcourt Brace Jovanovich, 1976.

Goodnight Willie Lee, I'll See You in the Morning: Poems. New York: Dial Press, 1979.

NONFICTION:
Langston Hughes. New York: Crowell, 1973.

WORKS EDITED:
I Love Myself When I Am Laughing . . and Then Again When I Am Looking Mean and Impressive: A Zora Neale Hurston Reader. Old Westbury, NY: Feminist Press, 1979.

ARTICLES/ESSAYS:
"The Black Writer and the Southern Experience." *New South,* 25 (Fall 1970), 23–26.

"In Search of Our Mother's Gardens: The Creativity of Black Women in the South." 1974; rpt. *Southern Exposure,* 4 (Winter 1977), 64–70, 105.

"One Child of One's Own: A Meaningful Digression Within the Work(s)." In *The Writer on Her Work: Contemporary Women Writers Reflect on Their Art and Situation.* Ed. Janet Sternburg. New York: Norton, 1980, 121–40.

"Saving the Life That Is Your Own: The Importance of Models in the Artist's Life." In *The Third Woman: Minority Women Writers of the United States.* Ed. Dexter Fisher. Boston: Houghton Mifflin, 1980, 151–58.

About Alice Walker

AWW, Vol. 3, 313–15; *DLB,* Vol. 6, 350–58; Brewer, Krista. "Writing to Survive: An Interview with Alice Walker." *Southern Exposure,* 9 (Summer 1981), 12–15; Christian, Barbara. "A Study of *In Love and Trouble:* The Contrary Women of Alice Walker." *Black Scholar,* 12 (Mar.–Apr. 1981), 21–30, 70–71; Gaston, Karen C. "Women in the Lives of Grange Copeland." *College Language Association Journal,* 24 (March 1981), 276–86; McDowell, Deborah E. "The Self in Bloom: Alice Walker's *Meridian.*" *College Language Association Journal,* 24 (March 1981), 262–75; McGowan, Martha J. "Atonement and Release in Alice Walker's *Meridian.*" *Critique,* 23:1 (1981), 25–36; O'Brien, John. "Alice Walker." In *Interviews with Black Writers.* New York: Liveright, 1973; Steinem, Gloria. "Do You Know This Woman? She Knows You: A Profile of Alice Walker." *Ms.,* 10 (June 1982), 35–37, 89–94; Washington, Mary Helen. "Alice Walker: Her Mother's Gifts." *Ms.,* 10 (June 1982), 38; Washington, Mary Helen. "Teaching Black-Eyed Susans: An Approach to the Study of Black Women Writers." *Black American Literature Forum,* 11 (Spring 1977), 20–24. REVIEWS: Pollitt, Katha. "Stretching the Short Story." *New York Times Book Review,* 24 May 1981, 9–15; Watkins, Mel. "Some Letters Went to God." Rev. of *The Color Purple. New York Times Book Review,* 25 July 1982, 7.

JOAN WILLIAMS

By Joan Williams

NOVELS:
The Morning and the Evening. New York: Atheneum, 1961.
Old Powder Man. New York: Harcourt, Brace & World, 1966.
The Wintering. New York: Harcourt, Brace, Jovanovich, 1971.
County Woman. Boston: Atlantic-Little, Brown, 1982.

COLLECTED SHORT STORIES:
Pariah and Other Stories. Boston: Atlantic-Little, Brown, 1983.

ARTICLES/ESSAYS:
"'You-Are-Thereness' in Fiction." *The Writer,* 80 (April 1967), 20–21, 72–73.
"Twenty Will Not Come Again." *Atlantic Monthly,* 245 (May 1980), 58–65.
"Remembering." *Ironwood,* 17 (1981), 107–10.
"In Defense of Caroline Compson." In *Critical Essays on William Faulkner: The Compson Family.* Ed. Arthur F. Kinney. Boston: G. K. Hall, 1982, 402–07.

About Joan Williams

DLB, Vol. 6, 367–70; SWBD; Mullener, Elizabeth. "Joan Williams and William Faulkner: A Romance Remembered." *Times Picayune, Dixie Magazine,* 19 Sept. 1982, 8–10, 12–14, 16, 18; Scafidel, Beverly. "Biographical Sketch of Joan Williams." In *Lives of Mississippi Writers, 1817–1967.* Ed. James B. Lloyd. Jackson: Univ. Press of Mississippi, 1981, 470–71. REVIEWS: Rev. of *County Woman. New Yorker,* 15 Mar. 1982, 143; Scholes, Robert. *New York Times Book Review,* 16 May 1966, 40; Warren, Robert Penn. "Death of a Salesman— Southern Style." Rev. of *Old Powder Man. Life,* 20 May 1966, 10, 18.

Notes on Contributors

DAPHNE ATHAS teaches at the University of North Carolina. She has won a number of awards for her fiction, including the Sir Walter Raleigh Award in 1979 for *Cora*.

DORIS BETTS is chair of the department and professor of English at the University of North Carolina-Chapel Hill. She is the author of a number of works of fiction including three volumes of short stories—*The Gentle Insurrection, The Astronomer, Beasts of the Southern Wild and Other Stories*—and four novels, *Tall Houses in Winter, The Scarlet Thread, The River to Pickle Beach* and *Heading West.*

MARGARET JONES BOLSTERLI teaches English at the University of Arkansas in Fayetteville. She is the author of a number of essays, as well as *The Early Community at Bedford Park.* She recently edited *Vinegar Pie and Chicken Bread: The Diary of a Woman in the Rural South in 1890–91.*

LAURIE L. BROWN is the acquisitions librarian at Millsaps College.

MARTHA CHEW, author of a number of articles on Southern women writers, teaches English at the Massachusetts College of Pharmacy and Allied Health Sciences. She will be a visiting professor of women's studies at California State University at Fresno for spring 1984.

THADIOUS M. DAVIS is an associate professor of English at the University of North Carolina-Chapel Hill. She is currently completing a biographical and critical study of Nella Larson.

MARY ANNE FERGUSON chairs the English department at the University of Massachusetts, Harbor Campus, Boston. She is the editor of *Images of Women in Literature* and author of numerous articles including forthcoming publications on Alice Walker, Erica Jong, and Eudora Welty.

ANITA MILLER GARNER has published fiction in *Intro 9, The Black Warrior Review,* and *Research in Action.* Recently she finished a collection of short fiction called *Delectable Waters.* She is an instructor of English at Virginia Commonwealth University.

NANCY D. HARGROVE is professor of English at Mississippi State University. She is the author of *Landscape as Symbol in the Poetry of T.S. Eliot* and articles on Eliot, Sylvia Plath and others.

ANNE GOODWYN JONES, assistant professor of English at Allegheny College, is author of *Tomorrow Is Another Day: The Woman Writer in the South, 1859–1936* (winner of the Jules F. Landry Award). She serves on the editorial board for the Feminist Press *(Reconstructing American Literature)* and on PMLA's advisory board.

NANCY CAROL JOYNER is professor of English at Western Carolina University. She has published articles in such journals as *Colby Library Quarterly, Journal of Narrative Technique,* and the *Southern Literary Journal,* and currently holds an NEH Regional Studies Grant to complete a book on Appalachian women writers.

CAROL S. MANNING, assistant professor of English at Mary Washington College, has published articles and read papers on Eudora Welty's fiction and is completing a book-length study.

PEGGY WHITMAN PRENSHAW, professor of English and assistant dean of the Graduate School at the University of Southern Mississippi, is editor of the *Southern Quarterly.* She is currently working on a book-length study of Elizabeth Spencer.

CAROLYN RHODES is professor of English at Old Dominion University. She is currently teaching American literature in Cluj, Romania, as a Fulbright scholar.

MARY ROHRBERGER is professor of English and Assistant to the Dean for General Education and Liberal Learning Projects at Oklahoma State University. She is the author of seventy-five articles in various journals and five books, including *Story to Anti-Story, Hawthorne and the Modern Short Story,* and *The Art of Katherine Mansfield.* She also serves as fiction editor for *Cimarron Review.*

MAUREEN RYAN, assistant professor of English and Director of the Writing Laboratory at the University of Southern Mississippi, is interested in Southern and women's fiction. She is currently writing a book on Jean Stafford.

CHERYL MCALLISTER SAUNDERS is managing editor of the *Southern Quarterly*.

DOROTHY M. SCURA teaches English at Virginia Commonwealth University. She is the author of numerous articles on American and Southern literature.

MERRILL MAGUIRE SKAGGS teaches English at Drew University. She has published a number of articles and is the author of *The Folk of Southern Fiction*, which won the Edd Winfield Parks Prize, and co-author of *The Mother Person*.

JEANIE THOMPSON has published poetry, book reviews, and interviews in *Antaeus, College English, The New England Review, Ploughshares,* and other journals. She has also published one chapbook of poems, *Lotus and Psalm*. She currently teaches English at St. Martin's Episcopal School in Metairie, Louisiana.

JUDITH BRYANT WITTENBERG is assistant professor of English at Simmons College. She has published articles on Faulkner, Thomas Hardy, and Ellen Glasgow and is the author of *Faulkner: The Transfiguration of Biography*.